FREDDIE MERCURY

Lesley-Ann Jones is a well-known features writer who is also the author of

Blade On A Mirror

Naomi: The Rise and Rise of the Girl from Nowhere

WOW!

Freddie Mercury

The Definitive Biography

Lesley-Ann Jones

CORONET BOOKS
Hodder and Stoughton

Copyright © Lesley-Ann Jones 1997

First published in Great Britain in 1997 by Hodder and Stoughton
A division of Hodder Headline PLC
First published in paperback in 1998 by Hodder and Stoughton
A Coronet Paperback

The right of Lesley-Ann Jones to be identified as the Author of the
Work has been asserted by her in accordance with the Copyright,
Designs and Patents Act 1988.

6

A CIP catalogue record for this title is available from the
British Library

ISBN 0 340 67209 9

Printed and bound in Great Britain by
Mackays of Chatham plc, Chatham, Kent

Hodder and Stoughton
A division of Hodder Headline PLC
338 Euston Road
London NW1 3BH

Este libro está dedicado a los amores de mi vida:
Gerard y Mia

CONTENTS

LIST OF ILLUSTRATIONS

ACKNOWLEDGMENTS

I am greatly indebted to the following for their help.

In London: Peter Freestone, Brian May, Roger Taylor, Mary Austin, Spike Edney, Tony Hadley, Leee Johns, Tommy Vance, Mike Read, Mike and Lulu Appleton, Paul Gambaccini, Bob Geldof, Ken Jones, Andrew MacGillivray, Fiz Shapur, Lindsay and Jude Martins, Alicia and Daniel Martins, Joy King, Hayley Young, Jenny Falconer, Nick Gordon, David Thorpe, Rolf Harris, Phil Swern, Denis O'Regan, Rick Sky, Martin Dunn, Peter Hillmore, David Wigg, John Blake, Edmund Preston, Richard Hughes, David Quantick, Tony Brainsby, Berni Kilmartin, Lynda Sheridan, Jennie Halsall, Phil Symes, Peter Lee, Lee Everett-Alkin, Debra and Gareth Mollison, Ken O'Neill, Jerry Hibbert, Charles Armitage, Liam McCoy, Chris Poole, Shernaz Screwaller, Michael Anastasios, Julie Glover, Dominic Denny, Jacky Smith Gunn, Ollie Lambert, WENN, Murray Chalmers and EMI Records; Hans Tasiemka Archives; News International; St Catherine's House; College of Psychic Studies, Kensington; Brookwood Military and Civil Cemetery, Surrey; Tanzania High Commission, Mayfair.

In Liverpool: Jim Jenkins.

In Munich: Barbara Valentin, Gerd Kochlin.

In New York: Mick Rock, Nick Elgar.

In Los Angeles: Stuart White, David Syner.

In Co. Carlow: Jim Hutton.

In Paris: Toby Rose.

In Montreux: Jim Beach, Anne Meyer.

In Zanzibar and Tanzania: Sandy Evans, Bonzo Fernandez, Perviz Darunkhanawala, Diana Darunkhanawala, Nancy Galloway, Nasser K. Awadh, Professor Abdul Sheriff, Hamari Omar, Kevin Patience, Zanzibar Museums, University of Dar es Salaam.

In Bombay and Panchgani: Sheroo Khory, Mr Innis and St Peter's School, Cyrus Ghandy, Janet Smith, Gita Choksi, Mr and Mrs Davis.

In Argentina and Brazil: Marcela Delorenzi, Jorge Fregonese, Patricio.

In Budapest: Hollow Skai, Tomas Petterson.

Any omissions are unintentional. I am sincerely grateful to all concerned for invaluable assistance. None of the above mentioned is in any way responsible for the author's views as expressed in this book.

'As Freddie once said to me, "If there's going to be a book about me, I want it to tell the truth, good and bad". This is the Freddie I knew'.

Peter Freestone, Freddie Mercury's personal assistant, 1982–1991

With special thanks to: Freddie Mercury; Robert Kirby, my literary agent; Simon Prosser, my editor; Anna-Maria Watters, his assistant; everyone at Hodder and Stoughton.

In loving memory of: Anne Margaret Jones; Glyn and Gladys Powell; Jack Tinker; Joseph P. Wheeler; Ted Hart; Olivia Cadman; Theresa Morgan; Alan Watkins. RIP

Chapter One

INTRODUCTION

It starts as a low rumble somewhere beyond the back of the stadium, and rolls steadily forwards like a mounting tidal wave until it breaks against the stage in a thundering roar. On cue, the band charge on to the stage to confront an audience seething with anticipation. No easing into the proceedings tonight: they launch frantically into the pounding beat of 'One Vision', their soaring sound seeming almost to lift the stage from its moorings and offer it up to the heathery evening sky. Here's lead singer Mercury now, standing out like a bandaged digit in snow-white military get-up dashed with red, hurling his body at the crowd. He strolls, struts, strums his sawn-off mike-stand in what is either a tribute to or a send-up of Brian May, you can never quite figure which. The air-punching, the defiant stabbing forefinger, the wide-legged posing and posturing, the bouncing left leg are by now globally familiar gestures that millions have come to expect of this performer, the very hallmarks of his style. Watch it as often as you like: Freddie Mercury never fails to enchant, to rip your breath away. Even seen-it-before cynics have to concede that he is unique. That Mercury is the quintessential rock-star.

It is a spectacle you will have watched only on video

1

or television these last ten years or more. For, incredibly, over a decade has passed since Queen gave their final live performance, and for five of those years Freddie Mercury has been dead. The legend that began to emerge shortly after his passing, however, gathers momentum with each passing year. His cult hero status rests assured. The word 'magic' is often used to describe what he had as a performer. Whatever it was, it seems never to fade or grow threadbare. It doesn't even really date in the way it has with, say, Peter Gabriel, Mick Jagger, or Sting. If there can be any blessing commensurate with the tragedy of dying young – forty-five is not exactly geriatric – might not it be the preservation of perfection in perpetuity? Age was never going to wither Freddie. He once even boasted that he would never make old bones. Indeed, the very notion of senescence was anathema to him. He had a point. If there is such a thing as rock 'n' roll Heaven, it must be swinging to the rhythm of the late and great: John Lennon, Elvis Presley, Marc Bolan, Janis Joplin, Jimi Hendrix, Phil Lynott, Sid Vicious, Kurt Cobain, Jim Morrison, Roy Orbison, Brian Jones, Keith Moon . . . To this day, Pete Townshend is forced to live with the indignity of having hoped against hope that he'd die before he got old. A septuagenarian axe-smasher is a pathetic idea. The pensionable rock-star is a figure of ridicule, and possibly even doomed. The remaining members of Queen – Brian May, Roger Taylor and John Deacon – stay behind to face the big birthdays, to ponder the past, to attempt to figure out the point of it all. And to wonder what might or might not have been, had the main man lived.

As rock superstars go, they don't come much bigger than Freddie Mercury. The rest of Queen, themselves masters of their craft, are hardly household names by comparison. They have all too often been disregarded as Freddie Mercury's backing group. Think Queen and the image you see is not four rock-stars, but one. It is Freddie Mercury, sporting the look which has become a globally-recognized cliché:

the tight denims accentuating his neat, muscular body, the skimpy white vest, the closely cropped hair and nail-brush moustache. Beneath this carefully honed 'clone' look, however, Freddie's discarded dandy image still lurks. In more Bohemian, Biba-conscious days the fleshy mouth was accentuated with gloss, the piercing dark eyes smudged seductively with kohl, the sharp shape of his cheekbones perfected with paint. Back then he lacquered his fingernails jet black, and curled his long wavy hair about his shoulders. The whole was an intoxicating, androgynous look bordering on girlish beauty; a stunning brunette version of Fleetwood Mac's Stevie Nicks which went well with the flared velvet loons, brocade jackets and lacy frilled blouses of the 1970s. And why not? It may seem to some a ridiculous look today, but it was in keeping with those times. Of course, the Freddie Mercury who left this planet in 1991 had a very different look from the Bohemian pop star of the mid-seventies. But images evolve and change, or they should do, if an artist's appeal is to last.

In 1990, when the band celebrated their 20th anniversary with yet another of their legendary riotous parties, it seemed a good time to stand back and take stock of an incredible career. Almost from the beginning, Queen had been breaking barriers, setting precedents, going boldly where no rock group had ventured before. It has been a deafening crescendo of success which even now shows no signs of abating. Their début album 'Queen' of 1973 made the American Billboard Top 100, a rare achievement for a new British band. Just one year later, Freddie Mercury was up there accepting his first Ivor Novello Award from the Songwriter's Guild of Great Britain for 'Killer Queen'. There would be countless Ivor Novellos, Britannias, Golden Lions, Billboards and Silver Clefs in the years to come – and even, one day, an inscription on the Greenpeace obelisk in Antarctica.

In 1975 the band had their first taste of Queen-mania. Not,

as one might have expected, in London or New York, but in Tokyo, when Japan became the first country to recognize the group as superstars. That year, with their first number one single, the classic 'Bohemian Rhapsody', they not only broke the one million sales barrier in the UK alone, but redefined the rules of rock, with haunting, innovative choral arrangements and unusual multi-layered production techniques. They also turned the tide of pop-music promotion with what is widely considered to have been the world's first pop video. The music business sat up and took notice; already, Freddie Mercury was making his mark. Freddie's powerful voice had an unearthly dimension, an indefinably unique quality which took it beyond the boundaries of conventional rock. It was a voice which gave formal credence, perhaps for the first time ever, to the idea that contemporary and classical styles can successfully combine. 'Bohemian Rhapsody' assumed a life of its own, destined as it was to become one of the world's best-known songs. Twenty-one years after its original release, it still tops All-Time Top One Hundred radio polls around the world. And its revival in the 'Wayne's World' cult movies introduced Queen to a new generation of fans worldwide.

Record-breaking has always been a favourite Queen theme. Their free open-air concert in 1976 still holds the record attendance for any free concert ever held in Hyde Park. By the end of 1980 they had entered the Guinness Book of Records as the highest-paid directors of a company. That year, their tenth anniversary, they had sold 45 million albums and 25 million singles. They have since lined endless walls with silver, gold and platinum discs; shifted records and CDs and videos by the billion; played in virtually every state in the USA, in every country on earth where rock music is a popular form of entertainment, and in plenty of places where it had never previously been performed at all. They made a point of doing so. They have filled most of the globe's vast arenas, from New York's Madison Square Garden to the Morumbi in São Paulo, Brazil – the second biggest stadium in the world.

The largest paying audience for one band anywhere in the world to date, 131,000 people, paid to see them there. On that 1981 South American tour alone, which grossed 3½ million dollars, Queen performed for a staggering 479,000 fans. Four years later they capped even that by headlining 'Rock in Rio', the world's biggest-ever rock festival – a colossal event. It was staged at the specially constructed Barra da Tijuca stadium in Rio which held a mind-boggling 250,000 fans. The post-gig party at the Copacabana Beach Hotel was, unfathomably, televised live to millions all over South America. That same year, on 13 July 1985, Bob Geldof was moved to describe them as 'the biggest band on the planet' when Queen performed at Wembley Stadium alongside the greatest line-up of rock heroes ever seen, for Live Aid's 'Global Juke Box'. While so many deserved credit for the once-in-a-lifetime show, everyone agreed that it was Freddie's day, the ultimate experience for the ultimate showman: all his life, Freddie Mercury had longed for just one chance to sing for the whole world at once.

In 1986, On the 'Magic' tour, Queen sold out two performances at Wembley, one at Newcastle St James's Park, another at Manchester Maine Road and yet another at Knebworth Park – a total in excess of 400,000 people and an all-time UK attendance record. That same tour, the year in which the band threw no fewer than 28 parties (five of which I managed to attend), Queen's 657th performance, on 27 July at Budapest's Nepstadion, became the first ever stadium concert in the Eastern Bloc. Throughout all this, Freddie Mercury was continually voted 'Best Male Vocalist' in polls everywhere, from the pop pages of British tabloid newspapers to international radio and television shows. Meanwhile, songs from Queen's incredible catalogue had made themselves as familiar to millions as the melodies of the Beatles or the rock riffs of the Rolling Stones: 'Killer Queen', 'Bohemian Rhapsody', 'Another One Bites The Dust' – number one in countless countries and adopted by several

American football teams and British TV's The Gladiators as their musical theme; 'We Are The Champions' – a rousing, tear-jerking anthem heard over and over around the world at football finals and other sporting events; 'Crazy Little Thing Called Love'; 'Radio Ga Ga'; 'Under Pressure'; 'A Kind Of Magic'; 'I Want To Break Free'; 'Love Of My Life'; 'We Will Rock You'; 'Friends Will Be Friends'. Everyone has their favourite Queen song. When, on New Year's Eve 1989, Queen's Greatest Hits album became the fourth best-selling album of all time (behind Dire Straits' 'Brothers In Arms' and Michael Jackson's 'Thriller'), even Freddie, who had never in almost 20 years been satisfied with Queen's achievements and had, more than any of the others, been the one to urge the band on and on to do more, had to sit back and admit that they had made it.

Not one of them could deny that they lived the millionaire rock-star lifestyle to the hilt. For the best part of 20 years, they partied like it was 1999. In Montreux, Switzerland, where Queen had bought Mountain Studios, their own recording complex, Freddie literally swung from the hotel chandeliers. In 1981 when he was living in New York's Berkshire Place Hotel and wanted to celebrate his 35th birthday at a moment's notice, he bought Concorde tickets for dozens of his closest friends and flew them all out to Manhattan. The celebration, held in his hotel, lasted for five days, only winding up when Freddie was forced to go to England to recuperate. They partied with presidents, cavorted with kings, hung out with heroes. But throughout, Queen made a point of 'giving back', paying assiduous attention to fundraising work and banking millions for charities like Save the Children, the British Bone Marrow Donor Appeal, the Kutlawamong School for deaf and blind children in Bophuthatswana, South Africa, the Terrence Higgins Trust, and Queen's own Aids charity, the Mercury Phoenix Trust, all of which benefit from considerable Queen royalties to this day.

Behind the larger-than-life public image, of course, were four individuals with families, foibles, private lives. The rest of the band made only occasional headlines down the years with an assortment of minor solo projects and stories about their private lives. The unwritten rules of rock 'n' roll appear to declare it entirely reasonable and acceptable for a man to live the wenching, wassailing life of the globally adored rock star on the road, then resume the comparatively staid domestic role of devoted husband and father at the end of each tour. Rock wives, on the other hand, have been known to think otherwise. There was Brian's marriage-wrecking affair with Anita Dobson, 'Angie Watts' from television's 'EastEnders'. Roger's fling with model Debbie Leng, the 'Cadbury's Flake' girl from that well-known TV commercial, for whom he dumped Dominique, the mother of his two children; that tale took a bizarre turn when he went back and married Dominique, then promptly moved out to live with Debbie round the corner and start another family. Staid, solid, family man John was rarely news, except for the time when he found himself overwhelmed by rock stardom and took off for foreign parts without his passport, having neglected to inform his family or management that he was on the move.

Freddie, however, had been a constant source of fascination, almost from the outset. He played along briefly in the beginning, and gave a few tentative interviews, mindful of the fact that a healthy relationship with the press was vital in the building of a positive image. He quickly realized, however, that this was a game he could not win. Rock and pop coverage was just entering its heyday during the late 1970s and early 1980s. Every British national tabloid newspaper had its rock writers and pop column, invariably fronted by a celebrity columnist whose job it was to fill a daily page with trivia. Competition was fierce, budgets vast. Minor members of staff at record and management companies, radio stations, restaurants, clubs, hairdressing salons and even doctors' surgeries were hunted down, 'put on the payroll' and encouraged to sell gossip about the stars. The daily comings and goings of the likes of Freddie Mercury became common knowledge, digested each morning along with the cornflakes. Freddie did not make a willing victim. No one knew better than he how much he had to hide. The shutters on his private life soon went up. The less he gave, the more they wanted. Speculation was rife and the mythology began to build. Of the handful of rock superstars who dominated the public's imagination during the 1980s – Mick Jagger, Madonna, David Bowie, Elton John, Bono, George Michael, Sting – only Freddie, irresistibly elusive, was up there in the Michael Jackson league. What the media didn't actually know about him, they guessed at and exaggerated. No smoke without fire, according to the old cliché – which is how so much fabrication went down in newspaper-cuttings libraries as fact. Not even the press could blame Freddie for retreating from view and drawing a veil over his private life. But it didn't stop them writing about him.

Freddie's efforts to protect his private life were not primarily self-serving. His main objective throughout his adult life was to protect his parents and other close members of his family, none of whom was party to, or, perhaps, would have been able to come to terms with, his wilder ways. In the early days of Queen, Freddie had fallen in love and moved in with a delightful girl called Mary Austin who would have made anybody's dream daughter-in-law. Although their romantic relationship dwindled over time as Freddie felt the urge to experiment further with homosexuality, their true friendship endured. The press were fooled for quite some time by the pretend image the pair maintained as Freddie and Mary the happy couple. What later appeared to the outside world, though not as a result of Mary's actions, to have been a great sacrifice on Mary's part had actually suited everyone. Freddie's devout Parsee parents would not have felt comfortable with his exotic and hedonistic ways, which at times could be at odds with their faith. To this day they are said to be bewildered by the fame and frippery and utter madness of the lifestyle of their adored son, even though they are openly and immensely proud of his musical achievements. In presenting Mary as the one true love of his life – which in many ways she remained – Freddie avoided offending them. Screened by this outwardly conventional heterosexual liaison, Freddie was able to indulge his homosexual promiscuity; Mary, for her part, might have lost her lover but had retained her best friend. She had also secured herself a job for life. As the band rose to a level of fame which exceeded all their wild imaginings, it was Mary who proved, almost single-handedly, to be Freddie's salvation. Having established herself as devoted, utterly trustworthy and completely indispensable, she was soon in charge of Freddie's retinue and organising virtually every aspect of his life, including his domestic finances. Thus was the 'Court of King Freddie' established, a rock 'n' roll version of the medieval monarch's household. Freddie's entourage either lived with him under his own roof or in property owned by him nearby. Each was employed for the sole purpose of attending to his master's needs. When he travelled it was with the band's manager Jim Beach or with trusted companions, and his own assistant, valet and cook. When Queen toured, Freddie's party was usually a separate entity. He would choose a different hotel from the rest of the band, and operate independently of them. With Mary's help he created his own hermetically sealed world. It was as if he faded, Doctor Who-like, into some alternative dimension when his professional presence was not required. Away from the stage, he would hang out with his pals, indulge in a few drinks, watch videos, disappear discreetly into gay clubs and bars and partake of every indulgence on offer. He would frequently be buttoned into an exquisitely tailored suit, fragrant and immaculate, and off shopping somewhere for paintings, porcelain or *objets d'art*. Accompanied by minders and whisked neatly from place to place, he would gleefully outsmart the snappers and outwit even the quickest hack. He soon learned to eschew the London gay scene in favour of more liberal cities, such as New York and Munich, beyond the gaze of the British media's all-seeing eye. For the most part he got away with it, and was able to enjoy an uninhibited private life. When publicity was required, he refused to work with anyone other than a couple of trusted journalists whom he had come to regard as friends. A kiss-and-tell style revelation in a tabloid newspaper by a former employee wounded him badly, and the rumours about his true sexuality and, later, speculation that he was HIV positive, never went away. But Freddie rose above it all.

There has never been any real relief for Mary Austin, in spite of the fact that she inherited the lion's share of Freddie's personal fortune. She resides to this day with her two children by interior designer Piers Cameron in Freddie's elegant Kensington home, Garden Lodge, which cannot help but be a shrine to her former partner. Neighbours who once complained bitterly to the Council about the incessant invasion now shrug and turn a blind eye. Day in, day out, there are fans to be seen loitering in Logan Place. They cannot even see the house from the street, but this does not appear to deter them. There is, after all, no other place of worship anywhere else in the world, apart from a statue of Freddie only recently erected on the shore of Lac Léman (Lake Geneva) in Montreux, Switzerland. Embarrassingly, no home for the statue in London could be found. There is no grave, no plate of remembrance in any crematorium, no plaque in any church. No one outside Freddie's immediate circle knows the exact whereabouts of his ashes, which unfathomably remained in the care of the undertakers for almost a year after his cremation. Some have claimed, among them Freddie's lover and 'surrogate widow' Jim Hutton, that they are buried beneath Freddie's favourite weeping cherry tree in the beautiful grounds of Garden Lodge. It is said that

Freddie once asked Jim and Mary Austin to promise that his remains would be buried there: 'so that I can keep an eye on you all!'

Perhaps the whereabouts of Freddie's remains have hitherto been kept a mystery to prevent theft or vandalism. My subsequent discoveries have proved more astonishing than I imagined.

Faced only with stark bricks and two unremarkable entrance doors, one main, the other trade, Freddie's fans continue to leave their mark in lovingly executed graffiti on his garden walls. As often as this is painted over by Mary's employees, the fans renew it again. The visitor will also see touching trails of flowers, and, on 24 November, the anniversary of his death, candles, prayers and poems laid at his door in Freddie's honour. But each year the numbers dwindle. Last November, on the fifth anniversary of his death, only about 60 blue-lipped, numb-fingered, weeping fans collected in the driving rain to pay their respects together. This was in stark contrast to the hundreds who had made the pilgrimage in previous years. Most of those present for the fifth anniversary had travelled vast distances, from Argentina, Italy, Japan. They sang together, prayed, looked on reverently each time someone new arrived with a carefully chosen or even home-made personal offering, and closely inspected the sodden flowers and smudged messages of remembrance and adoration. They huddled under umbrellas for hours together, awaiting the emergence of Mary Austin at about seven p.m., the approximate time of Freddie's passing. She steps out into the street on this day each year, flanked by two bodyguards. She spends a little time with the fans, thanks them for coming, and reads, in her small voice, a prayer that no one at the back can ever hear. A small box beside the door with a 'Please Take One' sign contains a pile of photocopies of another prayer:

On this, the Fifth Anniversary of the tragic death of

Freddie Mercury, may the Power of Almighty God bring Peace, Love and Joy to our immortal King of Queen, as he sings and dances among the Angels.

While love and joy may well be hers in the family life she enjoys with her sons, there is little by way of peace in life for Mary Austin. Time and again her mail has been intercepted, her letters stolen. She has now had to make alternative arrangements for her correspondence using a secret PO Box. There are more sinister aspects to being the keeper of Freddie's home: the obsessive Mercury fans who write to her demanding access to the house, who phone her at all hours. She refuses to change the number: 'That would be Mary Austin running away,' she says. 'If ever anything frightened me, I mustn't show it, because then they win.'[1] The most insensitive fans, including the odd Freddie lookalike, have been known to climb over her walls and invade her privacy – because they can no longer invade Freddie's? – in the most provoking ways.

While he never actually made a point of denying it, homosexuality was the last thing to which Freddie would ever publicly admit. Legs astride, fist raised, head thrown back and mouth wide open to reveal his protuberant top teeth, he flaunted a strong and blatantly proud stage image which could almost be taken as a proclamation of his gladness to be gay. He kept us guessing, however, while leaving us in no doubt that here was a man who was thrilled to be alive. His sexuality was at times dismissed as being as irrelevant to his performance as his preferred brand of soap; as not the most interesting thing about him, nor a yardstick by which he could be measured; that, as a facet of his personality, it was fascinating simply because it was that. But in many ways, Freddie's sexuality was and remains relevant. Although he was widely regarded and accepted as homosexual, Freddie's millions of female fans were not repelled. Indeed, their unswerving devotion to him could almost be said to be fortified by every new apparently scandalous newspaper revelation. Although he never officially came out and flaunted himself as a gay icon, he was a role-model for millions of gay men, in particular young men perhaps struggling with the issue of how to deal with their own sexual identity. Many showbusiness idols this century, such as film-star Rock Hudson, have concealed their true sexual orientation for fear of rejection by their audiences. While Freddie himself never did so, he never proclaimed his homosexuality either, which must have disappointed a vast number of his gay fans. But, for as many people who idolized him as one of the most successful gay performers in history, there were probably as many who believed that he was not really gay in the conventionally accepted sense. Significant weight is certainly lent to this theory by astonishing new evidence that, at the height of his homosexual promiscuity, he was still indulging in sexual liaisons with women. That Freddie was never fully understood by the world at large would undoubtedly have appealed to him.

There would come a time, of course, when Freddie's carefully guarded private world would crumble. The very media that he could nonchalantly take or leave were never off his case. The paparazzi would get him in the end. And the demolition, when it occurred, was monstrous. Following what would prove to be Queen's last performance at Knebworth Park, Stevenage on 9 August 1986, Mercury retired from public life and became a virtual recluse inside Garden Lodge. While he and the rest of the group continued to record studio albums, further touring was now out of the question. Speculation about the state of his health had consequently reached fever pitch. The Aids rumours had been doing the rounds for years, but Queen employees had closed ranks, issued terse denials and were refusing to be drawn on the subject. Now that the tabloid vultures smelled blood, however, there was no stopping them.

The exposure of Freddie Mercury as a gravely ill individual just months away from death was the day one photographer hit pay dirt. It was also the day ordinary people began to think twice about Aids. Having wondered for some time what had become of Freddie Mercury, photographer Jason Fraser, acting on a tip-off, went to find the star. Head bowed, designer suit hanging limply from his painfully thin frame, Freddie, oblivious to the snapper's presence, had joined his Harley Street doctor for a quiet meal at an exclusive West End restaurant. The couple of rolls of long-lens frames which Fraser shot that day had shocking impact. They depicted a haggard, wasted shadow of a once electrifying showman. When he developed the film, Fraser was stunned to find himself staring into the hollow eye-sockets of a walking corpse. For more than fourteen days and nights the photographer sat himself down with the tragic set of prints and searched his soul for justification to sell them, thus exposing to the outside world the agony of a superstar under sentence of death. He was in two minds. In the end his news-hound instincts got the better of him. Fraser opted to sell and suffer the consequences.

'I agonized over it for weeks,' Fraser told me. 'I discussed it with my family. My motivation, I wish to make absolutely clear, was *not* money. I did not need that exclusive to make my name or fortune.' Indeed, of the proceeds, which Fraser admits was a 'low five-figure sum,' he gave away over a third to charity. But he was clearly not convinced that he had done the right thing and admitted that they, of the thousands of photographs he has sold during a highly lucrative career, have given him the most grief.

'I was sort of a Freddie Mercury fan. He was always fizzy, smiling and on top of it. But something was up. He wasn't around anymore. This guy, adored by millions, had been struck down, as it turned out, by a terrible disease that can get you no matter how famous or rich you happen to be. He had gone to a very public restaurant. He was out there walking in the street. He could be seen by hundreds of people. At the end of the day, all I did was photograph him in the street, without malicious intent. I didn't stalk him. There is no way I would have broken into a hospital or climbed a wall in his garden to get the shot. But what I saw was as shocking to me as it was to everyone else.'

Had Fraser taken the alternative decision and filed the pictures away, he could have avoided much vicious criticism that subsequently flooded his way. With hindsight, as it happened, he is generally reckoned to have done the right thing. While not oblivious to the mercenary, ghoulish and potentially immoral aspects of offering such work for publication, Fraser claims he had a hunch that the shots might serve a significant purpose. Which they did. Public opinion is a fickle and unpredictable force. Take the Elton John case more than a decade ago. Executives on the *Sun* newspaper still wince at the recollection of their splash exclusives exposing alleged aspects of the star's homosexual behaviour, which backfired disastrously and expensively when readership tide turned against the tabloid for what it had done to Elton. The singer sued for libel, and *Sun* readers were behind him all the way. The newspaper was forced to back down, apologize, and pay up. By the same token, who would have thought that mass distribution of Freddie's tragic images would precipitate a radical volte-face in public prejudice over the Aids issue? This, however, is exactly what happened. Homophobia at that time was rife, and a widely held belief denounced the disease as holy retribution, a 'gay plague' delivered as deadly punishment for indulgence in vile behaviour. But no sooner had the star's plight been revealed than opinion, even among the most militant of so-called queer-bashers, appeared to soften. Nobody, regardless of their predilections, deserved to suffer like Freddie.

It is said that distinguished individuals who die before their time often achieve greater fame in death than they ever enjoyed in life. Once the mythology kicks in, it assumes a life of its own, and the facts and figures of history are all too often lost in the fray. The process is a runaway train.

While it might be too early to make such assumptions in Freddie's case, the predictions look positive. A legend in life, and sanctified in death, the only thing that time can do is consolidate his popularity. But what was it about the man that caused the legend to emerge in the first place?

Things are rarely what they seem. Behind the exotic-genius fantasy lurked an often confused and angry individual. Few would readily buy the image of Freddie as a sad and lonely man. But the enormous, all-conquering confidence he was able to project as if to order only served to disguise his at times excruciating insecurity. Despite the fact that he had achieved in a few short decades far more than most people ever dare dream of in a lifetime, he had never come to terms with himself. Freddie, by his own admission, was always 'Looking, dear, still looking.' But what on earth was he looking *for*?

This is the question which I set out to answer, and the reason that I wrote this book. Although not in any way disapproved of by those closest to him, this is not an 'official' biography of Freddie Mercury. Jim Beach, Queen's manager and Freddie's executor and trustee, graciously declined to make it such, explaining that he and the remaining members of the band had agreed years earlier not to become directly involved in any biographies, nor to be formally interviewed by any author whom they themselves had not personally commissioned.

But, in September 1995, I wrote to Brian May at the Queen office in Notting Hill, London, to see what he thought of the idea, on the grounds that I would not proceed if approbation was unforthcoming. We had been close friends in the past, and I had no wish to compromise that friendship. A good nine years had elapsed since we had last met, however, and I was not sure that Brian would even remember me. But he telephoned the minute he received the letter, and we arranged to meet. Lunch was an emotional occasion. So many years, so much sadness, no more Fred. We walked back to the Queen office where we sat around, reminiscing. Brian played me a few tracks from the then unreleased 'Made In Heaven' album. Freddie filled the room and we both wept. Shortly afterwards he wrote a long letter telling me that I was 'absolutely the right person' to write the Freddie biography, that he wholeheartedly approved, and that he would help me as much as he was able: 'I know you would approach it with sensitivity and professionalism.'

However, he was not sure what the rest of the band or Jim Beach would think: 'Whether our team will feel they can get involved at this time I really don't know.'

Since Queen have always functioned as a democracy, he said he would have to consult them. Thus began an epic exchange of faxes between my desk in Kent and Jim Beach's in Montreux, Switzerland. The first of his communications was cool. Queen were not considering any biographies at that time. Jim Beach was not prepared to be interviewed. Neither were the remaining members of the band. By this time, however, having read everything about Freddie that had been published to date, I was convinced that I should write the definitive biography. No previous writer, it seemed to me at that time, had gone back into the cobwebbed corners of Freddie's past and personality, and poked around for himself.

As one of a handful of journalists who had known Freddie personally, I was aware of certain aspects of his personality and character which had not been discussed at all in previous books. From the early 1980s until about 1992, I wrote more or less exclusively about pop and rock music for, among others, the *Daily Mail*, the *Sun*, and for the *Mail on Sunday's YOU Magazine*. It was as a young rock writer at the *Daily Mail* that I first met Queen. After being sent to interview Freddie and Brian at the Queen offices in 1984, I watched from the wings as they performed live at Wembley for Live Aid in 1985, and was then invited to various European destinations on the 'Magic' tour in 1986. I covered their show again at Wembley that year, attended a reception in their honour at the British Embassy in Budapest, and witnessed their historic Hungarian show behind the Iron Curtain, perhaps their greatest live moment ever. Then came Knebworth, after which Queen ceased to tour and we all lost touch.

I made it known to Jim Beach that I hoped to proceed with a definitive biography of Freddie that would be neither sordid nor sensational, but which would pay homage to a man who was arguably the greatest rock-star of all time. I planned to examine what drove him in his work while addressing every facet of the man's personal life in the most compassionate way possible. Beach's response was that he was now prepared to help me 'at arm's length', to put me in touch with key people. He spoke to Brian, Roger and John, Mary Austin and Freddie's parents. All of them except John contacted me. I received another letter and then a couple of telephone calls from Brian. Having spoken with Beach, he did not feel he could be interviewed further, although we had already discussed Freddie at length on the day we met.

For my part, there is much personal observation in this book, offered on the grounds that 'I was there'. I have also drawn extensively on new, exclusive interviews, material kindly given and lent, and a wealth of archive research. Although it is prudent to mistrust the contents of cuttings library files, I felt confident in the case of Queen's newspaper cuttings not least because of their meticulous attention to detail and the care they took when choosing interviewers, many of whom happen to be friends or former colleagues of mine. Queen were also, perhaps, the most proactive rock group of their era when it came to their relationship with the media. From the earliest days of their career they appeared to know exactly what they were doing with public relations, courted mutual respect with the press, and maintained a healthy control over their image, even when, at times, to say that the music papers didn't rate their albums was an understatement. It is also worth noting that although Freddie himself gave very few interviews, he was admirably eloquent and disarmingly honest whenever he did. His distinctive voice, with its elegant timing, phrasing and piquant sense of humour, was unique. You couldn't make it up. No journalist could have copied his style and got away with it.

The big seas of Freddie Mercury's dreams are calm now. Never again will he strut a stage, work an audience, lift us to frenzied sweat-soaked heights and leave us dangling on his every hum, his chin lifted in ecstasy. Freddie Mercury the man has gone. But the voice and the legend live, in millions of anonymous hearts and memories. Our pity is the last thing he would want. It is those left behind for whom we might feel sorry. People who devoted their best years to him, and whose lives remain irrevocably changed, not always for the better.

What of Jim Hutton, Freddie's loyal and devoted companion for the final seven years of the star's life, who published a book, *Mercury and Me*, in loving memory of their affair? The critics were swift to damn him; the Queen organization denounced him as disloyal. Finding himself lonely and without real purpose in London, reflecting more and more on the fact that he too is infected with the HIV virus and not altogether certain of his future, Jim planned to return home to Carlow in Ireland to spend more time with his mother. In June 1996, just as he was knotting the loose ends and arranging to have the last of his belongings shipped out, there came the news that his mother had passed away. He was then faced with the dilemma of whether to return to Ireland, and live in the house which Freddie's legacy had built, or to remain in London and try a calmer life. At times sad, a little directionless, disillusioned by Granada Television's cancellation of the movie version of his book – the Queen organization refused to grant the right to use their music in the film – Jim remains optimistic for the future. He cannot help but sometimes sit and wonder, however, how different his life might have been had he not been picked up by a famous rock-star in a London gay bar in the crazed long ago, while working as a barber at the Savoy Hotel. It was in Carlow that I eventually found Jim, and was able to spend some time with him there. He talks for the first time here about aspects of his relationship with Freddie which he did not address in his own book, and how dramatically his life has changed since.

Elsewhere, in Bavaria's bustling capital, a fifty-something German movie star maintains as flamboyant a lifestyle as her reduced means will allow. Big Barbara Valentin, once Germany's answer to Brigitte Bardot (though some bitched that she was more like Barbara Windsor) and latterly something of a cult figure, was Freddie's constant companion during his self-imposed exile to Germany in the early 1980s. More than that, she says, they were lovers in the true, devoted, sexual and spiritual sense, as she told me when we spent several days together in Munich. They invested in a property together which was to be their mutual European home, in which – after a lengthy legal wrangle with Freddie's lawyers following his death to prove her rightful ownership – she lives to this day. More than once, Barbara reports, she nursed Freddie through savage attacks of ill-health brought on by side-effects to the drugs on which he had grown dependent. The giddy couple declared undying love to each other, despite an unexplained period when he simply faded, without a word, out of her life. The tale ends sadly. Towards the end, as Freddie grew increasingly reclusive, Barbara was discouraged from visiting him at his London home, where at one point he had given her her own bedroom. Once, she revealed, she and Freddie had a circle of 'about a hundred' friends in Munich, with whom they shared a nocturnal lifestyle of lunatic proportions. Today, by her reckoning, there are barely fifteen of them left. Though a loving mother and grandmother, Barbara says there has been little meaning and virtually no fulfilment in her life since Freddie died. She embraces the notion of premature death as an opportunity to be reunited with the 'greatest love of her life': 'I cannot wait to see him again.'

And what of Peter Freestone, 'Phoebe', the former Royal Opera House assistant wardrobe master who went on tour with Queen to supervise their costumes and became Freddie's personal assistant and valet, later nursing the star until his final moments? Today helping to run the European Chamber Opera Company in London, Freestone gives here his first in-depth interview about life at the heart of Freddie's personal entourage.

There are many others, too numerous to name, who keep the Freddie dream alive. His personal domestic staff, his closest friends, the roadies and physios, the costume designers, dressers, and make-up artists; the record and video producers, the engineers, the record company employees, their heads all loaded with remembrances of things they can't always accept are past. And the rock contemporaries, some of whom perhaps lie in bed awake at night and think 'There but for the grace of God . . .'

Freddie was aptly named, since he could be the most mercurial of men. During the course of my research, I discovered many of the contradictory sides which shaped his character, and which he managed to keep so well hidden from the public. I respectfully make no apologies for portraying the 'warts and all' Freddie, as I am led to believe that it is precisely what he would have expected. Freddie, of all people, could not stand a job half done. To discover what lurks on the dark side of the moon does not render its bright side any less splendid. Indeed, the contrast merely enhances the brilliance. This was Freddie to a 'T'. He was a man of more sweeping extremes, of dark and light and little grey, than any other person I have ever met. He could be as hurtful as he could be kind; as self-indulgent as he could be unselfish; as offensive as he could be charming; as wretched as he could be ecstatic; as miserable as he could be hysterically funny; as humble away from the stage as he could be arrogant on it. It must be hard to be humble when a sold-out crowd of thousands is chanting your name. He liked the way it sounded as he leapt on to the stage. He looked perfectly as ease there, as if it were his preferred environment, his natural habitat. It was almost as if the man only became Freddie Mercury in front of a paying audience.

As Peter Hillmore of the *Observer* remarked in Budapest after we had spent the evening being entertained rather lavishly by Freddie in his own hotel suite:

> Sitting talking to him in the Presidential Suite overlooking the Danube, I found myself having a conversation with an ordinary guy. And he was nice. He treated me the way he would treat a guest at a dinner-party in his home. He was exceedingly waspish, in that way that gay men speak to heterosexual men. He was camp and acerbic and a wonderful bitch. But he wasn't strutting about in that little vest of his like some matador. I was seeing the paradox face to face. If he'd been as modest with his audience as with me on the balcony that night, I'd have hated him. If he'd been as arrogant with me as he was on stage, I'd have hated him. Freddie was unique in that he could drop stardom the way you take off an overcoat. He could be just an ordinary man.

It was he, Freddie Mercury the ordinary man behind the dazzling superstar, of whom I went in search in this book.

Chapter Two

SPICE OF LIFE

What better place for a legend to be born than in a land deemed a legend in its own right? For its modest size, Zanzibar, like Venice, occupies a large romantic space in the heart of world imagination. Its very name conjures hypnotic images of a romantic and turbulent history. Zinjibar or Zanguebar, the Land of the Blacks, was, during the Middle Ages, the term used to describe the whole of the East African coast. Fabulous tales such as those of Sinbad, Ali Baba and wild Arabian princes would emanate from its lore. Not only the moniker but all the marvels of Eastern promise were inherited by the place now bearing the name.

A mere speck in the atlas, approximately six degrees south of the Equator, Zanzibar actually comprises not one but two islands, Unguja and the even more remote Pemba, which float in the Indian Ocean off the East coast of Africa. Today, together with the neighbouring former German and subsequently British colony Tanganyika, they form the United Republic of Tanzania. This, however, has only been the case for a mere 33 years. For such a tiny territory, Zanzibar has seen more than its fair share of corruption, disruption, and violent loss of life. Invaded down the centuries by every race of intrepid explorers from the Assyrians, Sumerians,

Egyptians, Phoenicians, Indians, Persians, Omani Arabs and Malays to the Chinese, Portuguese, Dutch and British, the annals of its history read like a chapter from *The Thousand And One Nights*. Some came in search of trade, others looking for booty, others still on a quest for an exotic new life. All found what they were looking for, and more. Some, notably the Shirazi Persians – from the ancient walled city of Shiraz, now part of Southern Iran – the Omani Arabs, and much later the British, stayed on to settle and rule. There is evidence that the Swahili civilization in this part of the world dates back as far as the earliest centuries of the Islamic era. After the clove tree was introduced in 1818, giving rise to a thriving spice industry – islanders went on to cultivate other spices too, such as vanilla and cardamom, black pepper, ginger and nutmeg – the name Zanzibar acquired four little words from which it has been indivisible ever since. The Spice Island Of Zanzibar would see missionaries and explorers pass through its portals on their way into the Dark Continent. Harems, palace intrigues and the elopement of a Zanzibari princess to Europe all added to the romantic image.

Zanzibar acquired awful notoriety as a flourishing trading centre not only for ivory, but for slaves. Its reputation as the largest slaving entrepôt on the Eastern coast is something of which the modern Zanzibari is understandably ashamed. Every year until abolition, finally enforced in 1897, some 50,000 Africans drawn from as far away as the lakes of Central Africa, were dragged through its barbaric market in one of the worst violations of humanity the so-called civilized world has ever known. It is recorded that a young girl could be bought for 'a single elephant's tusk of the first class, a new shirt, or 13 English sewing needles'. Slaves were herded towards the coast in tragic cavalcades like the one described by a companion of explorer David Livingstone: 'I have myself seen bands of them – four or five hundred at a time – newly captured as one could see by their necks all chafed and bleeding, their eyes streaming with tears, principally young men of from 10 to 18 years, driven along in a most inhuman manner.'[1]

An increasingly popular tourist destination in the late twentieth century, the shame of its recent past is conveniently forgotten as modern travellers flock in droves to Zanzibar's exotic shores. They come to enjoy its diverse culture and architecture, to relax on more than two dozen talcum beaches, to float in its crystal waters. And they come, too, because Freddie Mercury was born here – a fact which those who control the tourist trade of Zanzibar have only recently begun to appreciate. There are no plaques, no monuments, no shrine to the singer's memory. This is no deterrent, it must be said, as there are none in London either. But he is invariably mentioned in the tourist guides and on television travel programmes whenever the place is featured. Freddie Mercury and the spice islands of Zanzibar are indelibly linked.

In this far-flung corner of the planet, a devout young Indian-born, Parsee wife of Persian descent, was delivered of her first-born child on Thursday 5 September 1946. Relieved to be able to report to her overjoyed husband, Bomi Bulsara, that not only was the baby alive and kicking but was male – which was a blessing in their faith simply because it would mean that the family name would continue – Jer Bulsara recovered from her exhausting labour and painful but mercifully routine delivery in the spartan surroundings of Zanzibar's Government Hospital. There, she mused on what they might choose for their child as a name. As Parsees, adherents of the monotheistic Zoroastrian religion dating back to the early sixth century BC, the couple's choice was limited. They settled on Farrokh. The name was duly registered by the baby's father according to legal requirements at the Government Records office.

That he had been born Farrokh Bulsara on Zanzibar appears to have been a source of embarrassment to Freddie throughout most of his adult life. Inexplicably it was a closed book, something of which he rarely spoke. He certainly refused to be drawn on the subject in interviews, which as we know he almost never gave anyway. PRs who had worked closely with him since Queen's rise to fame agree that Freddie was dismissive of his childhood, and generally displayed no inclination whatsoever to talk about the place or circumstances of his birth.

'It's true,' affirms Tony Brainsby, the independent publicist who handled their PR during the early years of Queen's fame.

He was very secretive about his background. He never even told me his real name. I certainly had no idea that he started out as a Farook, Farrokh, whatever – that was something he never admitted to. What's more, for years I believed his proper surname to be 'Bulsova' – and I was meant to be their PR. Funny thing was, he was fairly dark-skinned, almost a cross between Oriental and Asian, so there was no disguising the fact that he came from somewhere off the beaten track, or at least had exotic parents. Looking back, he must have been in denial about it, although it couldn't have been for sinister reasons, or that he was racist in any way. Not when you consider how he hero-worshipped Jimi Hendrix, who was his absolute rock idol of all time. I never got to the bottom of it then, and I certainly don't expect to now.[2]

Why Freddie should have adopted such an attitude remains a mystery. We can only speculate, since he left no obvious clues. Perhaps he believed that music fans in the 1970s would not readily accept a rock singer who owned up to Indian and East African roots. It would not matter at all now, of course – the more obscure your heritage the better. All the more to write about. But back then, in Freddie's mind, the facts simply did not fit the image he was trying to create. A rock singer, by definition, was ideally home-grown American, since the

United States was the birthplace of rock 'n' roll. At the very least he ought to have been born in London, or, thanks latterly to the Beatles, in Liverpool. White Anglo-Saxon was favourite, but Black American was good enough: at least you could argue that your blood ran blue with rhythm and soul. It was common enough in those days for pop and rock personalities to blur the details of their past anyway, to allow for the elusive dimension of glamour which top-gun publicity people were paid fortunes to project.

With the aim of uncovering the facts, there was no choice but to go to Zanzibar and check out Freddie's roots myself. So, On 19 January 1996, I set off on an unforgettable journey beginning with a flight to Dar es Salaam, Tanzania, via Nairobi in Kenya. The crossing to Zanzibar can be made by either small plane, hydrofoil, or boat. I made the one hour, 45-minute journey by boat, continuing on to the Mbweni Ruins about five kilometres along the main airport road, where, I had been advised, I would find a safe and decent hotel. Although Zanzibar is officially part of the United Republic of Tanzania, it jealously guards its autonomy, and makes plain the point by putting foreign visitors, on both arrival and departure, through its own immigration, health and customs procedures. A fine fuss will often ensue at the dockside in Dar, a few visitors managing to buy their way on to the boat by crossing an official's palm with US dollars.

Approaching the bustling harbour of Zanzibar Town by sea, one has the sensation of sailing back into the island's enchanted past. Surrounded by eighteenth-century-style dhows and fishing canoes, it is not hard to imagine the spirit of the place in its heyday. To someone born in some dull backwater, Freddie's dismissal of Zanzibar as the place of his birth seems all the more puzzling. To be able to wow the supper-party set with tales of an exotic, far-flung childhood – especially since wowing them was one of the things he did best – why did he not jump at the chance? There had to be a good reason for his choosing to wipe out that part of his past. But might not that decision to do so have been subconscious? Whatever the reason, Zanzibar was the best place to start looking for it.

On the shore stand the imposing Sultan's palaces, the ancient Arab Fort with its rusting cannons, colonial buildings and merchants' mansions galore. Those houses, some palatial, some of simple construction, but all with elaborately carved wooden doors denoting the riches of those who once dwelled within, are typical of the architecture of Zanzibar in general. One of the grandest mansions bore the not so modest epithet 'Mabo Msiige' ('Do Not Imitate'), the builder of which, according to one guide, used basket upon basket of eggs to strengthen its foundations. Behind the mansions lay labyrinths of bazaars and narrow, dusty streets, where the search for evidence of Freddie begins.

Most local people appear less than impressed that Zanzibar is the birthplace of Freddie Mercury. Some claim, inexplicably, to be insulted. A few seem mildly amused by it, and offer to help with contacts and locations. Word of mouth is the key, there being little forthcoming from official sources. The Zanzibar Archives on the main airport road looked promising, and Mr Hamari Omar, the Archives' Director, was both gracious and anxious to help. There was, however, nothing to speak of in the Archives which pertained directly to Freddie Mercury. Omar suggested the WAKF (or Probate) Department back in town, which houses all records of births, marriages and deaths, where it should have been possible to get a copy of Freddie's birth certificate.

The WAKF Department has now moved from its original home, a sadly dilapidated building which turned out to be the Labour Exchange. It is said to be common on Zanzibar for Government offices to swap buildings regularly. The visitor is casually directed to various others which again turn out to be the wrong ones. The right one, in this instance, was a large, crumbling place, dingy and dusty inside, and crammed with citizens waiting to register their particular hatch, match or dispatch. There were dozens of modestly-robed mothers cradling tiny newborns, and Scribe- and Pharisee-looking officials milling about, bossily dealing with the queues, attempting to create order out of impossible chaos, and making slow entries in huge volumes with proper pens. Ensconced behind ancient counters, separated from the public area by heavy metal grilles, they were attempting to assist people with registration or find paperwork pertaining to loved-ones, and looked worn and resigned. The whole was a scene from some epic Biblical movie.

They came, they listened, they went. The only course of action was for me to wait patiently and explain via my guide what was required. Finally, there came an invitation into the Chief Registrar's office.

His faced expressed no emotion as he handed over a piece of paper and a pencil, silently asking for the details.

Farook or Farrokh Bulsara
5th September, 1946 or *5/9/96*
Parents Bomi and Jer Bulsara.
Born Government Hospital, Zanzibar.

I took, for obvious reasons, the precaution of not mentioning the name 'Freddie Mercury' to anyone. I was told to return in two hours to claim a copy, for which I would have to pay. In the meantime, a visit to the Palace Museum in search of its Curator and leading authority on everything to do with Zanzibar, Professor Abdul Sheriff, proved to be a wild goose chase. My enquiry as to whether I might find anything at all about Freddie Mercury in the museum was met with the retort 'Freddie *who*?' accompanied by bemused giggles and shaking heads. Returning to the WAKF Department, I was not prepared for what I was about to learn.

'So, you are here for Freddie's birth certificate,' said the Chief Registrar, pulling out chairs and offering drinks.

Despite the fact that I had been careful not to disclose Freddie's identity and had only revealed his given name, not his assumed name, this gentleman was in no doubt as to whom I referred.

'It's not here,' he said.

It *was* here. The last time I remember seeing it was maybe three, four years ago. An Argentinian woman came here looking for it. She said she was researching a book about Freddie. A copy was made out for her and she went away. And the original has not been seen since – although it has been asked for on a number of occasions, I presume by fans who have come here to learn about him. That was how we found out that it was missing. When eventually we discovered that it had disappeared, it was too late to do anything at all about it. The main problem is, in 1946 and 1947, proper records were not being kept. Just pieces of paper, which are now in a jumble all over the place. Come, I'll show you.

Back in the main office, he slipped behind the counter, rummaged around on some shelves and in some filing cabinets, and came back with handfuls of loose birth certificates which he dumped on the reception counter. A good few dozen of them spilled on to the floor.

See? this is the kind of document that Freddie's was. But as I've explained to you, they were never kept in any proper order, and consequently it was easy for them to go missing. There is one other person, a physician, Dr Mehta, who is currently in Oman but returning next week. I know that he had a copy of Freddie's certificate, and he might agree to make for you a copy of his copy. You will have to speak to him about that yourselves.

But Dr Mehta proved excruciatingly elusive. A dead end had been reached.

It was indeed a mystery. It was common knowledge that the rock artist formerly known as Farook or Farrokh Bulsara had existed, and had been born on Zanzibar, but there was no official Government record to prove this. Those in authority had seen the document that proved his birth, but evidence of this had now been lost – perhaps for ever. As disorganized as the records office had revealed itself to be, it was hard to accept that such a document might have slipped unnoticed behind some disused desk or been discarded along with the daily rubbish. Could it be possible, as some thought likely, that Freddie's original birth certificate had been sold by some anonymous rogue with friends inside the record office, or some thieving outsider who had persuaded, bribed or frightened him into removing it in return for a handsome fee? And if so, where was it now? This could not be the end to the story of Freddie's birth certificate. There had to be more. And indeed there was. But it would be almost a year before I learned the truth.

There remained one more thread of hope in the quest for information. Some of Freddie's family and friends were said to be still living on the island, in the Shangani district of Zanzibar Town. Leaving the records office and heading directly down a narrow one-way street, one reaches a large, imposing white building with many small shuttered windows, all closed. The house, beside a hotel called the Serena Inn which was in the process of being built, dominated the entire street. A wooden bench ran the length of its front wall. A couple of Arabs sat staring into thin air, and an African lay there asleep. A battered old bicycle rested against it, and a big bundle of rags had been dumped at one end. There was a bell beside the vast wooden double doors, but it was too high to reach, and the ringing of it required assistance. No reply. Eventually, an African man who was lurking nearby came and banged hard on the door with his fists, before stepping back into the beaten-mud road to gaze up at the highest row of windows.

A couple of minutes later a female head leaned out, nodded, and pulled back inside. A good five or six minutes after that the young woman, perhaps in her late twenties, early thirties, opened one of the front doors.

The girl was stunningly beautiful. She had the classic fine-featured Parsee look and serene demeanour, and held herself like a ballerina. A skein of jet-black hair pulled back from her forehead hung down to her shoulders. She had large, round, dark eyes with Bambi eyelashes, a broad beaming smile revealing small white teeth, an elegant nose, the finest wrists and hands. It was as if somebody had drawn her for a fairy-tale film. Her style was simple yet elegant. She was wearing an emerald green dress patterned with a black and white cube design. Her feet were bare, and she wore no jewellery.

I introduced myself and explained the purpose of my visit, and that I had heard that Freddie's relatives lived in this house. She smiled as she introduced herself as Diana Darunkhanawala.

'Actually my mother and Freddie Mercury were first cousins,' she said with a smile, speaking impeccable English, except that she pronounced his adopted surname as if speaking about the famous Greek actress Melina 'Mercouri', with the emphasis on the second syllable: Mercouri. 'Their fathers were brothers.'

I asked if I could meet her mother, who she said worked for the island's Attorney General. But Diana explained that her mother had gone to Buffalo, USA, to stay with her sister for several months. Was there a number on which she could be reached? Diana insisted on going to ask her father. She closed the door and disappeared for 15 minutes. When she returned, she was sorry but they did not have a number; her mother called them from America, they did not call her. Would it be possible to write to her mother, and if so would they forward the letter? Diana agreed, and wrote her mother's name, Perviz Darunkhanawala, and their Zanzibar PO Box address in my notebook.

So what did Diana herself know about Freddie? She smiled at the question. 'Actually,' she laughed, 'I am not at all interested in Freddie Mercouri.'

But you were family, I said.

'Yes, but we didn't have anything in common.'

Nothing at all?

'Well . . . childhood, I suppose. Like Freddie Mercouri, my sister and I were sent to India for education, and stayed with an aunt and uncle in Bangalore. My uncle was in the Army, and we travelled all over India.'

The family had money, then?

'I suppose you could say that we were more privileged than most.'

Why, I persisted, was she 'not at all interested' in Freddie?

'He went away from Zanzibar when I was only a baby, if you want to know. He gave up his family name. He did not live like us – he was nothing at all to do with us. He never came back here; he was of another life. He was a stranger.'

It was the same story elsewhere. Everybody appeared to know about Freddie, but nobody really cared. One day a guide came dashing back in a pant, saying he knew exactly which house Freddie had lived in. We raced together through the winding backstreets past hole-in-the-wall stores towards the Post Office on the other side of the town where we'd been told we would find the little shopfront of Bubla, the old optician. 'Stop in there,' the guide said excitedly. 'The old guy knows which house it is!'

When I got there, the old man claimed, in English, that he didn't speak any English. And anyway, he hadn't got a clue which house it was. Nobody in the Post Office could identify the old Bulsara house – after all, it had been more than 30 years. Nor could anyone in the gift shop. Someone else suggested that they used to know which house we were talking about, over there somewhere, but it had now been pulled down – which turned out to be the truth, and I was able to return and photograph the building which now stands on the same site as Freddie's former home. Another dry-humoured Indian shopkeeper said,

No, I don't know. And neither does anyone else. Anybody who actually tells you they know is only guessing. Especially these guides who take you around the island and show you the sights. They don't really know anything at all, they just want money. There is no one left here on the island who does – so many people left suddenly at the same time. But if you ever find out, will you come back and tell me, please? Because I am heartily sick of people always asking me. I get asked frequently, yes indeed. At least every couple of days. Always by visitors. Nationality? Americans, of course. South Americans. English. German. Japanese. Local people simply don't understand this fuss. Who was this person anyway?

One could be forgiven for beginning to wonder. Here we stood in the birthplace of Zanzibar's most famous son – can you think of any other?—and Zanzibar couldn't give a brass razoo. To the outside Queen-worshipping world, this was hallowed turf indeed. But Freddie Mercury had never in his lifetime been accorded star status in the country of his birth, let alone in the town where his family had lived. It was not even forthcoming posthumously. No Freedom of the City for him. No official archive entry. No acknowledgment at the local museum. No former dwelling converted into personal shrine. No proud family member to boast about him. No waxwork, no effigy, no mass-produced ashtray or dog-bowl, not even a postcard bearing his likeness, although there were postcards of everything else. No 'Freddie Mercury

Desert Island Tour'. Not even, God forgive those responsible for its loss or theft, a humble birth certificate in the records office. If ever you were looking for the antithesis of Elvis Presley's Graceland in Memphis, Tennessee, this had to be it. The commercially-inclined Queen fan entrepreneur could clean up, on the above list alone.

Just before Christmas 1996, the mystery of Freddie's missing birth certificate was once again brought to my attention. Marcela Delorenzi, the Argentinian broadcaster and journalist, contacted me from Buenos Aires to say that she had something for me and that she was bringing it to London in person. It was a good copy of Freddie's original birth certificate. She had indeed been that Argentinian woman who had travelled to Zanzibar seeking a copy. At that time, she insists, the original was still in place in the official records office. She saw it herself. It was from the original that her copy had been made. With no further clues, we could only conclude that the certificate had been stolen, perhaps sold for vast profit, and today languishes in some private collection who knows where in the world.

The muddy waters were at last beginning to clear. The real reason for Freddie's initial 'forgetfulness' of, and subsequent indifference to, his roots was beginning to emerge: Freddie Mercury was not interested in Zanzibar because Zanzibar was not interested in him.

Chapter Three

FROM ZANZIBAR TO PANCHGANI, FROM ZANZIBAR TO LONDON

As much as Freddie might later perceive Zanzibar as having failed him, the fact remains that for most of the first 18 years of his life it was the place he called home. What happened there in his childhood years, and what eventually caused his family to leave the place for good, played a fundamental part in his development.

After Zanzibar had become a British Protectorate in 1890, all administrative power was vested in the British Resident who acted as Imperial Governor. Thus began a colonial heyday which would last for just over seventy years and which would eventually provide, for the likes of Bomi Bulsara and his family during the 1940s and '50s, all the trappings of the privileged 'expatriate' lifestyle.

Who better to talk about that lifestyle than a member of Freddie's family who was there at the time to share it? I was fortunate in that it eventually became possible to interview Freddie's first cousin Perviz Darunkhanawala, née Bulsara, who was Freddie's father Bomi Bulsara's niece, and the mother of Diana Darunkhanawala. Speaking in her own home on Zanzibar, she perched stiffly on the edge of a chair in her spartan sitting-room as she delved into the recesses of her memory for background about the Bulsaras' early years on the island.

My father Sorabji and Freddie's father Bomi were two of eight brothers. I was born here in Zanzibar, but my father was from India, from Bulsar, the small town to the north of Bombay in the state of Gujarat where they were brought up. That was how they got the name Bulsara. The brothers all came here one after the other from India to look out for jobs. My father got a job with Cable and Wireless, while his brother Bomi got a job in the High Court, where he worked for quite some time.

When Freddie's father Bomi first came to Zanzibar, he was not yet married. It was only later that he went back to India and got married to Freddie's mother Jer in Bombay. After that, he brought her here.

I remember very clearly when Freddie was born. He was so small, like a little pet. Even when he was a very young baby he used to come to my home with his parents. They used to leave him with my mother and go out. When he was a bit older, he would always play about in our house. He was such a naughty little one. I was much older than him, and I liked to take care of him. He was such a small boy, a very nice child. I loved him so much. Every time he came I wanted him to stay, but his parents would always collect him and take him back home at the end of an evening out.

The Bulsaras, according to Perviz, enjoyed quite the sophisticated social life within the confines of their Parsee religion and culture. On a salary which would have defined him as little more than a modest civil servant back in Britain, Bomi was able to support a very comfortable home and domestic servants, including Freddie's Ayah (nanny), Sabine. His family wanted for nothing. The living was easy and the climate good. When the boy still known as Farrokh was six years old, his mother at last produced a sister for him to play with. Kashmira, a bonny baby who would grow into a small but beautiful, slender child with large round eyes and glossy black hair, arrived in 1952.

As a High Court cashier for the British Government, their hard-working father Bomi was based at offices in the non-residential Beit-el Ajaib, the House of Wonders, built by the Sultan Sayyid Barghash in the late nineteenth century for ceremonial purposes. It had been, in its day, the tallest building in East Africa, and boasted impressive botanical gardens. It had survived bombardment by a British Fleet following a brief uprising, and has since undergone extensive conversion to become the main museum of Zanzibar.

Bomi's work required him to travel extensively throughout the colony and into India. His lengthy absences might have had some bearing on the decision to send their son away to school. But there was also the question of how far the child's education could be taken on Zanzibar. Despite the fact that his Parsee parents continued to practise their Zoroastrian faith, Farrokh attended the Zanzibar Missionary School from the age of five, where his teachers were Anglican nuns. His early influences were therefore predominantly female. He had rapidly taken to the basic 'three Rs': reading, writing and arithmetic; he was considered a brighter than average child, and had already shown considerable aptitude for painting, drawing and modelling. He was developing into a delightfully courteous if serious and precise little boy, with a twinkle in his eye and a mischievous streak which would now and then get the better of him.

But Perviz remembers her cousin most vividly as a very shy and secretive little boy. 'Yes, he was painfully shy. He would not talk much, even when he came with his parents to see us. That was his nature. As he grew older we didn't see each other so much, as he would be out playing with all the other boys.'

Educational opportunities were limited on Zanzibar in the

1950s. The trend among respectable professional families was to despatch their offspring approaching the age of ten to boarding schools, the finest of which were based on the English public school system and were to be found beyond a vast expanse of ocean in Commonwealth India. It was natural that Bomi and Jer Bulsara, both Indian-born Parsees, should look to Bombay when considering the further education of their son. Bombay had long been the adopted home of the Persian Parsees, a nation in exile.

'When our ancestors fled from Persia during the Islamic invasion in the eighth century AD, they landed, in 745 AD at Sanjan in Gujarat, Western India, to the North of Bombay,'[1] explains Fiz Shapur, a direct descendant of King Shapur of Persia, who ruled around 500 BC and whose artefacts are housed in the British Museum. A London-based musical director and composer, Shapur is of paternal Persian Parsee descent and fiercely proud of his roots.

There, the King of Gujarat decreed that the Parsees could only remain if they agreed to adopt the Hindu customs and lifestyle and speak the Gujarati language; all except the Priest caste, who could retain the Persian Parsee language, which was originated from ancient Arabic, for prayer. They would not pick up arms, and would not wear their own traditional clothing except for marriage ceremonies and religious occasions. He also ruled that there would be no inter-marriage, and no attempt to convert others to Parsee Zoroastrianism. Under these restrictions, the Parsees were allowed to practise their religion, and live harmoniously in their own community alongside Hindus and other religious groups. As such, the Parsees remained a pure race. The Towers of Silence were also permitted. We came to Bombay as bankers, shipbuilders and traders. Perhaps because of our flair with all things financial, we became known as 'The Jews of India'. The community grew down the centuries and migrated further south, until, in the 1670s, the largest Parsee community in the world was to be found in and around Bombay. In a cosmopolitan city of immigrants much like, say, New York, the Parsees were the best-known immigrant group. Eventually, exposed to India's colonial influences, the Parsees would become more and more anglicized, adopting British customs, dress and lifestyle. They learned Shakespeare, for example; they took to wearing top-hats, and played cricket and golf. Among the very first Indian undergraduates at Oxford and Cambridge were Parsees. It was a Parsee by the name of Tata who founded the airline which, in 1946, went public as Air India. Today's leading Parsees are often doctors, lawyers and writers. Nani Palkhivala, a Parsee and one of India's leading lawyers, served as Ambassador to the United States between 1977 and 1979. Of course, it was only natural that further-flung Parsees should return their children to India to be educated in the great British public school tradition. It was regarded as the best to be had.

The Parsee community in Bombay today remains incredibly tightly-knit, and India is the Parsee spiritual home. Their scriptures are in Persian, they speak Gujarati, and continue to give up their dead to the Towers of Silence. It was once rare for the Parsee to marry outside race and religion because the children would not be true Parsees. In such a small, élite and correct community, the only answer was inter-marriage. But today, although the Parsees maintain a patriarchal family and society, their community has dwindled to the point that they now have no choice but to marry outside the religion. There are fewer than 90,000 Parsees in the world today. Although their stronghold is still Bombay, they have also settled in England, Canada, and between Sydney and Melbourne in Australia. It has been remarked that, while the sane tend to be highly intelligent and extremely successful, 'there is a certain amount of battiness about'. Could this go some way to explaining Freddie's eccentric streak?

In November 1996, when the Freddie Mercury Photographic Exhibition was launched at London's Albert Hall to commemorate the fifth anniversary of Freddie's death, Freddie was exposed in the press as 'the Great Pretender' for having 'hidden his Indian roots from the fans'. According to widely discussed publicity, appearing under banner headlines such as 'Bombay Rhapsody' and 'Star of India', Freddie had been, in fact, Britain's 'first Asian pop star', and his Persian origins were disputed. But according to a spokesman for the Persian Parsee community in London,

> Just because our people have not lived in Persia since the ninth century, that does not make us any less Persian. If you are a Jew, and your family have not lived in Palestine for the past two thousand years, does that make you any less Jewish? There is a great difference between race and nationality, between roots and citizenship. The Persian Parsee may not have a place to call home (the terrain which was once their territory being modern-day Iran), but he remains truly Persian in his heart.

Physical features are another consideration. Compare a photograph of a Bombay-born Indian with a picture of a Persian and the differences are glaringly obvious. The classic Persian look is distinctly at odds with that which is commonly considered 'Indian'. Freddie's own reflection said it all.

Born, pre-Independence, in colonial India, Freddie's parents were British subjects and their nationality British-Indian. This is on record – they declared as much when they registered the birth of their son. But significantly, they gave their race as Parsee. Freddie himself was born on Zanzibar, part of East Africa, and was therefore Zanzibari by birth. It could therefore be argued that he was, in fact, more African than Asian. 'Britain's first Asian pop star' was a somewhat romantic notion, and merely a new hook upon which to hang a collection of old pictures of Freddie Mercury. Why did his immediate family not object to this blurring of their past, to such an overt dismissal of their sacred religious heritage? Their behaviour was often puzzling.

With regard to Freddie's despatch to Bombay for the purposes of education, his cousin Perviz remarked:

> Freddie's parents sent him away to school in India and it saddened me greatly to see him go. But here, at that time, the standard of education was not so good for the boys. Also, I believe it was about that same time that his parents were transferred for work to the island of Pemba, and there was certainly nothing of a high enough educational standard there. And so they felt that the best solution was to send him to Bomi's sister, also called Jer, that is, my Auntie, in Bombay, where he could study properly.

It was in 1955, when he was not yet nine years old, that Farrokh Bulsara was enrolled at St Peter's Church of England school in the hill station of Panchgani ('Five Hills'), an ecumenical establishment which promoted tolerance of many diverse religions, including Catholicism and Zoroastrianism. Freddie had already been indoctrinated into the ancient Parsee faith by then, having just experienced, at the age of eight, the Naojote (commonly westernised as 'Navjote') ceremony which, like the Christian Confirmation, embraces both boys and girls, but which more closely resembles the Jewish Barmitzvah. The procedure involves a cleansing bath to symbolize the purification of mind and soul, the wearing of a symbolic white shirt and wool cord, and the chanting of ancient prayers before an eternal sacred fire. Such fires are an integral feature of the Zoroastrian faith, and in some fire temples are claimed to have been burning for thousands of years. The Zendavesta, or sacred scriptures of the faith, contain no commandments as we understand them, simply the 'Three Good Things' which comprise the code by which Parsees live: 'Humata, Hukhta, Huvareshta'. Good Thoughts, Good Words, Good Deeds.

In the mid 1950s when Freddie arrived, Bombay was India's busiest, most industrialized and most progressive city. Since the majority of visitors travelling to India arrived by boat, Bombay was also its principal seaport and the true 'gateway' to India. As Freddie's cousin Perviz remembered:

> He must have gone by ship with his father, before taking the train up to Panchgani. A very long, tiring journey. Because in those days we all used to travel to India by ship, and not by plane. There were regular ships going from Zanzibar to Bombay, and we used to go often because we had our relations there. And, as planned, Freddie used to come to my Auntie Jer, Bomi's sister, during the school holidays. She was a very good, kind lady because she used to take care of the small children of another brother as well in India.

Although air traffic has now superseded sea travel and the port is in decline, Bombay's grand yellow basalt triumph arch, the entrance gate itself, still stands on the Apollo Blunder. Up on Bombay's Malabar Hill, these days a leafy, expensive residential area with impressive views of the city, respectable old Parsee families and ex-Maharajas find themselves living next door to diamond dealers and Bollywood movie stars. Also on the hilltop beside the world-famous Hanging Gardens are the Towers of Silence, where the Parsees, according to the rituals of religion, still expose their dead. Carefully hidden behind a high wall from the view of more ghoulish sightseers who occasionally attempt to photograph vultures picking over the human carcasses, the

Towers are closed to visitors, but remain one of India's most famous tourist monuments.

Bombay boasts a vast, sprawling Parsee colony, and Parsee culture continues to hold its own in the city. The highly commercial Parsee theatre, developed from British touring companies, produces popular lightweight comedy. The Jamshedji Navroz (Parsee New Year's Day) is celebrated in March according to the Farsi calendar with a colourful festival. While there are few specialist Parsee restaurants in Bombay, an invitation to the Parsee club, The Ripon, is always worth accepting if only for an opportunity to taste the cuisine, rich in meat and eggs. Special dishes include mutton dhansak and fish patia. Elsewhere, Parsee food may be sampled in the Irani chaikhanas, or tea houses, which are similar to Parisian pavement cafés and are mostly run by Zoroastrians who arrived in Bombay from Iran at the turn of the century.

Freddie's public school, St Peter's, founded in 1902, is still widely considered to be the finest school in Panchgani. Its appeal to Freddie's parents as potentially the best choice for their son was obvious: it offered a full English education including Cambridge University O level and A level examination sittings, and maintained consistently excellent results which attracted families from the Gulf, Canada and the USA as well as all over India. The school year lasts from mid-June to mid-April with the main eight-week holiday between April and June and a two-week holiday at Christmas. It boasts a strict routine with a good deal of discipline – hot water baths on Wednesdays and Saturday lunchtimes, the rest of the week cold; a strict matron to supervise bathing routines and the school's hospital; an on-call doctor and a resident nurse; its own church – although boys of all denominations attend the school, all are required to attend Mass on Sundays; boys not allowed off the school premises without being accompanied by a member of staff. But St Peter's was also known to be a caring establishment which promoted camaraderie and a close family atmosphere. It was one of four exclusive schools, two for girls, two for boys, in a remote but elegant hill station about 184 miles up from Bombay, and about five or six hours from the city by train and bus. Freddie's school is still there, thriving, and quietly proud of its most famous son.

As he headed for his first term there, moving further and further away from the safety of his mother's arms, Freddie must have felt increasingly alarmed, dejected and alone. Those close to him in later years have told how Freddie still harboured a deep resentment towards his parents for 'sending him away', although he had tried to come to terms with his feelings of rejection.

There was some comfort in the company of a handful of other, slightly older boys on the same Poona-bound train. One was 10-year-old Victory Rana, who, rather grandly, was related to nobility and went on to become a Brigadier in the Royal Nepalese Army. The others, who had also turned 10 already ahead of Farrokh, were Derrick Branche, who moved on to Australia and eventually became an actor, Farang Irani, who later became a restaurateur in Bombay, and Bruce Murray, last heard of working as a porter at Victoria railway station in London. Over the next few years these boys would become inseparable, sleeping next to each other in the same dormitory and getting up to the same schoolboy pranks. Packed off to either his paternal aunt Jer or his maternal aunt Sheroo for many of his term and half-term breaks, there was not even the relief of seeing his parents regularly during the school holidays. In reality, Freddie and other shy little boys like him were probably far too young to be sent such vast distances just to go to school. Some young children appear to deal with prolonged separation from their families better than others. For Freddie, a sensitive child who was particularly close to his loving mother and sister – he could even be described as a little clingy – the wrench, at just over eight years of age, was initially terrible. The thought of him crying himself silently to sleep in his narrow dormitory bed, surrounded by a quivering bunch of 19 other new boys as he pined for his mother and Kashmira, is unbearable. There is no question that his parents believed they were doing nothing but right by their adored son, giving him the best possible start in life. What could be more important than a sound education? What's more, he was being sent to a school with one of the finest reputations of its day. But the disadvantages were considerable. Freddie now found himself deprived, for the best possible reasons, of daily one-to-one affection and attention from his parents, particularly his mother, during the most crucial stage of his development; at an age when he was so deeply impressionable, his sphere of reckoning so black and white, that his schooldays could be said to be the one period that moulded the personality of the 'real' Freddie which he was to retain throughout adulthood. School dominates a child's most formative years. During that period, almost any experience, emotional or physical, can affect or even scar a child for life.

Freddie's maternal aunt, Sheroo Khory, a sister of his mother Jer and a spinster now in her late seventies, still lives in the Dadar Parsee colony to the north of central Bombay. When I spoke to her on the telephone she explained that she would have been more than happy to see us if not for the monsoon – it had rained incessantly for three days – or for her immobility due to a recent hip operation. But she talked frankly and fondly of her beloved nephew, telling what a good-hearted boy he had always been.

'Once Freddie was in England, that was it. He never wanted to come back to India. He called himself British, he liked the civilized lifestyle, and most of all he liked the justice system, especially in comparison to all the corruption here in India. But he kept in touch regularly with me, and even sent me money for an eye operation which I badly needed. He never forgot his old Auntie.'

So greatly indebted to Sheroo did Freddie feel for all the

love and kindness she bestowed on him during his boyhood years, that, she says, he begged her to come to the UK and on a tour of Europe entirely at his own expense, an offer which she had graciously declined due to her old age and failing health. But she could understand why Freddie wanted her there. She said that, even as a little boy, Freddie had always liked to be 'guided' by her, even when he was spending his holidays with his other aunt, Jer, his father's sister. 'He would stay with Jer but always come to me after breakfast, and spend entire days with me. He was very good at drawing and I encouraged him. When he was eight he drew an excellent picture of two horses in a storm, which was signed 'Farrokh' and which used to hang in his mother's house, I don't know if she still has it.'

Much later, Sheroo fell into correspondence with Freddie's former girlfriend Mary Austin, trading photographs of Freddie as a little boy and Freddie as a big rock-star. She told us that Freddie had enemies in England, and that she had often had cause to worry for his safety. When we touched on the subject of religion, and in particular more recent rumours that Freddie had in the final years preceding his death converted to Christianity, Sheroo became audibly upset. 'The whole family was extremely distressed by this news. It was a great blow. We were all fed up with so many heartbreaking things being said about our Freddie, all the lies being told, particularly this thing about him becoming a Christian. Which I am sure he did not. Certainly not to my knowledge.'

Sheroo appeared anxious to maintain what is left of the family's privacy, and declined to divulge too much, as if she were afraid of the consequences. 'Freddie's mother has warned that none of us is to deal with the press, nor give them photographs or talk to anyone at all from newspapers. She and Freddie's father have moved to Nottingham to be near to their daughter, and to get away finally from all the attention. Too many lies have already been written, and Freddie is gone. It is now time for all of this to end.'

Ensconced in his new school, it was now a question of stiff upper lip, of sink or swim. Ripped from the feminine security to which he had grown accustomed among the nuns at his Zanzibar primary school, and plunged unceremoniously into unfamiliar and predominantly male territory, Farrokh soon came to terms with his early misery. There was no choice. Talking about his schooldays years later, Freddie commented: 'You had to do what you were told, so the most sensible thing was to make the most of it. I learnt to look after myself, and I grew up quickly.'[2]

He realised that he would have to pull himself together and hold his own, particularly in the company of older boys who he soon learned would bully him mercilessly if they detected fear. Anything tease-worthy is always best avoided at boarding school. His name was the first thing that would have to go. 'Farrokh' was a bit of a mouthful anyway, pronounced the Persian way, 'Farroch', as in 'loch', to distinguish it from the North African version of the name, 'Farouk'. The boy was relieved when his teachers and pals began to use instead the diminutive of an eminently respectable English name, Frederick. 'Freddie' he became, and the nickname stuck. He decided that it suited him, and was soon signing himself that way. His parents and other family members appear to have raised no obvious objections to the assumed appellation, since they started calling him Freddie too, and still refer to him by that name to this day. The change of surname, of course, would come much later, and for different reasons entirely.

It was about this time that Freddie began, subconsciously, to develop an aloof streak which would stand him in good stead throughout his life. While not in any way an unkind or malicious child, he was simply not always the typical team player or one of the gang, preferring at times to indulge in more private pursuits. In sport, for example, he fared best at solo or one-to-one activities such as sprinting, boxing and table tennis – he became the school's table-tennis champion at just 10 years of age – than at the team sports of rugby, football and hockey. The one exception was cricket, which he is said by many to have loved at the time, although years later he would deny this, perhaps fearful of the effect that such an openly declared genteel preference might wreak on his hard rock-star image. His artistic temperament took hold at an early age, and as a consequence he began to feel somewhat isolated. His favourite class was Art, and much of his free time was spent painting and sketching, particularly for his aunt Sheroo and his grandparents, who lived not too far away from the school in the Parsee community in Bombay. When he did not go to stay with his paternal aunt Jer, Freddie sometimes spent his school holidays with aunt Sheroo when his parents were travelling. Because of the Bulsaras' lengthy absences from home, there were times when he had no choice but to spend shorter holidays on the school premises. But his parents did, apparently, try to avoid this as much as possible.

It was at St Peter's, too, that Freddie first revealed his musical inclinations. Even back in the late 1950s and early 1960s, Bombay enjoyed a more cosmopolitan East-meets-West culture than most Indian cities, and Western pop and rock were beginning to make their mark. Freddie was fascinated by the contemporary music he was getting to know as well as the classical works, in particular opera, which he was learning about at school under the guidance of the head teacher, Mr Davis. It was said that Freddie also had Mr Davis to thank for his music lessons. Aware of the young pupil's emerging talent, it was Davis who wrote to Freddie's parents with the suggestion that they might like to consider paying additional fees for private tuition. It was an extra to which the Bulsaras readily agreed.

His cousin Perviz remembers: 'Since he was very young, Freddie had always been interested in music, and in singing.

Much more than in studying. How did I know that? Well in those days, his parents and my parents were very close here in Zanzibar, and they used to talk to us about it. How he was learning to play piano and so on.'

Freddie studied the piano assiduously, encouraged to practise during the holiday breaks by his mother and his aunts, and passed his exams up to and including Grade IV in Theory and Practical. He also sang enthusiastically in the school choir, although some reckoned his motives for joining were more basic than a keen love of chorals. The choir, which numbered about 25, often featured girls from one of the girls' schools in Panchgani, and it is said that one of them, a local 15-year-old called Gita Bharucha, had been the object of Freddie's affections for some time. Although it has been widely assumed and commented upon that Freddie's self-exploration and subsequent physical precocity began at St Peter's when he was about 14 years old, and exclusively in the company of other males – fellow pupils and even a couple of hired hands at St Peter's – there is some evidence to support the theory that this assumption was somewhat erroneous; that, indeed, Freddie was not immune to the charms of the female of the species even then.

Whether Freddie's attraction to Gita was anything more than a purely unrequited crush, and whether any act of passion ever took place between them, is not actually on record. Attempting to trace the woman, I was told in Bombay that she is now married and held a senior managerial position at the Thomas Cook travel bureau's Head Office. But enquiries within at that time drew a blank, the desk clerks claiming never to have heard of her. It was only months later, quite by chance, that I came across the Thomas Cook number in my notebook and gave it one more try. By now, I had discovered that Gita's married name was Choksi, and I asked for her in both names. She had now left the employ of Thomas Cook. But as luck would have it, I was put through to a woman who had formerly worked with Gita, and who kindly gave me the number of her Bombay residence. I immediately telephoned.

'This is amazing that you have managed to find me,' Mrs Choksi said. 'I don't even live here anymore – I am now resident in Frankfurt, Germany, where I work for a private Indian tour operator, promoting tourism from Europe to India. I have just got in to Bombay today, a couple of hours ago, as we have some renovation to do on the house. It is truly extraordinary that you have tracked me down.'

She was reluctant to say much about Freddie at first, explaining that she had maintained a respectful silence all these years in loving memory of her old school friend: 'I just thought it wasn't correct,' she said.

'But I feel quite happy to talk to you now. Freddie and I had 11 years in school together,' – although according to the school records, it was in fact eight—'and we were good friends. It was terribly nostalgic for me, seeing all those pictures in the *Sunday Times* from the Freddie Mercury exhibition. A number of people sent me copies when it came out. I have all those original photographs, you see, in my little albums. I've had them for years.'

I first met Freddie in 1955, when I started at The Kimmins School in Panchgani, which was run by Protestant missionaries from England. I eventually left there in 1963. For most of the years that Freddie was in Panchgani – 'Panchi', as we used to call it – we were friends. The way it worked was that the little boys from St Peter's would attend the Kimmins kindergarten, then continue from Standard Three at St Peter's proper.

I was from Bombay, but I lived with my mother and grandparents in Panchi, and I was a day scholar. A group of us were in the same class together for many years. Victory Rana and I were always together right through school. And Bucky – that's what we used to call Freddie, because of his teeth, I suppose – was part of our same little group.

Derrick Branche was another one – he went on to be an actor, and had a part, I think, in the film *My Beautiful Laundrette*. He was the one who later gave an interview for a book about Freddie and said a number of things about me that were completely untrue; I can't imagine why.

It is all such a long time ago, but what I do remember is that Bucky and I were especially close, but always just good friends. Nothing intimate, nothing more. Very often during the May break we didn't go home to Bombay but stayed in Panchi. We all used to go cycling, which was very popular – we'd rent bicycles at three rupees per day, a lot when it meant parting with your pocket money. We also used to go out in rowing boats on Mahableshwar Lake and create mayhem. And Mum would allow that I could have a party, or a few friends over to lunch, after which we would go for walks or play games or whatever. Bucky often came during the holidays and spent time at our home. He was extremely polite and well-mannered in company, the perfect guest. My mother and grandparents liked him enormously. There was nothing more to our little friendship than that. You must understand that in those days, holding hands was the be-all and end-all.

One of the things that sticks in my mind the most was the way that Bucky used to wear his uniform. We had quite distinctive uniforms – I used to wear a white blouse and navy pinafore, and the boys were always in khaki shirts and shorts. Bucky's shirt was always hanging out of his shorts at the back. Later on, when we girls changed to what we called 'dusters', a sort of blue and white hounds-tooth dress uniform, the boys progressed to long trousers, which were referred to by the derogatory term of 'drainpipes', because they seemed so long and thin compared with the baggy short trousers. And still Bucky's shirt always hung out from the back. It was funny.

As for Freddie's personality, Gita remarks that it was best captured by the school photograph of him receiving the Junior All-Rounder trophy. Seated in a slightly hunched fashion on a plain fold-up wooden chair against lush foliage in the school grounds, the enormous trophy standing on the ground in front of him, Freddie, smart-casual in his piped blazer, open-necked shirt, khaki trousers and large, heavy lace-up shoes, leans forward slightly and stares directly and unselfconsciously into the camera lens. He beams with a modest pride. His arms are folded low across his chest and his hands tucked away out of sight. There is an unmistakable twinkle in his almost black eyes, and for once he does not attempt to shield his toothy smile.

'That picture was Freddie all over,' Gita says.

I remember that occasion so vividly, and how thrilled Freddie was to get the prize. That trophy was the school 'Oscar', and to win it was really something. He hadn't expected to win it at all, but he was of course very pleased that he did. He was really quite exuberant about it. Most of the time in school I remember him as being great fun, and occasionally a little wild. I have read since that a teacher called Mr Davis is supposed to be the one who first got him into music and playing piano, but I would like to set the record straight here. It was in fact this miserable but nevertheless rather sweet old lady called Miss O'Shea, who was of course Irish, and who had this wild, colleen-type hair. She was very elderly, but she absolutely doted on Bucky, and she was the one who encouraged him all the way in his music. I expect there were others too, but she was the one who really got him going at it.

Despite their close friendship, Gita never heard from Freddie again after he left Panchgani.

Very sad, I know, but that was it. He just didn't keep in touch, as if that part of his life was now over and he just wanted to divorce himself from life here in India and get on with the next stage. He alienated himself completely. I think I was a little disappointed that he divested himself of the past. When I eventually found out that Freddie Mercury was in fact Freddie Bulsara from school, it was about 20 years later, from a snippet I read in *Woman's Own* magazine. I was very pleasantly surprised, and pulled out all my old photographs to show to friends.

As for all that I have read about why he wanted to hide his Indian roots, I just don't know why so much rubbish has been written about this. I consider myself Indian, absolutely, but perhaps Freddie did not. We never discussed it – we were only children when I knew him. Of course it is very exotic to say 'I'm Persian', but the fact is that we were hounded from Persia a very long time ago. As I see it, we are Indians by nationality and that's it. It is of course quite possible that Freddie's family did not feel that way, at least at that time, and one must respect this.

After I realized who he was I did get hold of some of his recordings, and some of his music I enjoyed immensely – though not all of it. Friends were always giving me CDs, but I would give quite a few of them away. I never saw him perform live, however, I am very disappointed to say. This is also much to my 16-year-old son's dismay. Another of our old school chums once went to one of Queen's concerts, I forget where it was, and he tried to go backstage to see Bucky. But when he managed to put himself face to face with him, Freddie just looked right through this poor fellow, and said to him, 'I'm sorry, but I'm afraid I just don't know who you are.' That was when we all realized at last that he wanted nothing more to do with us.

What surprised me the most about him? That he achieved the fame that he did. I never knew that he was that talented. But nothing ever actually shocked me about him, so I was very pleased to see that he was doing so brilliantly well.

With regard to suggestions that Freddie was romantically besotted with his beautiful classmate Gita Bharucha, despite gossip and rumour it seemed unlikely. Given the era, the restrictions placed on boarding school pupils having contact with other pupils of the opposite sex, and the severe penalties imposed for misbehaviour out of hours and out of bounds, it appeared more probable that bashful glances and innocent chat were all that passed between them. Gita herself endorsed this when we spoke: 'For a start, I was never even in the choir! All these suggestions that Freddie was in love with me are simply a load of rubbish. I don't know what people must be thinking of when they make up things like that. We were just innocent platonic friends.'

Was it merely that pent-up pubescent frustration or the fact that he was gay which led Freddie to indulge, eventually, in sex-play with other boys? Freddie never answered that question. But, as he would later remark:

It's stupid to say that there is no such thing in boarding schools. All the things they say about them are more or less true. All the bullying and everything else. I've had the odd schoolmaster chasing me. It didn't shock me because somehow boarding schools ... you're not confronted by it, you are just slowly aware of it. It's going through life. There were times when I was young and green. It's a thing schoolboys go through. I've had my share of schoolboy pranks. I'm not going to elaborate any further.[3]

According to Gita, Freddie never gave any outward indication of his sexual preferences.

I never, ever thought Bucky was gay. Not at all. Mind you, he never had a separate girlfriend if ever any of us paired off at times in the later years. But nobody took any notice of that. There was no specific, permanent girlfriend-boyfriend arrangement. We were all just chums together. Maybe the masters knew about Bucky being gay, but were discreet. We friends were certainly not aware of it. It was never discussed, and in those days anyway that kind of thing was totally under wraps. He was quite the flamboyant performer, and he was absolutely in his element on stage – invariably he had the role of a girl. But I believe this was nothing at all to do with him being gay, it was just that he was an exceptionally good actor and nobody else could play the female parts as well as Bucky could. He had a very creative talent – he was the driving force of the band The Hectics. The academic side, in comparison, was not so good.

When I eventually discovered that he was gay, once he had become famous, it didn't bother me one bit. That, after all, is life today. But then again it didn't affect me personally. I guess if it were on my own doorstep I would be as equally affected by it as his family must have been. It has occurred to me since that maybe, quite possibly, he didn't actually know *what* he was. But that perhaps more has always been made of it because of the scandal element, which is always much more exciting to read about. It's a bit like when you read anything about India: it's always the cows on the road, the fumes on the tracks, the monsoons and the cyclones and the poverty. One never reads anything positive about my country, because that would be too ordinary and not scandalous. I imagine Freddie's life as an adult was a little like that. It could well have contributed to him being the way he was.

Although much has been written and repeated about his years at St Peter's, the information is often contradictory. Who could tell whether fact and fiction had traded places over time? Only a personal visit could aid in our attempt to unravel the truth about Freddie's Indian school days.

A nine-hour journey from Bombay to Panchgani above Poona was undertaken in August 1996, by four-wheel drive, during the monsoon season. It is a notoriously dangerous ascent, but we had been told that it was worth every heart-in-mouth moment along skinny hairpin bends for the views alone: enchanting waterfalls such as Chinaman's and the Dhobi, the beautiful Venna Lake, the impressive crumbling temples dating back to the fifth century. The challenging drive up through woodlands and often in torrential rain stirs deep-rooted storybook memories of Jack and his Beanstalk. Off the winding, narrow single-track pass which is, in places, little more than a ledge, lies the town of Wai on the river Krishna, the site of many of the ancient temples to which Hindu pilgrims have trekked for thousands of years. The exhilarating air seems almost to draw one onwards and upwards into the heavens. Through the fog, visibility is at times reduced to a mere 10 metres. One of the children remarks that she could put her hand out of the car window and eat the clouds. We pass through Mahableshwar, said to be the most desirable of all hill stations, once a popular summer retreat of the Bombay presidency during the days of the Raj, and renowned for strawberry farming and jam. Another 19 kilometres along the road and the soil begins to turn red. The fog clears, the casuarina trees and the silver oaks become visible. Panchgani has at last been reached, a slim settlement between vast tablelands and stark cliffs descending into the valley below. It is an idyllic and tranquil, clean and shimmering place, in stark contrast to crowded, slum-hemmed life on the teeming plains below. The Bombay bustle may be all but forgotten at this dizzy altitude of about 1,334 metres above sea level. The air is cool and tangy, the views through the mists truly spectacular. Panchgani's main street is quaint, a half-kilometre stretch of tiny shops, restaurants and cluttered bazaar stalls. We had heard the place described as gracious and restful with a pleasant climate all year, although Mahableshwar gets the second-highest rainfall in all India during the monsoon season, between June and September. It is famous for its fine schools and sanatoria, and is certainly a rarefied location. Derrick Branche, one of Freddie's aforementioned classmates, was once moved to describe it as resembling the English town of Great Malvern, nestling among the Malvern Hills another world away. Others agreed that it was absolutely the finest place in the world to which to send a boy to school.

St Peter's School is larger than one might expect, an almost hamlet-sized sprawl of modest buildings close to the roadside on both sides – dormitories, outhouses and staff cottages, the majority in need of substantial renovation, just like most Indian buildings. Thanks to the rains, the playing fields were a mud bath. Some of the buildings remain exactly as they were during Freddie's years there. Others have been rebuilt or renovated following fire and earthquake damage. The dormitories, classrooms and art room are extremely well-equipped if, by our standards, somewhat shabby. The main assembly hall is lined with polished wooden boards engraved with the names of distinguished pupils past and present. Although we scoured board after board, Freddie's name was nowhere to be seen. He had never been Head Boy, Captain of House or cricket team, senior monitor or champion of track or field. For such a world-famous pupil, it is perhaps surprising that the school neglects to display any tribute to Freddie whatsoever. There is not a photograph, not a poster, not a framed gold album anywhere. Much of the school, including the small hall stage where he performed in public for the very first time, remains intact as Freddie would have known it. It seems pitiful that his presence is not officially acknowledged in even one small corner of this foreign field.

The Principal's house sits adjacent to the school. In his office, we were warmly received by Mr Innis, who has been Principal since 1981 having taught at the school until 1978, returning three years later. Although he never met Freddie, Mr Innis feels he knows the school's most famous former pupil well, having spent years dealing with international interest since Freddie's death. He had to admit that he was glad, he said, when the Indian newspapers neglected to report in their Freddie obituaries that he was a former pupil at St Peter's.

'Apart from the cause of his death, I hear nothing bad about him,' reports Mr Innis, perhaps not meaning to suggest that the fact that Freddie died from AIDS was 'bad'.

I have always been told that he was a nice guy. That he was a good chap in general. That he had a natural talent at piano, and an aptitude for music in general. I don't believe he could actually read music to begin with, but played beautifully by ear. But you know something, at school, unless someone is really outstanding academically, or badly behaved, people tend not to remember them so clearly. And that was certainly the case with Freddie. He was no champion scholar, nor did he have a reputation for being wild or crazy.

According to the school's records, which had been marked up meticulously prior to our specific visit, Freddie was a boarding pupil at St Peter's from 1955 until 1963, and not from 1954 until 1962 as stated in previous biographies. He came from the Mission School in Zanzibar, and was admitted into Class Three on 14 February 1955. His name, on admission, was given as 'Farookh Bomi Bulsara' – note the change of spelling of his first name compared with the version on the birth certificate. The record books show that he was an average scholar with a particularly keen interest in all sports and extracurricular activities, especially music, elocution and chess. He was a member of Ashlin House. In 1958, aged almost 12, he took the annual prize for Best Junior All-Rounder, of which his family were extremely proud, and the following year, 1959, while a member of Class Seven, he took first prize for academic subjects and found himself top of the class. It was at around the same time that Freddie began to win roles in a number of school plays, his interest in theatre said to have been encouraged by Mr Davis, who would play the boys recordings of great British actors such as John Gielgud and Laurence Olivier reading from Shakespeare. The latent performer in Freddie was fast beginning to emerge. Also in 1959, he played a woman for the first time in the school's production of the play *Ghost By Request*, and won the singing competition in the Junior section. In 1960, in the play *A Night In The Inn*, Freddie played the priest. He lost in a lightweight boxing match against one R. Kapur, also of St Peter's, in 1962. That same year he put in a memorable performance in the Seniors' production of *The Indian Love Call*, singing a solo in a trio comprising Freddie and his two pals, Victory Rana and Bruce Murray. He also took a lead role in the amateur dramatics society's production of *Death On The Line*, the photographic evidence of which once graced the walls of the main lobby along with scores of others, but which is said to have since been stolen. Then there was his music. Plenty of schoolboys have made merry playing in their own school band, and Freddie and his pals were no exception. They were enthused all the more by the fact that the decade was on the turn, and pop music and sixties attendant culture were just about to boom. By now, Freddie and his close pals who were

61

also involved in the band, which they named The Hectics, were sharing a small dormitory of their own. Freddie's first ever performances as a musician were as the pianist with that fledgling band. His boogie-woogie style is said to have been particularly impressive. Encouraged by the other pupils and a number of the teachers, the band went from strength to strength, and soon had all but taken over the music room, where Gita Bharucha and a few other female friends used to be allowed to attend their rehearsals. They were permitted to play at all the school concerts, at the annual fête, and on a few other dates throughout the school year. Teachers remember a significant influx of females from the neighbouring girls' schools on such occasions, who would stand at the front, close to the edge of the stage, staring up at the band and screaming their lungs out. It was, apparently, as if they had heard that this was the way to behave in front of a group. The pop idols of the day were Elvis Presley, Cliff Richard Fats Domino, and Little Richard. Fats Domino and Little Richard were said to be Freddie's favourites, and he was always practising hard to emulate their style. Freddie was not yet fully prepared for his future role as rock front man. In those days he was more than happy to take a back seat and defer to Bruce Murray, who played guitar and sang lead. In fact, according to Gita and others who witnessed The Hectics' performances at the time, Freddie, who could be excruciatingly shy and even somewhat prim, did not look like front-man material at all. His louder, wilder, more daring side would only occasionally get the better of him. On rare occasions he was also known to lose his temper with both teachers and fellow pupils, particularly if he suspected that someone had taken something belonging to him, or that he had been wrongly accused of some misdemeanour. As Gita remarked previously, she and their other pals who were closest to him at school were later astonished to hear that he had become a world-famous rock-star.

By the time he reached Class 10, there is no further mention in the school records of significant academic achievement, and Freddie's standards appear to have begun to slip. He even failed his Class 10 end-of-year examinations, and left the school before entering Class 11, the year when O levels were taken. Nobody, all these years later, can throw light on precisely what happened. The most likely explanation for this would appear to be that Freddie had become distracted by his confused sexuality, as well as by more creative pursuits such as music and art. It would seem that he simply lost interest in his academic studies, and had begun to set his sights on more glamorous goals. Although it has been reported in previous biographies that Freddie left St Peter's with several O levels and with particularly good grades in Art, History and English Language, the fact is that he actually left St Peter's without any O levels at all. Quite why he would wish to distort history and claim otherwise emerged later, when I was able to set his academic achievements, or rather lack of them, into context alongside the incredibly impressive qualifications of the other three members of Queen. Later, in conversation with Jim Jenkins, co-author of *As It Began*, an 'official' biography of the band, I put it to him that, according to both Freddie's lover Jim Hutton and his sister Kashmira Cooke, Freddie had not been happy for *As It Began* to go ahead.

'Absolutely correct,' agreed Jim, also known in inner Queen circles as 'The Queen Encyclopaedia'. 'And the main reason was, he said, that he didn't want to come across as a prat or a dimwit, compared with the other members of Queen who had achieved so much between them. Perhaps that's why he said he had passed O levels when he hadn't really, which is understandable in the circumstances.'

Freddie's own Headmaster, Mr Davis, is still alive at the time of writing, and living with his wife in Nasik in the same province of Maharastra, a short distance from Panchgani. A frail octogenarian, Mr Davis remembered erroneously that

Freddie left St Peter's in 1962 to travel to the UK, where, according to what he was led to believe, it had been arranged for him to complete his final two years at a college in Kent. But I later established beyond doubt that Freddie had never studied in Kent at all. In fact, he had returned to Zanzibar in 1963 and completed those last two years in a Roman Catholic school there – St Joseph's Convent School. This fact had never been recorded in any previous Freddie biography.

Despite his memory having faded over the forty years since Freddie was a St Peter's pupil, Mr Davis touchingly remembered the Bulsara boy above all else for his pop group.

'Freddie was a very self-conscious boy. I remember him forming his own band called The Hectics, which performed for the pupils and the public around Panchgani. They also played in variety concerts. And I remember that he was a very good sportsman, and won the Junior All-Rounder prize at 12 for both academic and extra-curricular activities.'

Mrs Davis, his wife, worked alongside her husband teaching Drama and running the amateur dramatics society all those years ago. It was she who recalled a visit to Panchgani by Freddie's mother Jer in 1979, when Mrs Bulsara donated cuttings, records and other diverse memorabilia to the school. So who, precisely, took possession of all these precious things? For they are nowhere to be seen at the school.

Another Panchgani teacher, Janet Smith, who works at a nearby girls' school and whose mother (who died about a month prior to our visit) taught at St Peter's during Freddie's years there, relates her confusion at Freddie's apparent dismissal of his Panchgani days.

Later on, it was as if he washed his hands of Panchgani altogether. It never made much sense, considering how happy he appeared to be here. My mother was the Art teacher here for years, and she used to let Freddie and his little band practise in the Art room. Just above the Art room was the dormitory where they all slept. And attached to that dormitory was a small room where they used to play too, when it got too much in the Art room, because they made a ghastly amount of noise when they were practising. I remember Freddie well, although I was young at the time: he was an extremely thin, intense boy who had this habit of calling one 'Darling', which I must say seemed a little fey. It simply wasn't something boys did in those days. It was all 'Darling this' and 'Darling that'. But he was a very nice boy, very helpful. They were all nice guys in fact, but Freddie especially so. They'd make their own additional instruments out of crates and bits of wood and plink-plink at them, such a terrible din. My mother also taught music, but she didn't teach Freddie. After he left he did not bother to keep in touch with my mother or anyone else, and he simply disappeared into thin air. We never knew what had happened to him. Then, much later, when he burst onto the scene we all said 'My God, we know him, can he really be Freddie Bulsara?' We couldn't believe it.

With regard to homosexuality, Janet remembers that, while the fact was not exactly open and approved of, there was little doubt in her mind that Freddie and others among his friends were gay: 'I just knew it. If only from his "Darling Darling" attitude. It was accepted that Freddie was homosexual when he was here. Oh very much so, yes,' she says, quite matter-of-fact.

'Yes, very much when he was a schoolboy. Very much indeed. Don't seem surprised, because none of us were. It was fairly unusual in those days, admittedly, but somehow it was accepted in a boy like Freddie, I don't know why. Normally it would have been, Oh God, you know, it's just ghastly. But with Freddie somehow it wasn't. It was okay.'

Was it perhaps regarded back then as just a schoolboy

phase he was going through and which he might eventually outgrow?

'No, it was very much inside him, a fundamental part of him. I really feel that. He was simply very effeminate. I couldn't help feeling sorry for him, as the others would make fun of him from time to time. Funny thing was, he didn't seem to mind, exactly. And he wasn't the only one, you know.'

According to information gleaned by the school over the years, Freddie did not care to admit to his links with India, an opinion borne out by the fact that he never made any attempt to return to visit his school, or to put together any kind of performance to benefit his alma mater. They refer to Cliff Richard and Englebert Humperdinck, both of whom were born in India, the former in Lucknow, the latter in Madras. Neither of them appears to have attempted to conceal his roots. But did Freddie?

The eventual dwindling of Freddie's academic achievement must have come as a huge disappointment to his parents, given the time and money they had invested in his education; not to mention the great expectations to which his early success had given rise. Freddie quit St Peter's, not with a bang but a whimper, and returned to the Bulsara family home on Zanzibar.

'Eventually, my Auntie and Uncle brought him back from his school in India before he finished his studies,' confirms Freddie's cousin Perviz. 'This, I think, was partly because he was so interested in music, and partly because, at that time, my Auntie and Uncle were beginning to think seriously about migrating to London. So they felt that they would all be together here, and they would all leave from here together and go to London. So Freddie came back from India and was here two years more before they left Zanzibar. I know he went to school here after that, but I don't remember which school.'

* * *

Back in Zanzibar, many were asked but few other people on the island admitted to having known Freddie personally. One who did was Bonzo Fernandez, a former Zanzibar policeman who lost his job at the beginning of the revolution and today works as a taxi-driver. A kindly, smiling man, he gave this account of their friendship: 'When I met Freddie for the first time, I was around 16. We were students together at St Joseph's Convent School.'

The school, run by the sisters of the Sacred Heart, some of whom also taught there, was affiliated to the Roman Catholic St Joseph's Cathedral, completed by the French architect Beranger in 1896. The imposing towers of the church, set back from the island's fort, can be seen clearly from the shore if one approaches the island by dhow. The cathedral is, however, curiously hard to find along Zanzibar's narrow streets.

'I am Goan by race,' Bonzo said, 'and I had been living on the island of Pemba. Then I came across to finish my studies here on Zanzibar. That was when I met Freddie.'

> We used to play hockey and cricket together. He was a really good sportsman, and especially good at cricket. We had our own team at the school, as well as our own hockey and football teams, although Freddie wasn't at all interested in football. We were pretty good friends, but I must say I was never invited to his home. His family seemed to keep themselves to themselves. All I knew was that his father worked for the Government. I can't say for sure whether they were particularly wealthy. Yes, they had a servant, or servants, but in those days everybody had a servant, even if you were earning a small amount. I remember being aware that he had a good relationship with his family, and had a good sister, though we never really saw her, she kept inside. They were a good family, and Freddie was very

well brought-up. Their community of Parsees were very few, and they were very good, well-mannered people.

I knew that he had been away at school in India, but he never spoke about his years there. Not at all. That was strange. He came back to Zanzibar, and was sent to St Joseph's to finish his studies. That's all it seems I was allowed to know about that. He spoke very good English, and also good Swahili, although we did not study the language formally during colonial days. English was the first language, and then when you came to the secondary school, you could take French, which he also did. He was a very, very good pupil, that I would say. He was incredibly bright, and particularly good at mathematics, which he seemed to like very much. He never gave any indication that he would turn out to be a singer. I had to leave earlier than him as I had to go to work to support my family when my father died. I joined the police force and stayed until the revolution, when I lost my job, and we all left the island. I didn't return to Zanzibar until 1985. A few of our old classmates who live all over the world still return to visit Zanzibar – Freddie and I had a friend called Anthony who now lives in Canada, and another chap, John Fernandez, who is now quite near in Dar es Salaam. Ali, our other pal, who knows where he is now? I've got friends in the United States who are doctors, with big degrees, American citizens who actually came from here, from Zanzibar. Because St Joseph's School was one of the most respectable schools in those days, and offered a very good education. When they return, we meet. But Freddie never returned to Zanzibar.

Bonzo remembers Freddie as being 'very secretive'. Had Freddie enjoyed a close relationship in those days, he would never have talked about it for fear of being teased. 'If ever there was a party at the school, the boys would be on one side and the girls on the other side. It wasn't usual to have dances in those days. Freddie would occasionally come along to the Goan Institute, a private social club, but I never saw him with a girl there. And if he was interested in boys, he certainly never gave any indication of that to me.'

Bonzo and Freddie often spent their spare time together. Bonzo recalls trips to the beach, swimming: 'Sometimes after school we used to jump out of the window and swim in the sea, which Freddie loved to do. I can see him now! We also used to swim at the Starehe Club on Shangani Street, which had a very clean beach.'

They also enjoyed cycling excursions all over the island, to Fumba in the south, Mungapwani to the north-west, the site of the old slave caves, or to Chwaka way over on the far south-eastern peninsular. Cycling was one of the lads' favourite hobbies, and they would ride together for considerable distances. 'Sometimes a whole group of us would go. We'd get to the chosen destination, swim there, have our snacks, and sometimes we'd climb up a coconut tree and pinch some coconuts. We were mischievous, but not bad. No, we never drank alcohol. We never knew what alcohol was. Nor drugs, nor cigarettes, in our day.'

Bonzo remembers the Bulsara family as being faithful and committed followers of their religion, Zoroastrianism.

I think they were very good believers. Everyone in their small community respected the fire temple. I knew that Freddie did those things, because everyone respected the religion which their own parents followed, but we never discussed it. People didn't talk about matters such as religion in those days. Zanzibar is a cosmopolitan island, we have so many religions, so many castes, races living here. Nobody was excluded. Everyone was one of us, and whatever anybody got up to for their religion or anything else was their own business. I know that Freddie felt that way, and that this was his home. And it remains the same today. If I think of him now, I can still see that slim, happy young boy in his short blue pants and a white shirt. He was always smartly-dressed, especially for cricket, when he would turn out looking immaculate in his whites, which miraculously always seemed whiter than everyone else's. He loved to be out there on the cricket pitch. He was easy-going, and he'd crack plenty of jokes. But he could be a bit of a loner at times. He'd just move out from the crowd, fold his arms, and you knew that he wanted to be alone. But when he was in the mood, he was so much fun to be around.

After the revolution we all departed from the island. I went to Europe and to UK, but I never knew where Freddie went. I never knew what had become of him, and I had not realized that in fact we were in UK at the same time. It was only after his death that I came to learn that Freddie, my old friend and classmate, had become a world-famous rock singer.

I'd love to have met up with him again and talked about his adventures, heard all his stories. But it never happened. Well, that's the way the world is. Years later when my brother sent me a newspaper cutting from UK saying, 'This was our famous Parsee singer from Zanzibar,' I was at first confused. They put him as Freddie Mercury, but I never knew him as Freddie. I only ever knew him as Farrokh.

Perviz also remembers those days well, when Freddie the young teenager hung out with other local boys and passed the time on the beach. But not for long. The family's idyll under the sun was soon to be shattered, and life would change for good.

Zanzibar had been the scene of political unrest for some years. Post-war change had been echoing through the colonial world since the 1950s. Britain's loss of India and Pakistan in

1947, the independence of Burma and Ceylon in 1948, and China's social revolution in 1949, had all made a strong impact on East Africans. Recent nationalist struggles in North, North-East and East Africa were close enough to have affected many Zanzibaris directly. The 1950s saw the dawn of nationalist advance against British rule. Increasing unrest among the mainly African working classes had been causing the emergence of more and more trade unions, which were now organizing themselves into political parties to effect change. In 1956 the Zanzibar National Party was founded by the minority Arabs and Shirazi, followed swiftly by the Afro-Shirazi party, whose leadership was chiefly of African mainland origin. By 1960–61, increasing labour militancy was leading to strikes in many industries. Pro-Arab election results and poor clove and coconut harvests were frustrating the masses and hastening the end of British colonial order. Many riots ensued, and independence, at first typically resisted by Britain on the grounds that the country was not yet ready for it, was finally achieved under the Sultan Jamshid bin Abdulla on 10 December 1963. But imbalances in electoral representation infuriated the black African majority, whose anger soon flared in a radical left-wing coup. The violent Zanzibar Revolution of 12 January 1964 saw the new Sultan deposed, and Sheikh Abeid Amani Karume, President of the Afro-Shirazi Party, instated as the first President of Zanzibar. Thousands had been slaughtered in bloody street battles. Families like the Bulsaras all but ran for their lives. Leaving Zanzibar with little more than a few suitcases between them, they headed for England where relatives had offered to take them in, and never looked back.

'They all went together to England in 1964, when Freddie was 18,' confirms Perviz.

And that was that, as far as the family relationship was concerned. When I heard much later on that Freddie had become a famous musician, I was very happy to know that we had such a genius in our family. That was my reaction. We were all happy for him. But I never wrote to him to tell him how proud we were, because this was the thing: he was not communicating with any of us. He never sent any cassette or anything, although we were definitely interested in his music. It was a shame.

Despite the lack of contact for so many years, Perviz did make the journey to London with her daughter after Freddie died in 1991, and went to see her Aunt and Uncle, Freddie's parents.

They seemed very old to me now, my Auntie and Uncle. Auntie invited me and I went to their home. We had a nice chat, and I was happy to meet them again after so long. They showed us one of his video cassettes – and that was it.

They didn't discuss much about what had happened to Freddie, and didn't talk about his death. It's painful for parents to talk about losing a son, so I didn't bring up the matter myself, and neither did they. We just sat down and had a nice talk, that was all. They didn't take me to show me the house that belonged to Freddie, but my friends did, when we were just passing by on the road, on the way to Earls Court. I could only see from the outside, the wall only, I didn't get to go inside. I didn't see the house itself. Mary somebody is living inside there, I understand. That was my last contact with them.

Following the departure of the Bulsaras and many such families, Zanzibar dealt with the destruction and went on to form its union with Tanganyika on 26 April 1964 under the new name of Tanzania. Its people today are very laid-back and tolerant, and Zanzibar is widely acknowledged to be the most peaceful and stable country in Africa. But the revolution which took East Africa by storm and heralded a new age has not been forgotten. Africans throughout the continent still regard what happened in Zanzibar as the beginning of their own revolution; the culmination of the people's struggle against two centuries of aggression and oppression by foreigners, slave traders, Omani colonialism, and by seventy years of British colonialism. Enough was enough.

Chapter Four

EALING

Conflicting versions of the story of exactly how and when the Bulsaras came to live in London abound. One version has Bomi Bulsara changing his job and moving permanently to Bombay when Freddie was 'just a small boy'. Bomi was said to have taken his son to India with him while Jer 'returned' to England with their baby daughter Kashmira (although they had never yet set foot on these shores). Although it is true that they would later set up home in a Victorian terraced house in the Feltham district of Hounslow, Middlesex, a few miles south of Heathrow airport, it is erroneously reported that 'Bomi and Freddie would follow later, in 1959, when Freddie was 13'.

Only three living people could confirm the facts beyond all doubt: Freddie's parents and his sister. I wrote to Jer and Bomi Bulsara in Feltham – they had lived in the same house in Gladstone Avenue all these years – and shortly afterwards received a charming letter in reply from his mother, Jer. I had offered to visit them, explaining that all I wanted was to get details right and set records straight. Mrs Bulsara's gracious written response included the following paragraph: 'Thank you . . . for showing so much interest in writing a biography of our Son Freddie. We are sorry to say that we do not wish to interview [sic] anybody at the moment regarding the subject. In future if we feel the time is right, then we will let you know . . .'

Written on simple, cheap lined writing-paper in Biro, the handwriting neat, and properly laid out in the way that letter-writing was once taught at school, her words were dignified but loaded with pain. I was interested to note her use of the initial capital letter when referring to her 'Son', the precious boy she had idolized and whose death she has clearly never come to terms with.

I also wrote to his sister Kashmira, who modified her name to 'Cash' after her marriage to Englishman Roger Cooke, and is living in a respectable quarter of the Sherwood area of Nottinghamshire with their two children, Freddie's niece and nephew. Aunt Sheroo also told me that Freddie's parents had recently left Feltham to be closer to their daughter in Nottingham, particularly since Mr Bulsara was now very infirm. In fact they are living in the same road as their daughter and son-in-law and their grandchildren.

Kashmira never bothered to reply to my letter, which came as no great surprise. I had been warned that she was justifiably protective of the family regarding matters concerning her late brother. In particular, she was said to have no time at all for the media. Jim Hutton, Freddie's former live-in lover, reported that, while he always got along well with Cash, a diminutive, housewifely woman whom he genuinely liked, he never really felt that he knew where he stood. He also confessed to an unfathomable dislike of Cash's airline employee husband Roger, a feeling which he claimed was shared by Freddie.

It was not until nearly 15 months after I began researching this book that I had the opportunity to meet Freddie's parents, on the occasion of the Freddie Mercury Photographic Exhibition at the Royal Albert Hall in November 1996. Together with Queen photographer Denis O'Regan

I was shuffling round the circular corridor within the Hall, the walls of which were lined with the somewhat modestly displayed Freddie photographs, when I suddenly spotted a small group in front who were slowly moving from frame to frame. Realising that I might never again get the chance to meet Freddie's parents, I raced ahead and confronted them, explaining who I was. They were both tiny and frail, Freddie's father even more so than his mother. He was hunched and twisted like a small, gnarled old tree, and appeared no longer able to walk without a stick. When I introduced myself, they remembered the name immediately, and both greeted me warmly. Freddie's mother Jer said how pleased she was to meet me, but said little else. Freddie's father Bomi held my hand quite hard with his cold, stiff fingers as he murmured: 'It is wonderful to see all these photographs displayed, and to see all these people here in honour of our dear son. We feel very very proud . . .' At which point his wife pressed on his arm as if reminding him not to say any more. Having maintained dignity and silence all these years, the Bulsaras plainly feel disinclined to be interviewed at all.

As Brian May himself told me a few months ago, they had given an interview some years back and had been badly misquoted. Consequently, they had never gone on the record since. Who could blame them? Perhaps they also felt that every picture tells a story; that the fact that they had been persuaded, presumably by band manager Jim Beach, to open up their private family albums to the world for the fifth anniversary of Freddie's death, was more than enough intrusion into their lives. This collection of photographs looked loaded with a few choice tales. Everyone in the room that night (for this was a private preview and cocktail party with every invitee having some direct link to Freddie and Queen), from the band's first-ever manager, Ken Testi, to Freddie's old cleaning lady, Marje, had at least one amazing anecdote to relate.

Elsewhere at the gathering, Cash Cooke was giving Jim Jenkins, co-author of *As It Began*, a hard time for having had the audacity to write the book. One scowl from her was enough. Suffice to say that one was ill-advised to approach her for an interview.

If Freddie's immediate family were not prepared to verify information, it would be necessary to look elsewhere. Formal investigations at the Home Office regarding their arrival are officially prohibited. Immigration records do exist but are confidential, and public access to them is denied. I was, however, able to establish that the Bulsaras had definitely arrived for good in Britain in January 1964.

As we have seen, there are many conflicting stories regarding Freddie's education and academic qualifications. *As It Began* tells us, 'In 1962, at age 16, Freddie took his O levels at St Peter's, attaining good grades in Art, History and English Language, and decided that he wanted to leave school.' Several other books adhere to this version, although Rick Sky has him attending a 'secondary school' in Isleworth from age 14, '. . . where his education suffered . . . and when he left . . . the only subject he had really excelled in was Art.' But we already know that he left St Peter's in virtual disgrace without an O level to his name, and was forced to complete his studies at another school on Zanzibar. *As It Began* reveals that on arriving in England at the age of 17, Freddie had made up his mind that he wanted to go to art college, but discovered that he would need at least one A level to achieve a place. Therefore, in September 1964, just as he turned 18, '. . . he enrolled at the nearby Isleworth Polytechnic School to study for an A level in art.' This he apparently achieved with ease, leaving Isleworth in Spring 1966 with an A-grade art A level.

The question as to why, years later, Freddie would want to give the impression of having achieved so much more at school, remains hitherto unanswered. Could it be that he wanted to avoid offending his parents further, when they had obviously had such high academic hopes for him? Who had perhaps looked into a rosy future in which their only beloved son was reaping the considerable rewards of a flourishing career as a doctor, barrister or university professor?

Freddie's fellow band members, Brian and Roger had achieved first-class Science degrees. Brian had won a scholarship place at grammar school and left with 10 O levels and four A levels. He went up to London's Imperial College to study Astronomy, achieved his Honours degree and then commenced his PhD. Roger had attended Truro Cathedral School in Cornwall on a choral scholarship, and won a place at Truro public school (academically the best in the area), where he excelled at Music, English and Biology. He left with seven O levels and three A levels and headed for the London Hospital Medical School to study Dentistry. As for John, he achieved eight O levels and three A levels: in Maths, Further Maths and Physics, all at Grade A, results which were more than enough to secure him a place at Chelsea College, part of the University of London, to study Electronics.

By comparison, Freddie's departure from St Peter's without a single certificate must have looked very meagre indeed. He must later have been acutely aware of this – although perhaps not at the time when he had other, more glamorous and far more pressing matters on his mind, such as getting his new band up and running and on the road to stardom. True, he had gone on to study at Ealing College of Art in September 1966 at the relatively mature age of 20, leaving three years later at 23 with a Diploma in Graphic Art and Design. Ever loyal and generous to his hero, Jim Jenkins would insist in *As It Began* that this is 'the equivalent of a degree'. But it isn't – not quite. It failed altogether to equal the heights of scholarly brilliance and academic success achieved by the other members of Queen. But it was something.

The irony in all this is that Freddie came across as more of an intellectual than the rest of Queen put together. Roger, by his own admission, was lazy and not academically inclined, cramming for his exams the night before and scraping through them on the minimum of revision – which suggests that he took his enviable academic ability completely for granted. He has often admitted that he was far more interested in girls and sex and rock music than in boring old studies, and he has an extremely finely tuned sense of humour. (A dozen years ago, on a return flight from Germany, he happened to utter a line which I immediately committed to memory and use to this day: 'I'm so hung-over, my *name* hurts.') Brian has an unequivocally brilliant mind, but a somewhat gauche personality at times, in which all that subtle braininess can get horribly lost. Whether his self-projection as something of a 'Don't-ask-me-I-know-nothing' suburbanite is deliberate, it is hard to say. There has always been an aspect to his personality that is silent and studious; but he has at times revealed himself to be almost embarrassed by his cleverness. As for John, it would be savage to use the term 'anorak', but the trainspotter type is certainly what he appears to be.

Freddie, on the other hand, projected a splendid worldly air of self-confidence. Although, as we have seen, he must have been desperately insecure about his academic short-comings, he was remarkably skilled at creating the illusion of being otherwise. His flamboyant habits, his refined, gracious manners and his ability to charm virtually anybody were all impressive traits in their own right, and appeared to make up for a lack of formal exam passes. He was most certainly not lacking in intelligence. The opposite. If he managed to convince all who came into contact with him that he was a bona-fide intellectual, he would of course have been hugely amused by it. Freddie invariably had the last laugh.

*   *   *

When the Bulsaras arrived in Britain, they must have been daunted by the cruel environmental and cultural shock. The dull, grey orderliness of West London's flight-path suburbs was no match for colourful, exotic Zanzibar and bustling Bombay. Furthermore, the Bulsaras were somewhat down on their luck. They might have been big fish in a small pond out East, but here in London they were virtual nobodies. No status, no mansion, no servants, no generous salary, no privileges. With his government office connections and presumably adequate track record, it is not clear why Bomi Bulsara was unable to land an official accountancy job here. In releasing its protectorate, Britain had perhaps seen fit to turn a blind eye to a loyal workforce too.

Eventually, Bomi Bulsara found work at the Forte catering company, where he was hired as an accountant. Freddie, too, dabbled in the same line from time to time, at Heathrow airport's catering department, one of many local casual jobs he took to earn himself pocket money during the college holidays. He also worked in a container warehouse on the Feltham trading estate, although neither his physique nor his rather feminine hands were suited to heavy manual work. Freddie fobbed off jokes and jibes from his co-workers, airily explaining that he was really a musician just marking time and making a little extra money on the side. It was the first time he had spoken about his dreams of becoming a globally famous rock-star. Despite his somewhat camp, flamboyant ways he was soon, with customary charm, twisting his workmates round his little finger. Freddie managed to get by on the minimum amount of exertion for precisely the same remuneration as his colleagues.

Those who hung around with him at the time remember Freddie as somewhat shy and reserved but giving the impression of being a 'dark horse', with plenty bubbling beneath the surface. He appears to have been warm and generous, socially aware, and mindful of the plight and predicaments of others. His childhood on Zanzibar had instilled in him tolerance of

81

and compassion for people from every creed, culture and class. Such values would remain with him throughout his life. He was the first to lend money, and would put himself out to help a friend in need.

'Always generous, always thoughtful of others',[1] is how his mother Jer would later describe him.

Freddie attended Isleworth College during 1966 to obtain an Art A level, moving on to Ealing College of Art that autumn to begin his course in graphic design and illustration. He was 20 years old when he became a fully-fledged college student, in the middle of the swinging sixties. London was the self-appointed Mecca of youth culture, and Freddie could not have found himself living in a more exciting city. This realization alone caused him to feel restless and somewhat rebellious, just like most young people of his age who found themselves still living at home. There was so much going on which was at odds with what respectable parents had in mind for their children. Freddie was in a great hurry to get out there and take part. The pop boom was on the turn, the singles market just beginning to fade as LPs, 'proper' records, started to take over. Ballroom managers found that rock 'n' roll and 'beat' nights were no longer attracting the crowds, and began to switch to straight dancing sessions. Dozens of pop groups were trying too hard, and looked as if they would burn themselves out: competition on both sides of the Atlantic was at its most intense. The Beatles were still the most popular group in the world and, together with the Stones, the Animals, Manfred Mann and the undisputed 'king of clubs' Georgie Fame, ruled the pop charts. Tom Jones, a tall, beefy, black-haired singer with a very loud voice from Pontypridd in the Welsh valleys was the latest pop discovery. Sandie Shaw and Petula Clark were Britain's most popular girl singers. And the Folk boom which had emerged the previous year was also on the rise. Perhaps 'Protest' boom would be a more accurate description: it didn't matter what you sang about as long as you didn't like it. Bob Dylan and

Joan Baez brought their political messages about Vietnam to Britain. Donovan befriended Bob Dylan and leapt on the folk bandwagon. But whatever the 19-year-old Irish boy's claim to fame as a singer, his main contribution to teenage style was the fashion he set for 'Donovan jackets' – a hard blue denim battle-dress top – and peaked caps. Other American imports, including Peter, Paul and Mary, the Byrds, the Righteous Brothers, the Walker Brothers, Elvis, and Sonny and Cher were all holding their own in the British hit parade. Pirate radio stations were attracting huge audiences, and Youth Television was taking hold, the switch from miming to live singing for TV pop programmes being the most significant development (although many people failed to notice the difference). Pop TV was dominated by 'Ready, Steady, Go'. Cathy McGowan, the show's 'commère' (as female compères or TV presenters were then referred to) had made a big name for herself with her ideas on clothes and Mod behaviour, and achieved cult stardom as the British teenager's principal spokesperson, being voted 'Outstanding Woman Television Personality of the Year'.

In fashion, boutiques were booming, the younger set having found that *in* clothes were not to be had at the larger, conventional stores. Little shops in less expensive streets sprang up all over London, some designing and making their own garments. Quick, cheap changes were the order of the day for dedicated followers of fashion. Mary Quant and 21-year-old Angela Cash dominated the design scene, while John Stephen became the 'King of Carnaby Street', in those days the Mod centre of the world. Young fashion had acquired a voice of its own that was here to stay. Never again would teenagers be seen dressed in versions of the same clothes that their parents were wearing. Indeed, in years to come, the trend would be for it to happen the other way around. Denim was *the* fashion fabric, emerging in different colours such as pink and grey. 'Op Art' designs were daring, made up in dazzling colours, its craze for boys started by

The Who. They had appliqued shapes, especially bullseyes, on their T-shirts and sweaters, and wore jackets made from fabric printed with enormous Union Jacks. John Lennon hung out in black and white checked tweed peaked caps, and Dave Clark of the Dave Clark Five, later a close friend of Freddie's, popularized white Levis. Freddie himself was particularly lean and snake-hipped in those days and, like other boys his age, favoured tight hipster trousers, very skimpy and usually with a 'self-belt'. They were made from a wide variety of fabrics including jumbo cords and later crushed velvets, the forerunners of 'loon pants'. Jackets were long, often double-breasted and belted, with epaulettes and patch or button-down pockets. Leather and suede jackets were popular, especially the rough suede battle dress design. Shirts were the biggest fashion item, and came in two-tone, white with contrasting collars and cuffs, checks of all kinds, satins and silks, and florals for the truly committed Mod. Freddie's favourite colour for years had been black, although he started to experiment more flamboyantly with clothes and colours once he got to college. For Ealing College was nothing if not Freddie's first significant arena for self-expression. The student environment is a relatively safe place to start, whether you seek to blend in with your peers or dare to be different and stand out from the crowd. There would never be prizes for guessing which of these Freddie aspired to.

The year 1966 heralded many significant changes for Freddie. He decided, at last, to leave home and make a life for himself well away from his parents and sister. He quit suburban Feltham for the happening streets of London's Kensington, where he found a small flat to rent. It would mean a time-consuming journey each day, back to college in Ealing, but to Freddie it was worth it just to be living among others with similar interests in an infinitely more dynamic part of town. He wanted to have it all on his doorstep: the fashion boutiques, record- and book-shops, music venues, pubs and clubs, trendy Kensington Market and the celebrated Biba emporium. He revelled in the fact that he now lived a mere stone's throw from Chelsea's King's Road and Soho's Carnaby Street. He was free to come and go as he pleased. He was no longer answerable to his loving but strict parents who were finding their son increasingly difficult to understand and give guidance to, and with whom he now had barely a surname in common. It also meant that he could experiment with sexual relationships, a major preoccupation for a 20-year-old boy.

Ealing College of Art proved a good choice for a boy like Freddie. Former students included The Who's Pete Townshend, and Ronnie Wood of the Faces, later a Rolling Stone. Several other graduates had gone on to make a name for themselves in 'the print', on top national dailies in Fleet Street. Although not quite in the same league as the 'trendier' art schools – St Martin's, Camberwell, The Slade – Ealing was progressive and technical, and favoured the multi-media approach to ensure that students were more likely to land jobs once they had graduated.

Jerry Hibbert arrived at Ealing College from Oxford having just completed his first year of a graphics course, after a tutor advised him that Ealing was by far the superior college. He started two years below Freddie in 1968, but knew him well on account of their shared interest in music. Hibbert remembers Ealing as a thrusting, progressive environment, with students who dared to break the mould and be different:

My own personal plan was to go into advertising, and Ealing was exactly the right place because it encouraged that sort of thing. Ealing College was going through many changes at that time, and New York's Madison Avenue was the big thing. We even found it influencing our lifestyle, right down to the way we looked. There were a lot of us who said, 'Well, look, everyone's a hippy – let's do something else. We'd like to be like Madison Avenue advertising executives.' So we cut our

hair short, and came to art school in suits and ties
... simply because hippies were everywhere, and art
students like to do something different. It was sort of
a spin-off thing of the Mods movement as well ...
two-tone suits, snakeskin shoes. It was all pretty stylised
... we even had a thing about the way we walked. And
we were definitely not your Union Bar type of students,
because that scene tends to be more about rugby-playing
and beer-drinking, and we weren't really into that sort
of thing. Getting drunk on beer was not our idea of fun.
Mainly because, believe it or not, we were in the habit of
wearing expensive shoes. Snake-skin shoes don't really
want beer spilt all over them. We used to go to the
college restaurant though, which I remember as being
a sort of social centre and gathering place. Freddie – he
was still 'Freddie Bulsara' in those days – used to hang
out there with us all. He was definitely one, as we all
were I suppose, for style and clothes, and was always
very conscious of the way he looked.[2]

While undoubtedly artistic, Freddie was not by any stretch
of imagination the best student in the place. He lacked both
discipline and diligence, found himself bored to tears by much
of the compulsory course work, and quickly lost interest in
anything which did not immediately come easily to him. But
he enjoyed immensely the slightly hedonistic, self-indulgent
'hanging around' aspects of college life. As he would later
remark, 'Art school teaches you to be more fashion conscious,
to be always one step ahead.'[3]

He spent much of his time lolling about, sketching portraits
of his classmates and of his idol, Jimi Hendrix, whom he had
lately discovered, along with millions of other music fans, and
whose influence completely changed Freddie's life.

Hendrix, an African American just four years Freddie's
senior, had started life as Johnny Allen Hendrix in Seattle
on 27 November 1942. At the age of four, his name was

inexplicably changed to James Marshall Hendrix. After military service he worked as a backing musician for the likes of B.B. King, Ike and Tina Turner, Little Richard and the Isley Brothers, and moved to New York. He was playing the clubs of downtown Greenwich Village when a girlfriend of Keith Richards spotted him and talked about him to Keith, who in turn told the Animals' bass player-turned-manager Chas Chandler. Chandler went along to see Hendrix play and was so impressed that he decided to give up his own playing career, sell his bass guitars and buy equipment for Hendrix. He brought his new protégé to London in 1966, launched a massive and hugely successful publicity campaign, and persuaded the Beatles, Pete Townshend and Eric Clapton to turn up at all the *in* clubs to watch Hendrix's outrageously flamboyant performances. Hendrix left them all speechless. He was the ultimate showman, exploiting tricks he had picked up from a myriad of barely known black American musicians. He played his white Fender Stratocaster upside down, with his teeth and behind his neck, and experimented with an incredible range of playing techniques. He not only stunned the fans but amazed Britain's finest bluesmen with his brilliant guitarmanship and innovative style. Even stars like Eric Clapton began following Hendrix from gig to gig and drooling over every note. His band, the Jimi Hendrix Experience, was a 'power trio' based on the British group concept. Their drummer, Mitch Mitchell, displayed strong jazz influences, and Noel Redding, the bass player, was versatile and innovative, having played lead guitar in an earlier band. The Jimi Hendrix Experience, according to American music expert Robert Palmer, '... took blues-based, improvisational rock to perhaps its ultimate level of development. Hendrix himself expanded the tonal and sonic resources of the electric guitar so spectacularly that his work remains definitive a quarter of a century after his death. Subsequent rock guitarists have taken the instrument in different directions and redefined its role in the band, but nobody has come close to equalling Hendrix at his own game, let alone surpassed him.'[4]

Just four years later, a couple of weeks after Freddie's 24th birthday, Hendrix was found dead. Four years of relentless touring, recording, drink and drug abuse had taken their tragic toll. On 18 September 1970, Hendrix's lifeless body was discovered in his London flat. He had choked to death on his own vomit. Freddie had never had the opportunity to meet his all-time idol. He was absolutely devastated by the news.

Freddie now decided, thanks to Hendrix's influence, exactly how his future would be played out; he was convinced that he could, in his own way, take up where Hendrix had left off. Freddie was Going Somewhere. Not that Freddie was a brilliant guitarist, by any means. He was not yet even a professional musician. Although he would dabble with that instrument from time to time in years to come, his efforts were never anything more than mere accompaniment and just for fun. Freddie could pound up a storm on the piano whenever he chose. But his primary instrument would eventually prove to be his voice. Nevertheless, Freddie the performer owed more to Hendrix than most critics have ever bothered to acknowledge. Hendrix's guitar work challenged all conventional constraints of pop and rock; Freddie's future songwriting, arranging and vocal techniques would do the same. Hendrix's stage presence and outrageous performances had audiences eating from his palm and left them gaping in the aisles; Freddie would do the same. Hendrix could get away with playing the most ordinary of rock standards because, as Jerry Lee Lewis had done before him, he was able to do it with wild originality. He performed innovatively, with such energy and enthusiasm, that to see him do it ripped your breath away; Freddie would one day have the same effect on his own audiences. Hendrix could take any song, even something seemingly mundane, and make it sound unique, as if it were his own composition. In 1986 I was to witness Freddie do exactly the same live on stage in Budapest, when he brought tears to the cheeks of thousands with his rendition of a simple Hungarian folk ballad. He couldn't speak a word of Hungarian, the lyrics meant nothing to him, and the melody could not have been further removed from a rock song had it tried. But Freddie made it his own, performed it as if he really meant it, delivered it so directly from the heart that it was all but dripping with his blood. The audience were spellbound.

Dig a little deeper into Freddie's passion for Hendrix and it becomes easy to understand the primary source of his inspiration. There was old Jerry Lee Lewis, still projecting his explosive personality by using and abusing any old piano as a prop, while Hendrix had gone two steps further in taking one step back: every bit as explosive as Lewis, Hendrix was playing second fiddle to his own cherished guitars. It was a contradiction that worked wonders. On one legendary occasion, Lewis poured lighter fuel into his piano at the end of a show and set the thing alight in an attempt to upstage Chuck Berry, just for the hell of it. It didn't actually achieve anything beyond expensive destruction and mild, short-lived sensation. It was a mere stunt compared with what Hendrix pulled off at the Monterey Pop Festival in 1967, when he smashed and burned his guitar while the amplifiers were still plugged in and wound up to maximum volume. The sound of his guitar strings unravelling as the instrument scorched and disintegrated in the flames was not just another instrument-destroying mission: it made music. When Hendrix performed at the Woodstock festival in 1969, he played 'The Star-Spangled Banner' using his guitar to evoke the noise of bombs, sirens, all the screaming, suffering sounds of war. The chilling blend still echoes in the skulls of those who were there to hear it. Not that Freddie ever made a point of destroying instruments or deploying incendiary techniques on stage: such tricks of the trade had perhaps had their day by the time Queen were riding the crest of the global fame wave, rendered obsolete by highly technical light shows, elaborate, hydraulically operated stage sets and the occasional burst of pyrotechnics which were required to meet with every syllable of the fire safety regulations. The live gig had come a long way. But those essentially innovative elements of Hendrix's showmanship, coupled with his musical excellence, were the very factors which fired Freddie's enthusiasm and inspired him to have a go at rock stardom. For with Freddie, it was never simply a question of becoming a professional musician. World recognition and creating the same sensation as Hendrix were his goals. At Ealing College, Freddie was only just beginning to exercise his vocal cords. Even he had no idea that he had what it took to become the greatest rock singer the world would ever hear. All that would come much later. Originality. Flamboyance. Daring. These were the spangles of Hendrix's brilliance which had dazzled Freddie, and which he now planned to explore for himself. It was only a matter of time.

In the meantime, Freddie had plastered the drab walls of his tiny Kensington flat with images of Hendrix. He had practised drawing the star's portrait to perfection. Hendrix's slightly skew-whiff look, thick lips, Brillo-pad Afro hair, fleshy nose and soft, dark eyes were now as familiar to Freddie as the features on his own face. Freddie has also begun to adopt the Hendrix style, the basic elements of which were common enough on London's streets at that time: brightly coloured floral jackets over black or multi-coloured shirts, skinny coloured pants, Chelsea boots with black socks, chiffon scarves knotted at the Adam's apple, and chunky silver rings. Freddie's own wardrobe evolved until it contained much the same kind of gear. As skinny as a rake, the tight denims and crushed velvet pants he loved to wear made him appear even skinnier. Some former classmates recall that he definitely stood out in a crowd, as if getting himself noticed was a primary concern. Yet others do not appear to remember Freddie for any unusual flamboyance of personal style. According to fellow student Graham Rose, 'What he wore was no different from what we were all wearing at that time. On the whole, he was a quiet guy, although he was prone to fits of giggles. When that happened he would put his hand right over his mouth to cover up those huge teeth of his. I remember him as a terrific bloke who was very sweet and considerate. There wasn't a nasty streak in him. A lot of us were very pleased when he went on to become such a great success.'

Jerry Hibbert agrees that Freddie did not stand out in any particular way:

Except he was very keen on singing. He used to sit at his desk in class and sing. All day long. He was in the next room from me, in the year or two above . . . there were some double doors connecting us, and you could wander through and visit your friends. He sat opposite his mate Tim Staffell, and they used to sing . . . in harmony. That was actually very strange, since at that time we were all really into blues stuff. John Mayall and Eric Clapton, pre-Cream. Clapton played songs like Freddie King's 'Hideaway', which we all thought was great and which led to a great interest in all the Kings: Freddie King, Albert King, B.B. King. All very regal. Mississippi Delta blues. Blues music, blues culture. Delicious. Those musicians were all the more interesting to us because the American imports weren't that easy to get hold of. So there was an elitism attached, which of course appeals to students. Freddie Bulsara as a latter-day Freddie King . . . interesting that he should become a Queen instead.

We also rated Buddy Guy, whom Clapton loved: Eric used to say that Guy sounded like he was really on the edge, not in control, so that at any time he could hit a really bad note. He liked that rawness. Elmore James was another one – Ike Turner used to record him, in a makeshift studio at his own house. And there was a great, early Peter Green's Fleetwood Mac album, which basically ripped off Elmore James. We became quite obsessed with all the underlying influences . . . for example, we no longer wanted to see Eric Clapton play 'Hideaway', we were more interested in seeing Freddie King play it. Freddie Bulsara definitely had an interest in all that, along with the rest of us. But then he'd be in the classroom singing harmonies, which he seemed to be very interested in, despite the fact that no one else was into it and that it almost made him look ridiculous. The rest of us used to think that it was all a bit out of kilter with what everyone else was doing. But that didn't appear to bother him or Tim. They'd sit there working away, and they'd be singing together. Bizarre.

I remember Freddie's teeth, of course. You couldn't miss them. Especially when he sang all the time like that. He did have the most incredible buck teeth.[5]

As for Freddie's personality in those days, Hibbert refutes the idea that he was any kind of attention-seeker:

No, he wasn't like that. Freddie was the nicest possible guy. Nor did I have any idea that he was gay. He didn't show any signs of that at all. I don't actually remember him ever having a girlfriend, but then people tended to chop and change partners pretty quickly. Nor do I remember him being anything at all like his stage charac-ter. He was much more quiet, very friendly. Always polite, always nice. The sort of lad your Mum might say was 'well brought-up'. I don't have any memories of him being a show-off. Sure, he used to lark about and sing, using a ruler as a pretend microphone, that sort of thing. But that was just for laughs. Who didn't do stuff like that? I just remember him as being very pleasant indeed.

Even after they had both left college, and contrary to

Freddie's usual modus operandi regarding keeping in touch with people from whom he had moved on, the pair managed to stay in touch for some time afterwards: 'It was because of the music,' explains Jerry. 'I used to play blues with a bunch of people, at the college, at parties, at other people's flats. Freddie would come down and join in from time to time. This was all in the days before people played records at parties. If you wanted music, you'd get a band in. The word 'discotheque' hadn't been invented, and you went to clubs just to hear music.'

Eventually, Freddie confided in Hibbert that he planned to pursue a career in music.

After Freddie left college, I was in a band for about two years. He came round one day and told me that he was going to concentrate on getting a band together. He said to me that he was not going to bother with graphics. And I can remember telling him, 'Freddie, don't do it. Stick to graphics. There's no money in music. Stick to what you know.' But he had already made up his mind, and there was no persuading him.

'I think I'll have a go,' was all he said. And that was that. I did see him after that, at an exchange of equipment – I bought some equipment, or sold him some, can't remember which. In Barnes I think, at a flat in Ferry Road. He came back to play at the college more than once with a group – Wreckage, I believe they were called. They played in the common-room there. I didn't think much of them to be honest. They weren't that great, but that was partly because the music wasn't really my taste.

After that we just lost touch. It happens. I went directly into the animation business. I joined the company who made Yellow Submarine for the Beatles, and in about 1970 I completely lost interest in music. I found myself hating everything, never bought any records, never went to see bands. About four years later I heard a DJ on the radio talking about this band called Queen. I listened to the single, 'Seven Seas of Rhye', their first one: not bad. But I simply didn't associate the name Freddie Mercury with my mate Freddie Bulsara from Ealing College. All of a sudden, as if out of the blue, there was a lot of publicity, and you couldn't miss him. It was all Freddie Mercury this, Freddie Mercury that, here, there and everywhere. I was walking past a newsagent's one day and I happened to see his picture on the front page of *Melody Maker*. A huge picture, with a screaming caption about him. I looked at it and thought, Bloody hell, that's Freddie Bulsara. He's changed his name, the little bugger. I couldn't believe it.

But the old college chums and jamming partners were never to see each other again.

Chapter Five

<u>QUEEN – THE BEGINNING</u>

Their classmates could ridicule them all they liked. Had it not been for Freddie's two-part harmonies with fellow art student Tim Staffell, he might never have found himself tagging along to a rehearsal and coming face to face with the band who would be Queen.

Freddie and Tim had lately taken to hanging out, just the two of them or together with another student, Nigel Foster, to hold private jamming sessions for their own amusement. The two-part harmonies graduated to three-part; and much of their spare time was spent practising renditions of Jimi Hendrix's British Top Ten hits such as 'Hey Joe', 'Purple Haze' and 'The Wind Cries Mary', because Freddie had perfected such a brilliant impersonation of his idol.

'Freddie was already a star at college,' Staffell would later recall. 'He just exuded confidence in anything he did. He was committed to becoming famous. Art colleges in the late sixties were full of would-be musicians, yet Freddie really had what it took. Some people poked fun at him, but he always had a witty riposte.'[1]

Not that Staffell himself could be described as a humble down-home guy. He had his own sense of flair which made him stand out in a crowd. One tutor remembers a particular pair of metal-toed boots which Staffell would turn up to class in, the steel caps so highly polished that you could see your reflection in them. Staffell painted favourite cartoon characters onto the metal. He is also remembered for his obsession with science fiction, and with the nonsense poems of Edward Lear.

For a while, Tim and Freddie were inseparable mates. Together they made the most of their student days, enjoying to the hilt that voyage of self-discovery. Tim, along with other classmates, was only vaguely aware of Freddie's background and the circumstances which had brought him from Zanzibar to England. They all knew that their exotic friend was feeling somewhat estranged from his family. Freddie never made a point of taking friends back to meet his parents, for example, and so they were left with the impression that the Bulsaras were aloof, and reluctant to integrate or adapt. It was rumoured that they barely even spoke English at that time, and were anxious to preserve their culture and traditional way of life. This, however, was probably a biased and unfair assessment, given that Freddie himself had spoken perfect English since he was a toddler.

Tim and Freddie rarely discussed their family lives. Childhood is perhaps the last thing on a student's mind. After all, as author L. P. Hartley remarked in his acclaimed novel *The Go-Between*, 'The past is a foreign country: they do things differently there.' There were more pressing matters at hand. Self reinvention has always been a preoccupation of students, and why should Freddie prove an exception? His childhood was now completely irrelevant. Life was a vast, clean canvas stretching out before him. He would make of it whatever he wished.

Tim was already playing with a semi-professional band called Smile, and Freddie soon found himself tagging along to his friend's rehearsal sessions. The lead guitarist was Brian May, a tall, gangly physics and astronomy student at Imperial College. Unbeknown to Freddie, he and Brian had virtually been neighbours back in Feltham: Brian had grown up in a house just a few streets away from where the Bulsaras lived. Brian, a studious only child, had been playing guitar since he was just six years old, and had, while still at school and with the help of his father, carved his own Red Special guitar from an old mahogany fireplace and some cuts of oak. He played it with silver sixpenny pieces instead of a conventional plectrum. The guitar would later become his constant companion, accompanying him on tour all over the world. Brian, like Freddie, had started dabbling in amateur bands with school friends.

'None of the groups really got anywhere, because we never played any real gigs or took it that seriously,' he would later recall.

It was at a local dance one night that he and his musical pals spotted Tim Staffell, a lad from school, who was standing at the back of the hall singing away and doing impressive things on a harmonica. They asked him to join their group, and he came on board as lead singer and 'harp' player. The band, christened '1984', played their first official gig at St Mary's Church hall in Twickenham. They showed considerable promise, and in May 1967 found themselves hired as support act to none other than Jimi Hendrix at a gig at Imperial College. A few months later they won a competition at Croydon's Top Rank Club, and a professional career looked all set.

'1984 was purely an amateur band, formed at school, although perhaps at the end we once got fifteen quid or something,' was the way Brian would remember it later.

'We never really played anything significant in the way of original material – it was a strange mixture of cover versions, all the things which people wanted to hear at the time. This was about the time that the Stones were emerging, and later we did Stones and Yardbirds things . . . I was never happy about it. I left because I wanted to do something where we wrote our own material.'[2]

Brian told the others that his studies must come first, and that he no longer had the time to devote to being in the band. They reluctantly went their separate ways. Brian and Tim Staffell kept in touch, however. Staffell was now a student at Ealing College of Art. But they suffered withdrawal symptoms, and missed their band terribly. It wasn't long before they had begun to talk seriously about starting another. Eventually they agreed to advertise on the Imperial College noticeboard for a drummer.

Roger Meddows Taylor was almost too good-looking to be a boy. With his baby blond hair and Newman eyes, it was obvious to all who met him that the guy was sickeningly successful with women. Who was he to say no? Roger certainly never liked to disappoint. He had already begun to make a name for himself as a schoolboy drummer back in Cornwall, with an outfit called Johnny Quale and the Reaction, whose line-up he had joined in 1965. The group had won fourth prize in the local 'Rock and Rhythm Championship', and attracted quite a following on the Cornish circuit. When Johnny Quale ditched the band, Roger was elected lead vocalist too, and thus became a singing drummer long before Phil Collins. The band shortened their name to Reaction, and their tide of fans continued to swell. The following year they walked away with the championship, and were suddenly in big demand. Their musical style had hitherto been soul-based, but in 1967 they were blown away by the Jimi Hendrix Experience, and turned their backs on Otis.

Roger left Cornwall and headed for the capital in the autumn of 1967 to begin his Dentistry degree at the London Hospital Medical School. He soon became the fourth flatmate in rented lodgings in Shepherd's Bush, where a friend from Truro, Les Brown, already lived. Les was a year older and a student at Imperial College. Already hooked on the idea of becoming a rock-star – a rocker would never be short of a good woman or three – Roger's primary concern was finding himself another band. He was engaging and sweet, a little shy, and popular among the lads. His mates were all on the look-out on his behalf, and it was not too long before an ideal opportunity arose. Scouring the Imperial College noticeboard one day for something that might suit his friend, Les Brown found a very interesting card. It had been placed by a new group advertising for a 'Ginger Baker/Mitch Mitchell type drummer'. This was a precise and classy specification indeed: Baker had picked up a loyal cult following with the Graham Bond Organization, who had a strong reputation as a 'musicians' group', and had recorded with The Who before joining Eric Clapton's Cream. Mitchell was the drummer with the Jimi Hendrix Experience. This new band obviously knew what they were doing, had lofty expectations, and a clear idea of what kind of drummer they required to complete their line-up. Brian May's was the name on the card, and Roger wasted no time in getting on to him. Never one to leave anything to chance, Brian wrote back immediately, outlining exactly what he and Tim were looking for. Soon, Brian and Tim were heading for Roger's place for a jamming session on acoustic guitars and bongos; Roger's proper drum kit was still gathering dust at home in Cornwall. It wouldn't be long before they would be rehearsing properly at Imperial College in the jazz club room, where chemistry gelled and lifelong ambitions were sealed. They were three very different personalities who complemented each other perfectly: Brian was the quiet, gentle type; Tim, by his own admission, was a more vulgar, rough and ready individual; while Roger, according to those close to him, was a drummer 'both by name and by nature', whose energy and enthusiasm fuelled the band. Those were happy, hopeful days. The big dreams were as yet unfulfilled, and all three had everything to look forward to.

Smile, as this line-up soon began calling themselves, rehearsed in earnest throughout the autumn months of 1968. As well as covering songs by other artists, Brian and Tim had also begun to compose their own work. This was the true genesis of Queen: 'I could play you tapes of Smile which have the same general structures as what we're doing today,' Brian would say in an interview in 1977.

Brian had graduated with his honours degree that summer, and had been presented with his BSc certificate by the Queen Mother at the Royal Albert Hall. He stayed on at Imperial College as a tutor while studying for his PhD, and spent all his spare time on the band. Smile's début gig saw them supporting Pink Floyd at Imperial College that October, after which they hardly looked back. So in demand were they at Imperial that they were dubbed the Imperial College Band. Roger felt so confident of Smile's chances that he quit medical school after his first year. Smile supported T. Rex, Yes, and Family, and in February 1969 joined their first charity line-up at the Royal Albert Hall, alongside Joe Cocker and Free.

It was at the beginning of 1969 that Tim Staffell turned up to rehearsals one day with his art college pal Freddie Bulsara in tow. The attraction was instant and mutual. Freddie was in his element among accomplished and experienced musicians, and was convinced, the more he watched Smile rehearse, that this was what he wanted to do with his life. As for Brian and Roger, they immediately took to this exotic, amusing character with his razor wit and unusual personality. Once he felt at home, Freddie was always fun to have around, and they looked forward to seeing him. According to Tim Staffell, though themselves no strangers to sharp one-liners and witty backchat, Brian and Roger were most taken with Freddie's dry humour. Staffell commented, 'I thought he was more cynical than everyone else. He was mildly cynical at a time when people weren't cynical at all. He was not destructively so, it was just a humour device.'[3]

As Roger's friend Les Brown later recalled, 'I don't think I've ever met someone so outrageous since. He was very enthusiastic about everything. I mean amazingly so. I remember he once physically dragged me into a room and made me listen to this soul record he really liked. No one admitted to still liking soul at that time, it was all rock, so I suppose he was showing his catholic taste.'

Freddie took to showing up for most of Smile's gigs, and what's more would come armed with suggestions as to how they should perform, sit, stand, dress, style themselves. He was not exactly modest about it either. Coming from anyone else, such interference might have seemed offensive. Who did he think he was? But Freddie, as usual, managed to get away with it, with the usual charm and winsome grins.

'He offered suggestions in a way that couldn't be refused!' remembered Brian. 'At that time, he hadn't really done any singing, and we didn't know he could – we thought he was just a theatrical rock musician.'[4]

In the summer of 1969, Freddie left Ealing College with his Diploma in Graphic Art and Design. Not only did he lack a full-time job to go to, he had no intention of getting one either. He had other plans. Before long, he and Roger Taylor, who by now had discarded the cumbersome double-barrelled surname, would be running a stall in Kensington Market which they rented for £10 a week. At first they sold artwork by Freddie and fellow students at Ealing College. But this was not in great demand, and they soon found that it was not the way to make money. Unashamed clothes horses themselves, they decided to indulge a personal passion and try selling clothes. So they switched to trading in dandy paraphernalia, exotic scarves, cloaks, jackets, fur stoles, all of which was little more than tarty tat and out-of-town jumble sale junk, but was sold at inflated prices. 'Roger and I go poncing and ultrablagging just about everywhere and lately we've been termed as a couple of queens,'[5] Freddie wrote to a friend during that period.

They started having garments made up out of old fabrics and trimmings, and acquiring 'job lots': they were once offered a hundred fur coats by a Battersea rag merchant for £50, which they sold on for about £8 each. Their tiny 'telephone box' stall in the market, or the Kasbah, as many locals referred to it, was on Death Row, so called because most of the stalls in their part of the market traded in antiques. Many of the other stall-holders were also out-of-work artists and writers, and Roger and Freddie happily found themselves in the flamboyant company they craved. People who knew them at the time remember Roger as the more camp and flamboyant of the pair. One fellow stall-holder, a Turkish Cypriot called Michael Anastasios, has kept a clock, watch and sundry antiques business there since 1968, and is the only stall-holder left who remembers Freddie from those days. Elderly and eccentric, he tinkers away with his watches and chats about the good old days with passers-by.

'All very lively round here in the sixties and seventies,' he says with a grin in an accent dense as Turkish Delight, as he squints into the interior of an intricate antique watch and pokes around with a tiny screwdriver.

Lot of film directors used to come; all the filmstars. They all used to live around here, and the American actors all came in when they were visiting London. Michael Caine, he came in a lot of times. Norman Wisdom – always used to see him. Julie Christie. Olivia Hussey, you know her, the star of Romeo and Juliet; I fixed her watch for her, she sat here many times. The Rolling Stones were always in and out . . . you name them, they used to come. They all used to hang out in the market. This was the place.

Of course I remember Freddie. The Persian one, right? The singer. 'Oh, Dalling,' he used to say to everyone all the time. How could you forget him? He was crazy funny guy. Always dressing up, running about, always into this and that. Always laughing, screaming like a girl. Made you laugh just to look at him. Great. Nutter. Don't care very much about life. He had, what it is . . . ? Great spirit. He was always very 'I am' – full of himself and everything, but in a nice way. He wanted to be famous.

In those days, *everybody* wanted to be famous. That was why they all came to London, but not me! Freddie dead? No, Dalling, not dead. Still here!

T.C., a Dublin-born security guard who has worked the market for 11 years, also remembers Freddie, but in a different guise: 'Back in the eighties when he was by that time a big star, he used to come back here all the time as a customer. He just used to walk round, look at the clothes, hang out a bit. He seemed at home here, he wasn't looking over his shoulder and hiding away from people or anything. He obviously liked coming in. I talked to him once or twice and he was very normal, very pleasant.'

Tim Staffell would later recall that Roger and Freddie revelled in their market-trading, where they were absolutely in their element. 'They really enjoyed being outrageous,' Staffell said. 'Freddie developed this camp side of his nature – he regarded it as an amusing part of his personality. At no time was it suggested that he was gay. He was never overtly sexual.'[6]

Freddie had also started travelling with Smile on the road, as an accepted and expected part of their entourage. In April 1969, Smile had performed at London's Revolution Club, where they met A&R man Lou Reizner. Later to achieve fame in the music business as producer of Rod Stewart's first two solo albums, he was then a humble talent scout on the lookout for new bands. He offered Smile a one-single deal with Mercury Records which they virtually signed on the spot without pausing to consider the consequences, so desperate were they for professional recognition. Nothing much happened until June, when Mercury decided it was time to get their new act together, and booked Smile into Trident Studios in Soho where they recorded a few tracks, although no actual release dates were planned. Some months later Mercury put out a single called 'Earth', but unfathomably only in America, where they were complete unknowns and where it sank without trace, leaving the band hugely disappointed. Their live work was going well, however. Understandably, Mercury were reluctant to waste a signing with such obvious potential. Perhaps, it was decided, they were an 'albums band' after all. Brian and Tim had already co-written a wealth of material. The two of them were packed off to Wembley's De Lane Lea studios to work with a producer called Fritz Freyer. But nothing was ever released, the tapes consigned to the Mercury record vaults for more than 20 years before someone saw fit to release a Smile EP only in Japan, where Queen fans can never get enough of old curiosities. As 1969 drew to a close, the band were dejected and on the verge of giving up. Perhaps they had been foolish to surrender to their dreams. Perhaps they should have got proper jobs. Perhaps Roger should not have ditched his dentistry studies. Perhaps they were not cut out for rock stardom after all. It was certainly not the easy ride they had imagined, and was going to take a good deal more hard work if they were to be in with a chance of making it. Brian and Roger agreed that it was worth it, and were eager to carry on: as Freddie would one day remark, 'The harder you work, dear, the luckier you get.'[7]

Tim, however, decided to call it a day. Weary of the drudgery of the live circuit, he began to fret that Smile were not the right group for him. 'I was beginning to get a rather jaundiced view of the music we were doing, and my own approach to what we were playing on the bass,' he later said. 'It caused this sense of tension within me, and I was not enjoying the direction in which we were moving. I heard James Brown and thought, "God!" . . . Basically, I had changed musical tracks completely.'[8]

He quit Smile to join the line-up of pop group Humpy Bong, which featured a former Bee Gee drummer. It was all rather flash in the pan. One single release and one TV appearance, and Humpy Bong were consigned to the has-been shelf. Tim lingered on the music scene for a while longer, but eventually settled for a completely different career in television special effects. One day he would enjoy another brief spurt of recognition, this time for creating TV's Thomas the Tank Engine trains. Compared with his former band mates he has lived most of his life in relative obscurity, but appears to have few regrets. As the one-time rock front-man was to remark years later, 'I was never a showman like Freddie.' No hard feelings.

'I have regretted not being a musician, but not leaving Smile. It was good that I got out of the way, because otherwise Queen would not have existed, and the world would have lost a whole bunch of quality music. Smile wouldn't have done it.'

Without their lead singer, Mercury Records decided that Smile were no longer a band. Roger and Brian found themselves released from their contract and out on a limb. They were miserable, but not for long. Having forced themselves to look on the bright side, they persuaded each other that they must use this rejection as inspiration to try even harder. Heart-to-hearts were held, friends roped in, opinions sought. Brian, Roger, Tim and a couple of other musicians from a band called Ibex were now living in a tiny one-bedroom flat in a semi called 'Carmel' in Ferry Road, Barnes. So were two sisters, Helen and Pat McConnell, who had seen Smile play in their local pub and had fallen in with the same gang. Those were the days of their lives, romanticized beyond recognition in years to come. The flat would later be remembered as 'Bohemian', but in fact it was little more than a glorified squat: cramped, squalid, and devoid of anything edible. Its inmates were like sardines in a tin; most of them had to sleep on mattresses on the floor. To make matters worse, they had recently acquired yet another new flatmate: Freddie Bulsara. What did *he* think they should do?

Chapter Six

FREDDIE COMES ON BOARD

'Why are you wasting your time doing this? You should do more original material. You should be more demonstrative in the way that you put the music across. If I was your singer that's what I'd be doing!'[1]

So said Freddie to Roger and Brian in 1970, never one to mince his words. Well, they had asked. If he spoke with some authority, it was because by this time he was actually singing with a band of his own. Still smitten by Hendrix, and seriously impressed by Brian's guitar-playing, Freddie had got hold of a second-hand guitar which he asked Tim to re-fret and modify to suit his needs. Then he bought some Teach-Yourself books and started to learn to play. He probably knew even then that he would never make an axe hero. But that was never Freddie's primary objective. Songwriting was his latest project, and he needed to know enough guitar to be able to work out the chords. His initial attempts at composing were like everyone else's – clumsy, raw and excruciatingly personal. He would soon learn to be more abstract in his ideas, to look outside himself and his own experiences, and experiment with themes which had more universal appeal.

Just after graduating from college he had been intro-duced one night to a group called Ibex, who were down in London from Liverpool on a deal-seeking mission. Like Smile, Ibex were also a three-piece band – guitarist Mike Bersin, bass-player John Taylor ('Tupp'), and drummer Mick Smith ('Miffer'). Freddie also met their fledgling manager/roadie/head cook and bottle washer, Ken Testi, and Geoff Higgins, another bass player who occasionally played with Ibex so that Tupp, who idolised Jethro Tull, could have a turn on the flute.

They were a rather impressive line-up, and Freddie was pretty taken with them. Yet even he could not fail to notice that they lacked a decent lead vocalist. Just as he had done with Smile, he started turning up to their rehearsals and gigs, and occasionally got up to the microphone with Mike Bersin to sing. Eventually, during one rehearsal at Imperial College – which appeared to do rather well out of rehearsing and performing bands at that time – they invited Freddie to audition as their singer. Between them they agreed that Freddie had a fantastic voice with a marvellous range. All he needed was to learn how to control and project it properly.

If money was tight, it didn't hinder their having fun. Despite the damp, cramped flats and perforated pockets, those who were there recall heady days, with wild parties, marijuana in abundance (acquired from Kensington Market and mixed in with the jasmine tea), little sleep and less food. When he was not working the market, Freddie, who like everyone else was stick-thin because he was so undernourished, devoted all his time to rehearsing with Ibex, who played cover versions of hits by Rod Stewart, the Beatles and Yes. They were building their routine and stage act, and had started to work on a few humble trademarks: they'd always kick off a show, for example, with Elvis's 'Jailhouse Rock', a big hit some 12 years earlier. Freddie's flamboyance was at last manifesting itself in his performance, at times to the red-faced embarrassment of the rest of the band whose own stage presence was somewhat reserved by comparison.

'He gave the same kind of performances he did at the peak

of his career,' remembered Ken Testi. 'He was a star before he was a star, if you know what I mean. He'd strut around the stage like a proud peacock.'

Ibex played all over the country throughout 1969, and were particularly popular in the north of England, which meant tedious journeys up and down the M1 almost every week. The band soon grew tired of travelling. No recording deal was forthcoming in London, and so it was suggested that they move back to Liverpool. Freddie was not keen on the idea, but it suited everyone else. There was little he could do but grin, bear it, give it a whirl. Nothing much changed. They still slept on each other's floors. They were still starving, and still skint. Eventually, as Tim Staffell had done in Smile, the band began to wonder if it were all worth the effort. Mick Smith had family problems, and he suddenly found himself in need of a regular job paying decent wages to help out his needy mother. When he left, he was replaced with another drummer, Richard Thompson, a friend of the band. Together they played just one disastrous gig. Everything that could go wrong did go wrong: sound, lights, equipment. Even the microphone stand fell short of Freddie's expectations. He was used to twirling the thing around like a majorette's baton. This one came complete with a heavy old stand. At one point he seized the mike energetically and attempted to swing it, but the bottom fell clean away. Unfazed, Freddie simply used the top half, which he twirled and wielded to great effect. The trademark of a star was born.

The strange paradox of Freddie the performer and Freddie Bulsara the person was by now beginning to emerge. Even on the poorest excuse for a stage, Freddie projected a super-confident, larger-than-life persona, every gesture and movement flamboyant and melodramatic. You couldn't help but look at him. He was already majestic, and had an unforgettable quality. But offstage he cowered in kitchens and cupboards, the makeshift dressing-rooms with which bands made do on the pub and club crawl, where he'd coyly struggle into his hand-made, skin-tight trousers, so skimpy that once he had them on it was as much as he could do to sit down. He was relatively small and slightly built, and not conventionally handsome. He knew he stood out on account of his dark skin and swarthy looks, and these features at times embarrassed him. He hid his dark eyes behind a floppy fringe, and his buck teeth behind his hand whenever he felt the urge to smile. He would make the effort to chat with fans after the show, but he could never think of much to say; besides, although Freddie spoke the Queen's English perfectly, vowels crisp and pronunciation precise, his speaking voice was whispery and hesitant, with a vague lisp and a somewhat sibilant quality of which he was painfully conscious. Only when he felt he was among friends did his enthusiasm and humour, wild imagination and crackling personality shine through, when he would hold court and have them hanging on his every word. The rest of the time he'd just keep quiet and try to blend into the background. He never mastered the art of feigning confidence among strangers. In the years to come this would barely change; however relaxed and happy he was at his own parties, he was always a fish out of water at someone else's.

Another factor was that he was not yet in the habit of getting wildly drunk or out of his head on drugs. For one thing, he couldn't afford to. One or two friends remember him asking for port and lemon in pubs, which was, according to others of his generation, 'what all the nurses used to drink in those days. It was a girl's drink.'

Needless to say, Freddie soon grew tired of the Liverpool scene, of being bereft of cash, of making do with other people's floors. Just after his 23rd birthday, he kissed Ibex goodbye and made his way home with Mike Bersin in tow. But by now he was so hooked on the idea of being in a band that the wrench proved unbearable. He kept an eye out for 'Wanted: Singer' ads, but opportunities were thin on the ground. It made him more determined than ever that he wouldn't waste whatever chance came along. His very first audition landed him the job as lead singer with a band called Sour Milk Sea. Singer-guitarist Chris Chesney was only 17, but he and Freddie hit it off right away, and Chris soon moved in with Freddie and his gang in the already overcrowded Ferry Road flat. The other members of Sour Milk Sea grew jealous of Chris's relationship with Freddie, and the band fell apart after just a few weeks. Not long after that, so did Chris and Freddie's brief friendship. Chris headed back to Oxford with his tail between his legs to resume his neglected studies. Freddie was left, once again, to ponder a highly uncertain future.

As if he didn't have enough to worry about, Freddie had also started to grapple with his sexuality. Other members of his gang remember him showing a passionate interest in the whole concept of homosexuality and in meeting gay men, but never quite having the confidence to do much about it. He had certainly fallen prey to the charms of females from time to time. There had been particularly spicy gossip about Freddie and a girl on his course called Rosemary Pearson, with whom it was rumoured he had once spent the night, but had found himself unable to rise to the occasion. As one former art college friend put it, 'He thought he liked women, but it took him quite a while to realize he was gay . . . I don't think he could face up to the feelings it caused inside him. He was obviously terribly interested in homosexuality, but was afraid of it as well. I suppose he was squeamish and frightened of accepting himself as gay.'

Another friend remembers him paying regular visits to some gay flatmates in another part of Barnes, not far from Ferry Road. He hid these visits from his own flatmates, however. How could he explain his feelings to his friends when he hadn't even come to terms with them himself? Freddie started to worry about the impression he was making, and at times he would withdraw completely into his shell. Friends recall less attractive aspects of his personality beginning to emerge at around that time. He could be self-centred and egotistical, petulant and sulky, as if he were wrestling with some mammoth internal struggle. One woman even remembers him in those days as: 'Not a particularly intelligent person. He was frivolous and rather silly, not someone of great profundity. You had the feeling that he wanted to be famous, but wasn't really sure how to go about it.'

Everyone has his darker side. Freddie's, perhaps, was not all that dark compared with most. At least he was a fundamentally kind and generous human being. At least he was not ruthless. Freddie, it appears, never once used someone else to get what he wanted. On the contrary, he would happily allow himself to be used, expecting nothing in return. The most annoying thing about him was merely that he could be infuriatingly vain, endlessly fiddling with his hair and clothes and making sure that he looked 'all right', with what bordered on obsession. He had some odd habits which were at times hard to fathom and which made him look ridiculous if not pathetic. He would tell anyone who'd listen that he was going to be 'A Legend'. At the same time as he was living hand to mouth, he was very concerned with keeping up appearances: for example, he refused point blank to use public transport, and would rather spend his last couple of pounds on a taxi home than on a much-needed square meal. His friends began to despair of him. What, they wondered, would become of him if he never made it in the music business?

Lacking stability and direction in his life in every sense, it was understandable that Freddie had began to wonder if he were indeed on the wrong track. After all, he had qualifications and a potential career in graphic design, if only he could bend his head around the idea of a nine-to-five job. In his heart Freddie knew that he was simply not cut out for such drab, mundane obscurity. That he was not like everybody else. But he was beginning to feel that he should get off his cloud and try to earn a living, otherwise his future was going to be very bleak. The first few weeks of 1970 saw him trolling around the London agencies with his portfolio. Austin Knight's in Chancery Lane, Holborn, agreed to represent him, and look for publishing design work on his behalf. Unsurprisingly, Freddie soon lost patience. He couldn't bear the boredom of waiting for the phone to ring. He went freelance, placed some ads. But plenty of his evenings were spent hanging out with the guys from Smile at rehearsals and gigs, and it irritated him to distraction that he wasn't performing too. Frustration got the better of him, and there was only one thing for it: he would have to get his own band together. Pulling in Richard Thompson, Ibex's one-night-stand drummer, Mike Bersin and Tupp Taylor, Freddie turned Ibex into Wreckage. Their first live gig took place at Ealing College of Art, the same show Jerry Hibbert remembered attending and being completely underwhelmed by. Freddie was not bothered, he had his friends in that night: all his flatmates, including Roger and Brian, and the usual Kensington gang. If the band wasn't up to much, at least Freddie turned in a dazzling performance, and most of the audience went away amazed by what they had seen. He was some front man. Wreckage soon landed a gig at Imperial College, and rugby club bookings followed. Freddie, however, remained frustrated. He knew he had what it took, but something didn't feel right. Perhaps Wreckage were the wrong band for him. Maybe they were holding him back. After all, he should have been offered a three-album deal with a major record label by now – shouldn't he? He wanted it all. And he wanted it now. He told the others he was quitting, and that was the end of Wreckage.

As Ken Testi would later put it, 'I think Ibex filled a gap for Freddie. He wanted to be singing in a band, and Ibex benefited enormously from having him. It was a marriage of convenience for all parties. We were all very naïve, and there would have been some naïveté in Freddie at that time. To Freddie it was like his first second-hand car, the sort of thing you buy when you can just scrape a bit of money together. Eventually you want a better one.'[2]

No one blamed Freddie for the band's demise. There was no question that all involved had been profoundly affected by the man, his ambitious streak and his enthusiasm for life. Ken Testi spoke for everyone when he commented: 'It was an education knowing Freddie. He was very committed about everything. He had a certain tenacity, a single-mindedness, a desire for excellence.'

Bersin and Taylor shrugged off their disappointment and headed home to Liverpool. Thompson faded without trace into the swirling smog of the London music scene. That left the remainder of the musicians among them in an over-crowded West London flat. Roger and Brian without a lead singer. Freddie without a band. The solution was obvious.

Had Freddie not been so persuasive and downright stub-born, he might have found himself, in April 1970, fronting a band called The Grand Dance or The Rich Kids. The former was C.S. Lewis-inspired, taken from the trilogy of books *Out Of The Silent Planet* of which both Roger and Brian were fans. They raved about it as an ideal name for a band. The latter would be picked up in later years by Sex Pistol Glen Matlock as the name of his new group. Freddie was not having any of this. One-word titles worked best, he argued. They were punchy, memorable, and they had a superior edge. No argument, darlings, they would have to be called Queen. The others resisted at first, largely because the word had acquired a somewhat pejorative connotation in reference to homosexuality. 'Gay', at that time, was a word rarely used in that context, and probably emerged largely in defiance of 'Queer', its more disparaging predecessor. Freddie himself, although he had not formally come out (nor would he ever officially do so), had long grown used to being addressed as 'the old queen'. Far from being offended, on the contrary he was hugely amused by it. He liked its regal, androgynous, multi-layered implications; even better, the title would give him the excuse to camp it up to the hilt on stage – which after all was part of his act – and get away with it. Brian and Roger soon came round, once they had seen the funny side. No one would ever be sure whether they should take Freddie's antics seriously. As for them, no two males could ever be more macho or straight, so in their terms the name Queen was a riotous send-up. It was an inspired choice.

Having settled on a flamboyant name for the band, Freddie also set about discarding his own surname. Bulsara was dropped in favour of Mercury, the ancient Roman messenger of the gods. Identified with the Greek god Hermes, Mercury was also represented with winged sandals and a winged staff entwined with snakes. It is the name of the only common liquid metal, a dense, mobile, silvery fluid found free in nature and known to the ancient Chinese and Hindus. Mercury was also discovered in Egyptian tombs of circa 1,500 B.C., and is the name given to the planet closest to the Sun, the planet which has no moons.

Many theories have been put forward over the years as to why Freddie chose that name. But, according to Jim Jenkins, long-standing Queen fan and co-author of *As It Began*, 'Freddie told me himself, in 1975, that it was after the messenger of the gods. I remember it as if he's just said it to me. People have said since, that it was after Mike Mercury in TV's "Fireball XL5" – but I can tell you for sure that it was nothing to do with him.'

Although it is widely assumed that Freddie changed his name by Deed Poll around 1970, nothing exists on public record to prove this. Directed to the Public Records Office in Kew by London's Deed Poll Office, my investigations proved fruitless. Although they found Elton John's, there was no official entry for Freddie. But, as a spokeswoman told me, 'It has always been the case that only 10 per cent of name changes are registered through the Supreme Court and appear on our records. These days, in fact, about 5 per cent. It is not a legal requirement, as you can call yourself whatever you like. Chances are that Freddie Mercury changed his name through his solicitor. When the documentation is drawn up, he'd keep half and the solicitor would keep half.'

Freddie later displayed his interest in astrology when he designed Queen's world-famous logo. Incorporating the zodiac symbols of each band member, the logo featured two lions for Leos Deacon and Taylor, a crab for Cancerian May and a fairy for Virgoan Mercury, as well as a stylised 'Q' complete with elaborate crown.

On 18 September 1970, Roger and Freddie closed their Kensington market stall for the day as a mark of respect to their idol Jimi Hendrix, who had been found dead in his apartment. Freddie was devastated, and too depressed to work. But he soon became convinced that his mission in life was to take up where Hendrix had left off.

Next on the agenda, the hiring of a bass player. A number of bassists did time with the group throughout 1970 until the three almost despaired of ever finding their fourth man. The hunt for the right bass player continued apace. When they had virtually given up hope, they ran into John Deacon by chance at a London disco in February 1971. Deacon, Leicester-born, who had been involved with bands on and off since he was 14, was an electronics student at London University's Chelsea College, a man of few words but of buzzing brain and acute rhythm. He also turned out to be a dab-hand with amplifiers and equipment, and he happened to be looking for a band to join. More than that, though, said Roger,

'We thought he was great. We were all so used to each other, and were so over the top, we thought that because he was quiet he would fit in with us without too much upheaval. He was a great bass player too – and the fact that he was a wizard with electronics was definitely a deciding factor.'

There followed half a year of the most intense rehearsals as Brian, Roger and Freddie set about teaching their repertoire to their new band member. At that time, John was still a full-time student, and Brian was still working on his thesis. Only Roger and Freddie were at liberty to commit their time totally to Queen. Nevertheless, the band in its final guise were ready to play their first gig at a Surrey college towards the end of the summer term in 1971. Shortly afterwards, they played at Imperial College. Roger had by this time enrolled at North London Polytechnic to study biology, thus qualifying for a grant which would supplement his meagre income. That left Freddie, the only member of Queen who was no longer engaged in tertiary education. But he had other things on his mind.

The only way to achieve 'tightness' as a band was to play together as often as possible, and Queen threw themselves at the live circuit with renewed vigour. Thanks to Roger's following in the West Country they fared well for bookings in that neck of the woods, and often found themselves heading west for a few nights, where they slept on the floor at Roger's mother's house in Truro. As Win herself later remembered,

> Of them all, Freddie was the shyest and quietest one. He was not a conversationalist at all. His clothes were always spotlessly clean, and he seemed to be able to lay his hands on a pair of white trousers at any time. He was always effeminate, but we used to say, 'Oh, Freddie just get on with it.' He had longish black hair and they were all wearing fur coats at the time. They stood out a bit in Cornwall. If I was out shopping with my daughter and we saw the band, we'd sometimes hurry the other way.[3]

Eventually, as the entourage expanded to include girl-friends, roadies and liggers galore, Win had to put her foot down and the band were forced to look elsewhere for accommodation, sometimes renting small modest cottages.

Peter Bawden, a musician friend of Roger's at that time on the Cornish scene, also had fond memories of Freddie: 'I found him to be one of the genuinely nicest people I have ever met in my life. I remember I was walking through Kensington market a few days after I'd first met him. I heard someone shouting my name, and when I turned round it was Freddie and he just wanted to say hello. He had no need to do that, but he had made the effort. He was a delightful man in every respect.'

In September 1971 Brian decided to arrange a showcase gig for Queen at Imperial College, to which he would invite all the top London booking agents. Several turned up, but none was impressed enough to offer Queen a tour. It was yet another knock which the band, hungry for fame and success, took quite badly. But soon, Brian's chance encounter with an old pal from the past had them booked in to Wembley's De Lane Lea studios to try out new studio equipment in return for free studio time. Queen jumped at the chance, knowing that they were likely to meet all kinds of influential music business people at the studios who could perhaps help them get a record deal. The arrangement was not as simple as it sounded, and not without its technical problems, but at least it meant that they were able to record demos.

Roger, meanwhile, had been getting fed up with turning out to man a market stall. He felt it detracted from his standing as a musician. It had started to seem undignified, and anyway the novelty had worn off. He quit the stall, leaving Freddie to team up with another stall-holder called Alan Mair. Freddie was still enthusiastic about the Kensington scene, however. Apart from the fact that he still had many friends in the area, he had surprised everyone by falling in love – with a girl.

Chapter Seven

AND IT WAS MARY . . .

She could almost have been custom-made for the job. With her long, silky apricot hair, baby skin and Bambi lashes, Mary Austin was the image of Barbara Hulanicki's Biba hippy chick, the classic doe-eyed doll. When the fashion designer launched her Kensington store and the look on which an entire fashion was founded, she might have chosen Mary Austin, or someone like her, as her muse. The reality was not quite so glamorous. For Mary Austin, beautiful though she was, and even had she felt inclined to try her hand at that profession, did not have what it took to make a world-class model. Although petite and fine-boned, and blessed with that dewy, knowing innocence that epitomized seventies style, Mary lacked length of leg, strident confidence and that self-centred, almost aggressive streak which the modelling profession was beginning to demand.

As her old friend Mick Rock remembers, 'At the height of the Glam London scene she was a really cute-looking lady who could have had anyone, done anything. But she never saw herself as anything special. She never wanted to put herself forward in any way. She was self-effacing, sweet and charming. You just wanted to give her a cuddle all the time.'

Peering, pale and coy, from behind her shiny tresses, she had the demeanour of an earlier namesake, Mary Hopkin, the fresh-faced prodigy of Paul McCartney who had warbled so plaintively as to why 'Those Were the Days'. Both had a chaste, untouchable, ethereal quality that matched perfectly the floaty bohemian fashions of the day. What would be dubbed in hindsight the Stevie Nicks look after the Fleetwood Mac singer was already commonplace on Kensington High Street: midi dresses, maxi coats, suede platform boots, chiffon scarves, velvet chain chokers, purple lips, smoky come-hither eyes.

Mary was still a teenager when she found herself caught up in the maelstrom of the London rock scene. There could have been no better place for a fashion-conscious young woman to work than in the Biba boutique on Ken High. An incense-filled, fern-adorned Mecca of fashion followers of the day, the store was an exotic Aladdin's Cave of clothes, make-up and accessories and was the haunt of celebrities and anonymous groovers alike who couldn't get enough of the unique Biba style. In some ways, working in a trend-setting store might have seemed an odd career choice for a quiet girl like Mary. She kept herself to herself and never rocked the boat. Rumours did the rounds that both her parents were deaf and dumb; that, as a little girl, she had existed in a virtually silent world. Few around her knew many facts about her private life, however. Talking about herself never came easily to Mary.

Mary was a bewitching girl. But her beauty was not the most attractive thing about her. Her shyness and apparent introspection were perhaps her most magnetic qualities. Brian May was the first to notice Mary on the scene, and in many ways she was exactly his kind of girl. Being Brian, extremely tall, dark and 'dishy' in seventies parlance, he wasted no time in asking her out. Fascinated by her almost stoical streak, her serenity and an apparent wisdom beyond her years, he took her on a date in 1970 – and introduced her to Freddie. Curiously, while Freddie was to recall years later that he and Mary had first met in 1970, Mary herself would remember it as 1976.

'We met 16 years ago this month,' she is reported as having said in a newspaper interview in April 1992, although allowances must be made for the possibility of a misprint or a less than completely accurate quote.[1] It is common knowledge among those concerned that Freddie met Mary long before the band had made it. As she herself said, 'We had nothing when we met, so it was for richer and for poorer.'

The interview also stated that she had been 19 years old at the time. But years later, in 1996, when Mary and I discussed age and the problems faced by mothers contemplating childbirth in middle age, she told me that she was 45. This would mean that she had been born in 1951. I attempted to verify these facts by applying for a copy of Mary's birth certificate. But a standard 'five-year' search by the Office for National Statistics (assuming that she had not been adopted) turned up more than ten different Mary Austins in their indices, registered in the first two quarterly periods of 1951. Without more specific information, which Mary has always been so apologetically reluctant to divulge (gently reasoning that Freddie, not she, was the star of the family), there was no possibility of finding out more. So, if Freddie's memory had served him soundly in that they had first met in 1970, and Mary's in that she had been 19, they had actually found each other some six years earlier than she allegedly recalled – which would mean that they had been devoted companions for nearly 22 years, not 16, when he died. Whatever the facts, the attraction between them was immediate, mutual, and lasting, and Mary and Freddie would each prove to be the most important person in the other's life.

Puzzling, then, that Mary spent the six months following their initial introduction keeping well out of his way. It was only years later that she would explain the reason why – because she believed he was more interested in a close girlfriend of hers. One night after one of the band's gigs she even left him at the bar with her girlfriend, excused herself to go to the Ladies, and evaporated into the night. Freddie was dumb-struck. But it did not put him off. The opposite, in fact. The next opportunity he had to ask her out, he leapt at the chance. The pair became inseparable, and would remain so for the rest of Freddie's life.

In many ways, Freddie and Mary had much in common. Each had felt somewhat estranged from their respective parents, and had responded to the urge to assert their independence. Each had a 'tip of the iceberg' personality, in that what they revealed of themselves to others was but the minutest part of their complete character. Each could at times give the impression, however erroneous, of being a little shallow, flippant and frivolous, with materialistic tendencies and a live-for-the-moment style, particularly in their younger days. But most of this was little more than image – an act contrived to conceal their innate shyness. Both Freddie and Mary were sensitive creatures, naturally reserved, much deeper than they at times appeared. These were the common traits which first attracted them to each other, and which became the foundation of their everlasting bond. As time progressed, however, it was to be the contrasting, complementary and contradictory aspects of their personalities which would weld them. Mary looked a fragile, floaty, gentle soul who would not wound a fly. But her fragility concealed an incredible inner strength and serenity which Freddie admired deeply. In the years to come he would rely on Mary to remain strong for him whenever he felt himself spiralling out of control, increasingly unable to cope with the pressures of his demanding lifestyle. He might well have been the star of the family, but Mary, rock-solid and reliable, was the all-forgiving, all-accepting mother figure to whom he clung.

'I'm a man of extremes,' was how Freddie was once heard to describe himself. 'I have a soft side and a hard side with not a lot in between. If the right person finds me I can be very vulnerable, a real baby, which is invariably when I get trodden on. But sometimes I'm hard, and when I'm strong, no one can get to me.'[2]

Mary, who knew him far better than anybody else, and who could tell, instinctively, when he was being 'soft' or 'hard', had the tenacity of a limpet and made sure that she was always there for him. Freddie, for his part, flaunted a shatter-proof tough-guy image which concealed his insecurity and fear of being unacceptable, out of time, out of place. Almost from childhood he had suffered from something to which he rarely admitted: an intrinsic persecution complex. He strove to overcome it, but it would remain his fiercest inner demon almost until his death. It was perhaps a frustrated reaction against this irrational complex which at times caused him to flare in inexplicable bouts of bad temper and to be quite unkind and even cruel. While it has been suggested that Mary developed a defensive streak in later years to protect first Freddie and secondly herself from the media and hangers-on, and that she could frequently be untrusting and suspicious, she never lost the ability to put herself in others' shoes. And she was never knowingly unkind.

As much as the union of Freddie and Mary was a meeting of mind, heart and soul, the body in the equation was not to be ignored. Their sexual relationship began almost immediately, and was fulfilling enough to last for six long years. In one's early twenties, six years is a lifetime, and represents unequivocal commitment between lovers. Or so naïve, unsuspecting Mary believed. The two soon moved in together, into a one-roomed flat in Victoria Road, just a few minutes south of Kensington High Street in that same neighbourhood to which Freddie would return again and again throughout his life.

'We grew up together. I liked him and it went on from there,' Mary would later recall. 'It took about three years for me to really fall in love. I've never felt that way before or since with anyone . . . I loved Freddie very much, and very deeply.'[3]

Mary has, most of the time, kept her own counsel down the years, refusing to discuss even mundane aspects of her relationship with Freddie. On occasion, however, she has been known to let her guard slip and reveal intimate details. It once emerged, for example, that whenever Freddie felt the rush of songwriting inspiration in the middle of the night, he would pull his piano next to the bed and carry on composing. If this practice played havoc with both sex life and sleep patterns, who would be surprised to hear it? The average woman would not have put up with that for long. On another occasion, Mary confessed that she'd had her misgivings very early on about Freddie's sexuality, and even wondered when they first met if he could be gay. 'Then one day he told me he was bisexual,' she eventually disclosed in a rare newspaper interview with showbusiness journalist David Wigg, a loyal friend of Freddie's. 'I thought from that time that he would probably find someone else, but it never happened.'

It was not long, however, before Freddie was regularly taking male lovers. Surreptitiously at first, and all the while maintaining the inward as well as outward appearance of a normal loving relationship with Mary. The last thing he wanted to do was hurt her. Eventually, however, the subterfuge took its toll, and he was forced to come clean about the true nature of his sexuality. If she had known all along, she had denied it to herself. Such knowledge is loaded with pain. There were, after all, four separate entities in the relationship. Not only was Mary sharing Freddie with his bursting creativity, but with his ambiguous sexuality too. The dilemma she faced has perplexed many women in her situation. The outsider can only stand and stare. As one married woman of 20 years' standing, whose husband recently left her only to declare himself gay in middle age, revealed:

However perverse this sounds, the fact is that it is somehow preferable to lose your man to another man, or men, than to another woman. I can't really explain it, but it's not a competitive thing. It feels less of a slap in the face. You are at least reassured that it is not you who is lacking as a female. He didn't have to turn to another woman for all the obvious reasons. If he prefers a man, it's biological, as simple as that, and he was obviously wrestling with it inside all the while he was trying his damnedest to be straight for the sake of me and the kids. You do not feel that you personally have failed in any way. Of course, the same thing represents a challenge to some women, who will deliberately try to 'convert' a gay male as if to prove the power of their own feminine allure. It goes without saying what a dangerous game that is.

Perhaps Mary clung to the hope that Freddie was just passing through 'a phase'; that he would eventually 'see sense'. In the meantime, she was prepared to indulge him. As time went on, however, it became transparently obvious that he did indeed prefer male company for sex. Such preferences can only be concealed for so long, and the day soon came when their love affair ended in tears. One can only imagine the depth of Mary's sorrow and devastation. Freddie was her adored lover, her partner, her best friend. He was the one person with whom she could share everything and be her true self. Pre-motherhood, their relationship was her raison d'être. How alone she must have felt. How deeply she must have suffered over lost hopes and broken dreams, and how easily her love for Freddie might have disintegrated into hatred. It says much about the woman that she put her personal grief aside and refused to let the friendship die. If she couldn't have Freddie hook, line and sinker, she'd settle for the hook and line. Thus – and according to those who were there at the time, it was mainly due to Mary's efforts as Freddie himself

125

was consumed by guilt and would probably have kept his distance had she let him – the relationship metamorphosed into a deep platonic bond. Some described Freddie's feelings for Mary, and hers for him, as 'Mother Love'. Perhaps it was no accident that years later this would be the title of a plaintive hit song sung by Freddie on Queen's 'Made In Heaven' album, released four years after his death.

How quickly the speed of their relationship changed. Mary became a personal secretary of sorts, Freddie's Girl Friday, his right-hand. She later described herself as his 'general dogsbody', spending at least part of every day with him. He called her 'Old Faithful'. Mary was now free to seek other partners. It would be quite some time before she felt able to do so. There is little doubt that she hung on for dear life to the dream that she and Freddie would one day be reunited. That things would 'get back to normal'. She would even suggest to Freddie that they might at least have a child together – to which proposition he famously retorted, somewhat thoughtlessly according to some, that he would 'rather have a cat'. Mary was to give birth to two children, the second baby just after Freddie died. But her relationships with other men always seemed influenced by her relationship with Freddie, perhaps because she persisted, if only subconsciously, in keeping the Freddie-Mary dream alive. At the time of writing, her relationship with the father of her boys, interior designer Piers Cameron, is off. Mary resides in Garden Lodge, Freddie's palatial Kensington home, alone with Richard and Jamie. Cameron is reported to have complained that he could no longer stand living in a 'shrine' – it is well-known that Mary has gone to great lengths to maintain the house almost exactly as Freddie loved it.

As for Freddie, there would, curiously, be other affairs with women down the years as well as men, which Mary had no choice but to accept. What is certain is that she was never fully replaced in his affections. What they shared was as true as love gets. Freddie said so himself: 'All my lovers asked me why they couldn't replace Mary. But it's simply impossible. The only friend I've got is Mary, and I don't want anybody else. To me, she was my common-law wife. To me, it was a marriage. We believe in each other, and that's enough for me. I couldn't fall in love with a man the same way as I did with Mary.'[4]

Their friend Mick Rock, a London-born Cambridge graduate and linguist, fell into the seventies drug culture and became a rock photographer in 1972 after meeting David Bowie. He shot some of the first publicity stills for Queen in the early 1970s, made his internationally acclaimed name and fortune photographing Bowie and Lou Reed, and now works as a photographer/artist in his studio in New York City where he has lived since the late seventies. Rock maintains a relatively low profile these days, a far cry from the wildness of his and Freddie's youth. He was elusive at first, and most reluctant to be interviewed. I spent several months pestering him to meet me, and eventually he agreed to talk.

Rock remembers Mary as 'nothing short of a saint:

Mary's fabulous. Terrific. Very loyal. Unpretentious. Unintrusive. A good person . . . one of the best people I have ever known in my life. I knew both Mary and Freddie as a couple in the early days in London, '73, '74, '75, and I got on great with them both. After Queen had made it and I'd moved to Manhattan, I'd often see Freddie in New York and we'd hang out and talk. He was a good friend of mine, and I loved him dearly.

I hadn't seen Mary for some time until quite recently. I had tea with her last time I was in London, a year or so ago. She said a very strange thing to me then which I didn't understand at the time, but I think I do now. She said: 'First my father, then Freddie, now my sons. It would seem that I was put on this earth to nurture men.' She seemed to be saying that's her lot in life. A strange life, when you think about it. But it makes sense.

She is such a caring woman. I'm glad Freddie treated her right. Way back, when they were living together, they had what you could call a very interesting relationship. She was key to the whole thing that he became. She also knew him better than anyone on the planet. That's why he left her virtually everything. I remember him being beside himself over the whole sexuality thing, before he finally came out of the closet. Because there was a real true love there between him and Mary. The sexual thing wasn't nearly so important as their emotional and spiritual bond. Years later some people criticized her mercilessly for the way she hung in there, and they all questioned her motives. But I can tell you she was not there for the fucking money. I'd stake my life on that. I said to her when I saw her that the best part of it all is that she has got her sons' futures secured. I feel sad at times when I think about her. But she's so stoical. That was always her nature, I think.

Rock is the first to agree that Freddie was very fortunate to fall in love with such a sweet, easy-going girl. He could not have made the most quiescent partner.

Freddie was unique, a one-off, and anybody would have had trouble dealing with that. He definitely was gay, but not exclusively gay, and that screwed him. He was torn. It was almost as if he had to know whether he was one thing or the other for sure, but he was caught in this middle ground, in a kind of no man's land. In later years I was saddened to see that it was always 'Oh, Freddie was gay, Freddie was gay'. But the fact was, he loved women. He adored women as women, and he enjoyed their company immensely. While later in life it may have been predominantly men for sex, clearly he and Mary used to have sex, and I gather there were other female lovers from time to time. He may have been more promiscuous with men, but he loved to get with the girls. And Mary, of course, was the love of his life, definitely on the emotional level. It was clear that the relationship he had with her was the closest emotional bond he had ever known. The great irony of Freddie's life is that, though he was essentially gay, his greatest relationship was with a woman. Perhaps that had more to do with the woman in question than sexual preference.

'Also', explains Rock, 'he was more into his work than anything else. To compound the problem, he'd have these inexplicable crazy moments. All in all he must have been a nightmare to work with and to live with, and he knew that, he wasn't stupid. What Mary had to put up with was more than most people could take, but she never stopped loving him, not to this day. You could say she gave her life for him, and what's she's got in return is nothing compared to what she gave, believe me.'

Rock invited me to delve into a rather elegant book, *Mick Rock. A Photographic Record 1969–1980*, dedicated to 'A time not so long ago when to be young, glamorous, talented and wicked was a less lethal way of life'. The book contains some of the finest Queen photographs, and in it Rock recalls for posterity those fruitful years of working with the band, beginning in 1974.

'I still remember my first meeting with Queen,' he says. 'It was 1973, David (Bowie) was recording "Pin Ups" and I was spending a lot of time with him doing pictures. Ken Scott, who was Bowie's producer and engineer at that time and was always in and out of Trident, said that they had this new band who wanted to meet me. Queen were a sight for sore eyes, especially Freddie, who quickly became the one I related to most easily. I loved Roger too, though, and the other two were always great.'

In his book, Rock writes:

They were all unusually articulate and opinionated, and for an unknown band with no track record they were unashamedly confident. They had recently released their first album 'Queen' to little fanfare and insignificant sales, but they had no doubts about the inevitability of their success. They believed so much in each other. 'All for one and one for all,' I thought. There was no leader, they all had to be satisfied. When they played me their record for the first time, I immediately understood their confidence, they made very exciting and unique music.

Freddie and Mick recognized a mutual daring and off-the-edge streak. Both were uncompromising, and had the confidence never to accept no for an answer. Their friendship was based on reciprocal admiration.

'In the area of image, if not always in their music, if Freddie wanted something enough, he could probably badger the others into it,' Rock went on.

He was unquestionably the visual strength of the band. The others would tend to defer to him in that sense. It was his idea to get Zandra Rhodes to make clothes for them, that kind of thing. Getting his own way wasn't always the case musically, and I know he respected Brian's musicianship enormously. I believe he felt that he and Brian were pretty much equal musically, and naturally that caused conflict.

Freddie and I had many tastes in common. We soon became great friends. Maybe my work with Bowie had a little to do with it. I was aware that Freddie was absolutely fascinated by him.

It is not difficult to imagine Freddie falling under Bowie's spell. Revered by many as the most important rock figure of the era, Bowie had an innate sense of theatre and all the makings, even in those days when fashion, trend and The Next Big Thing were paramount, of a truly durable showbusiness icon. Not only did he continually alter and renovate both his image and his music, but he lived a heady, artistic lifestyle at such breakneck pace and so close to the edge that it thrilled and shocked even the most jaded inhabitants of the rock world. They had never seen anything quite like him. In a marriage which might as well have been made on Jupiter, David and his wife Angela were dubbed everything from 'The Multi-Sexuals' to 'Space-Faces' to 'The Aliens'. They were fierce defenders of sexual liberty during the seventies in a manner that challenged and even ridiculed all the dopey naïve permissiveness of the sixties. By this time, gay pride was also on the rise, the gay community having started to campaign against public intolerance and rejection of homosexuality. Freddie was intoxicated by it all.

'Glam was rampant,' wrote Rock in his book, 'and that was what Freddie wanted to project above all. Glamorous, androgynous, provocative – "and unforgettable", said Freddie.

'Freddie was living with Mary when I met him, so I got to know and love them both equally. I was always popping round to their little flat to hang out with them at teatime. Freddie was big on tea.'

Perhaps that was a habit harking back to the colonial lifestyle of Zanzibar in the late 1940s and early 1950s, attention to the more genteel aspects of English tradition being more assiduously paid among expatriates throughout the Commonwealth than ever at home. Freddie would never lose that clipped, colonial air.

Rock remembers:

Whatever else was going on, he was living this sweet little domestic life with Mary and it was all very cosy and charming. Freddie was always in his dressing-gown and slippers. We'd sit and talk for hours. I had a lot of fun

131

with him. You could talk to him about anything. He was much better informed than your average musician, and I wondered if he made sure that he was because he felt educationally inferior to the other three. It didn't necessarily figure – I mean, I studied at Cambridge and I met more congenital idiots there than anywhere. They'd have this fantastic in-depth knowledge of the one subject, but it didn't automatically make them brilliant all-rounders. I would say Freddie was the most knowledgeable and inquisitive member of Queen. He was so inquisitive – he wanted to know everything about everything. He was the most avid consumer of information. John Lennon was much the same. And David Bowie, too, in my experience.

There were an uncanny number of similarities between the three rock stars. All had left school ahead of time and were products of Art college – as, too, were Pete Townshend and Keith Richards.

'You could definitely say that Freddie was part of a British School of art students-turned-musicians,' says Rock.

Art was his thing. And music of course – especially, at that time, Joni Mitchell. He was always going on about how she was one of his biggest influences and how inspirational she was. He loved her melodies, her poetic lyrics, her paintings [virtually all Mitchell's albums featured her own original artwork]. And sometimes we would just sit there and gossip. He loved trivial gossip and nonsense. He was a lot of fun. He'd say to me: 'The most important thing, darling, is to live a fabulous life. As long as it's fabulous, I don't care how long it is.'

I'll go on the record here and say that he was just a fabulous person. He was so generous and warm. I can say that with a straight face and mean it. I can't think of any incident when he was mean to anybody. He had such an enormous heart. In fact, I can't think of one negative thing to say about him. If we're talking Bowie and Lou Reed, I can immediately think of negatives about both . . . not that it stops me being incredibly fond of them. But not Freddie. In my personal experience, he only ever exposed his most positive side. I have sometimes thought, since he died, that it could be the reason he died so young – like it was always on the cards. If people persist in bottling up their negative energy, that is not necessarily very healthy for them. Clearly, his was a very complicated and tangled life. Freddie certainly had a lot of internal anxiety. That was a vital part of his nature.

As far as work was concerned, Rock insists that Freddie was never the prima donna in the photographic studio. On the contrary:

He was very easy to work with. The only slight problem was that he had this thing about his teeth. It was always a factor when it came to deciding how a picture should look. There was no denying that they protruded, and that he was anxious to disguise this. He did actually open his mouth for me one day so that I could see the reason for the problem. There were simply too many teeth in there. He had four extra ones at the back of his palate which pushed the others all forward. I told him that a good dentist could easily put it right, but it was no use trying to reassure him. He would not even consider it, saying that he was worried that it might affect his voice: 'I need the extra teeth,' he said. It was all very baffling, and he never did have them out. Another thing was that he didn't much like the way his chin wrinkled and puckered at times. If you look at the photograph on the 'Queen II' cover, I can show you where a bit of retouching had to be done. [It is indeed noticeable when it is pointed out.]

133

And you won't see many set-up pictures of Freddie with his mouth open or where he's laughing.

Still, all that's irrelevant now. Freddie was one of my favourite human beings . . . He was a gem of a man, as gracious as any I've known.

As Mary herself would later remember, 'He widened the tapestry of my life so much by introducing me to the world of ballet, opera, art. I've learnt so much from him and he's given me personally so much.'[5]

Although his frivolous, mischievous side was much to the fore most of the time, his perfectionism could make him painfully difficult to live with. Not only did he feel compelled to make a drama out of any available minor crisis, but he could become almost obsessed with trivial details. Even flowers arranged around the home had to be just so, or he would throw them outside in disgust.

'That was all to do with his style,' Mary explained. 'He wanted things done his way and he could be very difficult, really. We quarrelled a lot. But he liked a good row.'

As in his personal relationships, so in his professional life. Compromise did not come easily to Freddie. He liked his own way, and always believed that his own ideas and interpretations were better than everyone else's. But the rest of the band did not give in without a fight, especially Brian, who, despite his otherwise gentle demeanour, was almost vehemently creative and understandably defensive of his own work. So much conflict would make for some uneasy episodes during Queen's glide to fame and subsequent two decades at the top. A couple of years later in 1974 when the band were on their way, Freddie made some telling remarks.

I'm very emotional. Whereas before I was given time to make my own decisions, now nearly all of us are so highly strung we just snap. We always argue but I think that's a healthy sign because we get to the root of the matter and squeeze the best out. But lately so much is happening, it's escalating so fast that everybody wants to know almost instantly, and I certainly get very temperamental.

You've got to know where to draw the line. But the public always come first – it's a corny thing to say but I mean it. Lately I've been throwing things around which is very unlike me. I threw a glass at someone the other day. I think I'm going to go mad in a few years' time. I'm going to be one of those insane musicians.[6]

The dynamics of the various relationships within the group could be so strained that they would from time to time discuss, in all seriousness, the option of calling it a day. Thankfully, they never got around to doing so. Meanwhile, with Freddie around, life was anything but dull.

Chapter Eight

EARLY DAYS, AND THE TRIDENT YEARS

As 1971 drew to a close, Queen were still going nowhere fast, and there were days when dejection and despair all but consumed them. As Brian remarked, 'If we were going to drop the careers we'd trained hard for, we wanted to make a really good job of music. We all had quite a bit to lose, really, and it didn't come easy. To be honest, I don't think any of us realised it would take a full three years to get anywhere. It was certainly no fairy-tale.'[1]

Said Freddie: 'At one point, two or three years after we began, we nearly disbanded. We felt it wasn't working, there were too many sharks in the business and it was all getting too much for us. But something inside kept us going and we learned from our experiences, good and bad.'[2]

Optimism flows easily with hindsight. As Roger remembered it, 'For the first two years nothing really happened. We were all studying, but progress in the band was nil. We had great ideas, though, and somehow I think we all felt we'd get through.'[3]

According to Freddie, 'There was never a doubt, darling, never. I just knew we would make it. I told everyone who asked just that.'

In the meantime, there was work to do. Confident in their ability as musicians, and convinced that they had what it took to succeed as a band, Queen went cap in hand to record company after record company. It is a notoriously rocky road strewn with endless obstacles, and the A&R guy has seen and heard it all before. Putting on a brave face, Queen continued to play college gigs, some well-attended, some attracting a mere handful of music fans. Tony Stratton-Smith, the head of Charisma records, showed an interest in the band. His record label was based in a tiny office in London's Dean Street. He had launched it in the late 1960s and it was responsible for the early Monty Python albums as well as Genesis, Peter Gabriel, Lindisfarne and Malcolm McLaren. Charisma was eventually acquired by Virgin Records.

Tony Stratton-Smith of Charisma offered Queen the not insubstantial advance of £20,000. But Queen reasoned, if they were indeed worth that amount then they were probably worth more elsewhere. They decided to use Charisma's offer and enthusiasm to drum up interest from other record companies.

As Freddie remembered in 1974, 'The moment we made a demo, we were aware of the sharks. We had such amazing offers from people saying, "We'll make you the next T. Rex", but we were very, very careful not to jump straight in. Literally, we went to about every company before we finally settled. We didn't want to be treated like an ordinary band.'[4]

Their logic appeared a little off-beat, particularly in the light of Stratton-Smith's declared intentions, obvious high expectations of this young new band, and a not indecent sum on the table. As Brian would later admit, 'We're basically very big-headed people, in a sense that we're convinced of what we're doing. If somebody tells us it's rubbish, then our attitude is that the person's misguided rather than we are rubbish.'[5]

Others certainly empathized with them for having the

courage of their convictions. 'We aimed for the top slot,' Freddie would eventually explain. 'We were not going to be satisfied with anything less.'

Queen did not think that they were good. They *knew*. That the entire record industry be made aware of the fact could only be a matter of time.

What has elsewhere been reported as Queen's serendipitous meeting with one of London's bright young record producers was in all probability less happy accident, more deliberate contrivance on Freddie's part. Freddie was nothing if not well-known in his manor for his diverse sartorial and musical influences. He openly raved about flamboyant artists such as Liza Minnelli, The Who, Led Zeppelin and David Bowie in his Ziggy Stardust incarnation, and would purloin aspects of their personal style. His preoccupation with dressing up continued, the more striking and exotic his attire the better; he would cruise Kensington High Street and the King's Road on a Saturday afternoon, having usually sweet-talked someone else into minding his market stall. He was known to justify the time he spent on his increasingly eccentric appearance with an airy 'You never know who you might meet'. He clearly meant to be noticed. Some had their suspicions that he had set his sights on an encounter with Trident Studios' John Anthony, and would not rest until he had achieved this. If so, Freddie's perambulatory perseverance paid off, for the two finally came face to face during one typical Saturday strut. In no time at all Freddie had charmed an invitation out of Anthony to bring the rest of band to his apartment in order to discuss their prospects. This resulted in Anthony persuading the owners of Trident Studios, Barry and Norman Sheffield, to join him at a Queen gig at Forest Hill Hospital in March 1972. The band proved such a hit that night that the Sheffields insisted on an official meeting at the Studios ASAP.

The meeting was not quite what any of them had been

expecting. The Sheffields were somewhat dominant, acutely business-minded figures. Their collective appetite whetted by the inflated sums being bounced at them, Queen were well and truly seduced. What they failed to spot among the small print was that their deal was nothing like the exclusive package the band more or less took for granted that they were being offered, but in fact involved two other acts. It was a crucial piece of information which somehow escaped the band's attention. What was glaringly obvious to others present that day was that this deal was purely business. There was also a tangible element of managerial control in what was on offer. It was not common practice for one management company to record, produce, manage and publish an artist, as well as negotiate a suitable record deal on their behalf. Anyone with the most basic knowledge of the workings of the music business would have raised questions about conflicting interests.

Not that Queen were hasty and incautious about signing their contract. On the contrary, they hesitated for almost eight months, until November 1972, during which time they did not give one live performance. In the absence of explanation, and given the fact that no one of significance really remembers, we can only speculate as to the reasons for their prolonged procrastination. Apparently there were no extensive legal wrangles. Perhaps the band were up to their old tricks again, wielding this offer in order to secure ever-increasing others. If they were holding out for a better deal with Trident, they were to be bitterly disappointed. What Queen eventually signed would be denounced by some as a poor excuse for a contract. They would, of course, only learn how unfavourable it was to themselves post-signature. How easy it is to be discerning with hindsight. Certainly Freddie was under no illusions following the eventual demise of their arrangement with Trident.

'As far as Queen are concerned, our old management

is deceased. They cease to exist in any capacity with us whatsoever . . . We feel so relieved!' he quipped in 1974.[6]

There was clearly no way to learn but the hard way. In 1977 Freddie spoke of the split from Trident thus: 'It brought on things I never realised . . . you just had to keep your defences up.'

In fairness to Trident and to the Sheffield brothers, it should be recorded here that their reputation in the business was sound. They ran one of the finest studios in London which was used regularly by many established artists. They neither ran up debts nor shirked responsibility, and they did invest considerable sums of their own money in the Queen-making machine. Only Brian could bring himself to acknowledge their contribution to Queen's success in later years.

Queen's time with Trident was spent under the care of a smooth operator, the American music business entrepreneur Jack Nelson, who had acquired his tactics at the sharp end of the US record industry. There was never any doubt that he was impressed by Queen and their output, and it was consequently decided that he would come to London and set them up with a suitable manager. Puzzled by the lack of interest that he encountered, he assumed the role of Queen manager himself. Since no record company was prepared to back them, Trident had no alternative but to fund Queen's recordings themselves, on their own studio premises. This all represented something of a come-down for Queen, who were forced to steel themselves to the indignity of access to a recording studio only when it was not required by more valued artists the likes of Elton John and David Bowie.

'They would call us up and say David Bowie had finished a few hours early, so we had from three a.m. to seven a.m. when the cleaners came in', Brian later admitted. 'A lot of it was done that way. There were a few full days, but mainly bits and pieces.'[7]

The arrangement was hardly conducive to creativity. But it's amazing what you can do when you try. Ironic, then, that a most notable recording from the Trident era, one of the collecting fraternity's most sought-after singles, occurred off the cuff and quite by accident. Hanging about in the studio one day, they were invited to contribute the backing to a cover version of an old Phil Spector number, 'I Can Hear Music', with which the Beach Boys had scored a top-ten hit in 1969. Freddie provided the vocals while Brian and Roger played and harmonised. It was mainly for fun, though each did receive a token session fee for his trouble. None of them had the slightest inkling as to the repercussions of that apparently innocent session. They had signed nothing, agreed to nothing, and had by virtue of their ignorance relinquished their right to any say over the finished product. That single was actually released under a made-up name by EMI Records the following year. The name was Larry Lurex, in both homage to and as a send-up of Gary Glitter. But most DJs failed to appreciate the gag and were offended by the dig, fiercely protective as they were of the Leader. There was virtually no air-play, the record sold just a few copies, and was soon consigned to the bargain bins. Years later it was re-released, and eventually became the coveted collector's item which it remains today, changing hands for hundreds of pounds. Growing wise to the ways and means of a cut-throat industry, Queen judiciously acquired the rights to the record en route.

September 1972 saw Queen pocketing a weekly wage packet from Trident containing just £20 each. The only way was up.

Chapter Nine

ALL THE YOUNG DUDES

Given the restrictions, indignities and irregularity of working arrangements that they were obliged to put up with at Trident, Queen's eponymous début album, diligently produced by Roy Thomas-Baker and John Anthony and completed by January 1973, was little short of a masterpiece. Pernickety perfectionists every one of them, the re-mixes and fine tuning had seemed to take forever. As one sound engineer involved in the project would later remark of Freddie, 'It was quite nerve-racking working with a born superstar.'

But Queen were still without a record company to press their efforts on to vinyl and release the album into the market. Despite the earnest attempts of Jack Nelson and Trident to stir up interest in Queen, response had been less than enthusiastic. As Nelson later remembered, 'It took me over a year to get Queen a deal, and everyone turned them down. I mean everyone. I won't name names . . . but they know who they are, every one of them.'[1]

Nelson did manage to secure a deal for the band with music publishers B. Feldman and Co., where there was virtual unanimous enthusiasm for the band, a rare occurrence indeed. The record companies remained underwhelmed, however. It was baffling. The consensus appeared to be that their sound

143

was too obviously reminiscent of other bands such as Yes and Led Zeppelin, which was a curious assessment since practically everyone who worked with Queen perceived their sound to be unique. Freddie, Brian, Roger and John were dumb-founded that a proper record deal still eluded them.

A showcase gig was duly scheduled for November 1972, at a trendy King's Road hang-out popular at that time, called The Pheasantry. Everyone involved had called in favours, borrowed and stolen address books, filched numbers, phoned round and begged support from every music business contact they could think of. In spite of all their efforts, the performance was poorly attended and a miserable night was had by all. Equipment failed, the band flagged, and to add insult to injury not a single A&R man bothered to put in an appearance.

Five days before Christmas they played the Marquee Club in Soho, one of rock's most hallowed venues. This was marginally better than their disastrous night at The Pheasantry, but still no major record deal. However, the MD of Elektra Records, Jac Holtzman, happened to attend the Marquee that night. Shortly afterwards Holtzman offered to sign the band for the United States. Here they were sharing a highly-respected label with The Doors and still they could not find anyone to release their album.

Queen kept their cool and waited patiently in the wings. February 1973 saw them recording a broadcast session for John Peel's progressive radio show, a coup indeed since it was virtually unheard-of in those days for Radio One to record an unsigned group. Things were looking up. B. Feldman and Co., meanwhile, had been acquired by EMI Music Publishing, to which Queen suddenly found themselves signed by default. Meanwhile, the chief A&R man at EMI Records, Dutch-born Joop Visser, was being wooed, having revealed that he was looking for a group to fill the gap left by Deep Purple. Visser was initially unimpressed by Queen. He had attended their pre-Christmas gig at the Marquee but had been left unmoved. He had watched them in rehearsal and pronounced them dreadful, and confessed privately that their personalities, both collective and individual, left him cold. There was serious work to be done. Unbeknown to Visser at the time, no band rose to a challenge quite like Queen.

Almost a year of ducking and diving paid off. Queen signed a major deal with EMI Records in the spring of 1973, and congratulated themselves that they had been right all along. Though they never actually declared the sum of their advance, this was rumoured to be a phenomenal pay-out. There could be no more blatant an endorsement by a record company of its latest signing. To justify such substantial expenditure, EMI were now required to bend over backwards to ensure that Queen were a success.

Yet overnight stardom continued to elude them. Queen's official début single, 'Keep Yourself Alive', was released on 6 July 1973. Radio One were unimpressed, it did not make the official playlist and the only DJ to give it any airtime was veteran Alan Freeman. The music papers were undecided as to whether they loved or loathed it. Meanwhile, lack of airplay meant that the single failed to chart. It was both the first and last time in Queen's career that this would occur.

Despite the fact that Queen's first single was disappointingly received, the EMI record pluggers, promotions people and press officers, ever mindful of the vast sum invested in the company's new signing, were assiduous in their attempts to publicize the band. Arguably the best exposure to be had at that time was on BBC Television's cult rock show 'The Old Grey Whistle Test' presented by Bob Harris, which, unlike 'Top Of The Pops', featured only album music. The programme was such a hit that it aired for some 16 years – a lifetime in television. Today's TV programmes of that genre rarely last a year, or even one series. Just one show in recent times compares to Whistle Test, and that is 'Later With Jools Holland'. It is the only music programme which has come close to Whistle Test's genuine feel. The success of the format depends almost entirely on the show not trying to be bigger than the artists featured.

A white label pressing of Queen's album, a blank LP in a flimsy white sleeve, was duly despatched to Whistle Test's production department. But, for want of a Biro, the masterpiece was almost lost. The plugger responsible had carelessly neglected to scrawl the name of both band and record company on the plain white label glued to the record, and there was no indication as to whom it was by or where it came from. Whistle Test creator and producer Mike Appleton takes up the story. 'At that time a lot of the strengths in album music were coming from the States,' said Appleton, formerly a 'lifelong BBC man'.[2]

Therefore, most of the bands were not available to come into the studio and play live. To get round that, I started this thing whereby I'd pick album tracks and have this talented guy Phil Jenkinson match the tracks with appropriate visuals. Nowadays, many people say that this led to the invention of the video. And with hindsight I can say that it was all rather detrimental to the music industry. It took all the money and emphasis away from the live performance, rock venues closed down, and ultimately all rock TV programmes began to look the same.

Anyway, the visualizations were a lot of fun. Fans began tuning in to 'Whistle Test' just to watch those. Regular featured artists included Little Feat, ZZ Top, JJ Cale, early Springsteen, Lynyrd Skynyrd – I could have featured their 'Freebird' every week and still been inundated with requests for more, it was the most popular thing at the time. We showed a broad range – cartoons, abstract films, experimental films, the lot. It worked incredibly well. One day I picked up this white label on my desk and noticed that it was unmarked. I might well have ignored it or dropped it straight in the bin, but as it happened I picked it up and put it on, completely unaware that this was a first pressing of Queen's first album.

I liked what I heard very much. I decided there and then that I had to get this one track, 'Keep Yourself Alive', on that week's programme. I started phoning around trying to establish name and source, all to no avail. In the end I just gave it to Phil and said, 'Let's put this on. We'll say on the programme that we don't know what the hell or who the hell, but if anyone out there knows, could they please call us.' Phil pulled out some black and white cartoon footage of a train doing a lightning speed, whistle-stop tour across America, this super silver streamlined train which had a cartoon of F D Roosevelt's face on the front. The footage had been used as part of a political campaign in the 1930s. The next day EMI called us to say that the band was Queen, and the following week we revealed all to the viewers. But during that week we received loads of phone calls. People were intrigued to know who it was. All this was quite unusual. Watching Whistle Test in the old days was a bit like belonging to a club. It was a private pre-occupation. We never publicized ourselves, we worked on the word-of-mouth principle.

Word-of-mouth was clearly doing the rounds. Queen's first album was eventually released in the UK on 13 July 1973. Then it was back to BBC Radio One, where Queen had recorded a session for John Peel only a few months earlier. The session was duly aired, but the band were still ignored by those who drew up the playlist. They were too busy to dwell on it. Trident had booked them into Shepperton Studios to develop new songs and rehearse existing material. Appropriately, it was during their spell at Shepperton that Queen found themselves making their first promo film, Trident having recently expanded into video production with their own company, Trillion. The film, made to accompany the album tracks 'Liar' and 'Keep Yourself Alive', was directed by another professional destined for legendary status in his field, Mike Mansfield, whose vast experience, technical knowledge and creative ability made him one of the finest directors in the business.

The promotional video, then in its embryonic stages, was to become such an integral promotional tool of the music industry that before long record companies were spending hundreds of thousands of pounds on top-gun directors, glamorous locations and dazzling special effects in their efforts to push their artists into the Top Ten. The promo video business with all its tricks and techniques would eventually spiral out of control and almost exhaust itself. The record industry would then remember the human element, and the whole cycle would begin again. But in the late 1970s it was still an exciting and fresh new medium which would greatly enhance the careers of dozens of artists, plenty of whom did not honestly boast the talent to warrant the hype, throughout the 1980s. The successful promo video relied on three essential elements: the music and lyrics of the song; the 'live' performance; and the distinctive imagery of the artist. When the mix of these ingredients was exactly right, a single airing of a promo video could do more to promote a record and establish an artist than any amount of 'blind' radio airplay. A three-minute epic commercial could satisfy a variety of requirements at once: grab a viewer's attention, make them watch as well as listen, remember the single, want to 'see' the song again, and hopefully buy the record. Before long, many artists were avoiding the live circuit completely. They were swift to realize that an illusion of perfection can be attained in a video recording which the live performance could never live up to, just as a photographed portrait can be retouched to the point that blemishes completely disappear. Thus, as Mike Appleton observed, small-circuit live music began to fast-fade. The downside is that filming is exhausting, especially for those unaccustomed to the rigorous demands of its schedules. Shoots often begin at sunrise and do not finish until well into the evening. But for a while, it seemed, the pros outnumbered the cons.

Queen's first experience of the medium, however, was not encouraging. The band felt uncomfortable in the studio and were at odds with Mansfield, who dismissed many of their artistic ideas in favour of his own. Queen were affronted. Freddie, in particular, was incensed. The result was unusable, and was never actually used or released – although it does appear as a 'rare bonus track' on Queen's 'Box Of Flix' (Greatest Flix and Greatest Flix II, which also records that the film was shot in St John's Wood Studios). For their attempt at a promo for 'Liar', Queen refused to work with Mansfield and directed it themselves, with the technical assistance of Bruce Gowers. Comparing the Mansfield film for 'Keep Yourself Alive' with 'Liar', however, there is not a vast amount of difference by today's standards. In both, Queen's look is very Kensington Market. In the first, they appear in a modest stage performance setting. Although basic and somewhat makeshift-looking – lights do not flash, smoke does not swirl – it is fairly effective for its time. Long-haired Freddie is flamboyant in black and white floral jacket and tight black satin pants, heavy jet choker, chain mail hand jewellery and belt. He bangs a tambourine against his thigh and smoulders about, macho and sultry, simultaneously masculine and feminine. But the focus is not on him: the overall impression of the promo is that it is a film of the band. In 'Liar', however, while also a stage setting, Freddie becomes the focal point of the performance, featuring in a sequence of sexy close-ups in which he is almost devouring his microphone, while the rest of the band fade into the background. Elementary soft-focus and kaleidoscopic effects have been introduced, and there is a slightly more daring, arty feel to the film, contradicted by the soundtrack which is distinctly heavy metal. In 'Liar', Freddie has swapped his flowery jacket for a black and white satin tunic. Brian gets to wear the jacket, somewhat ridiculously: it barely skims his waist, and the sleeves stop halfway up his long arms. The band display a discernible air of confidence – there is even the occasional to-camera smile. It had dawned on them by then that, only when they retained more or less complete control over their work, were Queen able to feel relaxed and courageous in their creativity. This was to set the pattern for a 20-year career.

'I wouldn't say that they were control freaks exactly. But they always knew exactly what they wanted, and they found it extremely hard to compromise or make do. They always had a perfectly clear idea of how they saw something, so it was generally pretty pointless to suggest that they go with something else,' remembers Tony Brainsby, in those days London's top publicist who had been brought in by Trident at considerable expense to act as the band's independent PR.[3] Brainsby once cut quite a dash on the music scene, and cruised around town in a Rolls-Royce. Lanky, bespectacled, mad-haired and usually dressed in a Mandarin-collared black jacket, drainpipe trousers and Chelsea boots, he was seldom without a cigarette, which he held between thumb and forefinger like a pencil, or a generously poured drink. Few can recall ever having seen him eat, and he was so thin that one could at times detect his bones through his clothes. He ran his publicity empire from his large, eccentric home crammed with televisions, dead plants, live rock chicks and pop memorabilia, not necessarily in that order, in Edith Grove between Fulham Road and the King's Road. His parties were legendary, and his walls were once decorated with Warhol originals: 'But they were nicked years ago.' Freddie's friend Mick Rock had been his wedding photographer. His client roster included some of the major artists of the day: Thin Lizzy, Mott the Hoople, Paul McCartney and Wings, Cat Stevens, Wizzard, Steeleye Span, The Strawbs.

'The approach came from Trident,' Brainsby remembers. 'Jack Nelson, the American manager, to be precise.'

It wasn't like me to take on relative unknowns – I was a bit of a star myself in those days. But Queen were different. Only two people spring to mind who, when you first met them, you just knew they were stars from the word go. One was Phil Lynott, the other Freddie.

I remember going to see them at Imperial College in London, where Brian went. I had already taken them on, but I wanted to take some people along. I remember there wasn't a stage, and Queen were just playing on the dance-floor, which was quite bizarre. Because no one was really there to see them, specifically, apart from us. There was Freddie doing all his posing in his white capes and what-have-you, literally inches away from people who were doing the Funky Chicken. That performance was far-removed from the way they ended up. But Freddie certainly had presence and presentation. He already had his act together.

What people tend to forget is that Freddie wasn't the main writer in those days. It was Brian who wrote most of the early material. And even though Freddie was very much the flamboyant front man, what I thought was commendable was that at no time did they style themselves 'Freddie Mercury and Queen'. It was always a group image. Freddie never tried to project himself as the leader of the band. As far as I could tell, relationships within the band were always very harmonious. They were unusual for a band in that they were incredibly intelligent, with God knows how many O and A levels and degrees between them. One could feel quite inadequate in their presence at times. But it was a great hook for interviews, as long as we played it down and didn't come across as too patronizing of the journalists. At the beginning we'd use Freddie a lot for interviews, but I learned to make sure that they did an equal amount. Later, we'd save Freddie for the major ones. After that, it was Brian for the major ones. He'd always talk about the guitar he'd made from an old fireplace, so that was easy, and got them into the more serious music papers. And Roger, who was always the pin-up, did well in the teeny girls' mags like *Jackie* and *19*. He was *so* pretty. At least the band weren't precious about where they got coverage, which was just as well considering so many journalists wouldn't give them the time of day. Although I must say they were rather fussy about photographs: they personally had to approve every single one before I could release anything. Freddie was the most sensitive: it was all to do with his teeth. He would never approve a picture where they showed too much. He was quite paranoid about his image. Not because he lacked confidence in his looks, I believe, but because he was such a perfectionist. A typical Virgo.

Everything about Freddie, in fact, fascinated Tony from the outset:

He was unique. He had many stylish little quirks that would stick in your mind. He'd paint the fingernails of just his right hand or his left hand with black nail polish. Or he'd just varnish one little finger. He'd say 'Darling!' or 'My Dears!' practically every other sentence, and he had this camp delivery which was highly amusing and very endearing. He was great to have around, never a dull moment. The girls all loved it whenever he came into the office. At the time, of course, he was living with Mary. His sex life was, to start with, a complete mystery to us all, we could never quite fathom it. I don't believe he understood it himself. But he was going along with the ride, suck it and see, so to speak. He never actually

spoke about it, not that I can remember at any rate. I
didn't have conversations of that nature with him, as
I didn't really socialize with the band. I never liked to
get too involved with clients. Mistaking them for your
best pals is a big mistake in PR, because they just take
the piss, and artists can become such a pain in the ass
if you get close to them. I left that sort of thing to the
girls in my office, that's what they were there for.

Rock 'n' roll is a very erratic, unstable, emotional,
ego-ridden business. Just like its stars. Work in it as
long as I have and you learn not to be surprised by
the fact that virtually every rock artist is a paranoid
eccentric. That's what it does to them.

Tony remembers very clearly one meeting with Queen in
his office when they were going to change the name of the
band. Thankfully, the change never occurred. But he says
they had very fixed ideas about everything else.

When they came in originally, they knew exactly how
they wanted to look and how they should be portrayed
for the press. They knew who they were and what they
were, which was rare for a rock group, believe me. It was
just another reason why you knew they were going to
make it. They had already designed their coat-of-arms
logo. The clothes, the colour schemes, it was all there.
You didn't have to get people in to style them. They had
really done their homework and knew exactly what they
were aiming for. Bands at that time simply didn't. It was
always 'Hey, man, we're musicians.'

Hardly surprising, then, that the music press were so
suspicious of Queen, and at first denounced them as a hype
band. It was all very well to dismiss such condemnation as
ignorant and ill-informed. But it was impossible to ignore
the massive influence of publications such as *Melody Maker*

and the *New Musical Express*. The damage they could inflict was as considerable as the good they could do a band's reputation. *Melody Maker*'s weekly sales regularly exceeded 200,000, and front page coverage could actually buy a band a hit. Nowadays, with circulation reduced and power diminished by competition, particularly by rock and pop coverage in the national press, getting the music papers on your side is no longer a vital consideration. Back then, affirms Tony Brainsby, it was everything.

> The trouble was, I just couldn't get them to take Queen seriously at all. They were a pop band in appearance, but they claimed to be real musicians. Which of course they were. Many music journalists simply refused to believe that Queen played their own instruments, and that can be the kiss of death for a band. They were called 'posing ponces', and were accused of getting session musicians in to cover for them, because people found it so hard to believe they could look like that and be talented. But you could almost understand why the music press were writing the band off as one gigantic hype. After all, they had come from nowhere, and all of a sudden everyone was talking about Queen.

Roger, in particular, was infuriated by all this, and said so in an early Queen press interview: 'There are really only two things that hurt: firstly, we're called a hype – that's one thing we're not. We're making it in the old-fashioned way, which is initially through selling records, through playing concerts, enabling the record company to get behind you for the second album. The other thing is that they cast doubts on your musicianship, which is one thing we're really sure about. Obviously we think we're bloody good.'[4]

Although he had well-planned strategies for dealing with such problems, what Tony was not prepared for was the reaction of the fans.

It was very peculiar indeed. Even before Queen's first hit record, I had old women phoning me up. It was so odd. Here was this band that no one really should have heard of, nor known anything significant about. And yet they already had a fan club. And there were housewives, of all people, in this fan club. Middle-aged women. Yes, they were authentic. One or two wags used to say that the band probably got their mums and aunties to ring in. But I could tell just by chatting to a few of them on the phone that they were for real. You just knew that something was happening. Queen had some kind of unique appeal. And there was a huge buzz, or something, going on, from the word go, that was causing all this to happen. I had never known anything like it in my career.

Another thing which astonished Tony, and which gave some indication as to how Freddie's star-struck mind was working, was that even in those early days, Freddie had his own personal hairdresser. Before long, he had also acquired a personal masseur: 'Freddie just knew that massive stardom was only a matter of time.'

On a personal level, Tony admits that, while he couldn't help liking Freddie, he was not the easiest of artists to deal with.

I suppose I liked other members of the band more. But I admired Freddie. Here was a man bursting with creative powers which were not simply in anyone's imagination, they existed. He knew he had it in him, however old he was at the time . . . 27, I believe. I mean, they were quite old for a band, weren't they, to be starting out. He'd had all this inside him for so long. How frustrating it must have been, knowing that he had what it took, trying desperately to make it big time and not getting anywhere for so long. He gave the impression of being someone who had known exactly what he was capable of since he was a child. He desperately needed a recognized outlet for his creativity, and it must have been such an enormous relief to him to know that he was at last getting somewhere. There were times when he was fighting tooth and nail to get what he wanted, which doesn't always bring out the pleasant side. Having to kick, struggle, scream, punch and shout in order to make an impact and get through is always going to take its toll. That's where Freddie was at when I got him.

By August 1973, Queen were back at Trident Studios to begin recording their second album. Brainsby's tireless efforts at publicity having raised their public profile considerably, Queen were now regarded as a bona fide band, and as such accorded the privilege of proper studio time. Being Queen, they had endless ideas and were keen to experiment with their sound. September saw them at the Golders Green Hippodrome recording yet another session for BBC Radio. And that month, American record company Elektra launched the band's first album in the US. Queen, however, did not over-excite themselves. They knew that they were a relatively unknown British band with a very long way to go. It came as a huge surprise, then, when American DJs right across the States hailed them as an 'exciting new British talent' and began to play tracks from the album on air. Before long the requests were pouring in, and the album soon made it onto the revered Billboard chart, climbing to a very respectable number 83. Success indeed for a brand-new band, and the achievement did not go unnoticed.

It was Tony Brainsby who had introduced Queen to another great act on his roster, Mott the Hoople, fronted by the wild, ringlet-haired Ian Hunter. Theirs had been a most chequered career. Despite a loyal following on the London club scene, their album sales were disappointing. They had even disbanded in 1972, and were only persuaded to re-form by David Bowie who introduced them to his own manager. With a little help from their friends, Mott The Hoople secured a new contract with CBS Records (now Sony Music). Bowie even wrote and produced a hit single for them, 'All The Young Dudes', which reached number three in 1972. They subsequently enjoyed three further Top Twenty hits, including 'All The Way From Memphis' and 'Roll Away The Stone' during 1973, which prompted them to look into the viability of a major British tour. Advance ticket sales were encouraging and the promoters duly booked twenty prime-venue tour dates, kicking off on 12 November at Leeds Town Hall and ending at London's Hammersmith Odeon just before Christmas. All they needed now was a support band.

Mott The Hoople's management could not be blamed for their reluctance to consider a relatively unknown group. The principal misgiving was that Queen were not experienced enough to handle a gruelling nationwide tour. The relentless Jack Nelson would not let the matter drop, however, and at that time proved himself to be the band's most ardent ally. He argued Queen's case, enthused about their talent and determination, pestered and cajoled until he had talked Queen's passage on to the tour. Some still speak in hushed tones of alleged cash incentives being involved in the transaction. Unsurprisingly, none felt inclined to elaborate.

Queen were now beginning to experience the first ripples of interest in their music outside Britain. EMI flew them to various European destinations for promotional broadcasts, in particular to France, Holland and Belgium. Then came the one-off live promotional concerts, their first international performance taking place in October 1973 in Frankfurt. By now, the band's British fan base was impressively strong, and their live shows always well-attended. Some fans were known to turn out with their entire families – kids and grandparents included. Queen's act was not exactly a mainstream family show, but this did not deter them. Their warm-up gigs for Mott the Hoople's tour were a resounding success, especially the one at Brian's alma mater, Imperial College, and a far cry from their flop at the Pheasantry such a short time earlier. At last, Freddie had just what he needed: guaranteed audiences, constant adulation, the crowds calling out for more. A couple of rave reviews in the music press couldn't hurt either, although these were few and far between. For all the enthusiasm generated by Queen's fast-growing army of fans, the music papers were predictably scathing, and more or less unanimous in their assessment of Queen as a mere and trifling 'Emperor's New Clothes' phenomenon.

'Fuck them, darling, if they just don't get it,' retorted Freddie to a baffled Tony Brainsby. Tony, who so often happened to be on the receiving end of Freddie's pent-up wrath and frustration, couldn't help but notice the dramatic effect all the fan worship was having on his charge:

In spite of the press, Freddie's confidence absolutely soared. But I could see that he did not enjoy doing interviews. And although he'd pretend that he was not bothered, bad reviews and bitchy write-ups really hurt him. In time, we stopped using him for interviews more or less altogether, apart from when there was an album release or a forthcoming tour. Those journalists who were interested in the band didn't seem to mind that they'd get Brian or Roger but not Freddie. His delib- erate elusiveness only made him appear all the more mysterious, of course, and I think that rather appealed to him. John didn't care about the press at all, and we hardly ever used him for interviews.

As Freddie himself saw it, 'I think, to an extent, we're a sitting target because we've gained popularity quicker than most bands and we've been talked about more than any other band in the last month, so it's inevitable. I'd be the first one to respect fair criticism. I think it would be wrong if all we got were good reviews – but it's when you get unfair, dishonest reviews where people haven't done their homework that I get annoyed.'[5]

Denis O'Regan, the award-winning rock photographer who made his first forays into the business photographing David Bowie at the Hammersmith Odeon with a camera borrowed from his uncle, and who would one day tour the world with Queen as their official lensman, saw Queen supporting Mott the Hoople at the same venue that year, and marvelled at the 'pretentiousness and confidence' of their lead singer.

'Freddie was an absolute star even then', insists Denis:

He was throwing the shapes and going through the poses even then – as a mere support act. He talked a bit to the audience between numbers, introducing the songs. And Brian May was fantastic. I'd never heard of Queen, but in those days one tended to go along and see the support band as well as the main act. I turned to my friend George Bodnar (today also a major name in rock photography) and said, nodding towards Freddie, 'Who does that prat think he is?' Because he was behaving as though he was the headline act. And then I found out why, of course, a year or so later, when I, along with the rest of the world, had got used to the idea of Queen. I only really got into the music when I heard them on the John Peel show. And I have been a big Queen fan ever since.[6]

'For me,' Joop Visser later observed, 'it was only after Queen toured with Mott The Hoople that they really got it together, and I mean got it frighteningly together. They scared Mott The Hoople at the end of that tour because they were stealing the shows.'[7]

The tour took in venues throughout the UK: Leeds, Blackburn, Worcester, Lancaster, Liverpool, Stoke-on-Trent, Wolverhampton, Oxford, Preston, Newcastle, Glasgow,

Edinburgh, Manchester, Birmingham, Swansea, Bristol, Bournemouth, Southend – where Queen minus John joined Mott the Hoople on stage for an impromptu rendition of 'All The Young Dudes' – and London. Although they started out nervously, Queen soon rose to the occasion and took the challenge in their stride, encouraged by audience reaction and by the fact that so many fans appeared to be attending the shows specifically to see Queen rather than just another support group for Mott the Hoople. Press reviews were generally ecstatic: atmosphere 'electric', band 'sensational'.

Asked to comment on their astonishing success on the tour which started out as Mott The Hoople's and finished as Queen's, Freddie himself shrugged: 'I've always thought of us as a top group. Sounds very big-headed, I know, but that's the way it is. The opportunity of playing with Mott was great. But I knew damn well the moment we finished that tour, as far as Britain was concerned, we'd be headlining.'[8]

Chapter Ten

KILLER QUEEN

From one extreme to the other. EMI Records could no longer cope with the avalanche of fan mail and requests for signed photographs and information on Queen, and attempted to hand over the responsibility to Trident Studios. But Trident could not handle it either. There was only one way to solve a very welcome problem. By the end of 1973, Queen had launched their first official fan club, having persuaded two old friends from Cornwall, Sue and Pat Johnstone, to run it. Although management of the fan club would change hands several times over the years, the band members themselves never lost interest. Freddie was the first to realize the importance of paying attention to and taking care of Queen's fans, and always provided whatever they requested, whether it be one of his stage costumes for a charity fund-raising auction or a personal newsletter for the fan club magazine. He also made a point of dealing personally with the girls who ran the club, encouraging them to call him at home with queries and, in later years, even inviting them to private parties at his home.

Despite their ongoing battle with the press throughout 1973, things started to improve in the New Year when music paper *Sounds* hailed them as 'Britain's Biggest Unknowns' and voted Queen the country's third-best newcomers. Album sales were looking good, and EMI stepped up their international promotional campaign, scheduling an Australian trip for January 1974. Disaster struck when Brian May developed gangrene in his arm following a routine travel inoculation. His reaction was so serious that for a while he believed he was facing amputation. His condition improved dramatically, however, and the band departed as planned. It was during the flight to Sydney that Freddie's extreme fear of flying first manifested itself. He also developed a serious ear infection for which antibiotics had to be prescribed, which resulted in a soaring temperature and temporary damage to his hearing. The trip, it appeared, was jinxed from the start. Neither Freddie nor Brian was up to performing. Queen did not make a good impression on local audiences. Reviews were scathing, and some completely false interviews appeared which portrayed Queen in a poor light. Their final gig had to be cancelled, and Queen, licking their various wounds and nursing their dented pride, beat a hasty retreat.

Encouragement awaited them back home, however, in the form of the *NME*'s readers' poll, which voted Queen second most promising new name – even without a hit single under their belts. In America, Elektra released a further single from the Queen album, but again, this sank without trace. Undeterred, EMI in the UK scheduled another single release. A last-minute vacant slot in the 'Top Of The Pops' TV schedule saw Queen rushed onto television, and Queen made their first appearance on 21 February performing 'Seven Seas of Rhye', before the single had even be released. As Tony Brainsby remembers, Freddie ran along Oxford Street to watch their appearance in a shop window because he didn't own a television set at the time. The single was rush-released a couple of days later, and at last, it seemed, the tide was starting to turn. Not only was their second album 'Queen II' now ready for release, but Queen were planning their first headlining UK tour, beginning in Blackpool on 1 March and closing at London's famous Rainbow Theatre 30 days later. Consequently they were rehearsing flat out at Ealing Studios. As Tony Brainsby remembers, it was Freddie's idea that they get acclaimed fashion designer Zandra Rhodes to make their rather sumptuous tour costumes, and the rest of the band readily agreed. Up to this point the old adage 'Don't Give Up Your Day Job' had stood Freddie in good stead. Only now, and not without a measure of sadness, did he feel confident enough to kiss his Kensington market stall goodbye.

Their 'Seven Seas Of Rhye' single charted four days after the Blackpool show, straight in at number 45, which was more than respectable for a first chart entry. Three days later saw the release of 'Queen II', which made number 35 on the album chart later that month to mixed reviews. 'Seven Seas Of Rhye' remains the only universally familiar track from the album, the others being 'Procession', 'Father To Son', 'White Queen (As It Began)', 'Some Day One Day', 'The Loser In The End', 'Ogre Battle', 'The Fairy Fellers Masterstroke', 'Nevermore', 'The March Of The Black Queen', and 'Funny How Love Is'.

The tour, sadly, was not without violent incident. When a fight broke out among the crowds at a Stirling University gig, two members of the audience were stabbed and the police called in. While Queen found themselves safely locked away in a kitchen, two members of their road crew were injured and taken to hospital. There was no choice but to cancel their performance in Birmingham the following night and reschedule it for later on the tour. Queen suddenly and unwittingly found themselves the subject of screaming riot headlines in the music papers, and a surge in publicity ensued. It continued after their Isle Of Man gig at the end of March, the success of which the band and entourage celebrated with a somewhat over-enthusiastic party which, in true rock 'n' roll tradition, left hotel rooms demolished and which was to set the trend in post-gig revelry for years to come.

Not only had Queen's second album now climbed to

number seven, but more and more fans were beginning to pick up on the first. Consequently that album too charted for the first time at 47, at about the same time as Elektra released it in Japan. It was received with enormous enthusiasm. Little did Queen, Trident or EMI realize then how big in Japan the band were destined to be.

The British live circuit fell under Queen's spell helplessly as the charts gave way to their records. There was now a great deal to live up to. And success, however much deserved, has a habit of taking its toll. At times the pressure caused Freddie to flare and Brian to lose patience. Their bitchy scraps were soon legendary, and usually resulted in a petulant Freddie flouncing off in a dramatic huff while Brian and the others simply stood around shrugging. More often than not Freddie would cool off and come back, but the time-wasting was pointless and tiresome when there was so much work to get through. Most agreed that Brian's irritation was justified.

Their confidence boosted by the massive success of their own début British tour, Queen were honoured but not surprised to receive the invitation to support Mott The Hoople on their imminent US tour, kicking off in Denver Colorado, and taking in several nights in New York. Freddie, especially, was champing at the bit. Despite his fear of flying, he could not wait to set off for America on 12 April, Elektra having released Queen's second album in the States a few days prior to the band's arrival. It promised to be a gruelling tour but not without its share of fun. Their first real American rock 'n' roll tour was exactly what they had been working towards all these years, and the four of them behaved like little kids the night before Christmas at the thought of it.

Disaster was to strike again, however, with Brian falling ill in New York during their run of shows there. It seemed he had never quite recovered from his infection in Australia. He eventually collapsed, and the band were told to forget about playing Boston. Before long, they were advised that they should drop the rest of their US tour completely, as

Brian had contracted hepatitis. In spite of the fact that he was so sick and incapable even of getting out of bed, Brian's disappointment and sense of guilt was indescribable. He couldn't help feeling that he had let the band down, and that, but for his untimely illness, Queen would by now have conquered America and be reigning supreme as the world's number one rock group.

Back in England, with Brian apparently recovered, the band set to work on tracks for their third album, which included 'Killer Queen', with master producer Roy Thomas Baker, who had been a Decca engineer in the early sixties and worked with the Rolling Stones, T. Rex, Frank Zappa and Eric Clapton. As a producer he had been responsible for the success of, among others, Nazareth, Dusty Springfield and Lindisfarne, and was one of the most highly acclaimed producers of the day. Which was all very well. Within weeks Brian was again back in hospital, this time with a duodenal ulcer. A further American tour scheduled for the autumn had to be scrapped, and Brian was beside himself. In darker moments, he even feared that the group might seek a replacement guitarist, although this was never on the cards. Compensation eventually arrived in the form of a music industry silver disc awarded to Queen for sales in excess of 100,000 copies of the 'Queen II' album. True to form, Tony Brainsby had organized a stunt for the presentation ceremony at London's Café Royal in the comely form of actress Jeanette Charles. Jeanette, Her Britannic Majesty's accidental double, appealed to Freddie's great sense of the ridiculous as she addressed those assembled in a manner fit for a Queen. One glance at Brian and a wag was prompted to jest at Brian, 'It hurts when I laugh . . .' Miss Charles, something of a national TV institution in those days, was an inspired Brainsby choice, particularly as Queen had been perfecting an inoffensive rock version of the National Anthem with which to close their live shows.

'Killer Queen', their third single, was released in October

that year, just before their next UK tour. Promoted by premier rock impresario Mel Bush, it promised to be more ambitious and elaborate than its predecessors. The new single was indeed a killer, tearing to number two and forcing all the music papers to admit, finally, that this unique group could not be written off as a no-hit wonder after all. Certain members of the press did the obligatory volte-face. But Queen were not about to throw themselves heaving with gratitude upon the hitherto indifferent media. The press were going to have to work rather harder than that, and Freddie could not help but savour the moment. Needless to say, Queen's third album, 'Sheer Heart Attack', was favourably received by most. A few journalists, perhaps hoping for the elusive interview, gave it dazzling reviews. Queen's Rainbow Theatre show was a complete sell-out, and extended to two nights. The after-show party at the Swiss Cottage Holiday Inn was an unholy riot and an indication of revelry to come. Queen were barely in a fit state for their first European dates, scheduled for the end of November; on the continent album sales were fantastic and most of the gigs a sell-out. In Barcelona, a city which for various reasons was to become close to Freddie's heart, and a place to which he would return again and again, the 6,000-seat venue was sold out within 24 hours.

For every up there comes a down. Queen would have been the first to admit that their arrangement with Trident had been far from ideal for some time. It was only now beginning to emerge quite how un-ideal it actually was. Come December 1974, relations were so strained that Queen felt obliged to appoint an independent music business lawyer to untangle the mess on their behalf. Up stepped legal whizzkid Jim Beach. Thus began a relationship which was to endure to the end of Freddie's life and beyond, with Beach heading up Queen's international management company to this day. In spite of his winning reputation, it was to take Beach some nine months to negotiate Queen's way out of their various signed agreements with Trident, who could hardly be blamed for wanting to hang on to the band. After all, considerable investment was now beginning to pay dividends. Queen were on the international rock map, and a bona fide US success. Both the single 'Killer Queen' and the album 'Sheer Heart Attack' had succeeded in breaking into the American Top Ten, and it was agreed that they were now more than ready to tackle their own major league US tour. New Year was consequently spent in quiet contemplation as they psyched themselves up for the big adventure, beginning in Kansas. Only John Deacon rocked the boat, on 18 January, by getting married. The entire tour was a sell-out, but the gruelling regime took its toll. It was on that first headlining US tour that Freddie first experienced vocal problems, an affliction which was to plague him from time to time throughout his entire career. In fact, he had caused the problem himself, by straining his voice. He had now developed throat nodules, and was instructed not to sing, nor even to speak if he could help it, for the next three months. As far as Freddie was concerned it was a preposterous suggestion. He defied doctor's orders, and stepped out on stage in Washington the following night. He did, however, take the trouble to consult another specialist, who opined that Freddie had a severely swollen throat but not nodules, and would not after all require surgery. Annoyed at having to cancel half a dozen gigs but relieved that he would not be incapacitated for several months, Freddie travelled on to New Orleans to relax and begin his course of treatment. But, typically of him, he went back to work too soon. The problem flared again, and Queen were forced to cancel further shows. What was becoming clear was that Freddie was giving far more on stage than the other three put together. It was more than his body, specifically his vocal cords, could stand. He would require more time off on the road if he was to maintain his voice and general health in peak condition. Especially since their thrilling affair with Japan was about to bloom.

While the American tour had been an exciting experience, and Queen had acquitted themselves well, they were under no illusions about their status. They were still just another rock band who had come, rocked, and gone again. It was not easy for a non-American group to make massive and permanent impact on a laid-back country which rightly regarded itself as the home of rock 'n' roll. While the best of British artists had held their own in the States since the days of the 'Great British Invasion' of 1964, when groups such as the Stones, the Kinks, the Dave Clark Five and Gerry and the Pacemakers effected something of a musical revolution across America, they could not help but detect a certain smugness in the average American audience. They tended to give the impression that they had seen it all before. Only the Beatles had entered the country as true pop demigods and remained unshakably so, especially to the millions of Americans who had tuned in to the Ed Sullivan Show and been captivated by the Liverpool boys' television performance. Bands like The Who, Rolling Stones, Bowie, Led Zeppelin, Genesis and Elton John would all achieve rock-legendary status in America, but only the Beatles retained universal appeal. Queen, of course, still craved rock superstardom. It remained the focus of their ambition. But when it finally hit them, they were somewhat unprepared for and bemused by its geographical source.

They were of course aware of their popularity in Japan, which was the first country to acknowledge Queen as fully-fledged rock-stars. Thrilled by their soaring album and ticket sales in that territory, and elated by the news that both their album 'Sheer Heart Attack' and single 'Killer Queen' were at number one in the Japanese charts, Queen were nevertheless totally unprepared for the heroes' welcome which awaited them at Tokyo airport in April 1975. The Arrivals Hall heaved to the deafening din of some three thousand hysterical Japanese rock fans, hundreds of them flapping home-made banners and waving Queen records at the beaming group and entourage as they strode through Customs. Some reported that it was a scene reminiscent of Beatlemania more than a decade earlier. Freddie rose regally to the occasion, waving and smiling enthusiastically and soaking up the adulation. One reporter joked that he must feel so at home there, and uninhibited about his teeth, because so many Japanese appeared to have buck teeth too. No one could resist a discreet giggle. There was a magnificent 'Tee Hee' factor to the proceedings which did not go unnoticed, and Freddie, at least, milked it for all it was worth. He warmed to the Japanese fans instantly. But it didn't stop there. Freddie was completely intoxicated by the place. Everything about this ancient, volcanic, far-flung land in the north Pacific appealed to his sense of the exotic, from her history to her distinctive art, particularly porcelain and paintings dating back to pre-Buddhist times of which he was to become an avid collector. He was also fascinated, not only by her quaint traditions and gracious culture, but by her prosperous, technological, 21st-century lifestyle. The country and the man, it would seem, had much in common. Like Freddie himself, Japan was a mass of contradictions, an old curiosity with a most complex and multifaceted personality. Even the names of her thousand islands rolled off the tongue like spells: Hokkaido, Honshu, Kyushu, Shikoku. Freddie was inspired by the notion that a culture could be so traditional and yet so progressive, so archaic and yet so futuristic. He was impressed by the gentle, stoical Japanese people who had come through centuries of feudal oppression and risen with such serenity from the ashes of the Second World War. As usual, his thirst for knowledge consumed him. He was again that small boy in a new theme park, he had to know and have a go on everything. He gazed upon Mount Fuji, feasted on sushi and saké, and bartered for dolls and sumptuous silk kimonos (the extravagant shopper in him was already beginning to emerge). He wanted it all. He would have made an even more unashamed tourist had Queen arrived there as relative unknowns. Unfortunately, from the adventurer's point of view at least, Freddie would never get the chance to be anonymous. This, however, did not deter him from visiting the notorious bath-houses and the kage-me-jaya (teahouses in the shadows, popularised by the American GIs), or hanging out with Geishas – boys rather than girls. He befriended Japan's classy answer to female impersonator Danny La Rue, Miwa Akihuro Maruyama, an amazingly beautiful and elegant man who produced and directed his own swish cabaret on the Ginza, Tokyo's equivalent of the Parisian Pigalle and London's Soho. The admiration was mutual, and after Freddie's first visit, Miwa began performing Queen and Mercury songs in tribute to his new bosom pal.

Queen's first sell-out gig at Tokyo's Budokan was an unforgettable experience, not least because, instead of ordinary security guards, the promoters had employed some Sumo wrestlers. But even their bulk was not mighty enough to hold back a 10,000-strong throng consisting mainly of hysterical teenaged girls. Just as the situation appeared to be getting seriously out of hand, Freddie halted the show and begged the fans, for the sake of their own safety, to calm down. Everywhere they played it was a similar story, frothing seas of small, black-haired fans beside themselves with excitement, trying to catch a glimpse of their idols. They came bearing excessively generous gifts, and they couldn't get enough of Queen. Not since the Beatles had Japan seen anything like it.

It was the good news and the bad news all over again when Queen returned to Britain. Good because not only did they now find themselves the toast of press, TV and radio, but Freddie had won a coveted Ivor Novello songwriting award for 'Killer Queen', proudly accepted in London at a celebrity-packed gala awards ceremony. This, to date, was Freddie's finest hour: as Elton John said, 'The Ivor Novellos are my favourite awards. They're the ones that mean the most.' The Ivor Novellos, founded in 1955, are organized by the British Academy of Songwriters, Composers and Authors and are so named in honour of the great Welsh actor, playwright and composer of musicals whose songs, such as 'Keep The Home Fires Burning' and 'We'll Gather Lilacs' represent an era when rock 'n' roll meant little more than the movement of a ship at sea. Of all the gongs presented annually, these are the official 'Oscars' of the British music business, and Freddie's delight at having earned one so early in his professional career was an enormous boost to Queen's morale. And there was more. The same hit also earned them a prestigious Golden Lion Award in Belgium, presented to Brian and Roger at a festival in July.

The bad news was that Jim Beach was still haggling with Trident over the band's contract. Nothing had been resolved. Queen were now growing very impatient. They liked to know where they stood. The business of being creative was difficult enough, without management problems dangling over their heads. But it would be August before anything was to be resolved. In the meantime, there was nothing for it but to get on with writing songs for the next album. All this uncertainty, as might have been expected, began to take its toll on relationships within the group. They could not help but feel the pressure. Arguments would flare out of nothing, and tempers ran dangerously high. Freddie, highly-strung at the best of times, found it harder to cope with all this tension and bad-feeling than the others, and suffered with a sick stomach. The gossip-mongers descended like vultures. A rumour started that Queen had failed to work out their personal problems and had decided to call it a day. The rumour soon reached the group, and was just what they needed to galvanize them into action. Putting aside their difficulties, they pulled together and called a truce. Trident eventually released Queen from their three contracts, but not without demanding compensation in the form of a £100,000 one-off payment and a one per cent royalty on their next six albums. Although Queen readily agreed to the deal, they did not actually have the cash to settle it. They'd worry about that later. In the meantime they were able to sign new deals with EMI in the UK and Elektra in the States. And they could begin their arduous search for a new manager. They did all this with the help of lawyer Jim Beach, a man they had not only come to trust and respect but to rely upon completely in their business dealings. The ideal manager was staring them in the face. Meanwhile, there were still a few frogs left to kiss.

Chapter Eleven

MONA LISAS AND MAD HATTERS

It was perhaps inevitable that the paths of Freddie Mercury, rock's 'next big thing', and Elton John, the most prolific rock-star of the seventies, would eventually cross. Just as Queen were beginning to make a name for themselves in the international arena, Elton was already the biggest solo artist since Elvis Presley, his singles and albums dominating the charts on both sides of the Atlantic. An incredible seven of his albums had been consecutive American number ones. Packing out vast stadia across the globe, Elton had achieved a rare universal appeal that defied constraints of age and class, culture and trend. Dozens of his melodies were instantly recognizable, even to those without the slightest interest in rock. Millions of fans knew by heart the lyrics to his massive hits: 'Your Song', 'Rocket Man', 'Crocodile Rock', 'Daniel', 'Goodbye Yellow Brick Road', 'Don't Let The Sun Go Down On Me', 'Philadelphia Freedom'. Little did it occur to anyone at the time how much he and Freddie Mercury had in common; how effortlessly each would come to identify with the other; what devoted friends they would make. Little did anyone know back in 1975 that Elton would be one of the few people to hold Freddie's hand as he lay on his deathbed just 16 years later.

To those on intimate terms with both men, there were a number of glaring similarities. Elton, just six months younger than Freddie, had always been devoted to his mother but somewhat estranged from his stepfather. He was a reclusive, sensitive child who had taken piano lessons from an early age. He had changed his name from Reginald Kenneth Dwight to Elton Hercules John – like Freddie, he had picked the name of a mythological Roman god. His road to stardom had also been long and not without obstacles. Like Freddie, too, Elton had always been at odds with his looks, developing an outlandish style – eccentric spectacles, outrageous platform boots – to disguise what he perceived to be ugliness. He was also confused about his sexuality. There had been girlfriends and even a rich, soignée fiancée, Linda Ann Woodrow, with whom he enjoyed an apparently conventional romance. Like Freddie and Mary, Elton and Linda shared a small London love nest, and all at first seemed idyllic. But their sex life appears to have fallen short of expectations, and should have provided some clues as to Elton's true orientation. He had a bad feeling about the marriage, and called off the wedding just three weeks before the ceremony. German recording engineer Renate Blauel would have no such lucky escape, and is said to remain heartbroken by her doomed marriage to Elton. He has been open about his homosexuality since 1988, and at the time of writing lives mainly in London and Atlanta, Georgia, with his American partner David Furnish.

Years later, as Freddie's and Elton's personalities developed in parallel and they grew to depend to some extent on each other's friendship, a more tragic dimension to their similarities would emerge. As one high-profile psychoanalyst would say of Elton in a TV documentary after the star had gone public over his personal problems, 'He was born an addict. He is a totally obsessive-compulsive person. If it hadn't been alcohol, it would have been drugs. If it hadn't been drugs, it would have been food. If it hadn't been food, it would have been relationships. And if it hadn't been relationships, it would have been shopping. And you know what, I think he's got all five.'[1] He was visibly unnerved to see this merciless dissection of his character and personality, but he chose not to disagree with any of the psychoanalyst's words. As a result of allowing these views to be aired, Elton John experienced an enormous upsurge in public support for his courage.

This, give or take, was the very mirror image of the person Freddie Mercury became in the mid-eighties, when fame and all its attendant diversions got the better of him.

In 1996 Elton John said: 'I've been through a hell of a lot in my life. It's been a roller-coaster ride of fabulous times, really low times, and terrible irresponsibility on my behalf.'[2]

He was speaking on the occasion of a gala for the Elton John Aids Foundation in America, his equivalent of the Mercury Phoenix Trust. When asked what he thought of politicians in America who claim that Aids is not a problem, he retorted: 'I just think they're misinformed. They're bigoted. And their anger is homophobic. Most of the Aids increase is coming via the heterosexual community at the moment. But bigots will be bigots, and they attack the people they hate the most. So it doesn't surprise me. I have always been comfortable with my sexuality. Living a lie is just not worth it. You only get one attempt on this earth, and it's just far better to be yourself. If others don't like it, tough shit.'

And to his wildly enthusiastic audience, he daringly and self-mockingly revealed: 'This is where I came out, in this country. I've slept with half of it. And I came out of it HIV negative. I'm a lucky, lucky person. It's now my job to repay that debt.'

Back in 1975, the most significant thing that Freddie Mercury and Elton John had in common was a feisty Scot called John Reid. The 26-year-old Paisley-born impresario had actually started in business at the age of 11, collecting used newspapers around his neighbourhood and selling them to local greengrocers to wrap vegetables. This proved so successful that he was soon employing other children and paying them a modest percentage. Just 15 years later the power-hungry Reid would be controlling a business worth an estimated £40 million, with one of the world's greatest entertainers as his charge. He had arrived in London via a circuitous route, worked in a men's outfitter's, and landed his first job in the music business as a record plugger. Rising through the ranks in a string of executive positions, he was also socially ambitious, cultivating important and high-profile friendships with all the zeal that he brought to his business dealings. For a while he was the unlikely social escort of bubbly Carry-On actress and BBC TV EastEnders star Barbara Windsor, and had his first official contact with Elton John in 1970 in San Francisco, a few days before Reid's 21st birthday. Before long he and Elton had become flatmates in a small apartment near Marble Arch. Few suspected the true nature of their relationship, well-known within the music industry and discussed at length in Philip Norman's biography of Elton. When word eventually leaked that Reid and Elton were lovers, it did not cause shockwaves. Perhaps because they were both completely relaxed about the situation, not trying to hide it, the affair was never a scandalous, newsworthy sensation. It was Elton's mother Sheila who suggested to Elton that Reid might make a decent manager. Reid was still only 21 years old.

Shortly afterwards, Elton found himself teaming up with another Scot who was also making a name for himself in the charts: Rod Stewart. Both had worked in the past with pop star Long John Baldry, and had agreed to do so again, producing an album for Baldry designed to revive his flagging career. Baldry had always been outrageously camp, and nothing appeared to have changed in the years since they had all last worked together. It was during those sessions for the Baldry album 'It Ain't Easy' that they hit upon the old theatrical custom of calling themselves by women's names. It was a gag that was to stick forever. Elton was dubbed

Sharon, Rod Stewart Phyllis, Baldry became Ada, and John Reid was styled Beryl, in homage to the actress Beryl Reid. When Freddie found out about it, he just had to join in. Before long he was calling himself 'Melina' after the Greek actress Melina Mercouri, and would one day employ an entire entourage who were known by girls' names: his PA was Phoebe (Peter Freestone), his chef Liza (Joe Fanelli), personal manager Trixie (Paul Prenter). Nor were friends and band members immune: Brian was Maggie, as in 'Maggie May', Roger was Liz, after Liz Taylor, David Nutter, brother of famous tailor Tommy Nutter, was Dawn. Music business manager Tony King was Joy. Mary Austin, in turn, was endowed with a *boy's* name: she became Steve, as in Steve Austin the Six Million Dollar Man. Did she mind?

'Nobody was *allowed* to mind,' chuckles Freddie's former PA Phoebe. 'More than that, you knew that someone was accepted if they got "a name". John Deacon never had one, curiously.'[3] Perhaps because he was so shy.

The joke lives: on his last tour, Elton's coiffure was the responsibility of the male hairdresser, Tina Sparkle. Elton's personal relationship with Reid survived various domestic upheavals and continued for a few years until it ended by mutual and amicable consent during 1975. World fame, acclaim and money had changed the two men irrevocably. There was never any question that Reid would continue to manage Elton, and his affairs are handled to this day by Reid's company John Reid Enterprises.

With Elton John in self-imposed temporary retirement from touring after an arduous six-year world slog, Reid, now also running Elton's own record label Rocket Records, was keen to consolidate and expand his empire. He had acquired an interest in the Edinburgh Playhouse. He had, with financial backing from Elton, opened a restaurant, 'Friends,' in London's Covent Garden. It was also perhaps inevitable that he would jump at the chance, in the autumn of 1975, of managing an extraordinarily impressive new band called Queen.

Elton John denounced it as a surefire flop. Music business executives voiced their misgivings, some even going so far as to ridicule Freddie for his crankiest composition yet. The radio stations wondered what the hell they were supposed to do with a six-minute single. Various rock reporters were prompted to ponder whether Mercury had flipped, and whether this was in fact the ultimate nose-thumbing send-up of the rock music industry.

Even band member John Deacon expressed his fears, admittedly in private, that to release the track would prove the greatest judgmental error of Queen's career. For a song which would enter the annals of rock history as one of, if not *the* all-time classic, it had the shakiest of starts. Even those who immediately recognized its magnificence hesitated to go on the record, so dramatic was the departure of 'Bohemian Rhapsody' from the accepted conventions of rock.

One can only marvel at whatever ignited Freddie's imagination and inspired him to create such a complex and brilliant work. Soaring and decadent, loaded with agony and ecstasy, it is an impossible juxtaposition of baroque and ballad, music hall and monster rock. Its incongruous elements are held together by a string of cacophonic guitar-grindings, classical piano sequences, sweeping orchestral arrangements and rich, multi-layered chorals, all dubbed, over-dubbed and over-dubbed again to the point that, depending on one's mood, it can be almost unbearable to listen to. Freddie's lead vocals, perfectly controlled, bell-clear and plaintive, lift the song along to a stark and sentimental climax which can move the most phlegmatic soul. With its poetic lyrics, daring tempo changes, its complex majesty and its aching simplicity, the song achieves in just six minutes all the highs and lows and fantastic emotion of any full-length classical operatic work. What's more, it profoundly reflects the clashing contradictions of the composer's personality. It could almost be an echo of Freddie himself. Unsurprising then that for years Freddie

Zanzibar town harbour, 1996. (*Collection: Lesley-Ann Jones*)

The beach where Freddie played, Zanzibar. (*Collection: Daisy May Queen*)

GOVERNMENT OF ZANZIBAR.

CERTIFICATE OF BIRTH.

Registered No. 3293

Date and Time of Birth 5·9·46

Place of Birth Shangani Gov't Hospital

Name Male Famoth

Sex Male

Name and Surname of Father } Bomi R· Bulsara

Name and Maiden Surname of Mother } Jer Bomi Bulsara Behramji Khory....

Race Parsee   Nationality Br Indian

Rank or Profession of Father Cashier High Court Z'bar

Name of Informant Harriet

Residence Z'bar

Date of Registration 20·9·46

[SEE REVERSE].   Registrar.

Freddie's birth certificate. (*Collection: Lesley-Ann Jones*)

ABOVE: St Peter's School, Panchgani, India. (*Collection: Lesley-Ann Jones*)

RIGHT: The house Freddie lived in with his family in Zanzibar, when he returned from India. (*Collection: Daisy May Queen*)

BELOW: Freddie's first band, The Hectics. (*Collection: Gita Choksi*)

St Peter's School
assembly hall,
where Freddie first
performed.
(*Collection:
Lesley-Ann Jones*

ABOVE: Freddie (sixth from left) cycling with school friends in Panchgani,
India. (*Collection: Gita Choksi*)
ABOVE RIGHT: Freddie (second from left) with school friends, boating on
Mahableshwar Lake, near Panchgani, India. (*Collection: Gita Choksi*)

BELOW: Freddie and Gita at a party in her home, Panchgani, India. (Freddie, back
row, second from right; Gita, back row, first on left).(*Collection: Gita Choksi*)
BELOW RIGHT: Gita Bharucha, Freddie's classmate, Panchgani, India.
(*Collection: Gita Choksi*)

From left: Perviz (Freddie's first cousin), Diana and Bomi Darunkhanawala, Zanzibar. (*Collection: Daisy May Queen*)

Queen's first publicity photograph featuring the astrological logo designed by Freddie. (*Collection: Tony Brainsby*)

Freddie's first publicity photograph. (*Photograph: © Mick Rock, collection: Tony Brainsby*)

Freddie and Mary Austin. (*Photograph: © Mick Rock 1974, 1977*)

Freddie and Mick Rock in New York, 1974. (*Photograph: © Mick Rock 1974, 1997*)

Freddie at the mirror. (*Photograph: © Mick Rock 1974, 1997*)

refused to explain the song, how he had achieved it, or even what it was supposed to be about.

'Does it mean this, does it mean that, is all anybody wants to know,' he once sniffed.

'Fuck them, darling. I will say no more than what any decent poet would tell you if you dared ask him to analyse his work: "If you see it, dear, then it's there."'[4]

Tommy Vance, formerly one of the biggest names in rock radio with shows on London's Capital, BBC Radio One and Virgin Radio, describes Bohemian Rhapsody, released on 31 October 1975, as 'the rock equivalent of the assassination of JFK': 'We all remember what we were doing when we first heard it. I was doing the weekend rock show at Capital at the time,' he said.[5]

It came out and I thought, this is an absolute lunatic asylum of a pop song. Most people at Radio One immediately dismissed it as a complete disaster, but – surprise, surprise – they played it. Queen, by this time, were considered to be a fundamental rock band, even at the Beeb, and so the rock people took a chance and gave it a whirl. And what was so brilliant about it was that it gave everyone a chance to shine and express themselves; it gave the rock cult DJs an opportunity to play something that was not obvious, and to use their imagination; it gave anybody who was involved in avant-garde radio the chance to make a statement, and a name for himself. It gave the public an excuse to rise to the occasion. I remember thinking that the most predominant thing about the record was that it was so magnificently obscure, it just had to make it.

Now presenting VH-1 rock television for MTV to 50 million international viewers a night, Vance affirms that what really made the record was its TV exposure.

*   *   *

The record's chart progress forced 'Top Of The Pops' to give it a chance. Because they *had* to play it if a record got into the Top Thirty, and Bohemian Rhapsody made it to number 30. Thereafter, every time they played it, it went further up the charts, and gave DJs, audience, everyone another chance to be expressive and creative. What was really incredible was that the video, directed by Bruce Gowers (now one of the most sought-after live directors in the US) and produced by Lexi Godfrey for Jon Roseman, was shot, at Shepperton I believe, for just $7,000. Gowers was making a performance video with the band, and shot the video for Bohemian Rhapsody on the same day, all together, in just four hours. It was truly creative stuff. He was using prisms, for example, to create certain visual effects he desired, long before electronics and computers started doing that sort of thing. Where did he get the ideas from? He was inspired by the record. It was a collective of so many thrilling concepts that Bruce's ideas just flowed. But the fundamental concept was based on a previous album cover.

It was 'Queen II' (1974), to be precise, featuring a stark black and white group shot on the album cover, heads-only of each band member apart from Freddie, who appears in the centre with his hands folded across his chest like wings. The idea for the shot had not in fact been their own, but was the brainwave of photographer Mick Rock.

Says Rock:

The band's brief for their Queen II album jacket *was* brief. It would be a gatefold. It would have a black and white theme. It was to feature the band. Beyond that, it was my problem. I would art-direct and photograph it. I had recently become friends with a Canadian gentleman named John Kobal, who was a keen collector of early Hollywood stills. In return for a photo session of himself, he gave me some prints from his collection, and among them was one I had never seen before, of Marlene Dietrich from the film *Shanghai Express*. Her arms were folded, and she was wearing black against a black background, and it was exquisitely lit. Her tilted head and hands seemed to be floating. I saw the connection immediately. It was one of those visceral, intuitive things. Very strong. Very clear. Glamorous, mysterious and classic. I would transpose it into a four-headed monster. They had to go for it. So I went to Freddie. He saw it too. He understood. He loved it immediately. And he sold the rest of the band on it.

'I shall be Marlene,' he laughed. 'What a delicious thought!'

In the editing process, Rock remembers, both the 'black' and the 'white' photos (the band members also dressed in foppish white outfits complete with silk scarves, flowers and furs and set against a white background during that shoot) were considered for the album cover. But,

Neither Freddie nor I doubted that the black image should be the one. But I recall amongst the other three there was some hesitation until the last moment. It wasn't that they didn't like the black photos, but there was some concern that they might almost be too strong, pretentious even, to some eyes. And they had a point. Fortunately Freddie was never scared of the accusation of pretension. He loved to quote Oscar Wilde: 'Often, that which today is considered pretentious is tomorrow considered state of the art. The important thing is to be considered.' So he wore the others down, and the right decision was made.

This, then, was Gowers's inspiration for the Bohemian

Rhapsody video. He took an image which they had previously created, embellished and developed it, and brought it as far forward as he dared.

As Tommy Vance commented:

Because the song was so bloody operatic, it allowed the band to express themselves visually in a fantastical way. By no extrapolation of the imagination was it a band doing what they normally did. It was pure fantasy. And 'Bohemian Rhapsody' became the first record to actually be pushed into the forefront by virtue of a video. Today, Queen are widely credited with also having been the first band to do a surrealist promotional video, but that was not actually the case. They were, I think, preceded by Devo, who had been doing experimental video work before 'Bohemian Rhapsody' was shot. But Queen were certainly the first band ever to create a 'concept' video. They stuck out their necks and went for it. They believed in it. Bruce Gowers, Lexi Godfrey and Jon Roseman all believed in it too. And somehow they made it happen. They did so by taking a song that was so out there, so different, then working and expanding that original idea and theme to the point that the video captured the musical imagery perfectly. What they did with it was not an obvious interpretation, but the end result worked brilliantly. And I have to say that it had bugger all to do with Freddie. The song was the song. The visual interpretation made it what the song became. Because every time the song had an echo, the pictures reverberated in the listener's mind. The two quickly became indivisible. You cannot hear that music without seeing the visuals in your mind's eye. You could say that 'Bohemian Rhapsody' was 'seen' everywhere. Because this was the first video ever to promote a song in such a way.

*   *   *

The edit, recalls Tommy, 'was done in an editing suite in Poland Street [in London's Soho] and I was there. You could only stand and stare. I watched some of it happen before my very eyes, and I remember thinking that they were doing something totally original, something that had never been thought of before: taking rock 'n' roll out of the performance circumstance and into the realms of the mysterious, the avant-garde.'

As for the song, Tommy's views remain unchanged:

Technically, the song's a mess. It's all over the place. It follows no known conventional nor commercial formula. And if you try to dissect the lyrics, the song is utterly meaningless. It is about nothing. It is just a string of dreams, flashbacks, flash-forwards, vignettes, completely disjointed ideas. It changes sequence, colour, tone, tempo, all for no apparent reason, which is exactly what opera does. But the intent was remarkable. I reckon that Freddie and the band took a chance because they believed that pop was better than it was. Theirs was the ultimate optimism. 'Bohemian Rhapsody' had an indefinable quality, some remarkable magic. It is brilliant. And it is still revered as an icon today, more than 20 years after its release. What other song stands up against it? Absolutely fuck all.

According to broadcaster and writer Paul Gambaccini, 'Bohemian Rhapsody' was, brilliant rock epic aside, the first significant and perhaps most important example of what held the band together for so many prolific years.

Okay yes, Freddie wrote the song, but Brian did that incredible guitar passage in the middle, Roger did the high notes, and John contributed, of course. To spread out the contributions in that way is fantastic, as they would later do with their own individual compositions, and I'm sure it's what helped keep them going as a group.

Of course, Bohemian Rhapsody has become bigger with the passage of time, and not only because there has been reduced ambition in popular songwriting. Those works which aspire to the great heights, such as 'MacArthur Park', 'Hey Jude', 'American Pie', 'Bohemian Rhapsody', seem more and more impressive as the years go by. And *Wayne's World* gave it a boost, of course . . .[6]

Had Gambaccini ever considered what Freddie might have made of a US Queen revival brought about by the cult rock parody movies starring Mike Myers as would-be cool dude Wayne Campbell and Dana Carvey as his hapless, bespectacled, gimpy sidekick Garth Algar, featuring a 'Bohemian Rhapsody' pastiche which brought Queen to the attention of a new generation of rock fans?

Oh, he would have loved it. Because the attitude was both reverential and fun. It's great – that there was such an achievement, *and* that the tongue was firmly in the cheek. That was fantastic, exactly Freddie's type of sequence. But it becomes a defining moment for hard rock. As well as being a send-up, it really does constitute a summary of guitar-based rock music. Which Freddie would have also loved because it gives substance to the music. It's Brian's hard rock roots. Freddie would have been thrilled.

Mike Appleton recalls the excitement generated at the 'Whistle Test' studio by the arrival of the 'Bohemian Rhapsody' video. 'I thought it stunning, brilliant – a truly wonderful concept,' he says:

It had the same sort of impact as seeing, for example,

Meatloaf's first video. I was utterly mesmerized. The thing spoke, sang and danced for itself. All I had to do was put it on the screen. And it did it for them, didn't it? There was already keen and rising interest in Queen by that time, but this was the icing on the cake. I can remember feeling blown away by Freddie, and by the sense that there had never before been anything like him. Nor has there been since. He was the ultimate rock-star – but he was amazingly private. He was the most flamboyant front man – but offstage he was not pushy in any way. I'd be almost tempted to say that he was shy and retiring. The strength and vitality that was there up on stage was still there, certainly, but it was controlled, contained. But the flamboyance was gone completely, to the point that he always seemed so much tinier, physically, offstage. The way I remember him is as a very private person in a very public field. I often thought of him as the only adult in a business dominated by spoilt, petulant kids. So many of the rock-stars I had to deal with at the time were infantile and ridiculous. Freddie was almost the perfect gent. He didn't actually behave the way many rock-stars seem to think they are required to behave. What's more he, and the rest of the band, really were extremely professional. They were always there on time for rehearsals, you never had to wait half a day for them to appear. They were always ready, there was no star-fucking. They knew exactly what they were doing, and they weren't going to waste a moment of it. I have never known a band work so hard. I remember liking Freddie in particular a great deal, although I found it difficult to assess him as a person. One never got the chance to get that close.

Appleton is the first to admit how easy it is to become blasé about the business of rock music.

* * *

185

I suppose it could be considered the aural equivalent of too many lavish executive lunches. After a while the palate jades. So, too, the ears. That said, I never grew tired of Queen. I loved the music. But I didn't appreciate quite how brilliant Freddie was until years later, when I saw the Freddie Tribute concert. So many fantastic singers got up to pay homage by singing Queen songs, but by and large all they managed to do was to accentuate how great Freddie himself was. Only George Michael, I think, ever came close to Freddie in a rendition of a Queen song. No other singer in existence could have brought quite the same magic to 'Bohemian Rhapsody' as Freddie. Even the most jaded, over-fed record company executive had to stop, look and listen.

Tony Brainsby's first reaction to the version of 'Bohemian Rhapsody' that he heard was 'bizarre'. 'Everybody thought so. The only person who genuinely, honestly liked and understood it, and championed it all the way to the top, was Kenny Everett. I must admit to loving it without really knowing why. But it represented a turning point for me. I had taken them from virtual obscurity and seen them through to one of the greatest hits of all time. I felt like a father who'd just given birth.'

Brainsby's ecstasy was short-lived. Queen's new arrangement with John Reid rendered Brainsby's position untenable: 'John Reid's made it difficult for me to work with Queen any longer. For whatever reason he preferred to use his own in-house PR set-up, and it became a no-go.'

There would be a come-back for Brainsby a little way down the line. But for now, if not forever, Queen were in orbit hand in hand with the man who made the Rocket Man fly.

Chapter Twelve

FAME

Queen's fourth album was released on 21 November 1975. According to Paul Gambaccini, 'A Night At The Opera', 'pole-vaulted [Queen] into Major Act status'.

I was at EMI Records' play-back party for 'A Night At The Opera', and what I remember most clearly is how very good the food was. Which might sound trivial and insignificant, but believe me, it was a statement: this was their manager John Reid bothering to declare that this album was first-class, and therefore there would be no expense spared. It was a true celebration of something brilliant. Here were Queen now leaving that rank of groups that might also include, say, Sparks and Mott the Hoople. There were many popular groups around, but John Reid had the biggest act in the world at that time, which was Elton John. And this lavish little party was like saying, here you go, Queen are now moving into Elton's league.

The interesting thing about John Reid, adds Gambaccini, was that he was obviously acutely aware of what he had with Queen, '—But he really didn't realize how lucky his timing was. If ever there was a time to get Queen onto your books, it was at the release of 'A Night At The Opera'. You have to remember that we were still basking in the glow of the four newly ex-Beatles, and that they were still *the* British performers who, along with Led Zeppelin and Pink Floyd, meant the most in the world. Compared to these glittering Beatles, almost anyone would look dull.'

The fact that Queen managed to stand out and make such a huge impression to the point that they had virtually made themselves as important as Elton John in the mind of the discerning John Reid, suggested that they were truly on their way.

Recalling his very first meeting with Queen, in Boston Massachusetts where he was working as Executive Producer of WBZ Radio, New England's largest radio station, Gambaccini says:

Queen were in town to promote the previous album to 'A Night At The Opera', 'Sheer Heart Attack'. The launch, if memory serves, was held in the bar that was later used in the 'Cheers' television series, in Boston, on the Green. They were doing the 'meet-and-greet' all across the United States. I had already seen them supporting Mott the Hoople at, I believe, Hammersmith Odeon. I was pretty impressed when I first met them because everybody was so down to earth, and Freddie was in my good books immediately because he had a long talk with Beverly Mire, who was my PA at the station. Of course, many people would have treated someone in that position as a lackey, but Freddie did not. He treated Beverly as a real human being.

Various little chance encounters at the beginning gave me a sense of having been with Queen for the ride – their chronological career and mine basically coincided in time. Much later, at Freddie's Tribute concert at Wembley, Bowie came out and did 'All The Young

Dudes', and it evoked that early Mott The Hoople tour, and I was quite overcome. It was as if we'd been in the same cub-scout troop together, and we'd now and again run into each other and be friendly, but basically we'd have our own lives to get on with . . . then, suddenly, here we all were, in one place, to honour the first of us who had gone.

While acknowledging and appreciating Freddie's humility, Gambaccini insists that Freddie always knew he was going to be an enormous star, and had risen to the occasion and assumed 'star status' in his mind long before Queen actually made it.

The analogy I always use here is with the Boston Red Sox baseball team. Their legendary hitter, Ted Williams, is still considered probably the best hitter of a baseball there has ever been. When he retired, the owner of the Red Sox team gave his young replacement the same salary, and consequently was challenged by the press. One reporter asked him 'Surely he doesn't deserve to be paid the same as Ted Williams?' to which the owner replied, 'If I pay him the same, I give him the same status as Ted Williams, and I tell everyone that he is a major player.'

I have known quite a few people in popular music who, themselves fans of popular music, have admired and even idolized genuine stars like Liza Minnelli and Shirley Bassey; and who, when given the opportunity to perform themselves, have assumed the attitude of ultimate stardom, even if they had not yet themselves reached that stage. It's very interesting. I also honestly think that Freddie was carrying on a bit of the Liza Minnelli-type of relationship with his audience: 'I'm a star – but we're in this together!' What a great combination of attitudes: you get them both to respect and like you. They look up to you, but you're letting them know that you consider them to be on your own level; you're a friend, but you're also The Big One.

Freddie always remembered that there is 'show' in show-business, which paid off enormously in the end because, after their great run in the seventies, not all of their eighties albums were great. But, because Freddie had established his persona, the fantastic image and the back catalogue saw them through the occasional rough patch of releases.

Apart from the professional relationship he shared with the group, Gambaccini formed personal friendships which were, in Freddie's case at least, to last a lifetime:

Strangely enough, I thought I did pretty well considering that they were four distinct people, four separate individuals. To me, they were always the model of rock musicians understanding what this crazy game was all about. They knew, absolutely, that it was a business. They didn't expect, for example, that they would be each other's best friends, and consequently they weren't disappointed in each other when they weren't. All they had to do was get on with each other, respect each other. They knew that you can like each other without being crazy about each other. This relaxed, even-handed attitude saw them through difficulties that would have split up other acts. In the eighties, so many popular groups who had become sudden sensations couldn't stay together for whatever reason: Culture Club, Wham!, Kajagoogoo. Queen, of course, were older, wiser, more mature. But, more significantly, they had business heads in the way that these others didn't.

I got to know Roger in a 'Hey, how ya doing' way. Enough to get invited to a party at his place. Brian I knew quite well: I remember he came over once to get my opinions about a new piece which eventually turned up as one of their singles. We became much friendlier later, when he started seeing Anita Dobson.

But Freddie was the one I was most intimate with, I would say. I do not claim to have been one of his *best* friends. I do not claim to have been a guest at his home many times, although I was a guest at his home. But he was one of those guys that, when you *did* meet him, you'd always go directly to the heart of the matter. He was just extremely personal and honest. Not one for small-talk. Part of this, I believe, is that I happened, like him, to be one of the rock world's gay people. Not that he was at all open about this at first: he knew that I was more 'Out' than he was . . .

Perhaps Freddie envied Gambaccini's courage in having openly declared his homosexuality, and longed, even in the early days of Queen fame, to do the same?

'Perhaps. He once said to me, 'One day we'll do an interview and we'll tell it all.' Which he never did. But I know that what he was thinking of going public about was the type of things he used to get up to, where he used to go, what the atmosphere was like in these places – the type of thing he never discussed.'

Because he was afraid to come clean about his lifestyle?

'It's possible. But, even though I am gay, that type of behaviour wasn't really my lifestyle at all. I mean, Freddie made me feel like a tourist. It was like he was the *real* homosexual. But while I was out there being up-front about it, he was keeping it quiet. He was gay with a capital G, and I was just this little pretender.'

While there is no doubt in Gambaccini's mind that Freddie was predominantly gay when they first met, he says he always had the utmost sympathy for Freddie for wanting to keep his true sexual orientation under wraps. But why did it take Freddie so long to declare himself, and what eventually caused him to feel relaxed about people knowing the truth?

Four things, I believe: one, sufficient success. Once you have that, you don't really care what people think anyway. Two, sufficient self-confidence, in which you feel you have something more to offer beyond some sort of heterosexual fantasy sex image – in other words, people will enjoy you for what you do, rather than some fantasy or other that they've got in their head about you. It took Freddie a good deal of success to reach that point, but he got there.

The third thing was, in fact, Boy George, who was always so brazen, though lovely with it, and I think that kind of made it easier for Freddie to say, 'Yes, well, I've always been gay too.' The fourth thing, which I don't pretend to know much about, but can only speculate, is to do with events in his personal life. You see, people clamour for these True Confessions from the rich and famous without realizing that there are constraints in their personal lives which may make it difficult if not impossible to be 'Out'. For example, their parents. Some people think that their parents will be embarrassed or upset, and they simply can't get themselves beyond that point. I know of one huge, internationally famous rock-star who has always been afraid of coming out because he has always lived in fear of his parents' reaction!

As for the fifth consideration – that Freddie was still involved in a deep relationship with Mary Austin in those early days, and was also known to have had affairs with other females – Gambaccini stresses that he does not pretend to know the distribution of Freddie's sexual activity.

Five days after the release of 'A Night At The Opera', on 25 November 1975, 'Bohemian Rhapsody' gave Queen their first number one single. They celebrated in style on their brief pre-Christmas UK tour, and played a spectacular Christmas Eve gig at Hammersmith Odeon which was televised live by 'The Old Grey Whistle Test' with a simultaneous airing on BBC Radio One, to record audiences. Fledgling photographer Denis O'Regan was there, and took his first commercial pictures of Queen:

A few days after that show I took my photographs to Queen's management offices, John Reid's place in South Audley Street, and, after blundering my way into the wrong office, I asked this young guy for directions. I was fully aware that the guy I was talking to was Elton John, but I didn't let on. He very kindly directed me to Queen's office, and was advised there to get my pictures to *Jackie* magazine. The magazine bought one of them for £12 and I was extremely proud of this achievement. It was the first picture I had ever sold, and I could now call myself a professional photographer.

Just three days after that Hammersmith Christmas show, 'A Night At The Opera' made it to number one in the album chart and went platinum with sales exceeding 250,000 copies. It also went on to hang in the American album chart for an incredible 56 weeks, Queen's longest run to date. None of this was any more than Queen had expected, of course. The new year brought them endless accolades, including the music press annual polls. This time they were nominated in, and won, many categories. Freddie also accepted another Ivor Novello award, for 'Bohemian Rhapsody' which, come 24 January, 1976, had been number one in the UK charts for a record-breaking nine weeks. It had now sold over a million copies in Britain alone, with 'A Night At The Opera' having exceeded 500,000. Queen's manager John Reid uncharacteristically took out ad-space in *Sounds* magazine to congratulate his protégés on their fantastic success.

Queen were now planning their second big American tour, this time as major rock-stars. The tour would prove their most gruelling to date, visiting as it did practically every state in the US, under the guidance of their new tour manager Gerry Stickells. It was a well-starred appointment: appropriately, Stickells had once worked as roadie and then tour manager for Jimi Hendrix. He was to remain with the band until the end of their touring career.

The tour was a massive hit. Audiences turned out in their hundreds of thousands, and Queen encountered a rapturous coast-to-coast reception. Not only that, but this was the tour on which Queen perfected the art of the after-show party. In time, these parties would become legendary throughout the music industry as the best post-gig bashes in the business. Originally conceived as wind-down therapy for the band, who tended to find themselves on such a high when they came off stage that they found it impossible to relax, let alone sleep, the parties soon became wild and memorable events in their own right. Wherever Queen played, local celebrities, dignitaries and party girls and boys would be invited along, and the organization of these events proved a virtual full-time job for Queen's management and publicity people. All manner of Bacchanalian delights were on offer, with hangovers guaranteed. Only the togas were optional.

America, especially New York City, turned the heads of Queen as a whole and Freddie in particular. Thus began a passionate fling with the place on that first major tour from which the star was never really to recover.

Journalist Rick Sky, whose tribute to Mercury, *The Show Must Go On*, was published shortly after Freddie's death, recalls a 'quiet, discreet bash' once thrown by Freddie and the band to celebrate the success of a memorable capacity crowd gig at New York's hallowed Madison Square Garden, a major league venue on the world rock and roll circuit.

'This was just backstage, immediately after a Queen show,' remembers Rick.[1]

The proper party was organized for later. There were a dozen topless waitresses who came round with magnums of champagne, filling up your glasses constantly. Nobody was allowed to run dry. I had been invited to New York for an exclusive interview with Freddie. The paradox about him, of course, was that he was such a flamboyant showman, the master of one-liners and witty back-chat, but he never gave away very much about himself. You always came away still wondering who this guy actually *was*. So I was excited at the prospect of the interview, but wasn't expecting to learn very much.

The fact that Freddie opened up about his personal life to Rick Sky on that occasion was perhaps an indication of how relaxed and at home the star felt in New York, a city he had come to regard as a second home.

Freddie was dressed in a white vest thing, and was holding a plastic cup of champagne in one hand and a cigarette in the other, and he seemed completely laid-back and relaxed, at ease with himself. He told me that the secret of happiness was in the living of life to the very hilt.

'Excess is a part of my nature,' he said. 'To me, dullness is a disease. I really need danger and excitement. I was not made for staying indoors and watching television. I am definitely a sexual person. I like to fuck all the time. I used to say that I would go with anyone, but these days I have become much more choosy.

'I love to surround myself with strange and interesting people because they make me feel more alive. Extremely straight people bore me stiff. I love freaky people around me. By nature I'm restless and highly-strung, so I wouldn't make a good family man. Deep down inside I am a very emotional person, a person of real extremes, and often that's destructive both to myself and others.'

This was Freddie owning up to his wild side, which fame and wealth had bought him the freedom to acknowledge. Now, he could indulge in it as much as he wanted, and it was obvious to me that he was really going for it. But it must have compromised the urge to settle down into a full one-to-one relationship, which is the thing we all crave, and I put it to him that his lifestyle must make this difficult to achieve.

'Well,' he said, 'when I have a relationship, it is never a half-hearted one. I don't believe in half measures or compromise. I just can't bear to compromise about anything. I give everything I've got, because that's the way I am.'

In his interview with Sky, Freddie also owned up to his helpless addiction to the New York nightlife.

'"I just love the clubs in New York," he said. "I remember once I wanted to go to a club called the Gilded Grape, which I heard was really exciting, but everyone told me I shouldn't go to. Or if I did, at least to make sure I had a fast bullet-proof car waiting for me outside. Everyone tried to warn me about this club, which of course made me all the more determined to go."'

Freddie's partner in crime that night was an unlikely choice of companion: the former Wimbledon women's tennis champion Billie-Jean King, who apparently took some persuading.

'Not long after we got there a massive fight broke out which ended up at our table,' Freddie told Sky.

'Chairs were being smashed, fists were flying, there was blood everywhere. Billie was petrified, but I loved it. I told her not to worry, and as the fight raged I grabbed her and took her on to the dance-floor. It was much more fun than having some cosy dinner back at my hotel.'

It was obvious by this time that Freddie had fallen for the city itself, and not only for the largely underground New York gay scene, once memorably described as 'a tumble of vice and depravity which seethed with mad dogs, rogues and wastrels'. In a discussion with pop writer John Blake about New York, Freddie revealed: 'When I go there I just slut myself. It's sin city. But you have to come away at the right time, because the moment you stay a day later it grips you. Very hypnotic. It's all tripping in at eight or nine every morning, taking throat injections so I can still sing. It's a real place. I love it.'[2]

While vaguely admitting to his incredible promiscuity, Freddie always kept quiet about his passion for cocaine. This was understandable: apart from the fact that the substance is highly illegal in most countries, certainly in Britain and the USA, Freddie had never fitted the druggie mould. Nor did he feel inclined to be perceived as such. In those early, poverty-stricken days, Freddie showed no interest in the marijuana his pals were passing round, and would have loathed to be regarded as the addict-type. What is certain is that he never became addicted to cocaine: when eventually he decided to stop using it, he was able to relinquish the habit just like that, quite literally overnight. But for now, he was living the sex-drugs-rock-'n'-roll cliché. Excessive quantities of champagne and cocaine were part of the deal. He was hooked on the instant high, the effect it had on his personality and, more specifically, on his libido. For this kick, he would part with literally hundreds of pounds a week, and he was by no means the only rock-star to be doing so.

The city that never sleeps had long been the nerve centre of the world and had seduced many before him – not only because of its sheer size and the scale of its architecture, but also because of the density and diversity of its population, its thriving business activity, its feverish street life, its vibrant, multi-layered culture, its vigorous attitude, its dynamism, its irreverence, its harsh, unforgiving humour. How do you get to Carnegie Hall? – Practise. One of Freddie's favourite gags involved the asking of directions by a foreign tourist to a native New Yorker: 'Can you tell me the way to Times Square or shall I fuck off now?' Freddie loved the city, the neon lights, the dazzling sights. By day he adored being up-town swanking it with the rest, hanging out in the luxurious stores and the salons of smart hotels. But by night he'd be off downtown to Greenwich Village and the cobbled streets of the old meat-packing district a few blocks from the Hudson River. It was there that New York's most notorious gay clubs and bars, most of which later closed down during the mid-eighties in the wake of the Aids epidemic, were in those days to be found.

The Village had long been known as New York's Bohemia, and, as such, was a magnet for gays and lesbians from all over America. The Stonewall Riots of June 1969 that launched gay liberation, later to be referred to as the Boston Tea Party of the gay movement, had kicked off at the most popular illegal gay bar in New York. The name of the seedy Stonewall Inn on Christopher Street off Seventh Avenue in the heart of the Village was from then on heard throughout the world as the cradle of gay power. The new homosexual glasnost consequently legalized a lucrative industry serving the New York gay community. Sex palaces, porn theatres, bath-houses, leather bars and so-called 'backroom bars' sprang up in abundance, promoting a seemingly empty (but presumably enjoyable) anonymity of sexual encounter. Boots, belts, beatings, bondage, 'water sports', fisting, humiliation, cigarette burns – in certain quarters, violent sexual activity constituted the norm. In those days, sexually-transmitted diseases were not thought of as a serious threat, as both gonorrhea and syphilis could be cured with a quick prescription. Hepatitis B was more of a problem, regular outbreaks ringing out a warning of things to come. Even so, it did not succeed in frightening gays into inactivity. Not yet.

The most squalid, godforsaken of gay establishments were

S&M bars such as the Mineshaft, where every unimaginable sex fantasy was realized. An upstairs room called 'The Playground' had ceiling slings from which men were willingly suspended to have unspeakable things done to them. Downstairs, a variety of debauched activity took place between pairs and groups, and one dark corner featured bath-tubs where men would sit and allow themselves to be urinated upon.

Then there was the infamous Anvil, where, one night, according to photographer Mick Rock who was with him at the time, Freddie first clapped eyes on one of the Village People, the late-seventies 'YMCA' send-up group which toyed with macho gay fantasy stereotypes: the cowboy, the policeman, the building site labourer, the biker. Freddie was said to be utterly mesmerized, along with a roomful of gay 'clones', by the sight of Glenn Hughes 'the leather guy' dancing on the bar, and, in Rock's own words, 'was never the same again'.

As Freddie himself was later to remark, 'I like leather. I rather fancy myself as a black panther.'[3]

The Anvil experience was presumed by some to have been the inspiration for both the 'leather' and the 'gay clone' looks that Freddie would later adopt. While the 'leather' phase was relatively short-lived, Freddie's 'clone' image (so far removed from his seventies Bohemian pose) – closely-cropped hair, clipped, bristly moustache, muscular upper body, tight denim jeans – was to last. The 'clone' look, in fact, had originated in San Francisco, and was referred to as the 'Castro Clone' image after the Castro district, a central, formerly dilapidated Irish neighbourhood of San Francisco which had once served the Haight-Ashbury hippies. It later became Gay Main Street, USA, thanks to a massive influx of homosexual refugees, housing the 'highest per capita population of gays in the world'. Most of these men were white middle-class, and they adopted their own 'conformist' look to replace the outgoing flowing robe/long beads/ hairy hippy style. A distinct new strain of gay male could now be identified, quickly dubbed 'The Castro Street Clone'. But the look was also, to begin with at least, something of a disguise. For a long time gays were protected by it, because straight people simply did not recognize it as an exclusively gay identity: it was just guys with short hair, moustaches and great bodies. But from that look grew an entire code for homosexual behaviour. A gay man could indicate his sexual preference by the colour of the handkerchief hanging out of his back pocket. What's more, whether the handkerchief was tucked into the left or the right pocket would denote active or passive. One of the most thrilling aspects of New York, to a newly world-famous Freddie in the late seventies, was that homosexuality was a veritable political triumph, and there was an infectious elation about the place. The mood had never more upbeat or celebratory. Gays were out, united, and firmly in charge of their own lifestyle and destiny. Things, so they thought, could only get better. The boundaries of experimental sexuality could be pushed to limits in ways that were probably not possible in any other city in the world at that time, except perhaps Munich. The New York gay contingent was more sexually active than any would dare to be elsewhere, because this was the capital of gay freedom, and they had earned the right.

It could be argued that Freddie, hitherto a relative innocent abroad, was corrupted by the blatant promiscuity (unpalatable to plain honest folk such as his own parents, whom he felt duty-bound to protect from his proclivities) that he encountered in New York City. But Freddie considered that he had no one but himself to blame: 'I didn't have to take my knickers off, dear. Nobody forced me.'[4]

As Paul Gambaccini points out,

Freddie played on the level to which he worked. This is where I'm a novice on the vices of life compared to him. My idea of a civilized evening after a long working day is actually a pleasant meal and an act of love with one person. For Freddie, there would invariably be a great consumption of various forms of things you can ingest. He liked his luxuries. This is one reason that I did not socialize with him as much as, say, someone like Kenny Everett, because Kenny was always more into Freddie's lifestyle than I was. What's more, he was quite well-behaved in London compared with how he was in New York, or later, Munich.

New York and Munich had far more decadent gay communities. Those two cities were the capitals of anonymous, one-time-only sex – which never interested me in the least. But Freddie undoubtedly enjoyed those places. It's a whole world, as rich in its magnitude as popular music is. It's just a part that there won't be books and videos about. I got the impression from him that his times in New York were always really wild, but the gay scene there at that time was much harder than anywhere.

One word comes to mind: fantasy. When you're having anonymous sex, or sex with multiple partners, there must be an element of fantasy involved. I think that you probably have to examine the role of the imagination in Freddie to understand that. It's not as if these things existing in the same person is so surprising. If anything, they make perfect sense. If you have an extreme amount of imagination in the public side, you're going to have an extreme amount of imagination in the private side. But I do think that at no point – and this is very important, because some people will be titillated or scandalized by your discussion of his private life – at no point did this *ever* take over or jeopardize his professional life. He knew it could go so far. It could consume Freddie, but it could not consume Queen. Again, it goes back to being about these four guys with business heads in a partnership.

According to Freddie's close friend, photographer Mick Rock, who emigrated there early in his own career, sex was only one aspect of the star's love affair with New York. The city appealed to Freddie on so many diverse levels:

Freddie was very at home in New York from day one. Mainly because, as outrageous as London was then, New York was that much *more* outrageous. The other main important factor for him was that you can get lost in New York very easily. All the stuff that happens outside Freddie's home Garden Lodge in London, fans worshipping at the door and graffiti everywhere, would *never* happen in New York – and this city is crawling with superstars. In New York, you can be as anonymous as you like. You can literally disappear, and whatever you get up to, nobody will bother you. Freddie was swift to realize that, and it appealed to him immensely.

I used to see quite a bit of him in New York in the early days of Queen's fame, and we'd sometimes be out strolling on Madison or Fifth or some place, and maybe a couple of people would come up and say Hi to him, and he'd say 'Hello, darlings' back, and that would be it. Never any bother.

Of course, he was really into his shopping by then, and New York was the ideal town in which to indulge that particular passion. It never ceased to amaze me how much money Freddie could spend. Incredibly extravagant. I'd never seen anybody shop like him. It was like watching a woman, he'd get these passions about certain things and he would just have to have them. He loved Tiffany's, for example, that was one of his favourite stores. He was always off buying presents for other people there, not usually stuff for himself. He was an incredibly generous guy. He so enjoyed being able to bring pleasure to others with his wealth. He especially loved buying for women. I was once with him when he got this adorable clock, really ridiculously over-priced but he just had to have it. That was Freddie.

Rock also remembers teatime forays around town which quickly turned farcical whenever Freddie spotted a young man who took his fancy: 'We'd always go out for tea, and he'd always end up flirting with the waiters. In a nice, amusing way, though, never in a trashy way. I had a lot of gay friends in New York in those days,' remembers Rock, himself now married with a daughter.

Believe me, I could camp it up with the best of them. I do remember being out with Freddie on one occasion when we mercilessly cruised. There was this one particularly good-looking waiter at the Waldorf Astoria, and I remember the guy spilling tea all over the both of us, we were behaving so badly and making him so nervous. Neither of us was looking to go off with the guy. It was nothing sexual. But we pulled his name out of him, and discovered that he did a bit of modelling, all that. For a laugh, Freddie and I went back there again to see him, and he avoided us like the plague, totally ignored us. I think we'd scared the shit out of him.

If Freddie metamorphosed into the ultimate hedonist in New York, it was mainly because he could afford to. Thenceforward, for years to come, he would leave no stone unturned in his quest for pleasure. 'Mercury by name, murky by nature,' quips Sky. 'There was a great deal of murkiness in his life, and that was exactly how Freddie liked it. He went where angels feared to tread. He was that classic refined person who loved to slum it. His ultimate fantasy would be to take a rent boy to the Opera. Rudolf Nureyev was very similar to Freddie in that he had that rare ability to adore high culture and low culture at the same time.'

Freddie was often perceived to be middle-class, but he had in fact moulded himself into the archetypal aristocrat. The reason he could not be labelled middle-class was that he was never cursed by that particular brand of snobbery which stems from not knowing whether one is up or down, in or out of favour. Freddie neither sought nor needed approval. He knew that as a star he was great, and that, as a man, he was as good as the next. He hob-nobbed, when it suited him, with his share of gentry. But the thing he did not like about 'toffs' was that they do not often take chances in life; that they are, by and large, totally predictable, even to the point of marrying their own kind for the sake of family fortune. This was exactly the kind of behaviour Freddie scorned. What he loved most about ordinary working-class folk was that they would now and then risk everything for the crack: the out-of-work father-of-four who skips a hot dinner and goes to the dogs to gamble the family's last tenner in the hope of winning a million. Why? Because you only live once. Because you are nothing, and you've nothing left to lose. That, as the song goes, is what freedom is all about. Freddie knew that. He greatly admired that attitude, and emulated it himself. If there was a risk to take, he would be the first to be out there, having a go.

Morality aside, what, then, was perceived as being so wrong with setting out to have a wild time? Few understood the motivation for Freddie's excessive promiscuity and decadence during his eighties rock 'n' roll heyday. But his public did tend to accept what they knew about, and mostly turned a blind eye. It was only the press who got excited whenever there was a whiff of scandal, and who were they to talk? What was certain was that Freddie was not by any means the only one doing it. Only much later did it become apparent that Freddie understood, more than any other rock superstar, that ordinary people actually adored him for being so daring. Many of them secretly loved it that he knew his way around the open sexual environment, endlessly savouring the sybaritic pursuits and deviations of the day. He tried and tasted everything to excess, in a way that most people would never dream of being able to. As well as providing his ever-swelling audiences with brilliant music and the grandest of over-the-top live entertainment, he was also treating them to the ultimate vicarious thrill.

'Something occurred to me on that trip to New York which I was to recognize many times in the years to come,' adds Sky.

I went to a Queen gig, interviewed Freddie, got to see the size and the amazement of all their excesses – and I got to eat the crumbs. That made me as privileged as they were, relatively speaking. They were never selfish in those terms. Queen were always anxious that everyone else should have just as great a time as they were having. There was this incredible generosity of spirit as well as a sharing of material riches which defined Queen as the best rock band in the world to hang around with. It wasn't just Freddie, because you didn't really get to hang out with Freddie, you were granted an audience with him from time to time and that was that. The rest of them, though, were usually totally accessible. You were always guaranteed a good night in their company. There were definitely four talents in that band, but, just as every man needs a good woman to help him to the top, every band needs a queen bee to be sure of superstar status.

Freddie was that: the queen bee of Queen. He was the greatest music hall act, an end-of-pier sensation, a true all-rounder. You could almost picture him on a Morecambe and Wise Christmas Special. He knew he could do anything. He had enormous confidence in his ability, and would take everything to the limit. He seemed to know instinctively where the limit was.

'The other three guys were incredibly talented, of course,'

Sky says. 'I'm forever amazed that Roger Taylor wrote 'Radio Ga-Ga', that John Deacon wrote 'Another One Bites The Dust'. But it was *Freddie* who made those songs hits. The greatest thing I had to admire about him was that all his weirdest and most wonderful fantasies came true in his lifetime. That was his triumph, and his tragedy.'

Photographer David Thorpe recalls several memorable encounters with Freddie, the first at the height of Queen's fame in the late 1970s, in which Freddie's less than gentlemanly side was beginning to show. It was not always a pretty sight. Perhaps, Thorpe concedes, Freddie's petulant, egotistical and at times tiresomely childish behaviour stemmed from the star's inherent dislike and mistrust of newspaper people. Perhaps it was due to the pressures of stardom and constant attention, the rigours of a seemingly endless touring and recording schedule. As Freddie himself said at the time, 'The higher up the ladder you go, the more vicious you have to be to stop yourself falling off.'[5]

Perhaps it was pent-up frustration at the realization that his life would never again belong to him completely. Or perhaps he was falling under the spell of more glittering stars than himself, as witnessed by Thorpe in a ballet rehearsal studio in London where Freddie the newly acclaimed rock hero was practising some routines with the greatest male ballet dancer the world has ever known.

'The first time I met him was in Covent Garden,' remembers Thorpe.[6]

He was working on some project at the time with Rudolph Nureyev, who, of course, was a world-class star, a legend. Even so, I don't remember thinking that this was any amazing, historic event that I was going off to photograph. It was not at all unusual for big stars to get pally with each other, and if you think about it, each had all the ingredients that should appeal to the other. I was working then as a freelance photographer for the *Evening News*, and Mercury's publicity people had OK'd it for me to go along and shoot some pictures of them together. It was at a rehearsal room, as I recall, in Floral Street, behind the main Covent Garden Opera House. Nureyev was showing Mercury all these moves. When I arrived, Mercury was his usual aloof self, the way he usually was whenever there was any press around. He was never overly friendly, nor unfriendly. He didn't laugh and joke while he was working, he took work extremely seriously, and he always appeared very committed to what he was doing.

He would certainly never communicate with the likes of us very much. In fact, he more or less ignored me, even though I had been given the impression that he was up for these pictures to be taken. Perhaps he was, really, and he was just putting on this annoyed little act for Nureyev's sake, to give the impression that he, too, was a world-class star, and how tiresome all this kind of thing really was, darling. Or perhaps it had rather been dumped on him, and he'd have much preferred it had I not been there at all. Nureyev, on the other hand, looked completely taken aback. I came in very quietly, very polite, said something like 'I'll just go and sit somewhere at the back, I won't disturb anybody.'

They were wearing ballet practice clothes and ballet shoes. Freddie was obviously taking it pretty seriously, there was no larking about whatsoever. Freddie could follow the moves Nureyev was showing him, and he seemed to pick things up fairly easily. He was obviously very intent on learning as much as he could. Knowing Freddie, the fact that he wanted to do it at all meant that he wanted to do it well, if not perfectly, because he was well-known by then as the ultimate perfectionist. Things seemed very harmonious between them. Freddie obviously deferred to Nureyev as the master of his art.

He was very respectful towards him, a sort of classic model pupil.

I thought I'd just work quietly and unobtrusively and not get in the way. But, it seemed, I just couldn't win. In the end, Nureyev literally exploded. It was a real sight for sore eyes. He came over to me, eyes bulging, red in the face, hands on hips, posturing and screaming, 'I just can't work with you here, it's absolutely impossible, you're putting me off. Please-leave-*now*.' It was quite a tantrum, and there was obviously something upsetting him. I don't think it could possibly have been just the fact that there was a little guy from the *Evening News* sitting unobtrusively at the back of the studio. I was really apologetic. But by that time I had already got a couple of rolls, so it didn't hurt me at all to clear off.

But something curious struck me later. That day, Nureyev, who became quite well-known for his tantrums, had behaved exactly the way Freddie would start to behave a little further down the line, when he became a really big, internationally famous star. It was almost as if he had picked up on that as a technique: This Is How A Really Famous Person Shows Off When They Are In A Mood.

When I heard much later that there was supposed to have been a raging affair between them, I wasn't at all surprised. Those two? Almost made for each other. And if there *was* ever a raging affair, it may well have started then.

Freddie Mercury had never made a secret of the fact that he had always wanted to be involved in more than just rock. I got the impression that he regarded himself as a much more multi-dimensional star. Because of that, he quite often befriended stars from other areas of the Arts, particularly ballet dancers and actors. He actually appeared to have very few close friends in the music business, which is quite telling. People like Nureyev were his passport to other worlds not directly associated with rock.

While it has often been denied by those close to Freddie that there was ever an affair between the two stars, Nureyev himself had written about it. On 21 June 1995 a book published in St Petersburg disclosed details about the dancer's many lovers. The book, *Rudy Nureyev Without Make-Up*, by Yuri Matthew Ryuntyu, is a highly intimate account which draws on letters written by the magnificent former Kirov Ballet star who had defected from the Communist Soviet Union of the Cold War to the West in 1961. In his correspondence, Nureyev admitted to a secret sexual liaison with his rock singer friend. Some of the letters, which contain nicknames or acronyms for Nureyev's innumerable sexual partners, begin by describing Mercury as 'Eddie', before going on to name the rock-star in full. Once, according to Nureyev, he cancelled all rehearsals and asked his theatre management for a week's leave so that he might spend time with Mercury. The pair appeared together in public for the first time in October 1988, in Spain, at the huge La Nit music festival, at which Freddie sang live with Montserrat Caballé with the Barcelona Opera House Orchestra and Choir. The fabulous concert was held in the open air in the city's Castle Square, where the Olympic flame was ceremoniously lit. But Nureyev and Freddie kept a discreet distance, to the point that people present wondered if they even knew each other at all. There was never scandalous revelation about the pair. But in the book, the author quotes a poignant extract from Nureyev's correspondence, in which he even implied that he had visited Freddie at home in London. Peter Freestone, however, insists that Nureyev never visited Garden Lodge, and does not believe that their affair ever occurred.

'He [Freddie] wanted to die alone in his house in London,' wrote Nureyev, 'which was alien to him. It rained, and I was crying at the hall of Great Freddie Mercury. He died quietly, without much pain. And I knew it was about two years or less until I would meet there.'

Nureyev, eight years Freddie's senior, was also dying of Aids. His prediction proved tragically right in that just two years separated their respective final curtains, the dancer finally losing his fight for life after lengthy illness in 1993. Each had lived in exile from the respective country of his birth. Each had 'sanitized' details of certain episodes in his life, and then maintained or turned a blind eye to various inaccuracies while knowing them not to be true: Nureyev, for example, never corrected the version of his life-story which had him born feet-first on a Trans-Siberian train, and even repeated it in his own autobiography. The question later arose as to whether he had deliberately and consistently lied about the place and date of his birth, and if so, why. Such anomalies were eventually put down to the dancer's 'theatrical and romantic nature'. We have already examined Freddie's reasons for allowing the perpetuation of similar discrepancies.

If Freddie epitomized Parsee eccentricity, Nureyev was the embodiment of the Tartar temperament. Both men were fiery and mercurial. Each was fanatical about his work, and possessed iron will and self-control in the workplace. Each was isolated by his artistic temperament, but was grateful for the compensation. Each had found his true metier, and was blessed with all the ability and application required to exploit it to the hilt. More fundamentally, each had demonstrated at an early age that he knew how to learn, applying himself assiduously to his craft, perfecting the art, soaking up culture, music, atmosphere and audience. Just as Nureyev would practise all the variations of a dance, including the female parts, and would often rehearse while the other dancers were resting, Freddie was perfectly aware of everyone's contribution to Queen's live performances, not least that of stage managers and riggers, lighting technicians and sound engineers. He was delighted by the efforts of others, while satisfying himself, even from a distance, that nothing was left to chance. In the recording studio, Freddie tended to take control of sessions, having usually done major pre-production work on song structure and harmony arrangements beforehand, which he would calculate with mathematical precision. Arriving at the studio dolled up as if ready to go on stage when the others simply came casually dressed, Freddie would have already assessed what he wanted to get out of a particular track, and would not stop until he had achieved it.

Both Nureyev and Mercury had phenomenal stage presence, unmatched by any living contemporary. Each was master of the spectacle, there being, after all, no great difference between the magic of rock and ballet when the various elements are dissected and compared. Each lived an absurd, extraordinary life, creating drama everywhere he went, in an exotic world that revolved around himself and his own personal interests. Each had an ambivalent attitude towards fame and celebrity. Each possessed a wicked and at times self-deprecating sense of humour. Each had lavish, extravagant tastes and a penchant for the good life. Each owned property in both London and New York: Nureyev lived in East Sheen and in Manhattan's fabled Dakota building on West 72nd Street at Central Park West, with Lauren Bacall and the Lennons for neighbours, a few blocks from the Lincoln Center and the Metropolitan Opera House. Freddie remained in his beloved Kensington, and in New York kept an apartment on East 58th St, a short walk from Central Park, Bloomingdale's department store, F.A.O. Schwarz toyshop, Carnegie Hall and the Plaza Hotel, a dozen or so blocks from Nureyev's home.

Each liked the idea of, and had occasionally enjoyed, stability of life with one special mate, provided it was offset by the freedom of promiscuity, by the variety and excitement of ever-changing sexual partners. Nureyev, while predominantly homosexual, believed that everyone is basically bisexual. For years, Freddie behaved as if he agreed. Each could be spectacularly promiscuous with men. Yet each had forged his most intense personal relationships with women: Freddie with Mary Austin and later with German film star Barbara Valentin; Nureyev with adoring 'nanny' figures, including Jackie Kennedy Onassis' glamorous sister Lee Radziwill, in cities all over the world. Some of these women, in the same way as Mary had for Freddie, were willing to renounce their own personalities and lifestyles to accommodate those of their 'true loved one'.

Nureyev once remarked, 'To have made love as a man and as a woman, that is special knowledge'.[7]

Neither made a habit of seeking out mentors in his life. Neither particularly cared for father figures. But both found the mother figure indispensable. Each was determined to get the most out of life. Neither seemed capable of monogamy or fidelity; neither found true, lasting all-encompassing and totally fulfilling love in the arms of another.

As one ballet critic remarked,

Theirs would have been a match made in heaven. But how could they be together, doing what they did, living the lives they lived? Contriving to be on the same continent at the same time would have been no mean feat in itself. If it happened, it must have been a huge, passionate affair, conducted in secret locations behind closed doors in glamorous cities around the world, because neither of them did anything by halves. They were kindred spirits. In truth, nothing either of them did in his career was that extraordinary. It had all been done before. But what they did was the best that anyone could do it at the time. Neither was unique, both were predictable, but at the same time they were brilliantly extreme. Just imagine if those two had had children . . .

A few years after his first encounter with Freddie, when David Thorpe owned a photo agency called Picture Power based in

London's Chancery Lane, he once again unwittingly incurred Freddie's wrath and glimpsed the darker side of the singer's nature.

My business partner, Bill Zygment, had some contacts with, I think, Phil Symes, Freddie's publicity people. Queen were doing several nights at Wembley and they were riding high. During that run of shows, Freddie had a birthday. Bill and I had the idea to have a birthday cake made for him and do a picture. We put it to his PR people, and they agreed. They got back to us and said that Freddie wanted a cake made in the shape of a huge pair of breasts. We commissioned the wife of a publican in Holborn, whose pub we drank in regularly. The cake was quite elaborate and probably cost £40 or £50: two great mounds covered in white icing, with red icing for the nipples. It was utterly gross, really, but suited Freddie perfectly, as he loved a bit of vulgarity.

I took the cake along to Wembley, went backstage, set up the lights and camera, so all Freddie had to do was walk in, sit behind the cake, lift the cake knife and say Cheese. I was also going to get a picture of him with the rest of the band. I got them in there, posed up, waiting for Freddie to arrive. He eventually came in, looked disgruntled, and it was immediately apparent that something was up. He just sat there. I said, quite politely, 'Could you just pick up the knife, Freddie, please, as if you are going to cut the cake?' Then, just as I'm saying 'Heads in close, guys', Freddie just explodes and goes 'What's the fucking crowd doing here?'

'Sorry,' I said, 'Beg pardon . . . What?'

'Who's fucking birthday is it?' he screamed.

'Well . . . yours. But I thought it would be nice if . . .'

'Look, I'm fucking sick and tired of fucking people fucking telling me what to do!' And with that, Freddie simply stormed out and slammed the door. Brian May, who is always such a nice, gentle, well-mannered guy, shrugged, looked embarrassed, and said, 'I'm terribly sorry.'

And there I was, high and dry, no pictures. I'm sorry, but I thought the guy was a total shit. Whatever was irking him, he didn't have to behave like that and spoil his birthday picture. The PR called a couple of days later to say sorry, it was before the performance, he gets very edgy, stage-fright, artistic temperament ... but I still though his behaviour was grossly self-indulgent. He didn't give a toss about anybody else.[8]

Thorpe later had a half-hearted stab at revenge, though Freddie never heard about it:

At that same pub on High Holborn, the barman told us he'd had an affair with Freddie Mercury. It didn't surprise me. Freddie was well-known for being a bit of a tart. When that barman heard I was taking this cake down to Wembley, he gave me a card in an envelope to give to Freddie, which I'd planned to hand him after I'd finished the shoot. Not only did I not give it, but in a huff on the way out I opened the bloody thing. It was a gay greetings card, with a picture of a nude bloke on the front. The barman had written inside something along the lines of 'That was a great time, Freddie, do you remember the night we had? Do you remember me?' I don't think he ever got the chance. I felt so angry as I made my way out of Wembley that I just dropped it on the ground and flounced off home.

Chapter Thirteen

QUEEN LIMITED

With all four albums simultaneously in the UK top 20 during February 1976, Queen were fired up for further live dates in Japan and Australia, where their product was outselling all predictions. Their return to Britain saw them back in the studio to begin work on their fifth album, from which Brian took time off in May to marry his girlfriend Chrissy Mullen. The following month, John Deacon's first Queen single was released. 'You're My Best Friend', a nice harmonious ballad, was something of a departure from previous Queen releases, but was well-received and quickly entered the top ten.

During the Scottish Festival of Popular Music that summer, Queen played two gigs at the Edinburgh Playhouse, followed by an open-air concert in Cardiff. And come September, in a typically touching Queen gesture which few other major rock bands would have thought of, they staged a massive free concert in Hyde Park to thank the fans for their support. In the event, nearly 200,000 turned out to enjoy the show. The day was co-organized by Richard Branson, the high-flying Virgin Records supremo, who at the same time unwittingly provided Roger Taylor with a new girlfriend in the gorgeous shape of his French personal assistant Dominique Beyrand. Soon afterwards, the couple set up home in a luxurious Surrey house set in several wooded acres with its own recording studio. The free concert was held on 18 September, the anniversary of the death of Jimi Hendrix. Brilliant weather held out, and it was a hugely successful day. Support act Kiki Dee, also a John Reid/Rocket Records signing, had been due to perform her new number one duet with Elton John, 'Don't Go Breaking My Heart' (which, despite his many popular releases, was actually Elton's first-ever number one). But Elton did not make it on the day, and Kiki had to settle for singing beside a giant cardboard cut-out of him instead.

Denis O'Regan, still striving to make a name for himself as a rock photographer but not yet the fully-fledged professional, attended the Hyde Park gig that day and, together with a friend, blagged entrance into the backstage enclosure and managed to wheedle his way actually underneath the stage.

'There I was, standing right next to Freddie as he was about to go on. He was getting into this cage thing and preparing to rocket up onto the stage via a little lift during the explosions at the start of 'Now I'm Here'. We were right underneath it when it happened. He seemed completely nonplussed. No photo opportunity, of course. I wasn't even supposed to be there.'

Freddie, resplendent in glittering white cat suit, addressed the audience in inimitable style: 'Welcome to our little picnic on the Serpentine', was the extent of his welcome.

O'Regan had now made it his business to befriend Rocket Records employees in an attempt to get closer to Queen, whom he hoped to photograph in an official capacity. One of John Reid's friends and henchmen, Paul Prenter, had taken a shine to Denis, and shortly afterwards started allowing him access to the photographer's enclosure at a number of Queen shows.

One of the earliest shows he gave me access to was in Paris. I was in the backstage area, and noticed that they had built another little stage behind the scenes. I immediately thought that Queen were going to do a little impromptu sesh . . . they had all these chairs laid out in front of it and everything. But the next moment, this girl came on and did a strip. Then another one came on and did a strip, and then another one, until there were about 12, 14 women on this little stage. Then they did this giant lesbian act in front of us all. This was just for the amusement and entertainment of those working and lurking backstage, and it was wonderful. I suppose it was all a bit seedy for its time, but that kind of thing became Queen's party theme – they would always go for boobs and bottoms and decadent sex. Nothing really that sordid about it, it was just their thing that they did for a laugh. Their preoccupation with sexy stuff was deliberately cultivated, and did seem to project a whole different side of Queen; and I imagine it would have put paid to any rumours at the time, not that I heard any myself back then, about Freddie being gay.

The most unusual thing that struck Denis about Queen at that time was that they were one of the only big bands who stuck around after their own shows.

Which I used to hate, because I just wanted to 'git going' – go out and have fun after the work was done. But they always used to have their dinner after the show. They'd all sit down round a table in the dressing-room and eat together. I'd never been around a band who did that before. Everyone else did a runner, limos waiting for them at the backstage door as they came off stage, ready to roar off to the airport or back to the hotel. Much later, I can remember thinking that there was a real element of camaraderie about that. I think they genuinely liked each other's company. There have always been stories about them not getting on and travelling in separate limos and so on, but everyone does when they're big news and they can afford it. Freddie in a tour bus? You must be joking.

The album title 'A Night At The Opera' had been inspired by the 1935 Marx Brothers film of the same name and Queen were keen to extend that same theme to their new album. It was consequently named 'A Day At The Races', the title of the 1937 follow-up movie by the funniest and most influential comedy team in Hollywood history, whom Queen had long adored. Some Queen fans amused themselves drawing parallels between the members of Queen and the four most famous of the five Marx Brothers: Groucho, so named because of his moody behaviour, rapid wit and ever-present leer, was Freddie; Harpo, the silent one, had to be John Deacon; Chico was the lame-brained, inventive pianist with the Italian accent, an image which did not really fit either Brian or Roger, apart from the fact that Chico had acquired his nickname from a strong and persistent interest in 'chicks' – so Roger it was. Which left Zeppo, who had only appeared in the first five of the Marx's 13 films, and who had collected his nickname from constantly doing chin-ups like 'Zippo', a popular vaudeville monkey act of the day. Which was not really Brian's image at all, but it would have to do. Groucho Marx himself got to hear about Queen's tribute to his films with the titles of their albums, and sent them a well-wishing telegram. The band were later able to thank him personally in March 1977 when they were playing the Los Angeles Forum as part of yet another American tour. Having heard that they were in town, the 82-year-old comic genius asked them over for tea. The band presented him with a tour jacket and a framed commemorative gold disc, and they all had to pinch themselves as they sang to each other in Groucho Marx's front room. Timing was everything: Marx died later that same year.

To promote the album in style, EMI Records took a

marquee at a Kempton Park race meeting and sponsored a special Day At The Races Hurdle. It was just another no expense-spared day, lavish food and booze and live music by the Tremeloes and Marmalade. The first single release from that album was 'Somebody To Love', which went straight to number four on the UK chart and to number one on Radio Luxembourg's. Christmas 1976 saw the band in huge demand on television and radio. The BBC repeated the Hammersmith Odeon Whistle Test concert from the previous year, and 'A Day At The Races', released on 10 December 1976, gave Queen their second number one album slot in the UK. And Freddie finally came clean with himself and the love of his life, officially ending his romantic relationship with Mary Austin. She was to remain his most devoted personal assistant, and was at his side almost daily until his death 15 years later.

Another New Year, another world tour. The latest American shows proved as successful as the last except for problems encountered once again by Freddie with his throat, causing a couple of West Coast shows to be cancelled. As Freddie said, 'My nodules are still with me. I have these uncouth callouses growing in my interior [referring to his throat]. From time to time they harm my vocal dexterity. At the moment, however, I am winning. I'm going easy on the red wine and the tour will be planned around my nodules.'

He had at one point come close to being operated on, but took a dislike to the doctor and was 'a bit perturbed about having strange instruments forced down my throat'.

The tour moved on to Europe, beginning in Stockholm, and then came the British leg, which kicked off at the Bristol Hippodrome in May. At the London Earls Court shows in June, they introduced their special 'Crown' lighting rig, a huge construction which rose from the stage in a massive swirl of dry ice and smoke. Then, once again, it was back into the studio to start work on yet another album. The various members of Queen would occasionally venture out into the solo arena, and also guest on albums and singles for other artists now and then by way of recreation. Fame and fortune were, by now, beginning to seem like one hard, never-ending slog. They still loved doing what they did best, of course, but there came a point when they could perhaps only get a real kick out of music if they were making it on somebody else's behalf.

Queen's next big single, 'We Are The Champions', would prove to be one of their best-loved and most enduring anthems. But at that time it was scathingly received by a British music press seduced by the Sex Pistols and so caught up in the Punk era that they were mightily scornful of anything that smacked of big band stadium rock. The last thing you wanted to admit to being in those days was a fan of Zeppelin, The Who or Queen. Despite the bitchy denunciations, the single made number two on both the UK chart and the American Billboard chart, and gave Queen their first American number one with its placing on the American trade paper Record World chart. Released as a double A-side along with 'We Will Rock You' in the States, the 'Rock You' chant was adopted by American football supporters, and 'We Are The Champions' was borrowed by both the New York Yankees and the Philadelphia 76ers. Revenge was eventually sweet. Originally released on 7 October 1977, with a promotional video featuring a loyal army of Queen fans, the song remains a huge classic throughout the world twenty years on, and is played constantly at major sporting events across the globe.

October 1977 also brought Queen a Britannia Award from the British Phonographic Industry for 'Bohemian Rhapsody' as the best British single recorded over the past 25 years. Two days later Queen were publicizing their sixth album, 'News Of The World', which they released to mixed reviews.

By this time, it had become apparent to all members of Queen that John Reid's mind was preoccupied with other things. Although Elton John was keeping a lower profile performance-wise, his recorded output was still prolific, and their own label Rocket Records was thriving. Queen, who now matched Elton in terms of star quality and status, were in desperate need of management who would concentrate on them exclusively. Lawyer Jim Beach of the legal firm Harbottle and Lewis was once again brought in, this time to negotiate a full and final extrication from the contract with John Reid Enterprises, a relatively painless if expensive procedure. The agreement being severed ahead of expiry, Reid walked away with a hefty pay-off plus 15 per cent of royalties on the sales of all Queen's previously-released albums in perpetuity. Queen could hardly be blamed for their desire to manage their own business dealings in future. Pete Brown, who had handled Queen's day-to-day affairs on behalf of John Reid Enterprises, jumped ship along with them and was made personal manager. Another friend of Reid's, Paul Prenter, also joined the team. Jim Beach would now handle all their legal and contractual affairs on a full-time basis, and Gerry Stickells would manage Queen on the road. Shortly afterwards, Queen Productions Ltd along with the affiliated companies Queen Music Ltd and Queen Films Ltd were officially established. Queen now owned as much of the rights to their own work and to themselves as it was possible to secure. And the dream team, so everybody thought, was now in place.

To boldly go where no rock band had gone before was fast becoming Queen's remit. There now being something of a been-there-seen-it-done-it element to their collective experience of rock stardom, new challenges would need to be sought if the band were to sustain creativity, and the enthusiasm required for the tedium of touring. For a start there were not one but two American tours in 1977. On the first, beginning in Portland on 11 November, Freddie performed the song 'Love Of My Life' live for the first time, inviting audience participation which was to become a staple of Queen shows everywhere, regardless of any language barrier. Queen also now felt confident and sufficiently in charge of their own finances to treat themselves to their first private plane.

By December they were back in New York, where Freddie, long an ardent fan, attended Liza Minnelli's sensational stage show, 'The Act'. There was more to Liza's appeal than her talent and showmanship. Minnelli's mother Judy Garland had been a beloved icon of that faction of the gay community which idolized tormented female entertainers. By an uncanny twist of fate, Garland was being buried in New York uptown on the same day as the Stonewall gay riots broke out downtown. This symbolism had not gone unnoticed. It was only natural therefore that Liza should have inherited some of her mother's following and become a darling of the homosexual community in her own right. Something of a tortured diva herself, Liza had also explored bisexual love as fictitious nightclub entertainer Sally Bowles in the cult hit movie *Cabaret*, itself derived from Christopher Isherwood's *Berlin Stories* in which the late, gay English novelist recorded the 'masquerade of perversions' that he encountered (and sampled) in 1920s Berlin. Freddie was surprisingly well-versed in this type of gay history and politics, and would occasionally let slip some seemingly minor detail which nevertheless demonstrated to others that he had thought very deeply about the meaning and spirit of homosexuality. It was as if he was on a private quest to unravel the tangles of his own complex psyche. The admiration between Freddie and Liza was mutual, Minnelli being one of the first stars to agree to perform at the Freddie Mercury tribute concert in London in 1992.

At Madison Square Garden, Freddie wowed his audience even more than usual by presenting himself for Queen's encore dressed in a New York Yankees hat and jacket. The Yankees had just claimed the World Series, and the New York fans were thrilled by this nod to their beloved ball game. The gesture was pure Freddie and from the heart, and it greatly endeared him to his audience. The personal touch was something he would introduce time and time again throughout Queen's stage career: a few words in Spanish here, a local folk song there, a British Union Jack for a cloak which happened to be lined with the Hungarian flag when he turned it round . . . Sometimes he would ponder for hours to think up precisely the right gesture to make, the very words to sing or say. This was Freddie's little way of giving something back, and his fans adored him for it.

Queen toured Europe again in 1978, and played five more shows in England during May, after which work commenced on the next album at Mountain Studios in Montreux, Switzerland. A charming and sophisticated lakeside tourist resort, Montreux was famous for its rock and jazz festivals. Otherwise, it was a delightfully refined and tranquil little town with spectacular views across Lake Geneva towards the Alps and the Matterhorn. Freddie would have found it to be not dissimilar to Panchgani in India in that it was a haven of sanatoria, clinics, and finishing colleges for wealthy young ladies. Queen, especially Freddie, instantly fell in love with the place. He would one day acquire his own home there. Queen's last-ever album, 'Made In Heaven', would be recorded there. When he knew that he had only a short time left to live, Freddie chose to spend as much time as he could savouring its pine-fresh air and heavenly views. His commemorative statue, at last unveiled in 1996, stands on the shore of Lake Geneva with the same outlook over the lake as depicted on the 'Made In Heaven' album cover.

Brian and Freddie had stayed behind in England. Brian for the birth of his first child, Jimmy, and Freddie to work on a project for his own newly-formed Goose Productions company: an album by his close friend, the actor Peter Straker. Jamaican-born Straker, whose acting credits included the original British stage production of the hip musical 'Hair' and late-seventies episodes of Doctor Who, also co-starred in the hit TV series 'Connie' alongside Stephanie Beacham, and took the lead on the West End stage in *Phantom Of The Opera*. He and Freddie had first met in 1975 at a London restaurant where Straker was having dinner with his manager, David Evans, who also happened to work for John Reid. By chance, Freddie and John Reid were dining together in the same restaurant. Straker would later recall Freddie's almost painful shyness and his habit of staring at the ground in the presence of strangers. After that they kept bumping into one another on the London scene, and Straker invited Freddie to one of his birthday parties in November 1975. The theme was 'Come As Your Favourite Person'. Freddie, who was at that time having an under-wraps fling with a young theatre hand called David Minns, apparently told Straker that he might make it (which he did), but warned him that he would not be wearing fancy dress because he was his own favourite person, and would therefore come as himself. The friendship developed to the point that Freddie and Straker were soon hitting the town together, enjoying excursions to the ballet and opera as well as the pubs and clubs, and playing a little irregular tennis at London's smart Hurlingham Club. Straker had asked Freddie to produce an album of post-Glam rock and vaudevillian cameos, and Freddie agreed, generously investing £20,000 in the record, entitled 'This One's On Me'. It spawned two singles, 'Jackie' and 'Ragtime Piano Joe', and Straker would go on to release further material for Goose Productions, although these were not produced by Freddie.

Queen were soon reunited in the studio in Montreux, and work on their new album continued in earnest. Recording then progressed to another studio, SuperBear in Nice, France, for tax reasons: Queen had been obliged to take a 'year out', and therefore could not risk recording an entire album in one country in case they incurred tax demands in yet another territory. Freddie's 32nd birthday party was held in the exquisite little French town of St Paul de Vence, where Rolling Stone Bill Wyman kept a lovely secluded home. The wild poolside party culminated in the usual everybody-in-the-water madness – all but Freddie. He and Peter Straker, who had flown over for the bash along with a number of Freddie's closest friends, serenaded the drunken throng with their rendition of some Gilbert and Sullivan arias later that evening.

The next single release was the infamous 'Fat-Bottomed Girls', a double A-side with 'Bicycle Race'. To promote the single they hired Wimbledon Stadium on 17 September, and paid 65 naked girls to stage a bicycle race therein. Hilarious footage ensued. The bikes had been supplied by Halfords, who unfathomably insisted that Queen pay for the replacement of 65 used leather saddles. The single was released the following month and rose to number 11 in the chart, but not without controversy: the bare bottom on the sleeve was deemed offensive, and future copies featured scanty black knickers sketched in.

October saw them back in the US for yet another tour where, on Hallowe'en night in New Orleans, Queen hosted yet another outrageous party to herald the release of their new album, 'Jazz'. The 400-plus guest list included press representatives from all over the States, Britain, South America and Japan. The band laid on a veritable orgy in a steamy, overgrown New Orleans swamp setting, created in a hotel ballroom. All the fun of the fair and more: dwarfs and drag queens, fire-eaters and female mud-wrestlers, strippers and snakes, steel bands, voodoo dancers, Zulu dancers, groupies, grotesques and prostitutes, some performing unimaginable and possibly illegal acts in full view of the revellers. One young model arrived on a salver of raw liver, others writhed in cages suspended from the ceiling. The mad goings-on made headlines around the world, and further confirmed Queen's status as the best party-givers in the rock industry.

PR Tony Brainsby, who was again handling the band's publicity, accompanied a posse of journalists from London to

New Orleans just for the night. Little did they know what was in store: 'Wild. We went straight from the airport to the party and the party to the airport, without having been anywhere near a bed as it were. I'd seen parties in my time, but never anything quite like that. Some of the journalists' eyes were practically hanging out by the time it came to leave. Freddie was even signing his name on strippers' buttocks – and that was the mildest thing I witnessed. Took me the best part of a month to get over it.'[1]

Across America, there was now a flurry of disapproval at the inclusion of a poster of the nude bicycle race in the 'Jazz' album sleeve. A public outcry denounced it as pornography, the poster was banned, and future albums came with an application form enabling fans to send for a copy of the offending poster instead. Queen were taken aback, as they considered the poster to be harmless fun. But, as they said, only in America. It didn't stop them bringing a bevy of bike-riding, bell-ringing girls on to the Madison Square Garden stage during their rendition of 'Bicycle Race'. Meanwhile, the 'Jazz' album went straight in at number two, and stayed on the UK chart for 27 weeks.

The band, it seemed, had by now forgotten how to relax, becoming restless if they found themselves away from work for too long. After the shortest Christmas break they departed for a mammoth 28-date European tour, taking in two performances in what was then Yugoslavia for the first time. 'Don't Stop Me Now', their twelfth single, was released later that January, and for once the music press came down on its side. Then it was back to Montreux to work on tapes made throughout the tour for a live album. Always at home in their favourite lakeside town, and happy at work in Mountain Studios, it was suggested to them by their accountants that they should buy the studios and help themselves out of a complicated tax situation. They jumped at the chance. The resident engineer Dave Richards came with the deal. That year, Queen were also asked to compose the title and theme for the futuristic sci-fi film *Flash Gordon,* about the classic comic character of the same name, to be produced by Dino de Laurentiis. Scoring a movie had long been a Queen ambition, and they leapt at the chance.

Now it was back to Japan, more mayhem and adulation, and then a live double album release, 'Live Killers', which rose to number three on the UK charts. When EMI Records received the Queen's Award to Industry, a special commemorative, limited-edition 200 copies of 'Bohemian Rhapsody' were pressed on blue vinyl, the first four of which were presented to the band. The single remains one of Queen's most collectable releases.

The summer months of 1979 were spent at the now defunct Musicland studios in Munich, which had risen to fame courtesy of producer Giorgio Moroder's disco-era success. Queen, still recording abroad for tax purposes, would now be working with a new producer, the acclaimed German record wizard Reinholdt Mack*, who had co-created Musicland with Moroder. Marc Bolan, Deep Purple and the Stones had all recorded there, and Musicland had an enviable reputation in the industry. Queen's time there was to have a profound and to some extent destructive effect on all the band, none more so than Freddie, who found the city and its dubious delights totally addictive.

For Freddie, Munich's main attraction was its gay culture, concentrated in a small, central area of the city which was known as the Bermuda Triangle. This enclave was a haven for homosexuals from all over Europe, just as the New York Village and San Francisco's Castro district had proved for gay refugees across America. The scene was laid-back and relaxed, and Freddie was able to experiment openly with his sexuality without the fear of the alacritous British press

---

* The spelling of the producer's Christian name remains a bone of contention, though he was universally known as 'Mack'.

breathing down his neck and exposing his every move. The disco club scene was at its zenith, gay bars were abundant and heaving with bodies seven nights a week. Nightlife was a thrill lived at break-neck pace, within the dark, deafening confines of clubs like the Ochsen Gardens, the Sugar Shack, New York and Frisco. People did not take any notice of outrageous gay behaviour in the Triangle, because everybody was enjoying themselves too much – the scene also attracted straight men and women out for a good time. As producer Reinholdt Mack would later recall, 'Freddie loved to be around a real mix of people. He never liked the purely gay world. He was a private person, and never behaved outrageously out of context. He didn't thrust homosexuality in your face. He would never cause a scene, and always behaved impeccably in mixed company. His attitude was very much "everything in its place".'[2]

Freddie was not the only member of the band profoundly affected by his experience of Munich. As Brian later explained to the authors of *As It Began*,

Munich had a huge effect on all our lives. Because we spent so much time there, it became almost another home, and a place in which we lived different lives. It was different from being on tour, when there would be an intense contact with a city for a couple of days, and then we would move on. In Munich we all became embroiled in the lives of the local people. We found ourselves inhabiting the same clubs for most of the night, most nights. The Sugar Shack in particular held a fascination for us. It was a rock disco with an amazing sound system, and the fact that some of our records didn't sound very good in there made us change our whole perspective on our mixes and our music.

In retrospect, it's probably true to say that our efficiency in Munich was not very good. Our social habits made us generally start work late in the day, feeling tired, and (for me especially, and perhaps for Freddie) the emotional distractions became destructive.

Despite Freddie's wild homosexual promiscuity in the Bavarian capital, Mack believed that the attraction of this type of gay lifestyle was beginning to pall. As the producer later recounted to rock writer Rick Sky:

Freddie told me a number of times, 'Perhaps I'll give up the whole gay thing one of these days.' I didn't think that was strange at all. He more or less decided when he was 24 or 25 that he was gay, and before that he was considered as straight. With him, nothing was impossible. I do think he could have given up being gay, because he loved women. I saw what he was like in their presence, and he wasn't the kind of gay man who didn't like them in his life. He was the opposite.

Freddie was a frequent visitor at the home of Mack and his wife Ingrid, being godfather to one of their children. Mack described how Freddie was not immune to the attractions of family life, and even suggested that Freddie had implied a desire to radically alter his lifestyle; that the star would have loved to marry and have children himself: 'Freddie's biggest thing was to have a family and a normal life,' Mack revealed.

I was once badly screwed and found myself having to pay a load of back-tax. I was very depressed, and I talked to Freddie about it. He told me, 'Fuck, it's only money! Why worry about something like that? You've got it made, you've got everything you need – a wonderful family and children. You have everything I can never have.' That's when I became aware that when he was at our house, he was watching everything and taking it all in. Seeing what a family life was like, and how it could have made him happy.

In New York the following year, however, Freddie confessed, to Rick Sky in an interview for the *Daily Star*: 'By nature I'm very restless and highly-strung, so I wouldn't make a good family man. I'm a very emotional person, a person of real extremes. And often that's destructive, both to myself and others.'

The conversation, which again took place backstage at Madison Square Garden, then turned to Mary Austin, with whom Freddie was still maintaining the illusion of a romantic relationship. 'We don't live together,' Freddie said. 'But she has a house only two minutes from mine. We see each other every day. I like my freedom and, luckily, she's very understanding. She's learned to get over her jealousy. My bisexual image is just for the public. It helps to keep some mystery going about me. I have a lot of gay friends, but I couldn't fall in love with a man the way I could with a girl.'

Mack also discovered, during the time he spent getting to know Freddie and from comments that he would make, that Freddie himself had been a lonely child. 'One day I overheard a conversation between Freddie and my second son Felix. Freddie was telling him, "I never had any of this. When I was young I spent a lot of time away from my parents because I was at boarding school. Sometimes I would hardly ever see them." He talked to my kids about his childhood quite a lot. Freddie adored children. As soon as they could walk and talk and respond, he got on with them.'

Mack described how his collaboration with Queen came about by accident, when he turned up at the studio at the same time as Freddie, who expressed surprise because he had not known the producer was available. Freddie had a new song that he wanted to work on there and then, 'Crazy Little Thing Called Love', and suggested that they get to work on it right away. Freddie was also to play rhythm guitar for the first time on a Queen track. He told Mack: 'I can't play guitar, but it won't matter.'

To Mack, Freddie seemed anxious to get the track down before Brian arrived to do his guitar solos: 'Freddie was looking for a different sound. I just put some rock 'n' roll echoes on it, and it sounded great.'

It was to be his approach for the entire 'The Game' album. As Brian explained:

We approached it from a different angle, with the idea of ruthlessly pruning it down to a coherent album rather than letting our flights of fancy lead us off into different areas. The impetus came very largely from Freddie, who said that he thought we'd been diversifying so much that people didn't know what we were about anymore. If there's a theme to the album, it's rhythm and sparseness – never two notes played if one would do, which is a hard discipline for us, because we tend to be quite over the top in the way we work.[3]

This new approach had caused anxiety at the outset, because nobody except Freddie was convinced that it could work. 'That was breaking new ground for us, because for the first time we went into a recording studio without a deadline, purely with the intention of putting some tracks down as they came out,' said Brian at the time.

'Crazy Little Thing Called Love' was one of them. Another was 'Save Me'.

Brian also revealed that Queen were not contractually obliged to release the material straight away, saying that this was 'something in the can' which 'at some future date we can perhaps fashion into an album'. The basic reason for this, he said, 'was to put ourselves in a totally different situation. It's a way of getting out of that rut of doing an album, touring Britain, touring America, etc. We thought we'd try a change and see what came out. You have to make your own excitement after a while.'

Meanwhile, Mack was raving about Freddie's technique in the studio, his on-the-spot inventiveness, his total commitment, his enthusiasm, the speed and dexterity with which he worked. The main disadvantage in the working environment, and possibly also in his personal life, was Freddie's limited attention span; the way he would suddenly lose interest if something appeared too laborious and long-winded. According to Mack, Freddie could never focus on any one thing for more than an hour and a half:

'With "Killer Queen", you can tell that he just sat down at the piano and did it. The end is a little bit unresolved. I think that was a typical Freddie quality. He just loved to get on with something newer and more different.

'I got on exceptionally well with Freddie,' Mack later remarked. 'I liked the fact that he was a genius. He really was, in terms of perception of music and seeing the focal point of where the song should be.'

Together, they added a new dimension to the Queen sound which matched the mood of the era and inspired the band towards new creative heights.

After Queen played at German open-air festivals in August 1979, Freddie went into rehearsals for a charity performance to be given by the Royal Ballet at the London Coliseum in October, on behalf of the City of Westminster Society for Mentally Handicapped Children. Wayne Eagling, a Royal Ballet principal, was a close friend, and he persuaded Freddie to star as a guest artist in the diverse dance programme. 'Bohemian Rhapsody' and 'Crazy Little Thing Called Love' were both choreographed, and Freddie also added live vocals. Freddie danced well, and received a standing ovation.

'I only really knew about ballet from watching it on television,' he confided at the time to John Blake, then a pop writer on the *Evening News*.

But I always enjoyed what I saw. Then I became very good friends with Sir Joseph Lockwood at EMI, also Chairman of the Royal Ballet board of governors, and I began to meet all these people who were involved in ballet and I became more and more fascinated by them.

I finally saw Baryshnikov dance with the American Ballet Theatre and he was just mind-blowing. More than Nureyev, more than anyone. I mean he can really fly, and when I saw him on stage I was so in awe that I felt like a groupie.

Referring to his performance with the Royal Ballet, he said:

They had me practising at the barre and all that, stretching my legs . . . trying to do things in a week that they'd been doing for years. It was murder. After two days I was in agony. It was hurting me in places I didn't know I had, dear. Then, when the night of the gala came, I was just amazed at the backstage scenes. When I had my entrances to do I had to fight my way through Merle Park and Anthony Dowell and all these people, and say, 'Excuse me, I'm going on now.' It was outrageous.

He also talked about his big moment, when he danced his scene while singing 'Bohemian Rhapsody': 'Yes, dear, I did this leap. A wonderful leap which brought the house down and then they all caught me and I just carried on singing.'

Asked if he would like to have been a professional dancer, Freddie replied: 'Yes, but I'm very happy doing what I do. You can't suddenly say at 32, I want to be a ballet dancer.'

And quizzed about his passion for the camper aspects of dance having led to rumours that he might be something of a 'man's man', Freddie roared: 'Oh God, dear. Let them think what they want. You see, if I actually said no or yes, that would be boring. Nobody would ask me any more. I'd rather they just kept on asking. Oh, it's all just so boring. My dear, the private life is up to the individual. I mean, with someone like Elton, I think: what can I say? He's more press-oriented, isn't he? I'm not that mad about it.'

In another interview, with David Wigg of the *Daily Express* in Cannes, on 5 February 1980, Freddie joked further about his Royal Ballet performance, milking the experience for all it was worth: 'Singing upside down is wonderful. I was shivering in the wings with nerves. It's always much harder when you are put outside your sphere, but I always like a challenge. I'd like to see Mick Jagger or Rod Stewart try something like that.'

He also let it be known, with customary cheek, that his most vivid memory of the evening was having his bottom pinched mischievously by ballerina Merle Park: 'She's outrageous, that woman.'

It was backstage at the Royal Opera House in October 1979 that Freddie first encountered a young wardrobe man and dresser by the name of Peter Freestone.

'Freddie came up to the Opera House to try on the outfits that he was going to wear for the Royal Ballet Gala at the Coliseum,' remembers Freestone, a large, amiable character with an almost permanent smile, to whom Freddie took an immediate shine.

He was extremely nice and polite. I'd later discover that he was always polite unless people really annoyed him, in which case he would let rip. And he was pretty in awe of the Opera House – he was out of his normal sphere of experience. This was a bastion of the Establishment, and he was the total opposite.

The Gala was brilliant. The way Freddie was manipulated around the stage by these dancers was superb. He sang 'Crazy Little Thing Called Love' and 'Bohemian

Rhapsody'. He came out in all his leather gear for the first one, then went behind a wall of dancers and reappeared dressed in sequins. It was the first insight I had into the showman in Freddie. Up until then I'd vaguely heard of Queen, and I'd once seen Freddie with Mary having tea in the Rainbow Room at Biba in about 1971. He had the hair down to here, a fox fur jacket, and it was unmistakably him.

After the Gala there was a party at Legends club, where I met Paul Prenter with Freddie, and had a chat with them both. Three weeks later Paul telephoned my boss Michael Brown and asked if he knew anybody who would be interested in a six-week contract to do wardrobe for the Queen tour. I was very keen to do it. After watching that performance on stage I just wanted that excitement. I'd watched *Sleeping Beauty* and *Swan Lake* a thousand times each, and for me the excitement wasn't there any more. Now I wanted to see more of this exciting person, see more of rock. Freddie was so thrilling on that stage. I had no way of knowing what I was letting myself in for. All I thought was that wardrobe for four people couldn't be nearly as bad as running wardrobe for the Royal Ballet Company. Little did I know. I left my permanent job 'with prospects' to take up the six-week contract with Queen, after which I was out of work. I then worked for three months as a telephone operator for British Telecom until Queen went on tour again, and I was invited back. After that I was kept on a retainer when they weren't on the road, because at that point I'd solely been doing wardrobe for tour. When they were not on the road, I'd do bits and pieces in the office. After the American tour, Paul and Freddie decided between them that it would be good if I just looked after Freddie exclusively. I'd still do wardrobe for everybody on tour, but otherwise I was only concerned with him.

Freestone was re-christened 'Phoebe' in time-honoured tradition. One of the first things Freestone discovered was that both he and Freddie had attended boarding schools in India, thousands of miles from their parents, which immediately provided a common bond. He also noticed early on an important aspect of Freddie's character:

He hated confrontation. He was never a rude man. If something started happening towards him, he'd appear to withdraw and let others get involved while he sat back and observed. Then he'd just throw in a line here and there. It's true that he and Mary did squabble a great deal. But that was mainly because he had expectations of people, and if people didn't live up to them, he'd get annoyed. You would tend to learn your lesson. If something happened once, he told you about it, and you'd make sure you didn't do it again. But that didn't stop Mary doing things again and again. Once she'd got something into her head, she would just do it, the best way she saw fit. But if that didn't fit in with Freddie's plans, there would be the big row.

Freestone never ceased to be amazed by Queen's professional excesses:

With each new tour, they had to have that many more lights, that much bigger a sound, a more and more fantastic set. Everything they did had to be never-been-done-before. It was the ultimate show. For that alone they were so exciting. A few years ago at Wembley I saw Michael Jackson in concert two days in a row. And everything was exactly the same the second day as it had been on the first. Not a whiff of variation. But Queen were totally different. You never knew *what* you were going to get. They also had to have the most expensive band meetings ever – actually in the recording studio. Nobody would do that now.

Freestone's duties as Freddie's right-hand man were soon defined:

I'd pack for him. I'd arrange the car to pick him up. I made sure he had money, cards, passport, tickets – in fact, I would hold on to the tickets. I'd get him on the plane. I was always with him, literally at his side, in the next seat on the aircraft. Considering the amount of time we spent in each other's pockets, we got on incredibly well. When we were in Los Angeles, where we lived for a while whilst Queen were recording, other people were always around, which took the pressure off. But when we were in New York, it was just Freddie and me. So many times it was literally just the two of us. The easiest way for me to describe the relationship was that there was a line: there's employer, and there's friend. The dividing part was never static. After a short period of time, I could instantly judge where it was, depending on what was happening, and whether he needed his employee there doing this or that for him, or his friend around to lean on. It had to be like that. That way, he knew he could shout at me – which he frequently did, mainly to work frustrations out. We both knew why, and that was fine. It would never be mentioned again, and Freddie never held grudges against anybody. He'd have his go and that would be it.

Always being at the beck and call of such a demanding master, one wonders whether Freestone was made to feel like a servant. Yet he insists that he never did:

Mainly, I think – and this is a dreadful thing to admit

– because Freddie never treated me in the 'do this, do that' way I used to treat the servants we had in India. He was incredibly nice to me most of the time. While he was paying a salary, all of us who worked for him never had to pay for anything. He never expected anybody to pay for a meal or buy him a drink. If we did buy him a drink he'd be very happy, but it wasn't expected. If he went out to a bar and there were 10 people in the entourage, it would all be on his bill. But he never carried his own money – we carried it. But no, it didn't make me feel awkward.

The way I look at it, I've had one of the luckiest lives going. I have lived Freddie's life without having had the responsibility of having to earn it. I haven't had to create music or face the press. But I have travelled by Concorde endless times, been in the best suites in the best hotels in the world, been shopping for him at auction houses with his signed blank cheques. I have lived and spent at his level. How could I feel like a servant?

Freestone says their close personal relationship that was to last until Freddie's death actually developed quite quickly:

Freddie didn't trust people that easily. He either trusted them within a relatively short time, or never at all. For him to have accepted me in that role was the basis of our friendship, and that happened within the year. We had only one huge falling-out, in about 1989, but it was pretty short-lived. I told him that I'd had enough and that I wanted to go. 'Please don't,' he said. 'I want you here. I *need* you.' That was all I needed to hear. Everything was instantly forgotten and I was there for the duration.

Those of us in his personal group were his family. We did everything for him. I would have done anything for him – and not just because he was paying me. I did what

I did out of respect. Freddie was up there on a pedestal to me. But I didn't do it because I was in awe of him. I did it because I was lucky enough to be a friend. I couldn't do it for anybody else.

Freddie was already enjoying a private life of such lunatic proportions by the time he and Freestone met that many have wondered since how he managed to conduct such a life without being exposed by the press. But, according to Freestone, it was simply a question of keeping himself to himself:

There are certain members of the rock fraternity who will go to the opening of an envelope. And if something isn't happening, they will create something, to keep themselves in the public eye. Freddie went out of his way not to appear in the press. He'd do the odd bits of publicity required of him, but he wouldn't go to any of these big showbiz parties or premières. He very rarely went to other people's gigs. He was a private person. Music was his work. The studio was his office. When he was not in the office, he didn't want to be working.

Freestone insists that he never felt afraid on Freddie's behalf for the lifestyle he was living: 'It was part of the times. This was the early eighties. Anything went.'

Freddie was in high spirits for another reason in October 1979: Queen's 14th single 'Crazy Little Thing Called Love', backed by 'We Will Rock You', was a hit with the press, and made number two on the UK chart. His floaty, long-haired Bohemian image was by this time long gone, and he was now relentlessly into his 'leather' look. Black or red leather pants and macho caps were his preferred stage gear, and his image was much harder and more aggressive. Yet this, too, would soon dilute down, to his final preference in stage wear of plain vest and jeans. Freddie in control, taking a defiant stance, putting on a new image for a new decade. The eighties were fast approaching, and Freddie was well-prepared.

'From now on, dressing up crazily on stage is out,' he remarked. 'I'm going to put our music across dressed more casually. The world has changed. People want something more direct.'4

Queen were now desperately seeking ways to keep the dream alive and maintain their somewhat flagging enthusiasm and energy. As Freddie commented,

> You've got to have nerves of steel to survive the pace. When you have success it becomes really difficult, because then you really learn the things behind the business. You find out the real baddies. Before, you don't know anything about it. You have to be very strong and sift them out. It's like playing rock 'n' roll dodgems. You've got to make sure you don't get hit too often. Anyone who is successful will always be burned once or twice. There's no such thing as a clean escalator to the top.

Queen were also nervous that their massive global success was causing them to lose touch with their fans. They then hit on the idea of shunning vast stadia in favour of smaller venues, some of them totally unsuitable for the antics of a rock 'n' roll band. It was dubbed 'The Crazy Tour' for the downright unsuitability of some of these venues, from Dublin, their first Irish gig, to Birmingham, Manchester, Glasgow, Liverpool (where Freddie wore one red and one blue knee-pad, to satisfy both Everton and Liverpool soccer fans), Brighton and London. The band approached it glee-fully, rolled up their sleeves and got on with the business of enjoying themselves. After the Brighton show, Freddie confessed to a friend that he was partial to 'the odd orgy': 'The night before last we were in Brighton and the road crew had one of their parties. One of Queen's things – we're very good at giving parties, apparently. It was full of naughty women, and everybody jumped in. I'm not going to tell you names but it was very well cast and there were props and goodness knows what flying about all over the place. It was wonderful.'

What he did not confess to was the passionate night he had spent in the arms of a young DHL courier by the name of Tony Bastin, who would soon become Freddie's first live-in boyfriend if not the antidote to his promiscuity. Their on-off affair limped along for two years, but Freddie was never under the illusion that he had met his match. He simply liked the stability of a permanent partner as a basis on which to play the field.

The New Year and a new decade were seen in with Queen's fifteenth single, 'Save Me', rising to number 11 in the British chart as 'Crazy Little Thing Called Love' was taking the rest of the world by storm, hitting number one in America (the first), Australia, New Zealand, Mexico, Canada and Holland. And work began on yet another album, and on the *Flash Gordon* soundtrack, at Musicland in Munich.

Meanwhile, back in England, Freddie's close friend and personal assistant Mary Austin had finally found Freddie the dream home he had always longed for. The endless, arduous search had paid off, as Mary presented Freddie with the details of a house he could not resist. Garden Lodge in Logan Place off Kensington High Street, just a short distance from 12 Stafford Terrace, the flat Freddie was living in at the time, was exactly what he had been looking for. What's more, as Paul Gambaccini pointed out, 'It was mighty convenient that it was within walking distance of all the gay pubs and clubs of Earls Court.'

Unusually for that 'prime real estate' part of London, the beautiful house was set in an acre of mature landscaped gardens and sat hidden behind high brick walls, which gave him almost total privacy. It had formerly belonged to the Hoare banking family. The play on words was not lost on Freddie, who mischievously re-christened it 'The Whore-House'. The asking price was more than half a million pounds, but Freddie was undeterred. He had to have it, and he paid cash. Extensive renovation and conversion was required before it was fit for Freddie to live in, however, and it would be a long time before Garden Lodge was the place Freddie called home.

Freddie talked proudly about his new mansion to Rick Sky in his *Daily Star* interview, and revealed that spending was one of his major vices: 'I don't believe in putting money in the bank,' Freddie said.

I like to spend, spend, spend. Recently I bought a new house. And I love buying antiques at Sotheby's and Christie's. Sometimes I could go to Cartier's the jewellers and buy up the whole shop. Often my sprees begin just like a woman buying herself a new hat to cheer herself up. Some days, when I'm really fed-up, I just want to lose myself in my money. I work up a storm and just spend and spend. Then I get back home and think, 'Oh, God, what have I bought?' But it's never a waste. I get an awful lot of pleasure out of giving presents.

To Ray Coleman in an interview for the *Daily Mirror* he said: 'I don't like life too easy. If I keep spending a lot then I'll have to keep earning it. That's how I push myself. I drink a lot, smoke a lot, enjoy my wines and good food. And I will never again eat hamburgers.'

And in a conversation with the former pop writer Nina Myskow, he confided:

I saw the house, fell in love with it, and within half an hour it was mine. It's in a terrible state at the moment with all the changes I'm having made. I won't be able to move in for about a year. I call it my country house in town. It's very secluded, with huge grounds, right in the middle of London. Once a month I get inspired and go there with the architect. 'Why don't we have this wall removed?' I ask. Everybody groans and the architect dies. I went in there sloshed the other day after a good lunch. There's a wonderful bedroom area at the top – I'm having three knocked into one palatial suite. In this sort of haze I said, inspired, 'What would be nice is a glass dome over the top of all this bedroom area.' The architect flinched, but went rushing back to his pen and drawing pad. I haven't seen the sketches yet, but they're on the way.

With his house, as with most things in life, Freddie was constantly looking for new ways to make it more exciting. To be bored, it seemed, was the thing that terrified him most:

Boredom is the biggest disease in the whole world. Sometimes I think there must be more to life than rushing around the world like a mad thing, getting bored. But I can't sit still for long. I've got all this nervous energy.

You become accustomed to different things. Your standards and your expectations become higher. If you know you need constant entertainment, you make sure you have it. When I tell people what I've been up to, they're amazed. But that's all I know. It's my way of having fun. That's why I can't sit down and read a book. I can read all the books in the world when it's all over and my legs are in bandages. I may be just being greedy, but I'm an entertainer. It's in the blood . . . I am just a trouper, dear. Give me a stage.

But in a way you've created a monster. And you're the one who has to live with it.

Queen's 16th single 'Play The Game' came out in May.

Female fans were outraged by the change of image Freddie flaunted in the video, complete with nail-brush moustache. In spite of the protests, the single still hit number 14.

Summer 1980 saw another American tour, this time a 46-date epic with every performance a sell-out. Queen's ninth album, 'The Game', was released in Britain at the same time. Slated by the music press, it entered the chart at number one. In Vancouver, the fans had stopped throwing flowers and underwear at their idol and had started lobbing razor blades and disposable razors, which left Freddie in no doubt as to what they thought of the moustache. He remained unrepentant, and the moustache stayed on his face. The 'Another One Bites The Dust' single was released in America in August, soared to number one where it stayed for five weeks, and proved an enormous hit right across the States. It also made number one in Argentina, Guatemala, Mexico and Spain. In the UK it went Top Ten at number seven. 'The Game', meanwhile, became Queen's first number one album in America, and sales of both exceeded all expectations. This tour had them playing four nights at New York's Madison Square Garden, at the end of their longest tour ever.

Queen's relentless schedule was all but wiping them out. They did take a holiday, but October alone was not long enough to relax. There was still the *Flash Gordon* soundtrack, their tenth album, to complete, and 'Flash' their 18th single, to release. Another European tour to prepare for, including three nights at Wembley Arena, all before Christmas. Like everybody else, Queen were completely unprepared for the news that John Lennon had been murdered in New York on the sidewalk outside his home, the Dakota Building. Not only did the band mourn the loss of a great rock hero, but they were now forced to take stock of their own vulnerability as celebrities, an issue they had hitherto never really addressed. The stark fact was that the same thing could happen to any of them at any time. They were virtual sitting targets. Queen were now forced to re-evaluate their own security arrangements and staff. Never again could they afford to be relaxed or blasé, and from that day on they would always be looking over their shoulder. As a tribute to Lennon at the second Wembley show, Queen performed 'Imagine'. The fact that Freddie forgot the lyrics and Brian lost track of the chords didn't matter to their weeping and devastated audience.

Still the awards continued to flood in, including two Grammy nominations, for best-produced album ('The Game') and best performance by a group ('Another One Bites The Dust'). 'Crazy Little Thing Called Love' and 'Another One Bites The Dust' both featured in the top five best selling American singles of 1980, the latter having sold more than three and a half million copies. As the year drew to a close, and Queen were planning their New Year dates in Japan, including five sell-out nights at the Tokyo Budokan and the Japanese première of *Flash Gordon*, it was calculated that they had to date sold more than 45 million albums and 25 million singles around the world. Queen also made their début appearance, as highest-paid company directors and their own primary asset, in the *Guinness Book Of Records*. Where on earth could they go from here?

Chapter Fourteen

QUEEN OF THE SOUTH

For Queen 1981 began well, and promised even more. Having made the decision that they would always strive to explore new avenues, they still had an eye on the atlas with a view to further killings around the globe. What about South America? Queen were currently the most popular rock band on that continent, and false rumours that they were coming down to play there had been doing the rounds for years. A few rock performers had previously ventured that far south, but never memorably, and never on the massive scale that Queen had in mind. If it could be done to their usual grand standards, in the finest football stadia of Argentina and Brazil, Queen could not wait to sign the contract. Neither country was short of such venues, thanks to the immense popularity of soccer: South American nations had at that point won six out of the 11 World Cup championships held since 1930. Local promoters were hired to negotiate deals, and fixtures were agreed: in Argentina at the Velez Sarsfield, Buenos Aires; Mar del Plata's municipal stadium; and the athletic stadium in Rosario.

As Brian once said to me, 'A Queen audience is a football crowd which doesn't take sides.'

Freddie, now in his 35th year – 'I'm the oldest in the

group, but only by one year' – proceeded to New York to finalize the purchase of his apartment. $1,000-a-day hotel suites were proving extravagant to a guest like Freddie, who might stay up to three months at a time. The magnificent balconied apartment, at 425 East 58th Street on the 43rd floor, boasted incredible north-south views of the East River and seven bridges.

'I remember how excited Freddie got during the New York celebrations for the 100th anniversary of the Brooklyn Bridge, which we watched simultaneously from his balcony and on the television,' Peter Freestone recalled. 'The apartment had belonged to a senator or congressman called Gray, and Freddie had bought it from his widow. And the whole place was decorated in grey: four bedrooms, five bathrooms and the den, all covered in grey material of the kind used to make men's suits. The dining-room walls were lined with silvery satin. Strangely Freddie, one of whose great passions was redesigning and redecorating his properties, left it exactly as it was.'

Meanwhile, 40 tons of equipment, rigging, lighting and sound, was being shipped from the US to Rio de Janeiro. The Queen road crew plus some 20 tons more equipment set off on the world's longest city-to-city flight from Tokyo to Buenos Aires.

When the band themselves landed in the searing summer heat of Buenos Aires on 24 February 1981, they realized for the first time what a 'heroes' welcome' was all about. Queen had known hysterical adulation in their time, but never anything like this. Since the announcement of their imminent arrival in Argentina, which was officially recognized by the government, the media had gone Queen-crazy and fans had been flooding into Buenos Aires in their tens of thousands. All of them, it appeared, had converged on the airport that day. There to meet them from the aircraft was a presidential delegation and a police escort, and the proceedings were covered live on national television. For once, even Freddie was speechless.

According to radio journalist Marcela Delorenzi, then a 15-year-old Queen fan who later adopted the professional broadcasting name Daisy May Queen in honour of the band:

This was the first big rock event ever in our country. It caused an unbelievable revolution across the land. In the press and on radio and TV, 24 hours a day for the month before they arrived, people talked about nothing but Queen. And in the wake of their tour, all our own rock artists were forced to change their image and adopt a completely new approach. All their equipment, sound, lighting, every aspect of the live performance had to be improved and upgraded. Suddenly, everything that had passed as acceptable before suddenly seemed pathetic when compared to Queen. This, in Argentina, was like the rock version of BC (Before Christ). From then on it was all Before Queen, and After Queen. Their effect on South America was profound. Hordes of people from Chile, Uraguay, Paraguay and Bolivia crossed the borders to see the Argentina shows. The Buenos Aires dates are engraved on my memory: 28 February, 1 March and 9 March. They also played Mar del Plata and Rosario.[1]

It was on that trip that Marcela met her idol Freddie Mercury for the first time, an experience which she tearfully explains changed her life:

He was staying at the Sheraton Hotel in Buenos Aires. I was there with a lot of other Queen fans, waiting for the band. They had to go to a press conference at the stadium which was to be televised on Channel Nine. There was a huge crowd waiting outside to see Freddie, screaming and chanting like it was the end of the world.

I remember that day as if it were yesterday, for this reason: I was dressed entirely in pale blue. And it was a great surprise, when the lift door opened in the hotel lobby, to see that Freddie was dressed from head to toe in exactly the same colour also. He was surrounded by bodyguards, but I felt this incredible urge to break through the people surrounding him and to hug him. I smashed through the circle and I did hug him, and I gave him a letter, saying that I'd like to meet 'Frederick Bulsara' (not Mercury) and put my address and telephone number, never really expecting him to call of course. I referred to him by his original name because I always regarded Freddie as having two sides: the good and the bad, the white and the black. Freddie Bulsara was the good, the white side. I felt even in those days that he was actually afraid of Freddie Bulsara. It would not be until years later that I discovered that I wasn't so wrong. Then one of the bodyguards hit me, and they pushed me away. I could not blame them for being anxious in case somebody intended to wound Freddie, but obviously I meant him no harm. I just had to touch him. I imagine there were millions around the world who felt exactly like me. The band left the hotel and got straight into their car to be driven away. Only Brian hung behind to sign autographs, and they had to throw him in the back of the car in the end. As they drove away, I watched Freddie open and read my letter, and I was so elated.

At the Velez Sarsfield stadium the fans queued from eight a.m. for all three shows, even though the performance, to some 50,000 fans each night, was not due to start until 10 p.m.

'Their show was an amazing spectacle,' recalls Marcela, who attended two of the Buenos Aires gigs.

Argentina had never seen anything like it. At the beginning they had something like a UFO descending on to the stage, amazing lights, smoke – it was like magic. Everyone had goose-pimples, and people were crying, literally sobbing, all around. The pitch was protected with Astroturf, and the security was extremely tight, police everywhere, mainly because we had such a strict, extreme right wing military government at that time, led by General Viola. The General said that he wanted to meet Queen, and sent an invitation for them to visit him. The whole band went except Roger, who objected, saying that he was in Argentina to play for the people, not for the government.

When Queen came to Argentina in 1981, our country was still very oppressed. But within two years of their first visit, we achieved democracy for the first time in nearly 15 years. A similar thing happened in Brazil. And shortly after they played in Hungary in 1986, the old regime was abandoned and Hungarians had a new democratic future to look forward to. Queen also went down to Sun City in South Africa on a highly controversial visit, and within a couple of years, Apartheid fell and the people had democracy. This is all probably coincidence, but it's a really amazing thing: wherever Queen went, it was as if they were bringing freedom and peace to the people. It was as if they were the band of Liberty.

Freddie looked particularly muscular in tight jeans and white vest with a scarf threaded through his belt loops, his thick moustache appearing to disguise his protruding teeth. It was a stage image that was barely to change until Queen retired from the live circuit, five years before Freddie's death. Pumping with energy, he conducted the audience with enthusiastic 'Yeahs', 'All Rights' and 'Okays', and told the crowds 'Cantan muy bien' (You sing very well). 'Love Of My Life' transformed the audience into a sea of swaying flames as a tearful, word-perfect crowd joined in the song. And Freddie arranged himself at the piano at one point to introduce another big favourite song: 'This is sometimes known as "Bo Rap".'

The band launched into 'Bohemian Rhapsody', leaving the stage during the backing track of the choral sequences – that was one part which could never be performed live.

One of a number of interviews Freddie gave in Buenos Aires was to *Pelo* (*Hair*), a music magazine with a massive circulation, and the Argentinian equivalent of *Rolling Stone*. Asked why he appeared always to be apart from the rest of the group, Freddie responded: 'As Queen play and record together, people see us as having a super-unit image. But Queen is a musical group, not a family. Each one of us does whatever we like.'

What were his expectations of this tour?

'I knew a lot about Argentina, but I never imagined that we were so well-known here. I am amazed by the nation's reaction to our being here . . . We had long wanted to do a big South American tour. The idea had been in our minds for a long time. But for the past six months we have been working hard, non-stop really. Queen is not just the band – it involves a vast number of people. And therefore it costs a lot of money for us to tour.'

What about the price of fame, and of having problems with the press? By this time, Freddie understood completely the value of the soundbite: 'It bothered me for a long time. But, as you can see, not anymore.'

To the now defunct Radiolanda 2000 he said:

I love the Argentinian people. I was accustomed to another kind of reaction and behaviour from audiences. But Argentinians are amazing, and I want to come back. I must admit I love it that people think I'm an idol. I do want to be a legend, but you must understand that our work is a joint effort. Queen is not just Freddie Mercury, it's the band. You just have to remember

'Seven Seas Of Rhye', 'Killer Queen', 'You're My Best Friend', 'Somebody To Love', 'Bohemian Rhapsody' – which actually was the most satisfying moment of my career. This was all Queen, not Freddie. I think the best proof of our respect for the audience is our work.

To avoid the possibility of kidnapping or terrorism, security on the tour was its tightest yet. Among the personal bodyguards was Jorge Fregonese, hired to take care of Freddie around the clock. Fregonese had landed this covetable appointment through his influential employer, businessman Alfredo Capalbo, who had organized Queen's Argentinian tour. He was a trusted employee whose previous responsibilities had included taking care of Capalbo's horses. This was his first experience of working as a translator-bodyguard, and he was keen to do the job well. But at first he had misgivings, as things did not get off to a good start. Fregonese tells how his first day among the Queen entourage was an unmitigated disaster:

No one knew each other at all. Each of us tried to do our best, but as the English bodyguards didn't know the Argentinian bodyguards, they tended to quarrel among themselves instead of getting on with the work of not letting people near the band.

I think that first day, my relationship with Freddie was very cold – mainly because we had not been formally introduced. The next couple of days were taken up with press conferences, interviews and so on, and we couldn't get time to know each other. So one day, I simply interrupted a conversation between him and his secretary, and I introduced myself. Things were by now beginning to soften between the English and Argentinian bodyguards. We had a meeting to organize ourselves, security and translators, and everyone started to relax and gain confidence.[2]

Fregonese remembers a distinct divide between Freddie and the band management – Jim Beach, Paul Prenter – in one camp, and the rest of the band in the other:

> Offstage, they lived completely separate lives, which I had not expected. But of course they were four people, four separate personalities. I had no real contact with the rest of the band; I only saw them at the stadium, at a press conference or at a dinner. I wasn't concerned by that: my job was to know where Freddie was and where he was going to be, at what time and at all times, which was necessary for security reasons. The other guys' security people knew the same about them, and we'd all know how to get hold of each other, in case anything strange or dangerous occurred. Meetings were being held all the time, and plans often changed. When they did, the managers let me know the new rules, and it was my job to inform the rest, including Gerry Stickells, who was in charge of the stage crew, and Mr Capalbo.

Part of Fregonese's brief was to control the fans who clamoured for Freddie's autograph:

> He never really commented on the fans. He just told me that he got bothered if there were a lot at one time. If there were just a few, he didn't mind. I'd have to ask him if he wanted to sign autographs, and if there were more than six people he would always say no, and I'd just have to get him through the crowd. Sometimes, while he was signing autographs, he would stare hard at me, and I knew the signal: it was 'That's it, enough.' So then I'd give the order and get him out of there fast.

On one occasion, Jorge and Freddie were taking tea together in the hotel bar when Jorge picked up a pen and piece of paper and began to doodle. Without realizing what he was doing, he started to scribble something he had seen his charge write a thousand times: the signature 'Freddie Mercury'. Freddie suddenly noticed, and seized the piece of paper in amazement. Far from being angry, Freddie laughed uproariously and told Jorge that he thought the forgery was just perfect. From then on, despite his initial refusal, Jorge was roped in to help with the autographs whenever fans left anything for Freddie to sign: 'Freddie wasn't going to take no for an answer. You could say that he made me do it.'

A favourite hobby of Freddie's was pushing all the hotel lift buttons at once: 'We always arrived late everywhere because the doors would open on every floor. But Freddie did not care. He found this enormous fun, he was like a small boy having mischief. And, as he waited for lifts to arrive, he would spend the time doing press-ups on the carpet, or organizing running races the length of the hotel corridors.'

Once, Fregonese recalls, Freddie forbade all the limousine drivers to smoke because he said it was bad for the health. Taking it to mean that he was worried about the condition of his own throat, the chauffeurs immediately complied. 'Imagine their surprise when Freddie got into the car and lit up a cigarette himself. "It's for the good of *their* health, not mine!" he'd retort with a great laugh. Not that Freddie smoked all that much. He liked just a few, and menthol cigarettes in particular, because he had convinced himself that the menthol was good for his throat. This was something of an ongoing problem, because menthol cigarettes are not at all easy to get hold of in Argentina.'

One unbearably hot night, Fregonese escorted Freddie to a post-performance dinner at an exclusive restaurant in Buenos Aires called *Los Años Locos* (The Mad Years):

I used to say that I couldn't let Freddie alone anywhere, not even to go to the bathroom. I accompanied him into public toilets every time he had to go. He did not like that situation at all, and seemed very uncomfortable about it. It was as if it was the ultimate invasion of his privacy, and I could understand what he meant. I wouldn't like to have a bodyguard leaning over me every time I had to pee. But that is part of the price of fame, and Freddie resigned himself to it.

But that night, at *Los Años Locos*, he made a stand and insisted on going to the bathroom alone. As we were on the second floor of the restaurant, and the men's room was very close to our table, I thought I had a clear enough view and would notice if anyone tried to sneak into the toilet while Freddie was still inside. So, for the first time on the tour, I let him go. The rest of us went on chatting and eating, and the minutes ticked by. Freddie was still in the toilet, and I soon realized that something must have gone wrong. So I asked another bodyguard to come with me into the men's room.

When we got there, we found two men and two women banging on one of the cubicle doors, which appeared to be locked from the inside. We could only assume that Freddie was in there. These people were terrorizing him, shouting and screaming at Freddie to open the door, open the door, they had to see him, they must have autographs. Freddie was not responding, and I could now see clearly that he had locked himself in. At that point I got frightened because I feared something must have happened to him. We yelled at these people to get away, to get out. When things had calmed down a little and Freddie realized it was us, he opened the door with a white face. He seemed terrified. He looked at me and said, 'Jorge, you were right. I can't even go to the bathroom alone, can I?' And from that evening on, we reverted to our old routine.

On the Saturday night preceding Queen's final date at Velez Sarsfield on Sunday, Queen were invited to a celebratory

'Asado' – a cross between a barbecue and a 'roasting', at the 'quinta' (weekend retreat) of Señor Petraca, president of the stadium. The estate was huge and very beautiful and Queen fell in love with the place immediately. Recalls Fregonese,

> There we all were enjoying ourselves when, as usual, the press appeared. Freddie was not at all fond of press. He did not object to the journalists themselves, it was just the unimaginative questions they asked him that he found so tiresome. He'd say, 'They've been asking me the same stupid questions for the past 10 years. Queen knew very well, then as now, that they didn't actually need the press to sell records and tickets; they managed that very well by themselves. But they were always polite, and went through the motions anyway.

On this occasion, however, Freddie seemed determined to make mischief:

> Two journalists were present that night, one, again, from *Pelo* magazine. This guy could not understand a word of English. So it fell to me to act as interpreter, which was part of my job anyway so I didn't mind. But Freddie and I had cooked up a little deal. I would translate the question for Freddie, who was playing pinball very enthusiastically at the time – just so that he would know what he was being asked – and then, while Freddie rattled on about anything at all, I replied to the journalist whatever came into my head. The questions, as usual, were incredibly dumb, so the guy got what he deserved. When I got the magazine the following week, I saw the answers were all my fictitious ones, except one, about Diego Maradona.

A sensitive subject. Argentina had been world football champions since claiming the trophy for the first time in

1978, on home turf. Soccer was sacred. The young star who would have a hand in shattering England's hopes of World Cup glory in the quarter final of the 1986 championship was already little short of a national god. Queen had long admired Maradona: as Brian once remarked, 'The spirit of the pursuit of excellence lives in the man.' Maradona and Freddie had met at a party in Castelar, where Freddie put to him the idea of appearing on stage with Queen during the last Buenos Aires show. It was an exciting proposition to which Maradona readily agreed.

'Freddie hadn't really known who Maradona was, as he was not what you could call a football fan,' laughs Peter Freestone. 'Footballers' thighs, maybe. Rugby thighs, even better.'

Nevertheless, Freddie could not help but he amused by the cheeky young footballer. To a certain extent, he could also identify with him. On the surface, it seemed, they had little in common, except perhaps a cast-iron crotch, limited height and a hunger for success. Maradona duly appeared on stage with Queen to ecstatic applause, where he and Freddie exchanged tops: Maradona peeling off and swapping the Number 10 Argentinian international team shirt he was wearing for Freddie's T-shirt of 'Flash'. He then introduced 'Another One Bites The Dust', and left the stage as Queen tore into one of Argentina's all-time most popular hit records. Perhaps the *Pelo* journalist was not so stupid. He started quizzing Freddie that night at the Asado on the subject of Argentina's greatest sporting idol, and his questions were provocative to say the least. He put it to Freddie that the shirt-exchange with the soccer star on stage in front of the Velez audience had been a 'demagogic' act. Freddie was incensed by the implication.

'Freddie told the journalist he thought his question was ridiculous,' Fregonese reports. 'He said, "It was a friendly gesture, nothing more. If the audience thinks it's okay to do such a thing, and appreciates it for what it is, I don't give a damn what the press might think. I'm going to do what I like, regardless of whether the press label it demagogic or wrong."'

Fregonese's working relationship with Freddie was relatively calm. The bodyguard agreed that Freddie was not particularly demanding by celebrity standards, and had no strange habits to speak of.

Off-stage, he behaved like any other person with one fundamental difference: that he was constantly having to deal with being followed and harassed. He was forced to spend too much time hiding and running away, and that is going to affect anyone. He was immediately recognized everywhere he went, and he could never have peace and quiet, not for a moment.

As for his personal habits, he ate very little. He liked to have tea, but his dinners were quite frugal. He was not what you could call a hearty eater. Nevertheless, satisfying his eating requirements was a complicated business, because he wanted to go to a different type of restaurant every night. We ate Italian food, French food, Argentinian food, you name it. He slept a lot, and never, ever left his hotel room before one or two p.m. so nothing could be scheduled before then. He had fancy shopping habits, and he obviously liked to buy his clothes himself. On one occasion he bought 25 pairs of socks, 10 identical T-shirts, 20 pairs of similar trousers . . . when I asked him why, he told me that, when he was a teenager, he had never had the opportunity to be a kid and wear whatever fashionable stuff he wanted; that this was his way of catching up.

Apart from all that, Freddie was a simple man. He would occasionally like to go for a drive and look around the city. And now and then he would have a childish turn, such as the day we visited the Japanese Garden in Buenos Aires. One afternoon, we paid a visit to the lovely garden, which is situated in the main city park. It has a little nursery, and you can walk along the pathways and over the bridges. Freddie thought it was enchanting, and took a lot of photos there, saying that he wanted to create a similar garden at his home in London. At one point, despite the fact that it was prohibited, he clambered to the top of a waterfall to take a picture, and one of the Japanese guards saw him, blew his whistle furiously, and ordered Freddie down. I had to rush over to the guard, explain who Freddie was, and managed to persuade the guard to let him stay up there and take the photos. Freddie would only come down when he was ready. He fed the Koi carp, and said he was delighted with the place. In the little nursery where you could buy food for the carp and so on, he graciously left two autographs in the visitors' book.

But he could never really enjoy his time off. It was always spoiled by him being recognized everywhere he tried to go. Sometimes we would literally have to run out of a place as fast as we could, because someone had recognized him and almost immediately a massive crowd had started to build up around him.

Fregonese and Freddie grew quite close during their time together in Argentina, and towards the end of the tour, each had started to fret about their 'last day'.

We both admitted to each other that neither of us liked farewells. We had a really nice relationship by then, one of those strange close friendships that blossoms in 20 days. People tend to believe that a friendship requires years to mature and be worth anything, but sometimes, in a few days with the right person, you can achieve something that you might never reach over 20 years with someone else. We could discuss things like how we would say goodbye, but we never actually resolved that one. He had given me a couple of presents, though: his cap, and a photograph of him, signed 'To Jorge, A Million Thanks, Freddie'.

It was one Freddie Mercury autograph that Fregonese had not had to sign himself.

When our car drew up at the airport, I got out, went straight to the check-in desk of Aerolineas Argentinas, and informed them that Freddie Mercury was there. They confirmed the reservation of the VIP lounge, and three seats in First Class. I went back to the car and told Freddie that everything was arranged, took everyone's passports back to the check-in desk, and an assistant escorted them off to the VIP lounge. When I noticed that Freddie was about to disappear into the lounge, I simply said 'Bye. See you,' and shook his hand. 'Goodbye. Ciao,' was all he said, and that was it – the end.

Months later, out of the blue, I received a post-card from him, quite casual, which simply said 'Jorge, how are you? I'm fine. Best regards, Freddie Mercury.' Nothing more. But I had no regrets about our time together. I feel enriched for having known him. He was one of the biggest stars in the world, but he came across as a simple and mostly undemanding person. He had been around the block and back, and now he just wanted to live. I got the impression that he had grown a little tired of his artistic side. I had known other artists who were stars offstage as well as on – they acted like celebrities all the time. But that was not Freddie. On stage he was this amazing, electric machine, it took your breath away to look at him. But off it he was completely different. People always seemed surprised by that. He was a completely day-and-night character. The show might be over, but as far as he was concerned, the star could stay right there, on that stage. The Freddie who made off for the dressing-room afterwards was just this humble ordinary guy.

I always felt that he was such a good person. To borrow his own definition of himself, he was a grown man now enjoying the life he had never been able to enjoy as a child. He had reached a stage where he could have whatever he wanted. I want it all? At times, to me, it was as if he was making himself want things, even when he didn't really want them at all.

Queen's elation at their historic rock triumph over Argentina was somewhat deflated by the news, mid-tour, that their ambition to perform at Rio de Janeiro's fabled Maracana stadium, which, with a capacity of 180,000, is the biggest in the world, had been dashed by red tape. The technical, legal and political difficulties encountered in Brazil could hardly be understimated, but the show would go on. They settled for the Morumbi stadium in São Paolo further south, where, on 20 March 1981, they would play for 131,000 people, recorded as the largest paying audience for one act anywhere in the world to date. The following night, another 120,000 would turn out to take part in the magic, hemmed in by riot police on skittish horses while armed plain-clothes policewomen moved among the completely over-awed throng, most of whom had never seen anything like this before in their lives. Again, in a city where few spoke English, the sight of over 100,000 people joining the band to sing word for word 'Love Of My Life', Queen's anthem in South America, was spectacularly moving.

The massive success of the South American tour was nothing if not a personal triumph for business manager Jim Beach, who had talked himself dry over the five months that it took to convince authorities in both countries that everyone would benefit from Queen's pioneering rock adventure.

In seven concerts Queen have been seen by over half a

million people who were totally unfamiliar with rock concerts,' Beach said in Brazil in 1981.

The actual costs of appearing down here are so enormous that the profit margin for the band is quite small. But the promotion is marvellous. During our last week in Argentina, every one of Queen's 10 albums filled the top 10 positions in the charts. Before we came, everyone said that no group could play successfully in South America, but we have proved that they can. In Brazil, 50 per cent of the population is under the age of 21, which is a massive potential audience.

Added Brian, 'We had no idea how they were going to react to us. In Europe and America we know what to expect, but for these fans down here it was a completely new phenomenon. In Argentina, where they are relatively more sophisticated, they did have some idea of what to expect, but for the Brazilian fans everything was totally new. One of the most exciting moments in my life was when I looked out and saw 130,000 people waiting for us.'

Many Queen critics had posed the provocative question as to whether the band had a moral obligation to shun performances in such countries as Argentina and Brazil. It was argued that Queen might be accused of supporting their political regimes in so doing. But Jim Beach was unrepentant: 'If we took that attitude then there would be very few countries in the world outside Western Europe and North America where we would ever be able to play at all.'

Chapter Fifteen

BAVARIAN RHAPSODY: MY FUNNY VALENTIN

I hate mixing with lots of showbusiness personalities. I could do a Rod Stewart and join that crowd, but I want to stay out of all that. When I am not in Queen I want to be the ordinary man in the street. I've changed. In the early days I used to enjoy being recognized. Not now. I spend a lot of time in New York where a lot of people don't know me. I may be very rich, but the days of posing and pretending to have money have long gone. I'm a jeans-and-T-shirt man around the house and everywhere else. I don't put a show on anymore when I leave the stage, because I'm secure in my own knowledge of who I am and what I have. Gone are the days when I wanted to walk into a room and stop everyone's conversation. I can't predict whether we will go on, but as long as we keep breaking new ground, the fire will remain in Queen. And if I lost everything I had tomorrow, I'd claw my way back to the top somehow.[1]

Thus spake the retired peacock towards the end of 1981. Perhaps his most honest publicly-spoken words to date, that statement was confirmation from Freddie himself that his metamorphosis was more or less complete. The world could think what it liked. The multi-millionaire rock-star was finally comfortable in his own skin, and at home with what he recognized to be his true personality. He had recently celebrated his 35th birthday in inimitable style at an estimated cost of £200,000, by flying a posse of favoured pals including actor Peter Straker on Concorde to New York's Berkshire Place Hotel on East 52nd Street, on the corner diagonally opposite to Cartier, where he temporarily occupied a lavish suite. Some £30,000-worth of vintage champagne was swallowed, and the gang partied on for five drunken days. By the end of it, Freddie was so wiped out that he was forced to fly home to London to recuperate.

'I remember the absolute mess that our suite got into,' Peter Freestone recalls with a grimace. 'And I remember Freddie sprawled out on a huge heap of gladioli. Those were what you could call "parties". Queen knew how to throw them better than anybody.'

As well as yet another amazing if hazardous South American tour, this time taking in Venezuela and Mexico, 1981, Queen's official 10th anniversary year had also seen the release of their 11th album, the lukewarm 'Hot Space', which included the single 'Under Pressure', Queen's famed collaboration with Montreux neighbour David Bowie.

'He'd often come over to see us, to chat and have a drink,' explained Brian. 'Someone suggested that we should all go into the studio and play around one night, to see what came out – which we did, playing each other's old songs and just fiddling around. The next night we listened to the tapes, because we'd left the tape recorder running, and picked out a couple of pieces which seemed to be promising, and then we just worked on one particular idea, which became "Under Pressure", for a whole night. An extremely long night.'[2]

Years later it was rumoured that Bowie himself had hated the number one record, believing it to have been not up to his usual standards. He allegedly remarked that he wished it had never been released.

In 1981 the *New York Times* reported the phenomenon of a rare form of skin cancer among some 41 previously healthy homosexuals. At least nine of them, according to the New York University Medical Center, suffered an unexplained lowering of the immune system. Kaposi's sarcoma had, until now, occurred more commonly in elderly men of Mediterranean descent. Other cases were reported in San Francisco and Los Angeles. The *New York Times* report was published on 3 July. By the end of August, according to the city's gay newspaper the *New York Native*, the number had risen to 120, most of them in New York. Shortly afterwards, it was confirmed by the Atlanta Center for Disease Control that cases of Kaposi's sarcoma, as well as a rare parasitical form of pneumonia known as pneumocystis carinii pneumonia (PCP), were inexplicably on the rise across America. Of all reported diagnoses, more than 90 per cent related to gay men. Thus began highly controversial speculation that a new 'gay plague' might be linked to a promiscuous homosexual lifestyle, and/or to drug abuse. It would be some time before investigation provided conclusive evidence that the new disease, originally referred to as GRID (Gay-Related Immune Deficiency), also affected millions of heterosexual men, women and their children, notably occurring in haemophiliacs and intravenous drug-users. It was finally established that the disease now referred to by the medical profession as AIDS – Acquired Immune Deficiency Syndrome – was spread via blood or blood products, the sharing of hypodermic needles, and through unprotected sex.

Meanwhile, commemorative 10th anniversary Queen products were being released: the 'Greatest Hits' album; a collection of all their promo videos, 'Greatest Flix'; and portraits of the band by Princess Margaret's former husband Lord Snowdon. Queen also starred in their own first feature film of a live concert, filmed in Montreal. The final weeks of 1981 saw Queen's return to Munich, as they were still officially tax exiles, where production was to begin on yet another album.

It was also, for Freddie, the beginning of a frantic episode in which he would become embroiled in no fewer than three quite desperate love affairs. Two of these lovers were men. The first, Winnie Kirchberger, was a bluff, uneducated Austrian restaurateur, so rough and ready that few of Freddie's personal entourage could fathom the attraction. This, though, was how Freddie had come to like his men: the more they resembled unwashed truck-drivers the better. The second, Irish hairdresser Jim Hutton, was picked up by Freddie in London, regularly flown out to Munich and paraded like a puppet to make Winnie jealous and consequently more devoted. Ironically, a much deeper bond was to develop between Jim and Freddie, and it was Jim who would remain Freddie's faithful companion for life. The third lover in this equation was female: but the sensation did not end there. German filmstar Barbara Valentin could never be described as 'just another woman'. With the famous former soft-porn actress as his almost constant companion and latterly live-in partner in crime, Freddie's life in Munich would never be the same again.

Although it has been recorded that Freddie made his home at the Arabella-Haus Hotel, Peter Freestone says:

Freddie stayed there only for a night or two, because he hated it so much. It was above Musicland studios, and was yet another dreadful concrete block. Most of the rooms there were on a long-term let, and it had a rather large Arab contingent. At night, the corridors were filled with the pungent smells of their cooking. It wasn't a very comfortable place to live. At first, Freddie spent quite a lot of time living with Winnie Kirchberger at his place. Later on, he settled at the Stollbergplaza apartment hotel on Stollbergstrasse in a more elegant part of central Munich. Barbara Valentin lived just across the street – she had a fabulous apartment. Paul Prenter used to come out every now and then, and Joe didn't come out until '84, '85. Most of the time it was just Freddie and me.

With his loyal personal assistant to see to his whims and fancies and accompany him on his escapades and nightly prowls, Freddie's lifestyle in the German city seemed charmed. Worryingly for the others members of the band, however, he appeared to have lost the taste for work.

'Possibly Fred was then getting interested in other things and a bit bored with being in the studio . . . he got to the point where he could hardly stand being in a studio, and he'd want to do his bit and get out,' Brian comments.

The main reason for this was that he had developed an insatiable taste for Munich's frenetic nightlife and naughty, glamorous cast of thousands. It was always bound to replace as his primary passion, if only temporarily, the routine business of rock.

'It was all a crazy time, far better and worse than anyone could ever imagine,' said Barbara Valentin when I visited her in Munich in May 1996, where she still lives in the comfortable apartment she and Freddie purchased together, on HansSachs Strasse in the increasingly seedy Bermuda Triangle district, and for which she had to endure a lengthy legal battle to keep after Freddie's death. She had proved a reluctant interviewee, and it took several months to persuade her to see me: 'You have to be careful what you say about someone, and about your life together, after they have died,' she explained.

Because other people have to live on, you know? I don't want to hurt anybody by talking about Freddie. Let Mary Austin be the widow, I have always said. It's fine by me. I don't want to take from her. I have been offered fortunes over the years since he died to write a book about our relationship, but I have always said no until now. It's important to me that, if I talk about Freddie, you tell our story in a sensitive and caring way. Because after he died, so many people claimed to have been best friends with him, so many people claimed to have been in bed with him, so many people wanted to get on the bandwagon.

Barbara Valentin retains the allure well into her 50s that Freddie was entranced by all those years ago. Austrian by birth and a one-time baroness, everything about her is big and impossible to ignore: the breasts, the bones, the blonde hair, the voice, the presence. The one-carat diamond stud in her right earlobe was the first present Freddie ever gave her. A short walk with her along the street – she strolls slowly and serenely, with her nose held high – is enough to see how she still turns heads. Dozens of people stop to speak to her. Everybody knows who she is, especially along HansSachs Strasse, a trendy little street with its barbershops and drugstores, bars, saunas and jewellery studios, exotic florists, B-movie cinema, and Parisian-style street cafés with marble-top tables, umbrellas and cane chairs. Once a soft-porn model and actress with all the requisite assets, Valentin's career soared in the seventies when she was chosen as the muse of cult German film director Rainer Werner Fassbinder, who died in 1982. Fassbinder was noted for his enormous productivity (over 30 films) all stylized pieces about love, hate and prejudice, such as the acclaimed 1974 movie *Angst essen Seele auf* (*Fear Eats The Soul*). In all, thrice-married Valentin herself starred in some 70 films, and has been described as 'the German Brigitte Bardot'. What Freddie saw was a strong, determined female in charge of her own destiny. Barbara Valentin could not have been less like Mary Austin had she tried. He was attracted by the larger-than-life image which concealed an intense sensitivity and fragility within. In fact, Barbara's image reminded Freddie in many ways of himself. What you see is not necessarily what you get. Perhaps for the first time in his life, Freddie had connected with another human being with whom he was able to be himself – utterly and completely, on every level, no holds barred. There was nothing about Freddie Mercury, his life and times, that he felt afraid to reveal to this woman. There was no need to protect Barbara from aspects of his personality and behaviour the way he had felt obliged to do with Mary. Barbara understood – she was exactly the same herself. She went her own way, and she had never cared what people thought. Who are others to judge? Let he who is without sin cast the first stone. Barbara's attitude to the world, to people, to life in general was, to Freddie, a breath of fresh air. Who was this bizarre female who looked all-woman but who acted like a man, who'd think nothing of knocking people down and had been known to make bodyguards run away? He was intoxicated by her majesty, her 'devil-may-care-and-screw-the-lot-of-them' attitude. He responded to the longings of her soul – and she to his. To say that they were soulmates, therefore, is no exaggeration. That Barbara was willing to give up a potentially lucrative theatre career to be with Freddie, and the fact that he allowed her to do it, knowing what her acting career meant to her is, by her own reckoning, the ultimate proof of their mutual dedication. Their firm friendship was to take Barbara on a whirlwind journey through Freddie's world. As well as accompanying him on Queen and private business to Rio de Janeiro, Montreux, Ibiza and Spain, she visited his home in London 'some 40 or 50 times', and was even given her own bedroom under his roof.

Contrary to earlier biographies, Freddie's relationship with Barbara Valentin did not begin until January 1984. The actress met Freddie through his puny, sly-looking personal assistant Paul Prenter (Trixie) whom she had literally bumped into quite by accident one night in one of the most popular clubs on Munich's Bohemian Triangle gay scene.

'I used to see them out night after night, every night. I vaguely knew who Freddie Mercury was, but the fact that he was a famous rock-star was no great shakes here in Munich. I was probably more famous here than he was at the time,' Barbara recalls in her deep, throaty voice as we plough through box upon box of meticulously-kept newspaper and magazine cuttings about her prolific career and her relationship with Freddie. Sifting through her memories does not come easily, and she soon appears exhausted by the process. Kind and hospitable, she invites me to look around the apartment which she and Freddie bought together, where they each had their own bedroom, and which was to have been their permanent Munich home. The third-floor apartment with its plain white door could belong to anybody. Only the initials 'FM', in gold metal script, glued crudely onto the wall to the left of the door, are a giveaway. The apartment has a chintzy, Laura Ashley-meets-Liberty feel. The walls are painted a soothing shade of lemon, and hung with valuable paintings, etchings and carvings. There is also a fine antique chandelier, and some heavy rustic Bavarian furniture. Her sideboard is crammed with framed photographs of her nearest and dearest: her children, grandchildren, Freddie. And her coffee table is cluttered with silver trinkets, candlesticks, pill boxes, most of them gifts from Freddie:

'I also have a lot of jewellery that he gave me: hearts and stuff, from Tiffany and Cartier, so many things that I can't even wear them.' There are rugs and tapestries, elegant drapes and velvet-covered sofas. Tarzan the 16-year-old cat, the 'child' she shared with Freddie, and her most beloved companion, snoozes on a plump armchair. There is a collection of Queen and Freddie Mercury videos and CDs, but Barbara can never bring herself to watch or listen to them. Today, however, fuelled by Cognac and much besides, she forces herself to sit through a screening of the 'Living On My Own' video, partly to point out her own bleach-headed dervish-like performance, and partly to reminisce about all those friends who appeared in the short promo film and who live no longer: most of them.

The small kitchenette, in which Barbara says she never cooks, is lined with bright tiles. The tiny guest cloakroom features a toilet with a seat made of coiled barbed wire set in clear Perspex, supplies of condoms and toothbrushes in little packets, and a framed photograph of Barbara in provocative pose, leaving nothing to the imagination, draped sexily over the back of a chair and dressed in exotic red lingerie, négligée, stockings and red high-heels. She later remarks that she 'revealed all' for the first time for *Penthouse* and *Playboy* at the age of 46: 'You've just got to believe in yourself.' Not a swatch of fabric nor a single item of furniture in the apartment was chosen or purchased without Barbara first having sought Freddie's approval: 'I mailed him pictures of every corner of the room. I sent him samples of everything to London. Every time I moved a plant, I sent Freddie a photograph.' The tragedy, for her, was that in the end he never actually set foot in the place, and was never able to call it home.

At times clearly in pain at these remembrances, Barbara continues the story of how she and Freddie met:

I saw them practically every time I was in the 'New York' disco, maybe three times a week, and whenever I went in, there was Freddie Mercury and his crew, a bunch of bodyguards or Phoebe or whoever the hell he had with him that night. He was always surrounded, he always had an entourage. Freddie was like an industry all by himself. I was often in that club because I knew the owner – I know all these faggots, you know? I live here. It's hard to say why I know so many gay people – who knows? Through Fassbinder, probably. Fassbinder was gay, and you couldn't work with Fassbinder the way you work with other directors. You were not hired for the day and then you went home. You had to live his life, go out with him, eat with him, spend time with his friends. It was like a family. You didn't have to go to bed with him was the only thing. I made a lot of films with him, and my second marriage broke up because of him. I found that I could not be happily married to this heterosexual lawyer with little children at home and enjoy this wonderful normal life in a villa with a swimming-pool and sauna and all the grand things I used to have, while I was so deeply involved with Fassbinder. He was God, you know. Most of them are gay, and if you know one you know 10, and if you know 10 you know 100. And so it went on. It seemed to me that every single one of my friends was gay, but so what.

I was in 'New York' one night, and I was smoking a cigarette, when Trixie passed by, brushed up against me and I accidentally burned him. He shouted at me, and I shouted back. 'What the hell, I didn't do it on purpose, Buster. Watch yourself in these places.' It was in a corner of the club, The Family Corner, they called it, because Freddie had his own special place where he and his gang always sat. There was Trixie and Freddie together with Winnie – those two were already seeing each other. Winnie came from the Tyrol, he was Austrian-born like me, and had come to Germany with his parents. He was a good friend of mine around town. He was not sophisticated like Freddie, and spoke with a heavy dialect. Freddie spoke very little German. He was not much of a linguist, but could understand quite a lot, and always made the effort to communicate. Freddie had met Winnie about a year before he met me, and they had quite a long relationship, with several breaks. They just couldn't keep away from each other. It was ultimately very destructive. They made an unusual couple: Winnie was a little butch, a little primitive, the truck-driver type that Freddie preferred. They'd have terrible fights, and

Freddie relaxing on tour.
(*Collection: Daisy May
Queen*)

Freddie in Tokyo, 1975.
(*Collection: Daisy May
Queen*)

Freddie and Mary at customs, May 1979. (*Collection: Daisy May Queen*)

RIGHT: Freddie performing live in Argentina, 1981. (*Collection: Daisy May Queen*)

Brian, Freddie and Roger in Los Años Locos restaurant, Buenos Aires (where Freddie was mobbed in the gents). (*Collection: Daisy May Queen*).

Freddie with Barbara Valentin on the balcony of the Montreux Palace Hotel, Montreux, Switzerland. (*Collection: Barbara Valentin*)

From left: Graham Hamilton, Freddie, Barbara Valentin, Jim Hutton and Phoebe at Roger Taylor's house, Ibiza. (*Collection: Barbara Valentin*)

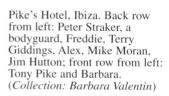

Pike's Hotel, Ibiza. Back row from left: Peter Straker, a bodyguard, Freddie, Terry Giddings, Alex, Mike Moran, Jim Hutton; front row from left: Tony Pike and Barbara. (*Collection: Barbara Valentin*)

On the steps of a gay bar in Ibiza. Back row, third from left: Phoebe; front row, left to right: Barbara, Winnie Kirchberger and Freddie. (*Collection: Barbara Valentin*)

Freddie, Barbara and Peter Straker
in the sitting room at Garden Lodge.
(*Collection: Barbara Valentin*)

Freddie on his birthday with Paul
Prenter. (*Collection: Peter Freestone*)

Freddie's 45th birthday party, Garden Lodge. From left: Piers Cameron (father
to Mary Austin's children), Mary, Phoebe, Freddie, Joe Fanelli, Barbara, and
Dave Clark. (*Collection: Barbara Valentin*)

Queen performing live 1981. (*Photograph: © Denis O'Regan*)

Jim Hutton in his garden, Co. Carlow, July 1996. (*Collection: Lesley-Ann Jones*)

Freddie at work (far right), Power Plant recording studio, Los Angeles. (*Collection: Peter Freestone*)

Freddie live with Queen.
(*Photographs above and right:*
© Denis O'Regan 1982, 1986)

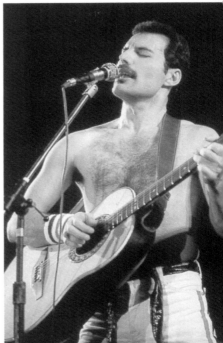

We were intoxicated by each other. We couldn't tear ourselves away. He'd laugh a lot – and usually he did put his hand up to his face when he laughed, as he was so self-conscious about his teeth. But once he'd got drunk, he would laugh openly and loudly, and not care about his teeth any longer. He always refused to have them out. He'd say, 'Why should I? They're healthy teeth!'

When eventually the gossipy pair decided to rejoin the crowd, they discovered that the club had long since closed and that they were locked in for the night. They simply sat down and carried on talking until the cleaning woman arrived and let them out. It was the beginning of a deep, powerful relationship which thrived despite Freddie's gay tastes and Barbara's lack of them. She claims there is no question that they were passionately in love.

'That's quite possible, yes,' agrees Peter Freestone, who witnessed virtually everything that went on between Freddie and the actress. 'They were certainly very close. I did, and I do, like Barbara enormously. They had a lot in common, by way of status and fame. Barbara didn't *care*. She had that whole, wonderful, take-it-or-leave-it attitude which Freddie found so refreshing: 'Let people think what they want of me.' Freddie was the same. He knew what he was like, and he never cared what people thought he was like. They had similar tastes, and both were very classy. Barbara was very, very important to Freddie, and never let anyone tell you otherwise.'

As for Barbara, she says that it took a little while for her to realize that she and Freddie were in love:

We were both trying to work each other out for a long time. Did I think he was normal when I first met him? Well. Normal wouldn't be the best word, but then you couldn't have called me normal either. I had four or five faggots around me, and he had his crowd around him.

It took some time, being alone with him, to find out how he was really. In public, in the bars he was the crazy gay person who ripped off his shirt and danced and did outrageous things. Freddie was always performing. But in private, as I would later find out, he was like another person.

Barbara was not in the least surprised to hear from Freddie about the monumental bond he shared with Mary Austin:

Freddie was always talking about her. He seemed to adore her. He trusted her. He told me everything about her: things like, she desperately wanted to have a child with him. Apparently he had once promised to marry her, but he never did. And because of that, he always felt guilty about it. Freddie was a very dutiful man. He had this sense of obligation. That had been what was expected of him, and he'd gone back on his word. That's the way he saw it, and the guilt never went away – although I wondered, to some extent, how much of that guilt she herself subconsciously made him feel. It wasn't Freddie's fault that he turned out to be mostly gay, that's life, but he couldn't ever get over the way he had let her down. That was so typical of him. He used to talk about this whole thing, and I could see how terrible he felt. He said that he hadn't been gay, not in the beginning, but then he just turned around, flipped out completely, and started to live a gay life. It was a choice, not a biological thing, with him.

'That is absolutely true,' agrees Peter Freestone. 'Freddie was very emotional at that time.'

'At the end, he didn't care about sex anyway,' says Barbara. 'He'd get together with people just for tenderness, affection. It was soon the case that his longings had nothing to do with the body anymore. He was like a little child. He would cry like a baby. Oh my God, to see him that way would break my heart. He'd say to me, "Barbara, the only thing they can't take from me is you." He'd write me little notes: "Dear Barbara, drop dead, love Freddie."'

Although Barbara says that she never had a problem with Mary: 'She's a wonderful person' – she always felt that her own goodwill was not reciprocated: 'She was cool, and quite wary of me. She'd often come over and stay in Munich, but she always kept her distance. Not that she wasn't nice to me; she was, extremely. But it was reserved and polite, not warm. We did exchange Christmas presents . . .'

Barbara delves in her handbag and produces a leather credit card holder bearing her initials. 'She gave me this one year. Or it would be a scarf, or cosmetics. And I sent her presents for the baby. But I couldn't say that we were ever close.'

Perhaps Mary knew that she occupied a special, untainted place in Freddie's heart, and had no desire to share that with another woman?

'Perhaps,' concedes Barbara.

'But she had to acknowledge that I had a relationship with him too. One thing I must say for her is that she always had Freddie's best interests at heart.'

Peter Freestone agrees.

'Once,' continues Barbara, 'she phoned me from London to say that one of Freddie's cats had died. "You break it to him, Barbara," she said to me, "but go gently, find the right moment." I agonized for ages, then finally I told him. He broke down uncontrollably, and said, "We're flying to London right now." "Freddie," I said, "the cat is dead." But he wouldn't hear otherwise, and back to London it was. He was devoted to his pets. Another time, when Jim had to kill one of his fish, Freddie went crazy and blamed Jim: "How could you kill a poor fish, you monster?"'

Barbara says that the one word which immediately springs

to mind if she thinks of Mary is 'thrifty': 'She certainly took care of Freddie's money. The kind of thing she would do was to get a toothpaste tube back out of the wastebin after Freddie had thrown it away, saying, "You could clean your teeth two more times with that!" I'm sure Freddie really liked that about her, because he could be so wasteful himself.'

Barbara remembers as if it were yesterday the night she knew they had fallen in love:

> One of Freddie's lovers grabbed me off the bar one night where I was sitting, and started to wash my hair in the sink behind the bar where you wash the glasses. Can you imagine? That night, Freddie hit me for that, I don't know why. Because he was jealous, I suppose. I glared at him, and I must have looked so shocked because his face started to crumble and he said to me, 'I love you, you crazy woman, you know that?' I was bewildered. I said to him, 'But Freddie, you are supposed to be gay.' 'Fuck the gays,' he said. 'I love *you*. Let's go home.'

It was not long before Barbara realized that homosexual promiscuity was not what made Freddie tick after all:

> It was a role he chose to play: the Great Pretender. But I think, in a sense, it excited him, because it was kind of forbidden fruit. I mean, while all this was going on, he and I were lovers in the true sense. We did have sex together, regularly. Yes. Yes. It took a while, and when it happened it was beautiful, almost innocent. There was, how can I say this, a delicate quality to it. Anyway I was completely in love with him by this time. Of course he still continued to pick up dozens of gay guys and bring them back night after night, but I didn't mind. Sounds insane, doesn't it, but that's the life we were living at that time, and anyway I couldn't stop him even if I wanted to. And I continued to take lovers myself. Well, to a certain

point I was allowed. But then Freddie start to show off about it and would kick them out, or embarrass them, put them down, or make life so difficult for them that they would leave anyway.

It all sounds so far-fetched when I talk about it now, but at the time it was just the way we lived. I would say to you, don't try to understand the lifestyle that we had. You had to be there to make sense of it. It sounds crazy to the outsider, but it made perfect sense to those who lived it. Actually crazy is too minor a word for it. Too primitive. There was something very special about it all, and crazy is too stupid, too cheap a word. I can't think of another one.

There were times when Barbara found she simply could not cope with Freddie's indiscriminate behaviour:

Sometimes I used to say to him, 'Darling, there's more to you than your prick, you know.' Why did he sleep with all those guys? Because they were there. He would say to me very often that he didn't even enjoy it. But he thought nothing about using people in that way, because he knew very well that so many of them were using him. Sometimes I had to be cruel with him, and throw out his lovers, or advise him not to go with this one or that one. 'Don't have him,' I'd say, 'he's stupid, or he's this or the other.' But you couldn't tell Freddie. 'Don't you tell me who I can sleep with!' he would yell. 'What does it matter if he's stupid, anyway? Don't tell me the only people you fuck are Sigmund Freud or Albert Einstein!' 'OK,' I'd say, 'so just tell him to shut up and not open his mouth.' He'd have his way and that would be it. It would then be up to me to get rid of all these guys from the apartment. I was always having to translate between Freddie and them, and sneak around covering for him, and a lot of the time it was very embarrassing for me because these were people I would see around town every day. The things I did for Freddie. Hah! Sometimes Freddie did come on like a total nymphomaniac. It seemed he couldn't help himself. Anyone who didn't know him as well as I did might despair of his behaviour. But I'm telling you it was put on. He wasn't really that way at all.

At first, Barbara suspected that Freddie was trying to prove something to himself. What bothered her was that she could not quite figure out what:

After a while, when I took a long hard look at my own behaviour, I realized exactly where he was coming from. I was coming from the same place myself. Later I came to understand him very well; he did all that because he was so lonely. I sympathized with that, because I was lonely too. We were both trying far too hard to be happy, because we were *not* happy. It's almost as if you say to yourself, 'Right, now I am going to be happy.' And you get drunk, you take blow, you play the monkey, you lay as many people as you can, night after night, as if you are daring your body to stay alive. It *is* a sort of death-wish, and it seems like fun, and you can kid yourself that you are having a fantastic time. But the more you do it, the more miserable you become. It's a form of self-protection, but in the end it just makes you *more* lonely, *more* empty. In the end it is stupid behaviour, but you don't know that at the time. And then one day you discover that it has taken over your life.

Freddie and I were both as bad as each other. We identified with each other. In the end, we were the only one that each one of us could turn to. If he hadn't had me, and if I hadn't had him, I think we would both have been dead much sooner.

All over Munich, Barbara and Freddie were known as The Crazy Couple who were always getting into scrapes. Once, Barbara knocked down a taxi-driver because he said Freddie was drunk, and he refused to take drunks. In fact, the singer was stumbling because he had broken his leg. Both got their kicks in the arms of others, but for the most part they were known to be inseparable:

Rumours even started to go around that we were going to get married, and made headlines in all the newspapers. There was nothing we could do to stop it, so Freddie and I just laughed it off. And in the end Freddie started saying, 'Well, yes, actually we *are* married already . . .' You only have to make a joke like that once and the next day it's 'World Exclusive' headlines all over the press. I'm a hotshot in this town, you know? Well, maybe not anymore . . . but at that time it was like, Oh! the big star. The combination of Freddie and me might not have seemed like much to you over in England or in the United States or wherever, but here it was *very* big news. Freddie Mercury and Barbara Valentin, my *God*, that was something for the press. They were chasing after us wherever we went.'

After a while, in spite of themselves, both Freddie and Barbara found themselves falling for their own public image, a well-known trap:

Well. It was a pretty idea. And at times we did talk about this crazy fantasy, the beautiful big wedding, the fairy-tale white gown. We both started to think, well, maybe . . . but in the back of our minds I think we both knew it was nothing more than a fantasy, and that the reality could never work. But it was nice to dream, to have a bit of fun with something we knew we would never have. The reality was that we both liked our freedom. And I must admit I was never that good at being a wife, taking care of children and slaving over a hot stove. What I do believe is that a part of both Freddie and me craved a simpler, more organized, more secure and conventional lifestyle – that kind of wholesome thing you see in movies. I think it was a reaction to this crazy unnatural life that we actually had. You can have too much of a good thing to the point that it becomes a *bad* thing. And you never know if you have a friend, because actually you are just a monkey for the crowd. Your life is a show. The reason that Freddie and I became so close and dependent on each other is because we were both in the same boat. It would be, 'Are we relaxing tonight or are you going out to do yet another performance?' And yet in some ways neither of us could help it. Because if you're an actor you *like* to do a performance. And your insecurity stems from knowing inside that your audience enjoys you more as a big performer than as the real *you*. It destroys your sense of self-worth, and it takes a devoted friend to build that up again for you. That is what Freddie and I did for each other.

While acknowledging that they were on a dangerous tread-mill, despite their inner feelings Barbara insists that she and Freddie did derive some enjoyment from that mad Munich lifestyle they lived to the hilt, and which they went for so shamelessly and deliberately:

It was the best defence. From what? I can't tell you, really. A number of things. Every day something new. Freddie and I were always up against it for one reason or another. But at least we had each other. We would never let anyone else see when we were wounded, but we'd show each other. We both had things to hide from our families, for example. Freddie was protecting his parents and sister, and I certainly did not want my children to know everything about my lifestyle. Now and again it might happen that I'd run into my son at a disco and go, Oh my God, *wrong* disco. But Freddie and I became each other's second family. And we always left our private family sides private.

Meanwhile, the troilist escapades between Barbara, Freddie and Winnie continued apace. Once, recalls Barbara,

On 26 November – Winnie's birthday – we are all three in bed together, stark naked, and the doorbell goes, seven o'clock in the morning: tax police. 'Come back later!' yells Freddie. 'If you don't let us in, we're breaking the door down now!' they yell back. Freddie was frantic. He came screaming back into the bedroom crying 'Get up! Get up!' The next minute, the police were inside and stationed in every room, and there was Freddie naked except for a little towel around his waist. We three were told to stay exactly where we were. We couldn't make a move while they tore the place apart. Finally Freddie says 'I really need to take a piss, guys.' So they let him go. And suddenly, the policeman beside the bathroom recognizes him: 'It's Freddie Mercury!' Freddie got cheeky then: being Freddie, he couldn't resist. He said to the policeman, 'If you're nice to my girlfriend, I'll sing a song for you. Come on, mate, let's have a glass of champagne together.' It was still not even eight o'clock, and the policeman sheepishly said, 'Sorry, we're on duty.' 'Okay, then, go fuck yourself!' retorted Freddie. 'You're all too ugly to be sung to anyway!'

Such amusing moments in Freddie's company were many. 'Another time I found him naked on the balcony singing "We Are the Champions" to a group of construction workers down below, and shouting "Whoever has the biggest dick, come on up!" He loved to shock people, but not in an offensive way, just for fun. It was charming.

'He was absolutely special,' smiles Barbara.

Gentlemanly, tender, thoughtful, amusing . . . and totally unpredictable. With him, you never knew what was going to happen next. Being with him was the most exciting time of my life – and I'd had a life, you know?

So many things about him came as a total surprise to me. As hard as he partied – 'I'll have a long time in my grave when I can sleep', he used to say – in Musicland studios he was calm, professional, he got on with what had to be done. But before he went on stage he was shitting himself with nerves. He'd have to be taken to the loo 20 times, but then he'd get out there and he'd explode, like Superman, and he had thousands eating out of his hand. He had such charisma, which nobody can learn. That you are born with.

It amazed me, with all the travelling he was accustomed to, that he absolutely hated flying. He'd cling to me like a little child, hold my hand and shake and sweat. He was terrified of take-offs and landings. Once, when they couldn't get a plane from London to Munich because the flights were fully-booked, Freddie hired a private plane. So there we were on this plane and found that it was getting so incredibly hot. We were stripping off our clothes, and we could hardly breathe. Eventually we went up to the flight deck and said to the captain, 'There's obviously a problem, the plane's overheating.' The captain said we would have to turn back towards London, and as we did so we had such a terrible near-miss with a jumbo jet that we were absolutely terrified out of our skins. Then they said it would be a three and a half hour wait at the airport while they fixed the problem. I said to Freddie, 'Let's go home to Garden Lodge. Maybe God is trying to tell us something. We'll go in the morning, what difference?' I would have thought, the way I knew he felt about flying, that it would have put him off completely. But no, he was determined to get to Munich that night, for whatever reason. So we waited and waited, and eventually we got back on the same jet, and everything was okay.

Freddie could not stand elevators either:

Once we got stuck in one at the hotel in Montreux. Freddie was petrified. I said, 'Look, just breathe deeply.' That didn't work, so I said to him, 'Why don't you sing then?' And there he was in this lift, singing 'We Are The Champions'.

The thing I loved about him most was that he knew always exactly how to behave, in any situation. He was the perfect gentleman from top to toe. He had impeccable manners. He was extremely well-bred and he never forgot that, even when he was completely drunk. You'd never see him do something like belch at the dinner-table. He'd always treat me like a lady, like a princess, even in the worst leather bars, the shittiest whorehouses, where you wouldn't touch anything without gloves. And you could really get hassled in those places at times. If anyone ever taunted me and said, 'Who do you think you are, Barbara Valentin, you're just the same as anyone else,' Freddie would always stick up for me and say, 'No – she's not. She's special. Arrogant arseholes. So, if you don't care who she is, just leave her alone!' He was very chivalrous – he'd open doors, help you on with your coat, light your cigarette before he even had his own in his mouth.

Once he was in the kitchen with my mother, having a conversation. She was speaking in French, and Freddie was speaking in English, so I went out there to try to help. 'Get out! Get out!' he cried. 'Leave us alone, we are communicating perfectly well the way we are!' There they were, gesticulating with hands and feet and all, and having a wonderful time, and my mother simply couldn't get over him:'*What* a charming man!'

Such conversations, and misunderstandings, always made for fun when Freddie was around. On one occasion, Barbara remembers, the phone in the apartment rang for Freddie from Los Angeles, and the caller said he was Elton John.

'Oh yeah', said Barbara, 'and I'm Liz Taylor,' slamming down the phone.

'But when I told Freddie he said, "My God, you're an idiot! I was waiting for that urgent call, you stupid cow!" Luckily, Elton called again. This time he said, "It's Sharon, can I please talk to Melina." That was when I knew it was really him.'

Freddie had become fairly helpless by the time he was living in Munich. The full complement of staff he employed to fetch and carry and cater to his every whim had rendered him virtually incapable of doing anything for himself. He barely had to make a decision or even do his own thinking. By Barbara's reckoning, this was the single most lethal threat to Freddie's sanity.

Freddie never carried a key, never had money in his pocket – like the Queen! – and he didn't know the difference between one Deutschemark and one thousand dollars. He'd go into bars and say to people, 'Drink whatever you want, it's all on me.' But he had no concept of money. He was always surrounded by hustlers, pimps and whores, complete strangers wanting to take advantage of him.

He never went anywhere by himself. He couldn't. Not even to the toilet – he'd always make me go with him. Wherever Freddie was, there was a mess. But he was perfect at delegating people to clean up.

Still, things did not always go according to plan.

Once, Joe Fanelli went off to the gym to work out at about six p.m. saying to me, 'Can I go off for two hours and you take care of him?' Off he went. Freddie and I had hardly been up for one hour, and there was nothing at all to eat in the place. Quite often we would get food sent in from a nearby restaurant, but on that occasion I decided that I had to go shopping quickly, and make a meal. Maybe we were bored with the restaurant food.

The apartment was an absolute bombsite, ashtrays overflowing, a filthy mess everywhere. I said, 'Okay, Freddie, I'll be an hour, don't move, here's the TV remote, just sit there and watch until I get back.' All this because Freddie just couldn't be trusted not to get into mischief. I tore round the supermarket anxiously and even asked the store manager if I could use his office to make a quick call, as I realized that I had been gone a little longer than the hour I'd said I would be and I was worried about Freddie. We had a code where we would ring once, hang up and dial again, and I made the call.

But, when Barbara returned laden with shopping, Freddie was nowhere to be found. Yet the bed was made, the ashtrays emptied and washed, the whole apartment sparkling and pristine.

When he eventually appeared I said, 'What, have the fairies been in?' He laughed out loud. 'No,' he said, 'it was me. *I* cleaned up the place. I even vacuumed.' 'How on earth did you find the vacuum cleaner?' I asked him. 'I didn't.' He winked. 'I used the toaster.' I was just amazed at how clean the place was. I didn't even know that he knew how to do such things. But later on as I walked round the apartment, I noticed that all the electrical sockets were hanging out of the wall on their bare wires. You had to press a button to release the electric cable six metres, but Freddie hadn't worked that out. He was trying to vacuum the entire apartment with a cable one metre long. We had to get an electrician round and pay him DM250, for which we could have had the place spring-cleaned professionally. But Freddie was like a little boy, so proud of his efforts that it was impossible to get angry with him.

On another occasion, in Rio de Janeiro in 1985, Barbara recalls, they had made such a mess of their hotel suite that they were afraid to let the maids in: 'We actually called Housekeeping and sent down for brooms, buckets, cloths and polish. The place was a disgraceful mess. "We'll do it," they said. "No, no," we insisted. It was in such a bad state that even we were embarrassed. Freddie was never consistent about being clean and tidy. Sometimes he'd fold his clothes neatly, sometimes he left them where they fell, sometimes he didn't even remember to take them off before he had a bath'.

One December, the day before Christmas Eve, Freddie suddenly panicked because he had not done any Christmas shopping for his friends. 'He decided that he wanted to go into town to buy all these gifts,' remembers Barbara. 'So he drew himself up a list of about 20 people, and by the time he had done so it was 11.50 a.m. and Cartier was due to close at 12 that day. I had to phone ahead to the store to get them to stay open for him. When we got there in my car, there was nowhere to park, so I just had to dump it on a grass verge so that we could run straight into the shop.

'Freddie was sitting in the seat where you are now,' she says to me as we drive through Munich peeking into the corners of Freddie's and Barbara's old stomping ground: the Teddy Bar on HansSachs Strasse, a short walk from their apartment; the Deutsche-Eiche Hotel, also a favourite of Robert de Niro and

Richard Chamberlain; the Car restaurant – a 'Cheers'-type American bar; the Petit Café, Freddie's best-loved bar. In a number of his old haunts, Freddie's pictures grace the walls

'I said to Freddie, "Lock the door." "How do I do that?' he said. "Just press the button!" I yelled. Freddie just flew into this terrible tantrum. "I am a rock 'n' roll star!" he raged. "I am not supposed to know how to press a button! Call Phoebe and get him down here to do it for me – right *now*!"'

'It's perfectly true,' smiles Peter Freestone. 'And yes, they did call, and yes, I went down there and went off shopping with them. It is so wonderful hearing all these memories, as if I am living them again.'

This was not an uncommon reaction from Freddie, and as usual, Barbara chose to ignore it. The mini-crisis dealt with, and the button pressed by Barbara herself, they went on into the Cartier store and Freddie started to look around. But he soon became agitated, and could barely contain his frustration.

'"*I* don't know what to buy," he wailed. "*You* know what would suit everybody, Barbara – *you* do it."

'"But I have to go down the road to the pharmacy," I said. "I need to buy some Tampax."

'"Don't worry," said Freddie. "*I'll* do that. You stay here and buy the gifts."'

Although he loved to shop, Barbara explains, he did not have the first clue when it came to choosing anything. This went some way to explaining why he always spent so much money: if he couldn't decide, he'd take the lot; if he couldn't settle for a colour, he'd go with every shade in stock. It was then that Barbara was able to witness at first hand a fundamental reason for Freddie's legendary extravagance. Some time after he had left for the pharmacy, she reports, Freddie returned with a vast shopping bag, and she stared at him in amazement.

'What on earth did you get?' she asked.

'Well,' replied Freddie, 'you didn't tell me what sort to buy, so I got some of everything!'

'He'd bought three different brands, light, heavy regular, super, super-max, packets and boxes of every kind of towel and tampon in existence. You could have supplied the whole street and taken care of their periods for a year. All I'd wanted was one little handbag-sized pack.'

Chapter Sixteen

LOVE OF MY LIFE?

It was in 1985 that an Irish-born, London-based hairdresser by the name of Jim Hutton began to make regular appearances on the Munich scene. He and Freddie had met first at the end of 1983, in the Cococabana, a South Kensington gay club. Freddie had made an overt pass, but Jim, a barber at the Savoy Hotel, was not available – he had a regular boyfriend at the time Two years later, in March 1985, they bumped into each other again, this time at the notorious gay London superclub 'Heaven' – the place where, in 1984, broadcaster Paul Gambaccini says he 'realized for the first time that Freddie Mercury was going to die':

In 1984, we were standing in a particular spot in Heaven, and I asked Freddie if he had altered his behaviour in light of recent developments. And with that characteristic flash of the arms he said, 'Darling, my attitude is, fuck it. I'm doing everything with everybody.' And of course 'everybody' is not limited to men. I would assume that meant that he was probably still having sex with some women somewhere . . . but I don't know. All I knew was – there was a lot of whoever it was. And I had that literal sinking feeling. I'd seen enough in New

York to know that Freddie was going to die. I associate certain spots of the club with friends who are no longer with us, and it's so profound, I can't be glib about it. I can't. Oh, there are too many ghosts for me to pretend that Heaven can ever be a carefree environment.

The fact that Freddie was picking up and having sex with, at times, dozens of men a week while openly flaunting his relationship with Barbara Valentin would suggest that he had come to regard himself as bisexual rather than gay. But, argues Paul Gambaccini,

Remember that the concept of homosexuality only came about in the 1860s, when a German psychologist invented the word 'homosexual'. Before that, people tended to be 'sexual', and I've always thought that, in this sexual spectrum, at one extremity you have people who never make love to people of the same sex, and at the other extremity people who never make love to somebody of the opposite sex. But you'd best believe that in the middle there are a lot of people who make love to both sexes. It doesn't mean that it's a 50:50 thing. I've known many people who would call themselves straight, who have had same-sex lovers, and I've known many people who would call themselves gay who have had opposite-sex lovers. It's the rule rather than the exception that gives them their name. True bisexuals would be 50:50 folk, and I rarely encounter 50:50 folk. It's usually a matter of individuals, which is as it should be. Love turns your head. For those going outside their majority activity [as it appears Freddie did with Barbara], there is usually a great emotional contact.

I don't wish to speculate on matters of Freddie's heart, but I don't see any contradiction between the statements that, in the course of his life, Freddie would have had sex with more men than women, which I believe is probably true, but that in the end he would recall his love for Mary. These are not contradictory positions. It just means that she was one of his exceptions to the rule. It just means that emotion came into play as well as lust. I'm not saying that Freddie did not love some of the men that he loved, but she could easily have held a special position in his heart. There is no reason for that not to be true.

But women were the last thing on Freddie's mind when he hit on Jim Hutton in Heaven that night. Not unlike his German lover Winnie Kirchberger with his thick dark hair and moustache, Jim was somewhat taken aback by Freddie's chat-up line: 'How big's your dick?' Nevertheless, he was persuaded to join Freddie's gang, which included Peter Straker and Joe Fanelli, and spent the rest of the night dancing with Freddie before returning with him to Freddie's Kensington flat around dawn. Hutton would not hear from Freddie for another three months, partly because the star was living in Germany as a tax exile, and only returned to London at irregular intervals; but also because Freddie had been out on the road, to Australia, New Zealand and Japan with Queen. When his call was least expected, Freddie phoned and invited him to a dinner-party at his home, where Jim was astonished to see Peter Freestone. Jim and Peter had once worked together at Selfridges. Neither could believe that they had met up again through Freddie Mercury.

In his autobiography *Mercury and Me*, Hutton reports that he fell for the rock star almost immediately: 'I fell in love with so much about Freddie, regardless of what he did for a living. He had big brown eyes and a vulnerable, child-like persona. He was quite the opposite of the sort of man I'd ever fancied before: I liked big men with stocky legs, but Freddie had a waspish figure and the thinnest legs I'd ever seen. And for all that he had apparently achieved, he appeared to be remarkably insecure. He seemed totally sincere, and I was hooked.'

Soon afterwards, Jim and Freddie fell into a routine whereby Freddie would fly home to London one weekend, and fly Jim out to be with him the next. The first time Jim arrived in Munich, he found Freddie, Joe Fanelli and Barbara Valentin there at the airport to meet him. But it quickly became apparent that he was being used to make Winnie Kirchberger jealous, a situation which Hutton did not care for at all.

Recalls Barbara,

Yes, Jim was here in Munich to make Winnie jealous. Jim was a puppet. Sometimes Freddie would call him up: 'Come over.' He'd arrive at seven o'clock in the morning, and at four o'clock in the afternoon he was sent back. I heard many sad stories during that time. Jim would cry very often, and I'd say to him, 'Just resist. Say no to Freddie for once. Don't let yourself be used.' 'Yes,' Jim would say, 'but I love him.' And I'd say, 'Okay, look, he is just using you to make Winnie jealous, you know? Stick up for yourself.' Jim was shoved around like a monkey. He'd do whatever Freddie said. I could see the attraction – he'd take off his shirt and he had quite a nice body. There is no doubt that Freddie was attracted to him. But it was always on Freddie's terms, when Freddie felt like it, and he just came running every time. And then Jim would be sent back, and Freddie would get on with whatever he was up to here. Sometimes it was quite pathetic, and often very mean.

But the relationship was perhaps deeper and more meaningful than it appeared to almost everybody other than the two involved. According to Peter Freestone, who observed all Freddie's affairs at close range.

I believe Jim and Freddie did love each other – each in their own way. From reading Jim's book, and knowing

him as well as I do, I would say that the book is to
some extent idealized. But it was actually written and
edited by someone else. Jim wanted a one-to-one happy
relationship with someone. And I don't think he could
ever appreciate how much more there was to Freddie's
life than a relationship, and later on his home life at
Garden Lodge. Freddie had his life, and it was a big,
extravagant, multi-faceted life. Everybody knew that
you had to adapt to Freddie's life. He was never going
to adapt to yours. Part of their problem was that Jim
was too stubborn to accept that. Consequently, their
relationship was very 'upstairs-downstairs'. Jim wanted
Freddie to come downstairs, but Freddie wanted Jim
to come upstairs. Having said all that, Freddie would
certainly not have had such good years at the end
without Jim. Overall, Jim was right for Freddie at that
time in his life. He meant a great deal more to him than
a lot of people have suggested.

When Freddie had finally put his London house together,
decided to change his life and leave Munich behind for good,
it was Jim, not Barbara, whom he chose as his live-in partner.
Although Jim remembers an eight-year relationship with the
star in his book, they had met briefly in 1983. Their actual
affair did not begin until 1985, and lasted until Freddie's
death in 1991. They were actually together for six years.
Even so, this suggests that Jim meant rather more to Freddie
than Barbara implies:

Jim was just a puppet on a string. Jim had nothing to
say. When they went back to Garden Lodge, he was good
for Freddie's cats and the fish and for the garden, that's
it. Freddie would sometimes really lose his temper with
frustration over the whole thing. Once, in Garden Lodge
when I was staying there, Freddie went completely crazy
and rushed into the garden. He tore up all the tulips Jim

had planted and threw them around on the ground. I said to him, 'What are you *doing*, poor plants!' And Freddie said, 'I *hate* him, this asshole.' Sometimes Freddie said that Jim was good for nothing.

And yet there was obviously something unique in Jim to which Freddie related; something between them which did not exist in any of his other relationships – not even with Mary. Even Barbara concedes, 'We often thought of Jim as no more than a servant really. But in one way, I know Freddie loved him. He kicked Jim around, but then some people need a kick in the ass. They thank you for it. In the end it was good that he was there. Six years together – that's quite a time. That means more than nothing. Freddie moved back to London, and Jim stayed with him until the end. Thank God, in a way.'

Meanwhile, across the United States throughout the early eighties, hospitals were seeing more and more cases of Aids. They were mostly young, sexually-active gay males, suffering from HIV-defined illnesses: weight loss, lesions, swollen lymph glands, herpes, cryptococcal meningitis and toxoplasmosis – characterized by jaundice, enlarged liver and spleen, and convulsions. Doctors noticed more and more evidence of cellular immunodeficiencies. New manifestations of immune disorders, including exhaustion, shingles and nightsweats, were appearing all the time. Many victims were fighting candidiasis (thrush), turning up for treatment with mouths full of white spots. In some cases, the yeast infection in their throats was so advanced that the patients could hardly breathe. Paranoia was also now being reported, and a growing number of patients appeared increasingly forgetful and disoriented. Of all the cases of Aids diagnosed across America, the New York City area accounted for half.

In Munich, Barbara and Freddie were still so close that they were now spending virtually all their time together, and were consequently planning to purchase a property together which they would pay for 50:50. Outright ownership would pass to the one on the death of the other, and paperwork was drawn up. Meanwhile, although nothing was ever said, Barbara could not help but notice that all was not as it should be with the state of Freddie's health.

'It started with little things,' she recalls with a crack in her voice and with great hesitation, as if these are the things of which she should not speak.

I mean, you couldn't really say that Freddie was losing his appetite or anything, because he had never had much of an appetite to begin with. He'd always say, 'I eat like a bird and shit like a bird.' And it was true. He really ate very little. His favourite food was caviare and mashed potato. And these little cheese crackers that his mother used to send him – I still have the box. He did like Italian food, Indian, Chinese. He never ate much at all, but there were always people around to eat for him. He always had Stolichnaya vodka.

Freddie would get sick for no apparent reason. Once, he was taken ill in my apartment, and I didn't know what to do, so I called my gynaecologist, whom I trusted more than any other doctor. I felt sure that he would know what to do. He came right over, and found Freddie quite delirious. He was taking a look at him when suddenly Freddie woke up in a terrible state, and I said, 'It's okay, Freddie, this is my gynaecologist.' 'Oh my God,' said Freddie, 'I'm not pregnant, am I? I can't believe it.'

It was around this time, remembers Barbara, that Freddie started to bitch about the other members of the band, which she had never previously known him to do. Then came Freddie's famous falling-out with his old friend Peter Straker. The relationship, which had lasted many years, would never be restored:

'Straker was funny, he was a clown, he was good for

Freddie because he kept his spirits up in a warm, light-hearted way. He made him laugh,' explains Barbara.

But Straker was not settled. He drifted from place to place, and he always seemed to be 'living with friends'. Eventually he got a flat in one of Jim Beach's buildings in London (Peter Freestone believes in Clapham). But the bathroom badly needed doing, new tiles, new bath, new sink, everything. Well, five times Freddie gave Peter the money to do up his bathroom. But the work never got done. Finally, Freddie just lost his rag and banished Straker from his life. He never actually explained his rage to Straker, it was just 'Out! Out!' Straker was dumbfounded. I felt he never actually understood what had happened, or why he had fallen out of favour. But that kind of thing became so typical of Freddie. He would give and give and give, and never count the cost, and then finally there would be some small, insignificant thing – the straw that broke the camel's back.

'Freddie's friendship with Straker collapsed over something stupid,' agrees Jim Hutton.

There are various stories about why, although I think in fact it was a build-up. One of the stories is that they were supposed to have lunch at Joe's Café, and Peter arrived a little bit late, slightly inebriated, and started performing: singing and chatting up the waiters and generally having a jolly good time, just like he would do at Garden Lodge. And that time Freddie got pissed off, and that was that. It didn't make any sense: Straker and Freddie had been such good friends. Straker was always around. He would come into the house, and of course as soon as he arrived, Freddie would say, 'What would you like to drink?' And then he'd scream at Joe or Peter, 'Okay, a glass of champagne for Straker,' or a brandy or whatever. My attitude was, since he was there so often, why the bloody hell can't he help himself? But I wasn't in a position to say that. That was Freddie all over. The guy had to be 'served'.

Peter Freestone, who says he knew Peter Straker almost as well as he knew Freddie, confirms both stories.

There wasn't any one specific reason, although both of those things, which are absolutely true, were contributory. Straker arriving late at the restaurant – it was actually Ponteveccio, not Joe's Café – *was* the last straw. He was showing Freddie up. I love Peter Straker dearly, but I have to say that he was acting more drunk than he really was, just for the effect. Later, when Freddie was giving up drinking and so on, he found that he was getting through just as much brandy and champagne at home, which he wasn't seeing any of, and that irked him a little. He knew he was sort of set up for that kind of thing. Freddie was the kind of guy who, if he knew they were doing it, he didn't care. But if it was being done behind his back, he hated it so much. Still, like Barbara, Straker was very good for Freddie.

Barbara remembers another occasion when Freddie cut off a friend:

Freddie had 'lent' this guy endless money, knowing only too well that he would never get it back. One day at Garden Lodge, this guy just went to the fridge, helped himself to a bottle of champagne, opened and drank it – without asking. Now, Freddie would give anything to anyone. He was the most generous person I ever knew. But he was somehow offended by what that guy did. Freddie would have given that guy *ten* bottles of champagne to drink all by himself. But he

was offended that he just took one without even asking
if it was okay. Freddie just flipped. And that was the
end of *that* friendship.

There came the time, in Munich, when it was impossible
not to notice what Barbara refers to as 'the growth in
Freddie's gullet':

It would well up in the back of his throat, just like that.
We called it 'the mushroom'. After that, it never went
away. Sometimes he said he felt as if he was rotting away
from the inside out. One night I was in bed with Freddie
and one of his boyfriends, and Freddie got a terrible
coughing attack, which was what this thing used to
do to him. He got up in the bed to cough into some
tissues, and then he leant right over this guy to reach
the wastebin to put the tissues there. The guy woke up:
'Oh my God,' he says, 'I never thought that I'd have a
naked dying rock-star lying on top of me in the bed!'

Aware of the information that was coming to Europe out of
New York, as were gay communities throughout the world,
Barbara must have long suspected that Freddie was likely to
be HIV positive when they first became lovers.

'Well . . . when we first met, he was either denying it to
himself, or he didn't know it. After he made the first test, it
changed his life.'

Was she not afraid for herself?

'No.'

Never?

'Well, not after the first test.'

So Barbara actually took an Aids test herself?

'Sure. I had only one test, and that was it. Negative. And
since there would be no more sex, and no further risk, I
wouldn't be having any more tests.'

Ask her when she actually realized that Freddie had Aids

and Barbara falls silent for a long time. She eventually composes herself, swallowing a large gulp of Cognac:

Once, after we'd been out, he went to the toilet and he cut his finger by mistake. There was a lot of blood. I was trying to help him, and I got the blood all over my hands, and he was screaming, No! Don't touch me, don't touch me! And that was the first time I realized that he must have the virus. He never actually told me. But I knew. And I had known for some time, because he had these marks on his face, like dark blue bruises, and I'd covered them for him with my make-up when he did a TV or a video shoot or so, before the professional make-up girl arrived.

We never actually talked about him having Aids. But he knew that I knew. And I knew he knew that. He'd start making casual remarks like, 'Well, I might not live that much longer anyway,' and so on. But he never actually told me to go and get tested too. I was aware, from what was said, that Freddie never found out which of his lovers was responsible for giving him Aids. But a long time ago, when one of his very early American gay lovers died of Aids, Freddie said, 'Oh my God, this is it,' and got very worried. I'm sure he knew from that moment on that his days were definitely numbered.

Freddie's departure from Munich towards the end of 1985 was abrupt, inexplicable, and excruciatingly painful for the woman he left behind.

'One minute we were all over the place together, insepa-rable, and then out of the blue came this break,' says Barbara with a hurt and puzzled look.

Looking back, I'm almost sure it had something to do with 'the test'. And then he disappeared from Munich. And in the meantime I was in London, because I was supposed to do 'Blind Date' with Cilla Black, for German TV. I was there, in a hotel, and I called Freddie, and he didn't answer. As far as I knew, I hadn't done anything. But he just disappeared out of my life. I couldn't understand it. I sent the birthday card, I wrote, I called, he was never there. I knew it didn't make sense. What he was doing was a lie. But okay, I thought. If he wants it over, then it's over. Don't think about it. It really was a break without a reason.

I realized that the actual night he left Munich, he was leaving me. There he was, organizing the transport of his ice machine, and paintings and so on – because he did have quite a bit of stuff here already. He was quite settled. That night we had been out, and then we went back to his place, the apartment hotel across the street where they were all based because my apartment was too small for everyone. And there was Joe saying, 'Okay, we have to be by 11 o'clock to the airport,' and the night was getting later and later. So I said, 'Okay, we go for one drink to my place.' It was just a few feet across the street. And they said, 'Sure, but we have to get some sleep because we must go . . .' Actually, it was such a lot of fuss for a two hour flight to London that it should have made me think. I just shrugged and said, 'Okay, off you go to bed now, I'm going home, bye-bye, bye-bye, we'll talk tomorrow' – all these little lies. Freddie knew exactly by that time that he had no intention of ever talking to me again.

But then he changed all of a sudden and said, 'Actually, I will take you home.' So he did. Once we got there, I said, 'Freddie, you must have a sleep,' and I took off my clothes. But it was all strange. Because then he said, 'Oh come on, let's go back to my place,' and I had to take him home again. We did this to-ing and fro-ing practically all night, and it was eight o'clock in the morning by the time we had finished. I'd had enough,

I was saying, 'Oh damn it, call Joe, tell him to cancel the flight and take an evening one or whatever.' By this time I was lying in bed, and Freddie was on his knees at the end of the bed just crying. He couldn't even talk to me anymore. And I said, 'What's the matter? What do you have? What is it?' But he said nothing.

Barbara whispers this, her voice raspy and tearful.

'He just sat there looking at me. That's it. That's it. And then, he disappeared out of my life.'

Adds Peter Freestone,

'Yes, but only out of her life for a while. He had intended it to be permanent, but he couldn't handle it. He missed her too much.'

Did Barbara ever find out why?

'*Now* I understand'.

Because he was sick? Because he didn't want to tell her? Barbara nods. 'It was hard at the beginning, because I didn't understand. But after a few months I just tried not to think about it any more. Because it just hurts, you know?'

According to Peter Freestone:

Garden Lodge was by that time ready to move into. I'd stayed in Munich for about a year and a half, and when Garden Lodge was completed, somebody had to be there for security and insurance purposes. I moved in with the cats, Oscar and Tiffany, and Joe Fanelli went out to Munich to be with Freddie. One day out of the blue, Freddie decided that he'd go back and live at Garden Lodge. Jim had replaced Winnie, but it was complicated with Barbara, and I think Freddie had simply had enough. Also, stories about Freddie and Barbara were beginning to appear in the German press with alarming regularity, and Freddie foolishly got it into his head that Barbara was the one leaking the information. I don't believe she would do that, but

Freddie was convinced. Enough was enough, and he left Munich. I think at the time he really believed he was leaving for good.

Soon after Freddie moved into Garden Lodge, Jim was evicted from his flat, so Freddie invited Jim to join him. 'Freddie and I never talked about how long we'd be together,' said Jim. 'We accepted that we were and would be. Now and then he'd ask me what I wanted from life. "Contentment and love," I'd say. I found both in Freddie.'

But did Freddie find those things in Jim?

There is no doubt that Jim Hutton's selective 1994 auto-biography *Mercury and Me* started out as a tender tribute by a devoted and bereft lover. But Jim's good intentions became slightly blurred, perhaps thanks to a journalist/ghost-writer who tended to focus on the more sensational aspects of the relationship and the less palatable details of Freddie's dying days for maximum tabloid appeal. If the reader was left with a sense of never having encountered the real Freddie anywhere in the book, Hutton – once famously described as 'the Sally Burton to Mary Austin's Elizabeth Taylor' as well as 'Freddie's breath of fresh air' – is not to be blamed. Sickened by much of what he read in the press during those dark empty weeks following Freddie's death, and angry that he himself, as well as the other members of Freddie's household, appeared to have been obliterated completely from the singer's life, Jim resolved to set the record straight. His aim had been to produce the most accurate account of his life with Freddie. All things considered, he is not unhappy with the result. But he remains bewildered by the objections raised, the abuse hurled, and his ostracism by the 'Queen camp' following the book's publication.

Roger Taylor, for one, made known his disappointment that the book went ahead: 'Freddie would never have allowed the publication of *Mercury and Me* in his lifetime,' Roger explained. 'Anyway, it was just one aspect of the last few years of his life. It is not the whole man. I knew Jim Hutton fairly well, and I thought the book was okay, but written very much from one viewpoint. I didn't object so much to the book as to some of the publicity around it. I don't think Freddie would have particularly wanted the book out. He was never one to parade his private life – it was no one else's business.'

Having met Jim, after tracking him down to picturesque County Carlow in the South East of Ireland, where he lives in a comfortable bungalow built with his £500,000 inheritance, I am left in no doubt that the love he claims to have felt for Freddie was genuine. Hutton is a warm, decent and friendly man content with his lot in life, getting on with what's left of it and making the best. He is also that rare Celt who has no regrets. And he remains eternally grateful for the taste of the superstar lifestyle that Freddie treated him to.

Fifty-something Hutton certainly saw the good life on Freddie's arm. Prior to meeting the rock-star, Jim, one of ten children born to an Irish Catholic baker and raised in a small two-bedroom council house, lived in London and worked as a £70-a-week barber at the Savoy Hotel. He would eventually share Freddie's bedroom at his home Garden Lodge, where, keen to 'earn his keep', he also worked as the gardener. It was clearly an attraction of opposites. Freddie, according to Hutton, was 'sensitive, shy, had terrible mood swings and wanted his own way. Whereas I'm quiet and don't have much of a character – unless you want to pour a few gallons of beer down my throat.'

The pair remained devoted companions until Freddie's death. Freddie even referred to Jim as 'my husband'. But only the star's closest friends were aware of the situation. To the outside world, even when they travelled together, Mary Austin was still paraded as the great love of Freddie's life. It was she, not Jim, who decorated the singer's sleeve at parties and public gatherings. And it was Mary who was paraded as 'the widow' at the end.

Jim was often credited with being the person who caused Freddie to change his lifestyle, turn his back on the wild gay scene and curb his excessive ways. But the truth was more complicated. Freddie's radical change in behaviour was brought on by the confirmation of his greatest fear. It was not until 1987 that Freddie was officially diagnosed as HIV positive – a fact which neither he nor the rest of the band or his entourage would publicly admit to until the eve of his death – although each had long had his suspicions. He confessed to Jim immediately and said he would understand if his lover preferred to leave. But Jim flatly refused to desert his man. They stayed together, and the word 'Aids' was never mentioned in the house again, to the point that it became a taboo subject. Jim first tested HIV positive in 1990, but did not inform Freddie until a year later, just before Mercury died. Hutton admits he now has 'someone special' in his life again, but claims that sexual activity is altogether a thing of the past.

'Freddie was the main love of my life,' he says, his words an eerie echo of Barbara's. 'There was no one like him beforehand, and there never will be now that he has gone. In the meantime, Freddie always said that you must get on with life. I could live for a year, or another 50, but I'm not particularly worried about dying. I know that when I do, Freddie will be on the other side, waiting for me.'

Once again, as with Barbara Valentin and all before her, many months of negotiation would pass before I was invited to Ireland to meet Jim at his home. I eventually made the journey in July 1996, driving out through Carlow town, the 'Celtic centre of Ireland', into rich, vibrant farming country. His bungalow stands at the heart of a network of overgrown country lanes. In his garden, the exquisite, lilac-coloured 'Blue Moon' roses that Freddie adored and which are notoriously tricky to cultivate, are in glorious bloom.

Jim chats about the other rose relating to Freddie, the

'Mercury Rose', which is pink and yellow and which, he believes, you can order through Harrods. He apologizes for 'the state' of the place: he has not quite finished unpacking, and many of his belongings are still in boxes. The house itself, although not palatial by Garden Lodge standards, is homely, respectably furnished, and quite spotless.

Given Jim's Catholic family background and the fact that his mother was still alive when he wrote it, *Mercury and Me* must have taken enormous courage to write.

'I did actually speak to my family about the book before I wrote it,' says Jim. 'And I did, in a way I suppose, ask their permission. Being my family, they said, "What you want to do is what you want to do. We are there for you, and the rest doesn't matter."'

Yet, considering the behavioural expectations and restraints of Catholicism, and the extent to which sin and guilt are emphasized, Jim's family were remarkably understanding about his homosexuality. Freddie, on the other hand, faced a more monumental dilemma, because of his devout parents' Zoroastrianism:

'Well, number one, Freddie didn't practise that religion.'

'Correct,' says Peter Freestone.

'But because Freddie's parents had him cremated according to the Zoroastrian faith, it was wisely assumed that Freddie himself practised.'

In all the years Jim knew him, he says, 'Freddie never worshipped in or practised that faith. I know nothing at all about Zoroastrianism. Freddie and I never discussed religion at all. Since he knew I was Irish, he probably assumed that I was Roman Catholic, but it wasn't a subject we ever discussed. I don't know if his family's religious values affected his life in any way – they may have. I do remember lying in bed beside him half asleep at times, and hearing him praying.'

In which language?

'In English'.

To God?

'To whom, I don't know. I'd sometimes say to him, "Who you talking to?" and he'd just shrug me off: "Saying my prayers." To me, and to him I think, it's all one God anyway.'

It was shortly after their affair began that Freddie took Jim to see the house which would become their 'marital' home. In his book, Jim describes the house, which Freddie had gutted, renovated and decorated to his own taste.

Jim speaks of 'large, light hallways', 'elegant wide staircases'; double doors leading to 'spectacularly spacious rooms, parquet-floored with expansive windows gazing out over the garden'; a minstrels' gallery, Italian marble bathrooms, a 'jacuzzi bath big enough for three'; and what he describes as 'the jewel of the house', the garden, which made the house totally private.

The couple lived together until Freddie's death in 1991.

'I am certain that Freddie's idea of their relationship was not standard "man and wife"', insists Peter Freestone.

We were *all* so important to him – but there was a different part of Freddie's heart for Jim. Although to even say that is strange, when I think about it: Freddie had had a relationship with Mary, and with Joe, but never with me. The thing was, Freddie's capacity for guilt was enormous, which was why Joe and Mary were still around. Freddie felt responsible for them. He felt that he'd upset their lives by having relationships with them, and therefore it was down to him to take care of them, as if to compensate in some way. When you think about it, that's ridiculous. But that's how Freddie was.

Freddie's permanent household of Phoebe, his personal assistant and valet, Liza (Joe Fanelli), the cook, with whom Freddie had an extremely volatile relationship, and Jim, who eventually gave up his hairdressing job at the Savoy to become the gardener, was quickly established. The payroll also included two members of staff who did not 'live in': Terry Giddings, the chauffeur, and Mary Austin, the go-fer, who had her own Freddie-financed grace-and-favour home nearby. Of all Freddie's close friends and staff, Mary was the only one with whom Jim ever had a problem.

'Mary never really let go of Freddie,' says Jim, and Peter agrees.

She never really accepted that it was over between them. In many ways, she was a bit of a driving force for Freddie. She didn't let him get away with anything. She was very strong in that way, and so in that sense it could be said that she was absolutely what Freddie needed. In a way, she was like a mother to him, and he trusted her for that, and relied on it. She ran his life. That's how their relationship lasted. Freddie used to say that even when they were together, they were not like lovers, they were more brother and sister. It was a long, long time before he met me that Freddie went public with his promise that he would leave most of his worldly wealth and goods to Mary. And Freddie was one that, once he'd made a promise, he stuck to it. He didn't go back on his word.

Chapter Seventeen

UNDER PRESSURE: SUN CITY ROLLERS

The observer could be forgiven for concluding that, throughout the eighties, Freddie's personal life and domestic preoccupations took precedence over both the creative and business interests of the band. While it is true that Freddie's fascination with work had waned to some extent, the same could not be said for the rest of the group, who soldiered on relentlessly and, when required, swept Freddie along with them. There was never any serious question that they would go their separate ways: all were only too well aware of the fact that Queen *was* Freddie. That Freddie *was* Queen. But of all the band members, he *knew* that he had made it; that he did not have to try so hard; that he could sit back and enjoy the fruits of his labour a little. Whenever his attendance and input were required, however, his contribution was as committed and as effortlessly brilliant as ever. In spite of this, the press had a field day with 'Queen Split' stories throughout 1983. In reality, wiped out by life on the road, the band had simply decided that it was time to take a rest from the tour circuit and from each other, and perhaps concentrate on a few solo projects. It was Brian who admitted:

I think each of us thinks of leaving quite a lot. But we all know that, even though we might get our own way if we left, we'd still lose something. We'd lose more than we'd gain at the moment. It's a stimulating environment, and because we don't always agree, it's good for us . . .

If you split up, then you lose your vehicle. It has a certain balance of talents, a name which people identify with . . . if you look at most people who've split off from a successful group, they very seldom find a situation that's either commercially successful or personally satisfying. Getting your own way doesn't always make you happy in the end.

But as Brian told me in a personal interview at the Queen offices, 'I don't want to quit playing live. I might want to quit Queen. It gets damned annoying. You only get a quarter of your own way. I like to get it all.'

Freddie chose to put it another way:

I used to think we'd go on for five years, but it's got to the point where we're all actually too old to break up. Can you imagine forming a new band at 40? Be a bit silly, wouldn't it?

The reason I personally needed a rest was because I just got too tired of the whole business. It got to be too much. I decided I really needed a long break.

I don't think we'll ever split. It would seem like cowardice. I suppose if people stopped buying our records, we'd call it a day. And I'd go off and be a strip-tease artist or something.

The decision came after one of their most demanding years ever: a contract with EMI Records for a further six albums had been signed in April 1982, just before Queen commenced another European tour, including several dates around Britain in May and June. It concluded, predictably, with erotic revelry: a 'Shorts and Suspenders' party at London's Embassy Club. 'Hot Space', their 12th album, had also been released. Somewhat disco-orientated, perhaps due to the influences of Reinholdt Mack and the ghosts of Musicland Studios, Brian later admitted to his disappointment in the album, which, despite criticism and a royal panning in the USA, reached number four on the UK chart: 'I think "Hot Space" was a mistake, if only timing-wise. We got heavily into funk and it was quite similar to what Michael Jackson did on "Thriller" a couple of years later and the timing was wrong. Disco was a dirty word.'[1]

American dates had followed throughout summer 1982, including two further shows at Madison Square Garden, a venue which Queen were by now rather blasé about playing. They were handed the keys of the city by the Mayor in Boston in July, the 23rd being declared the official 'Queen Day', and made special guest appearances on two hugely popular American TV chat shows in September: 'Saturday Night Live' and 'Entertainment Tonight'. On to Japan, and the customary Queenmania, after which Freddie retreated to the 43rd floor of the New York skyscraper and the apartment he would henceforth call home. Come November, Elektra Records in the USA had such a resounding flop with 'Staying Power', the final Queen single of their existing contract, that renegotiating the deal was a highly complicated and expensive affair. The Elektra contract also covered Australia and New Zealand, where Queen felt they could be doing better than they were. Elektra and Queen went their separate ways, Queen paying a million dollars for the privilege. Not long afterwards, Queen's Elektra Japan contract was also terminated. EMI would handle significantly more output, while a new recording deal would not be struck in the US until October 1983, when Queen signed with Capitol Records.

In 1983, free to explore his personal creativity, Freddie

began work on a solo album at Musicland Studios in Munich. For a change of scene he would often adjourn to his beloved New York playground. During one such trip he decided to fly to Los Angeles to visit Michael Jackson with the intention of toying with some tracks, which apparently they did, although nothing was ever released. Unlikely rumours did the rounds that Jackson ceased to be enamoured when he accidentally discovered Freddie's penchant for cocaine. Two years on, Freddie had never managed to persuade Michael to go public with any musical collaboration.

Says Peter Freestone:

Freddie certainly did a couple of demo tracks with Michael in his studio at the house in Encino, California. I was there – I even played video games with Michael. On one of the tracks, I can be heard slamming the bathroom door, as it made a good bass drum sound. I've recently been told that a couple of tracks with Freddie are coming out on Michael Jackson's 'History Part II' album. An unlikely friendship? Well, it was only the once. It never developed to the extent that some newspapers built it up to be. Their schedules never allowed them to pursue it further. But they liked each other, and recognized each other as geniuses in their own right.

Back in London Freddie indulged his passion for opera, attending, in May 1983, a Covent Garden Opera House production of Giuseppe Verdi's *Un Ballo In Maschera* (*A Masked Ball*), starring the formidable Italian tenor Luciano Pavarotti and the equally impressive Spanish soprano Montserrat Caballé, then, amazingly, in her 50th year.

'Until that point,' explains Peter,

Freddie has always adored the tenor voice – Domingo, Pavarotti. I had a huge collection of opera records, and Freddie was tremendously keen to learn as much as he could about opera. One day I said to him, 'Okay, if you claim to like Pavarotti so much, he's singing at the Opera House soon, why don't we go?' He thought this was a splendid idea, and got me to book tickets straight away.

Pavarotti came on and sang an aria in the first act, and Freddie thought it was brilliant. In the second act the prima donna came on, and it was Montserrat Caballé. Because we had been so taken with the idea of seeing Pavarotti, we hadn't taken much notice of who else was in it. She started to sing, and that was it. Freddie's jaw dropped. He only wanted her from then on, and just about forgot that Pavarotti was on the stage.

Freddie was mesmerized, particularly by the famous love duet between the ardent Riccardo and the beautiful Amelia, a woman tormented by guilt but unable to resist – a sentiment with which he readily identified. And for the rest of the performance he could not tear his eyes or ears from the strong but musically delicate Caballé, so impressed was he by her limpid tone, impeccable technique, and exquisite vocal versatility:

'Now, that's a *real* singer,' he later remarked.

'If I were asked to come up with 10 images of people being happy in my life, I would have to say that one of them is Freddie about to see Montserrat perform at Covent Garden,' says Paul Gambaccini.

I have, in my mind, in one of those snapshot stills which we carry through the photo album in our brain . . . a Covent Garden performance by Montserrat. She's just about to come out on stage, and I'm sitting in the middle of the orchestra stalls, and to my left, sitting in the front row of the box seats, is Freddie. And there is a look of such wonder and delight in his eyes . . . his left hand makes a gesture towards the stage, indicating that she's about to appear, and there is such happiness in his face.

Just like a child! It's a great moment – and proof that, no matter what success he may have had, he *never* lost his respect and admiration for his great and favourite stars. Even the stars have their stars.

Little did Freddie know that, before too long, he and the internationally acclaimed soprano would be performing and recording together as one of the music world's least likely dynamic duos.

Even rich and famous rock-stars can have too much of a good thing – rest and relaxation, for example. An aborted attempt to write and record the score for movie director Tony Richardson's motion picture adaptation of John Irving's novel *The Hotel New Hampshire* whetted their collective appetite. It was time for Queen to get back to work. They would convene in Los Angeles forthwith where, business matters dealt with, they checked into LA's Record Plant recording studios to begin pre-production on their next album, 'The Works', the first release from which would be a Roger Taylor composition, 'Radio Ga-Ga', in January 1984. A number two in Britain, it hit number one in 19 countries across the globe, and was one of the cleverest Queen compositions ever released. Within its bland, pop-chant lyrics lurked a thinly-disguised snipe at the way the pop radio medium had 'sold out', its image and function greatly at odds with what it had once represented: Roger had listened religiously to the worthy Radio Luxembourg under the bedclothes in his teens. An epic record in every sense, it required equally epic visuals to promote it. With the help of the Queen fan club, some 500 fans descended on London's Shepperton Studios where they donned silver boiler suits, stood in straight lines, clapped and raised their hands in time to the chorus-line – a sequence soon to be mirrored by

Queen fans at gigs the world over. This, their most expensive promo to date, also proved to be one of the most impressive videos Queen had ever attempted. The single shot directly to number four in the UK. February 1984 saw them joining a line-up which included Boy George and Culture Club, Paul Young and Bonnie Tyler for the laugh-a-minute San Remo song festival in Italy: something of a gauche fiasco for such long-in-the-tooth performers, but a cute location – a sort of Bournemouth for the Italians – and a few days' fun in the sun nonetheless. It was a combination which Queen had rarely found themselves turning down.

'The Works' their 13th album, made its US and UK début in February. While their American fans appeared underwhelmed, the British contingent watched it chart at number two.

Another famous if controversial Queen video was inspired by a track on The Works album. For their single 'I Want To Break Free', Queen dolled up in women's clothes, with Freddie, perhaps unsurprisingly, the most outrageous in inflated tight pink sweater, leather mini, fishnets and stilettoes. The video also incorporated a 45-second ballet sequence, inspired by Debussy's *L'Apres-Midi d'un Faune* for which Freddie, ever the incurable balletomane, rehearsed with the Royal Ballet corps until he dropped.

May 1984 saw them performing for the Montreux Rose d'Or pop festival and making the announcement concerning their forthcoming European tour, to commence that August, after which Freddie withdrew to Munich to live it up and to continue working on his own album. It was during that episode that the accident referred to by Barbara Valentin occurred, which resulted in Freddie breaking his leg.

'Rock Star Freddie Injured In Bust-Up', yelped the *Sun*, reporting how the '37-year-old singer' had been 'kicked in the leg during a night-club binge'. The incident referred to was said to have taken place at the now defunct Henderson's nightclub, or 'Mrs Henderson's' as they referred to it, a favourite watering hole of Freddie's and Barbara's and once the riotous scene of one of his many birthday parties.

'It was actually at the New York bar in Munich, but the confusion must have arisen because it was owned by the same couple who owned Henderson's,' laughed Peter.

What had started as a bit of fun got madly out of hand, and culminated in a drunken brawl during which Freddie sustained a bad fall and wrenched the ligaments in his right leg. Trying to rush her friend to hospital, Barbara had her aggressive encounter with the taxi-driver who refused to take a 'drunk' to the hospital. As luck would have it Freddie's bones were not fractured, but the injury was nevertheless very painful and he 'remained plastered' for three weeks.

In June came a very special accolade – the Silver Clef Outstanding Contribution to British Music award from the Nordoff-Robbins Music Therapy Charity. The charity, founded on the theory that severely handicapped children may be taught a variety of motor and communicational skills through music, had, since its inception, been warmly supported by the pop and rock music industry. Its annual London fundraisers and award lunches are always enthusiastically attended by the biggest stars as well as industry personnel.

Shortly afterwards, Queen unwittingly found themselves embroiled in the most politically compromising phase of their career, when they agreed to perform 12 shows in October at the then controversial South African resort, the Sun City Superbowl. The multi-million dollar Bophuthatswana desert resort, ostensibly a Vegas-style gambling complex partly financed by the Government while apartheid was still firmly and shamefully in place, represented to the outside world a vulgar sneer by the privileged white South African minority to the many poverty-stricken black inhabitants of the country's squalid townships. In Britain, the Musicians' Union had imposed a ban on performances by any of its members in Sun City. Bruce Springsteen, plus Little Stevie and friends, captured the anti-apartheid mood on the single 'I Ain't Gonna Play Sun City'.

According to Brian, 'We had heard so much about South Africa, about the troubles there, but we had also heard a lot about Sun City, and we wanted to go and see it all for ourselves.'

Controversy against Queen over the planned South Africa gigs continued to rage in the press as the band prepared to embark on their European tour – on which, for the first time ever, they welcomed along a fifth musician to perform with them on stage as part of the band. Amiable, talented, hard-working and fun-loving, Spike Edney had made a name for himself with Bob Geldof's Boomtown Rats, and had previously lent his keyboard-playing skills to a variety of big-name groups. His refreshing lack of ego, his laddish cheek and his ability and willingness to muck in made him an instant hit with Queen, who had lured him to Munich to audition, an occasion Edney recalls with not inconsiderable embarrassment:

Queen had this fearsome reputation for being sensitive and difficult, and I really didn't know what to expect. I thought the only way to safeguard the cause was to be as prepared as I could be, so I made sure I learned all the songs from their previous tour and from the current album, 'The Works', inside out and back to front.

Freddie was already in Munich, and I travelled out with the others. We arrived the day before we were due to start rehearsing, and Crystal (Chris Taylor, Roger's personal roadie) said to me, 'Okay, Spike, we're having a kind of getting-to-know-you dinner tonight.' So me, Crystal, some of the crew, Roger, Brian and John hit Munich. In a very big way. Of course I was very wary; I was the new boy, and I didn't know the rules. There I was, on my best behaviour, trying to be Mr Affable. We had a damned good time – far too good. Toured Munich the length and breadth. Come four o'clock in the morning, we were in the Sugar Shack club, and by six o'clock in the morning we were back at the hotel, in Roger's suite, where the champagne was flowing. It had all been very fabulous, and I thought, well, this is a bit of a laugh – better than work. Then I suddenly remembered that 11 o'clock was meant to be rehearsal time. I thought I should go off and get some sleep. Although I was well-prepared, I really thought I should be on my toes because I hadn't even met Freddie yet. I trolled off to bed, put in an alarm call, and I was fairly wasted, I have to say. When I woke up it was still dark, and I thought I could only have been asleep for an hour or so. I must have woken up so soon because I was nervous. So I phoned down to ask the time, and the front desk said, 'It's eight o'clock.' 'But it's dark,' I said. 'Yes, sir,' they replied. 'It's eight o'clock at night.'

Spike still recalls the experience as the worst moment of his life. Believing he had missed the entire first day of rehearsals, he thought there was nothing else for it but to pack up and go home. Before he did so, he put in a call to Crystal's room.

'You c–t,' came the greeting. Because he'd been the one who'd got me the gig. Utter venom was pouring at me down the phone. I thought, Jesus Christ, he's really mad, and quite rightly so, I've let him down. I said, 'Look, I'm so sorry, I overslept, I booked an alarm call . . . why didn't somebody call me? You could have given me a shout when I didn't turn up . . .' He said, 'You c–t, you woke me up!' I said, 'But it's eight o'clock at night.' He said, 'Yeah, well, we didn't go to bed until four o'clock this afternoon.' 'What about the rehearsal?' I said. 'What *about* it?' he yelled. 'Rehearsal *nothing*!' and slammed the phone down. An hour later he rang back and said, 'Right. We're all meeting in Roger's room, and we're all going out.' And we hit the town *again*. Nobody had yet done *any* work. But this time we took it a bit easy, and the next day I met Jim Beach and Fred for the first time.[2]

At that stage, Queen had not actually played together for the best part of two years, although they had been in the studio together recording 'The Works' album. Although it was not their favourite pastime, it had never been Queen's habit to rehearse casually: if the job was worth doing, it was worth doing well. So into the most sophisticated hangar they would go, equipped with state-of-the-art production, sound, lighting equipment – the works, in fact. The band had never made a secret of the fact that they hated rehearsals. Consequently they usually confined themselves to the bare minimum.

'The very first thing I played with them in rehearsals was 'Tie Your Mother Down',' recalls Spike.

Which was fine, because they'd been playing that for a hundred years. Then something else—'Under Pressure' – and then they said, well, let's try one of the new ones: 'I Want To Break Free'. Not really a very difficult song, you might think. So we got going into the first verse of it, crumbled, stopped, and it occurred to me that they had never actually played it live together. I had everything written down, of course. So I said, 'Well, actually it goes . . . da da da . . . then John came over to the piano, then Brian, and they sort of stood there. Then Freddie pitched up and said, 'You wouldn't happen to have the *words*, old chap, would you?' And I did, actually. So there we all were round the piano and I suddenly thought to myself, 'This is gonna be okay. I can do this.'

I was very wary at first of making contributions. But after a while I'd just stick my neck out and say, 'Why don't we try this?' And the great thing was, none of them seemed to mind.

Munich was Spike's first taste of the clearly-defined division between 'Freddie's Scene' – 'The Mafia', as his so-called personal travelling circus was referred to by members of the Queen entourage – and 'The Rest Of The Band's Scene' – 'Hetero Towers' being the name applied to whichever hotel they were based at.

'There was no problem with that arrangement,' insists Spike. 'It was no kind of "Us And Them" nonsense, everybody was very relaxed about it. We had our separate parties. It wasn't always like that on the road. But later on in Rio it was certainly so, mainly because there were so many pop stars down there, and Fred *needed* to have the best suite in town, so he stayed in one flash hotel, and we stayed in another, equally flash hotel. In South Africa, it was a different situation entirely, and we pretty much all pitched in together.'

Prior to the South African excursion, Queen performed their UK shows, including three nights at the Birmingham National Exhibition Centre. It was on this occasion that bright young Londoner Tony Hadley, the pop-singing sensation with Chrysalis signing Spandau Ballet who had stormed the Top Ten with hits such as 'Lifeline', 'True', and 'Gold', had the opportunity to met Freddie for the first time, and discovered just how generous the great Queen front man could be towards young, up-and-coming performers. Hadley, then only in his early twenties, had such an incredibly powerful and versatile voice that he had already been compared to the young Frank Sinatra. Unbeknown to him, Freddie was one of his biggest fans. The admiration was entirely mutual, as Hadley had grown up listening to Queen records, and was already a committed fan.

'Freddie was the world's greatest front man,' affirms Tony.[3]

'Plus, Queen records always made you feel good. There was always this underlying sense of fun. I'd been dying to meet them, especially Freddie, for ages.'

The first time I actually met him was at the Birmingham NEC in 1984. I travelled up with Leonie [his wife] – we had tickets, passes and everything else. At that time I was famous enough that I could get a backstage pass to virtually anything! We went backstage, met the lads, and they were really friendly and polite. They said they were having a party after the show at the hotel next-door to the NEC. So we went along, I walked in with Leonie, and Freddie had a spare seat next to him. 'Come on darling,' he said to me. 'Come and sit next to me, dear.' Leonie ended up sitting somewhere else at the table! We were chatting away when all of a sudden a couple of strippers came on to entertain the troops. It was brilliant. It seemed to me that Queen always had more fun than anybody else. The parties were always big, the records were big, the personalities in the band were bigger than in any other group you came across. Even someone like John Deacon, who was a really quiet guy, had this incredibly large personality. Sit down and talk to him and you find out he's a terrific geezer, surprisingly deep. There are very few people you meet in this business who are completely genuine, and Freddie was one of them – as were all the Queen guys. Top geezers.

That night in Birmingham was the first time Freddie and I really discussed the on-stage persona. 'Never make excuses for being there on stage; never apologize,' he'd say. 'The audience have come to see *you*, so it doesn't matter if you're a bit off one night. You've just got to front the whole thing out.' And Freddie was the best person at doing that, without a doubt. All he had to do was walk out on stage and swing a few of his gestures, and he had them. He wasn't the tallest fella in the world. But he looked every inch a star. I was 23, 24 years old back then, singing in a band that was doing okay. Freddie didn't have to bother with someone like me. But he was very enthusiastic, and always keen to impart his knowledge and experience. He was incredibly generous in that way. I really appreciated it. No one before Freddie had ever actually taken me aside and said, 'Look, now these are a few dos and don'ts ... this is how to get the best out of yourself and make the most of a show.' He was the only bloke who ever did that. I really respected him for it. He wasn't patronizing me or being condescending; he was genuinely trying to help me.

'Every artist is wracked with self-doubt, Tony,' he'd say. 'Even you?' I'd say. 'Especially me,' Freddie would reply. We talked about the fact that there are two sides to every artist. The one who goes out on stage, you have to psyche yourself up to. The one who remains offstage is vulnerable, needs a cuddle, a bit of affection – and needs to be told that he's good. I know for a fact that Freddie was no different. If you are as large as he was onstage, you can guarantee that you are going to be equally vulnerable and small *off*stage.

The UK shows having been the expected hit, and with one of the Wembley shows falling on 5 September, Freddie's 38th birthday, he celebrated with a huge party at London's Xenon nightclub. A few days later, Queen's 26th single 'Hammer To Fall' was released on the same day as Freddie's début solo single, 'Love Kills', recorded for the movie *Metropolis*. As the band arrived in Germany for their Dortmund gig two days later, it was noted that nine Queen albums currently featured in the UK Top 200, an incredible achievement. A little way into the tour, Freddie sustained another fall during Queen's Hanover gig, which again resulted in the strapping-up of his leg in hospital. Ignoring doctor's advice, Freddie was back on stage two days later, although the shapes he threw that night were somewhat subdued.

Early in October, against Musicians' Union advice, Queen

and entourage, including Mary Austin and her new live-in boyfriend Joe Bert, the bass player in Tom Robinson's band, departed for Bophuthatswana for their 12-gig Sun City run.

'The South Africa situation was a bit tricky because officially, nobody was allowed to go there,' recalls Spike Edney.

I actually denied at the time that I even went. It was safer to, because I was just a session musician. The Union had a block on going there, and if you breached Union rules and went down there to play, you could find yourself expelled. The consequences for me would have been catastrophic. The Union took exception to Queen going, which was so hypocritical as Stevie Wonder had already been down there to perform, as well as Diana Ross, Rod Stewart, and various others. So why make an example out of Queen? But, they did. Queen were told that they had broken the rules, and that their product would henceforth be blacklisted, nothing allowed to appear on TV and so on. Which is all pretty serious.

It was as if the band were jinxed when, on the very first night, 5 October, Freddie's voice gave out just a few numbers into the show. Among the desperately disappointed audience was Rolf Harris, the all-singing, all-sketching, didgeridoo-playing veteran Australian star: 'I had made a special trip to Sun City just to see Queen,' confirms Rolf, who recorded his own wobble-board version of 'Bohemian Rhapsody' in 1996, although it failed to match the chart-busting success he had achieved with his rendition of Led Zeppelin's 'Stairway To Heaven'.

'It was all fantastic. I couldn't believe the volume – these monumental decibels pounding from the stage and damn near blowing the roof off. I had the earplugs in, I can assure you. I was thinking to myself, how can all these other people in the audience stand this noise? Queen did about two songs, and it was brilliant, but the next thing we knew, someone came out on stage to announce that Freddie had done his voice in, poor bugger. What a disappointment.'

According to Spike Edney, the night Freddie's voice gave out 'was really a very sad, black night. I think it was the first-ever time Queen had had to stop a show, and Freddie felt really bad about it. But it was beyond his control. The rest of us all went off for dinner and a few drinks to console ourselves, and Roger ordered a very large bottle of champagne and sent it up to Freddie with this little card saying, "Don't worry, Fred, we all still love you."'

The shows resumed after four days. It was impossible to reschedule those which had been cancelled, however, and the cost to all involved was considerable, which depressed the band deeply. The trip, however, had not been without its humorous moments:

'One night', remembers Spike:

They took us all out to a hide, a water hole, to see some local wildlife. Off we went 10 miles down the road, dragging the picnic hampers of champagne behind us. All the band, all the crew, security – everyone was there. This was everybody's first go at being on a wild animal jaunt, so there was a certain amount of excitement. It was all 'Sssshhh . . . mustn't make any noise, because the animals will bugger off.' So for about 10 minutes we all sat there completely motionless and silent. You could have heard the proverbial pin drop. All of a sudden, this moth comes flying across in front of our faces, and Freddie goes, 'Well fuck me, is that *it?*'

Of course, everybody just cracked up. We were howling with laughter, the animals had all been driven away, and the guide said, 'We might as well go back now. We're not going to see anything tonight!'

Overall, in spite of the cancellations, we had such a great time that I for one didn't want to come back.

On their return to London, Brian and Roger went along to the Union to plead their case: 'It was not as if the trip had been a complete jamboree,' reasons Spike.

Queen had done quite a bit of charity stuff out there . . . including significant fundraising for Bophuthatswana's Kutlawamong school for deaf and blind children, for whom Queen later released a special live album in South Africa and donated all royalties to the school . . . And the reaction to them was so fantastic that I still don't believe it was the wrong thing to do. The punters out there were so starved of decent musical entertainment. And of course within a couple of years the whole political thing had changed and it was kosher to go to South Africa after all.

Queen did not escape without a heavy fine, however. But the band held out for their money to be donated to charity instead of swelling the Union's personal bank balance. They remained puzzled by the fiasco for years. As Roger Taylor pointed out to Martin Dunn of the *Sun* in April 1986, 'Our songs are very popular in South Africa. "I Want To Break Free" is an unofficial anthem among the Africa National Congress movement. And "Another One Bites The Dust" is one of the biggest-selling songs in South African black history.'

It was on that trip, recalls Spike Edney, that he realized for the first time what a tightly-knit group Queen actually were:

Queen were a real band – very much so. They were all such strong characters in their own way, and they'd all be in their digging and digging, and they all did a very good job of sticking up for themselves and for each other. I do think Fred usually had the last word. When it came to, say, the live procedure, it was he who had to carry the can, and so he called the final shot. By the time I joined them, Queen had been doing all this for so long that everybody knew what they were up to, they could almost do it with their eyes shut. The tantrums would only come – and I personally witnessed very few – during the recording process. It would all generally get resolved in the end when Freddie said, 'No, I'm not doing that – I'm doing this!' But in my experience he didn't rule with an iron rod. Nor did he try to. He would always listen to other people's opinions and try out everyone's ideas. He certainly wasn't a control freak.

Slowly, I began to learn just how many sides to the man there were. He could be incredibly strong and forceful sometimes. Then again he could be easy-going, playful, fun – completely approachable. He tended not to trust people when he first met them, for obvious reasons. That was why we got into that thing on the road of all hanging out in Fred's suite. Because he couldn't really *go* anywhere. If he did, he would be on show, he couldn't relax or have proper time off, so what was the point of going out to be surrounded by hundreds of people wanting yet another autograph? For him to relax, he had to be in his own private world surrounded by his gang. And we were like a bunch of kids really – a boys' club, out on tour. The rock 'n' roll tour is a boys' game, after all. In that private world he could be incredibly relaxed, and you could say anything to him, and have a lot of fun. He liked the camaraderie and the merciless piss-taking, which was invariably two-way. There was no worrying about 'job security', as we called it; you didn't have to defer to The Boss. Towards the end of his touring life, Freddie was pretty much confined to the hotel, which was a terrible existence really.

The thing I loved about Freddie was that he had such *style* – even when he was slagging you off. I never had too many problems with him. If I suggested something and he thought it was crap, he'd turn around and say, 'That's crap.' You always knew where you stood. You couldn't take offence because he had such a good sense of humour. But I must say I would have hated to be on the receiving end of one of his seriously bad moods. I think he was a difficult man to reason with if he'd made up his mind about something.

Spike concedes that Queen had a reputation for incredible arrogance:

That was true. They *were* arrogant. But it was because, most of the time, they were right about what they did. I got the impression they believed that they had been unfairly treated when they first started out, and that had taught them to be self-sufficient – to rely on their own judgment. The only downside to Queen's arrogance was that it filtered down through the ranks of their organization. People who worked for them started being arrogant on Queen's behalf, when they didn't actually have a right to be. It could all get pretty unbearable at times.

Following the South Africa experience, Freddie returned to his Munich haven. And that Christmas, Queen decided to produce their first-ever Christmas single, 'Thank God It's Christmas'. Something of a send-up of the genre, Queen's 27th single was produced mainly in London with Freddie's vocals added in Munich. It failed to make the UK Top 20. But, because it has yet to appear on any Queen album, the single remains a rarity.

Chapter Eighteen

QUEEN OF THE ROAD

It was billed as the biggest rock music festival the world had ever seen. Coming as it did, pre-Bob Geldof's Live Aid, 'Rock In Rio', a sort of 80s South American answer to Woodstock, more than lived up to the hype. Queen had been invited to be the main stars of 1985's eight-day New Year summer festival, which would also feature some of the greatest contemporary music acts: Rod Stewart, Yes, Iron Maiden, Def Leppard, Ozzie Osbourne, George Benson and James Taylor as well as various top Brazilian artists. Planned on a size and scale which thoroughly met with their approval, it was a festival to which Queen could hardly say no – not least because the man in charge of the festival was none other than their own faithful tour manager, Gerry Stickells. The band duly departed for Brazil on 6 January. Freddie was accompanied by Peter Freestone, Barbara Valentin, Paul Prenter and a minder. Just six days later Queen would perform live for the most massive live audience in rock history: between 250,000 and 300,000 fans, many of whom had travelled for two days or more through blistering heat to witness the spectacle.

Spike Edney, who joined Queen on the Rio trip to play keyboards, remembers sizing up Freddie's predicament and feeling very sorry for him indeed:

You've got to remember what a massive star Freddie was in South America by that time. He was a God. The Queen song 'Love Of My Life' had been number one in Argentina as if forever; it was Queen's version of 'Stairway to Heaven'. Consequently, Fred was a total prisoner once he got down there. He more or less couldn't go anywhere, not even with armed guards. It must have been so distressing for him. I think he did manage to slip out once or twice, but in the end, quite frankly, it just wasn't worth the aggro.

I believe part of the reason for his popularity in that part of the world was his looks. I don't know if this is true, but I heard it said that when Fred shaved off his hair and grew the moustache, he turned into the epitome of the good-looking South American male – a sort of Latin Clark Gable. Perhaps there was a bit of that in what they adored about him. But I think in the main it would have to be the music.

Spike remembers being blown away by the Rio experience:

I had been involved in some things in my time, but never anything on such a scale. I knew that Queen's earlier South American tours had been really pioneering adventures, but I have to say that this was fairly pioneering as well: The biggest show ever. Nearly 300,000 people in this Brazilian field. The memory is a little blurred, but what I do remember is that the night before the show, the Minister of Culture threw this party, which we all trolled off to attend. His house was mind-bogglingly massive, in the middle of this private estate absolutely smothered in security. All the stars were there: Rod Stewart, George Benson, Yes. Most of the house was covered in white fur – the floor, the ceiling, even the walls! And my most vivid memory is of some top Brazilian star sitting at the piano, with George Benson up there giving it loads of crooning, and us all standing round going 'this is a bit of a laugh', when up rocks Nena Hagen to the piano just as George is doing his best warbling, and she starts wailing along very loudly at about 150 watts. Hilarious.

The event did indeed take place in a wide open field. Over several months, the festival organizers had constructed the Barra da Tijuca Rockodromo site, which featured a gigantic semi-circular stage with a fountain on either side. These, in the event, proved particularly useful, as the day before the festival was due to commence it rained heavily all through the night. Mud-splattered fans were able to wash themselves clean in the fountains.

It was as if a small town had mushroomed in the middle of nowhere. The Barra also featured large press stands in which international telephone lines had been installed for the thousands of journalists and photographers attending, along with wiring facilities, shops, burger bars, all mod cons. At night, huge searchlights criss-crossed the sky, Hollywood première-fashion, lighting up the site for miles around. Nearby, a special heliport had been constructed, which proved an absolute necessity: all roads leading to the Barra having been jammed for days, the only way in, and out, for the performing artists was by helicopter – a mode of transport which Freddie did not fancy at all.

Queen were due to appear after Iron Maiden the first night of the festival, as the main headlining act. In the event, two hours elapsed between Maiden's performance and the long-awaited appearance of Queen, the latter finally taking the stage at around two a.m. By that time, the crowd were almost beside themselves with anticipation.

Observer columnist Peter Hillmore was in Rio to witness the spectacular event:

Jim Beach had arranged everything – but not quite well

335

enough. I'd already thrown a tantrum, insisting that they change my hotel because I wanted to be staying where the band were staying. Otherwise, what was the point? I can remember sitting beside the pool, idly picking at a melon, when Rod Stewart came down for breakfast, going, 'Gosh, what a hard life we all lead.' By way of a sweetener, Jim Beach had now fixed it for me to be actually on the stage, in the wings, when Queen went on. When I got there, I peered out and saw this colossal audience. It was mind-blowing. I turned to Brian and said, 'What's it like being out there, on stage?' and he said 'Well go and have a look.' I went on – and I have never felt like a bigger prat. I wasn't performing, of course. I was just standing there. Thousands upon thousands of faces staring up at me. All of them screaming for Queen. And by definition, screaming for me, because I was there with them. It was an extraordinary moment. I felt the raw power of Freddie Mercury, and tasted what it was like to have a quarter of a million people wanting nothing more than for you to open your mouth and sing. I remember feeling very scared, because I couldn't actually *do* anything. In the meantime, Queen amble on and it all starts to happen, and those quarter of a million people scream out '*Yes*!' Roadies are rushing about, nobody even notices me, and I just float away to one side. I knew, there and then, that I wanted to be one of Queen more than anything in the world. I wanted to *be* Freddie Mercury. He'd lift his hand and they would sing along with him. He'd drop his hand and they would immediately fall silent, because he'd said so. The effect was unbelievable: like seeing a nuclear reactor split the atom.

He was not natural. He was different. He'd have people jumping out of cars at traffic lights, salivating over his limo, going 'Freddie – you're *God*!' He, and the rest of Queen, had an entire organization pumping away and costing a fortune, just to make sure they were absolutely comfortable wherever they went, before they even did a day's work. They'd never unpack. They'd never have to worry about 'Excess Baggage', or queuing at airports, or lining up for their Duty Frees. It was all VIP lounges and first-class transatlantic flights – and someone at every end to cater for their every whim. Which all adds up to why I think it is impossible for a star like Freddie to have a private life. In the end, that is going to have an effect on even the most normal person's sanity.

That night, on stage, came Freddie's widely-reported 'Brazilian boob'. Strutting on to the stage in the same pneumatic girlie get-up in which he had posed for the video of 'I Want To Break Free', Freddie was amazed, as he launched into the song, to note that the audience did not appear to see the funny side. In fact, his posturing all but started a riot, as the fans began to pelt the stage with cans, stones and other rubbish in protest. When a huge piece of cardboard hit Freddie at the front of the stage, Brian retreated from the firing line, taking several steps back until he was level with Roger's drum riser. But Freddie stayed defiantly where he was – and proceeded to lose his temper. He reacted very angrily, and began to taunt the crowds in return, which was perhaps not the wisest move. He had not been aware of the fact that the locals had adopted the song as a kind of anti-dictatorship anthem, and did not approve of it being sent up in this way. In the ensuing video, however, the unfortunate incident was edited out.

Installed in great luxury at the Copacabana Palace hotel in Rio de Janeiro, Freddie, in customary style, held court. He managed a visit to Alaska, the most popular gay disco in Rio at that time, with a few chosen members of his circus, including Paul Prenter, to whom fell the dubious task of picking out men that Freddie fancied the look of, and persuading them back to the star's hotel suite. It was not the most demanding job Prenter had ever had. Few could resist such an attractive invitation, especially as Prenter worded it so seductively: 'Freddie Mercury would love you to come to his personal private party at his hotel . . .'

All who witnessed this had to agree that Prenter's duties had by now taken on a somewhat sordid dimension. Not only did he have to round up the talent – for many of the likely lads that Freddie chose were 'taxi boys', young male prostitutes – but he was also responsible for organizing copious supplies of alcohol and cocaine. The procedure quickly fell into something of a routine:

Boys were chosen, and joined Freddie back in the privacy of his hotel suite, which was very luxurious and over-looked the hotel pool. First they drank, and then they snorted some cocaine – there was a little low, wooden table with the lines of cocaine already chopped out, all prepared. Next, they shed their clothes and entered Freddie's bedroom, where Freddie would greet them, wearing just his dressing gown. Throughout the pro-ceedings, Paul Prenter was the only one who remained fully-clothed. Freddie then engaged in sexual activity with each of them in turn, and each time in front of all the others. Then, he would tell Prenter that he was tired. Prenter paid off the boys, and they were invited to leave.

Such were the reminiscences of one such former taxi boy, a masculine blond, blue-eyed Jew named Patricio who joined Freddie for such antics on several occasions. Patricio was not what you could call tall, but he had a large, muscular body and everything else it took, and appeared to be very attractive to gay men. He had travelled from Buenos Aires to Rio, Dick Whittington-style, to make a name for himself, perhaps as an actor. But, like so many others, he had tumbled into prostitution through destitution and despair. Patricio, who would eventually make one final journey to Israel to die of Aids, had sex with Freddie on several occasions. He reported that Freddie himself was always passive, on the receiving end: 'When you start being gay, you tend to be active. But if you are popular, and everyone wants to go with you, you then turn to passive as it is the easiest way to have fun. To act like "the man" is very tiring. Most gay men come to prefer the more "feminine" role.'

The only conclusion to be drawn from such revelations is that Freddie, for whatever reason, had acquired an insatiable taste for loveless, pointless sex. According to Patricio, he was not even turned on by any of what he tried. The wilder such activity grew, the more impassive Freddie appeared. He did not even seem to be enjoying himself. Many such parties took place down in Rio – and all concluded the same sorry way. There were also various other events with a broader-spectrum appeal, which would be attended by a more diverse range of guests, including women.

Freddie's quest for kicks had by now clearly exceeded what he could reasonably handle. He had always craved the outrageous, if only for its own sake: he once revealed that his fondest dream was to be held aloft by Negro slaves. But his relentless indulgence in every kind of excess proved just one thing: that he was tired. He could have anything money can buy, but he found himself having to work harder and harder for a specific kind of pleasure – the kind which would always elude him. Zipless sex was all very well, but the excitement had long since faded. The reality, which Freddie was loath to admit, was that he was sick of it. He was sick to death of it all. And yet, the more he despised himself for such gross self-indulgence, the more he was driven to indulge. It was, by now, as if he could not stop himself. Something very soon would have to give.

'This is a very fair assessment of what he was like at the time,' Peter Freestone concedes. 'Sadly, it was no worse than what we expected. When Paul and Barbara were both around, it became a competition as to who could provide the more outrageous spectacle, until it all reached burn-out point. Freddie had long ago lost interest, but he was too polite to say anything. He'd always had such enormous fun doing those things before, and of course people didn't expect him to have changed.'

Marcela Delorenzi was also present at Rock in Rio, and joined Freddie for a record company celebration soon afterwards:

I was invited to the party thrown by EMI for Queen because by this time I was the president of the Community of Queen Subjects, Queen's fan club in Argentina. The party was held around the pool at the Copacabana Palace hotel, and many stars and VIPs attended: David Coverdale from Whitesnake, the Scorpions, Rod Stewart . . . Rod was still very angry that night, particularly with Freddie, because he had his birthday (his 40th, in fact, on 10 January), and Freddie and Roger had eaten the cake before Rod had a chance to light the candles and have everyone sing him 'Happy Birthday'! And David Coverdale was causing mischief, teasing all the groupies by showing them his room key number, and pretending that they should show up at his room at half-hourly intervals.

Brian, Roger and John were all there when I arrived, but no Freddie. He did eventually get to the party, and made a very grand entrance with his whole group. Accompanied by Paul Prenter, Freddie was dressed in a green T-shirt and white trousers. He entered the party, looking quite serious, and just stood there. I was talking to Roger close by at the time, and I just turned to talk to Freddie. As it was a private party, and everyone was very laid-back, this was a perfectly natural thing to do. I told him that I was now President of the Argentina fan club.

'Oh! Argentina!' he said. 'How wonderful!' He spoke very quietly, and sometimes covered his mouth with his hand when he was talking. We gave him some presents – an Argentinian boleadoras – it's a type of lasso with which the Gauchos trap the animals on the pampas. Freddie took one look at it and said, 'What on earth is this?' I spoke a little English then, not as well as I do now, and I wasn't able to make him understand.

I chatted a bit with Paul Prenter, and I got the impression from the things he was saying that he was, or had been, Freddie's lover. But that, in fact, was the most surprising thing I learned all evening.

A much bigger party, held at the other hotel being used by artists including the rest of Queen, the Copacabana Beach, was thrown on 12 January for all performers who had played the festival. That party, a much rowdier affair during which a sizeable contingent including Brian May wound up in the swimming-pool, was televised live throughout South America to countless millions.

Queen took the stage once again on 19 January to close the festival. By this time the sorry site was awash with mud due to incessant torrential rain. But it dampened neither the fans' enthusiasm nor Queen's performance. Once again, the band had made history.

It was on 5 April 1985 that the Queen machine descended on Auckland for the first time, more than ready to take New Zealand by storm. Always revved up by the prospect of playing in a country which had not previously had the opportunity of falling to their charms, every member of the band was raring to go. Their visit was marred slightly in the beginning by the protestations of a handful of anti-apartheid demonstrators, still inflamed by the Sun City fiasco, at the airport and outside their hotel. Freddie, in any case, was more preoccupied by the release, back home, of his second solo single 'I Was Born To Love You', from the début solo album which many believed would never actually see the light of day. The single did eventually rise to number 11 on the UK chart, but interestingly made no impact in America.

Queen's début in New Zealand, at Auckland's Mount Smart Stadium, almost went disastrously wrong thanks to the arrival of an old friend of Freddie's from England: one Tony Hadley of Spandau Ballet. As Spike Edney pointed out, 'It was very rare indeed for Freddie to go on stage drunk. That night in New Zealand following the ridiculous afternoon he had just spent with Hadley (who these days performs regularly with Spike's All Stars band when not working on solo projects) was one of the few times.'

Tony Hadley winces at the memory as he picks up the story:

I'm a bad influence, see. Spandau were really big then. We had just completed a two-month tour of Europe, only two days off, and were down touring Australia, 60, 70,000 people in every city, then a similar tour lined up for New Zealand. It was relentless, and we were completely knackered. For some reason, to this day I don't know why, our New Zealand tour got cancelled. But I'd heard Queen were down playing New Zealand, so I thought, Oh great, I'll nip over and see the lads anyway. I went over to Auckland with a minder – only because I wasn't allowed to go anywhere without one – checked into their hotel, went to the sound check, had a chat ... For some reason I remember big bowls of Smarties in the dressing-room. Then Freddie and I went back to the hotel, and went to the bar for a drink.

It was all downhill from that point.

The next thing, Freddie's saying, 'Let's get some

Stolichnaya.' It was his passion, that vodka. We sat at the hotel bar, talked and talked, put the world to rights, exchanging cliché rock 'n' roll war stories, all the bit, while we did the whole bottle of Stoli. Neat. The next thing I knew he was saying, 'Come on, darling, up to my room, I've got a bottle of port up there. That's what we'll hit next.'

'Freddie used to say that port was "good for the throat",' Peter added.

So they did. Tony continues:

By which time we were both off our heads. Freddie then says, 'You've *got* to come on stage tonight.' 'Well, I don't want to intrude,' I said. 'No, no, no,' he insisted, 'it'll be great.' He then got straight on the phone to Roger and John individually to say, 'Tony's coming on stage with us tonight, okay darling? Wonderful.' And it seemed to be fine by them. 'The only problem we might have is Brian,' Freddie confided. 'He tends to get a bit funny about these things.' So he called Brian and came on all diplomatic, and said, 'Brian, darling, Tony's coming on stage with us tonight and we're going to do "Jailhouse Rock" – okay?—Tony, love, Brian's on, and he's absolutely fine about it.' Well then I said, 'But I don't know the bloody words, mate. I ain't got a clue.' And Freddie said, all jolly, 'Never mind – I don't fucking know them either!'

They sat down to try and learn the song, completely drunk. Half of the words they made up, and the rest they guessed. Then Tony went off to get some sleep.

'Got down the gig that night, and everybody was going to me, "What the hell have you done to Freddie, he's out of his head!" I said, "Well, we've been boozing big time," and they all looked at me weirdly and said, "But Freddie *never* boozes before he goes on stage!"'

Freddie's assistants had never had a harder time getting their man together to go out on stage. Recalls Spike:

At that time everybody was wearing these Adidas boxing boots, which tie up quite high, lots of laces, because they really feel good and are great for running and jumping about on stage. So that night, Freddie was laid out on the sofa. Tony Williams (another wardrobe assistant whom Queen had hired for tour work when Peter Freestone became Freddie's personal assistant) and Joe Fanelli had been dressing Fred together because he was too out of it to do anything. They'd got his gear on, and his boots, and he stood up and went to walk forward, and he couldn't walk. At all. The announcement came over – 'Tape's starting now!' – by which time we were all supposed to be at the side of the stage, and Freddie went, 'You stupid c–ts, you've put my tights on back to front!' The next thing you know, he was lying on his back like a beetle with his legs in the air, with Tony and Joe going like maniacs trying to undo these laces to get his boots off then his tights off. Eventually they got everything back on the right way and we went hurtling down these stairs, the intro tape having finished and all this fog and smoke filling the stage, and we had to rush right on . . .

And Fred, bless him, was so out of it that he was going to *fly*. He was out there ad-libbing, making things up, singing crap – for about the first half-hour of this show, *completely* fucking with the songs. Roger had his head down, couldn't look at anyone, and Brian's staring wildly, like 'What the fuck's going on *here*?' Fortunately, by the time we'd made it about halfway through the show, Freddie had sobered up a little bit, and amazingly it all went great. That is until Hadley came on . . .

It was one way to do an encore. Smarting from a telephone argument with his former manager Steve Dagger, who had insisted that Tony keep as low a profile as possible in New Zealand, Tony had not sobered up in the slightest but was dying to get out in front of an audience with Freddie.

'The next thing I knew,' he says, 'I was standing at the side of the stage while Queen were playing, still trying to remember the bloody words to "Jailhouse Rock". Freddie came across and draped himself over Spike's piano, and he was hissing, 'Hadley you bastard, I am *so* pissed' – in front of 45,000 people.

There I was mumbling away to myself like an idiot, with a few key words scrawled on my hand – 'Wardens . . . county jail . . . party . . . jailhouse rock'. I just couldn't get the lyrics into my head. Eventually, Freddie said something to the audience like, 'Ladies and Gentlemen, Mr Tony *Hadley*!' The crowd all went crazy, and I rushed on and launched into the bob-bop bit of 'Tutti frutti' . . . *Wrong song!* And Freddie's going, 'Yeah! All right!' and Brian's going 'What the fuck is *this*?' And the rest of them were just pissing themselves. A classic moment. Freddie and I didn't care, we were just giving it loads . . . simulating sex with Brian's guitar while he was playing it, the lot. Spike has been taking the piss out of me over it ever since.

The Melbourne gigs proved decidedly low-key by comparison – not that Queen had ever had an easy time of it in Australia. Four nights at Sydney Entertainments Centre towards the end of April, to be followed by six further shows in Japan, were rendered even more enjoyable by the fact that Elton John was in town. Freddie, Elton and Roger wasted no time in painting the town pink, in advance celebration of the launch of 'Mr Bad Guy', the Freddie Mercury solo album the critics and cynics had said would never be released. After the Japanese shows, having said his Sayonaras, Freddie headed home to Munich for a rest.

Chapter Nineteen

WE ARE THE CHAMPIONS

It was between Queen's 'The Works' tour and the 'Magic' tour that Bob Geldof launched his campaign for the most ambitious rock and roll project of all time. Having already highlighted the plight of Ethiopia's starving millions with the Band Aid fundraising single 'Do They Know It's Christmas?', Geldof was not prepared to stop there. D-Day for Live Aid was 13 July 1985. Wembley Stadium and the John F. Kennedy Stadium in Philadelphia were booked. Now it was only a matter of persuading rock's biggest names to participate and help the dying where governments across the world had failed.

'Queen were definitely disappointed that they hadn't been asked to appear on the Band Aid "Do They Know It's Christmas?" single,' admits Spike.

I was out doing a Rats tour with Geldof, and I mentioned this to Bob. It was then that he told me he was planning to get this show together, and he was going to ask Queen to play. I remember thinking 'Bollocks. He's nuts. It'll never happen.' Bob asked me to ask Queen if they'd be up for it, which I had the opportunity to do in New Zealand. To which they replied, 'Why doesn't he ask us himself?' And I had to explain that he was afraid they'd turn him down, blah blah. They didn't sound that convinced, but said they might be prepared to consider it. I told Bob, and then he approached Jim Beach officially.

Geldof tells how he persuaded Queen in inimitable style:

I traced Jim all the way down to some tiny little beach, some little seaside resort that he was staying at, and I said, 'Look, for Christ's sake, you know, what's *wrong* with them?' Jim said, 'Oh, you know, Freddie's very sensitive.' So I said, 'Tell the old faggot it's gonna be the biggest thing that ever happened – this huge mega thing.' So eventually they got back and said okay, they would definitely be doing it, and I thought, Great. And then when they did do Live Aid, Queen were absolutely the best band of the day. Whatever your personal taste was irrelevant. When the day came, they played the best, they had the best sound, they used their time to the full. They understood the idea *exactly* – that it was a global jukebox, as I'd described it. They just went and smashed out one hit after the other. It was just unbelievable. I was actually upstairs in the Appeals box in Wembley Stadium, and suddenly I heard this sound. I thought God, who's got *this* sound together? I went outside, and saw that it was Queen. I looked down over this crowd of people just going crazy, and the band were amazing. I think they were delighted afterwards – Freddie in particular. It was the perfect stage for him: the whole world. And he could ponce about on stage doing 'We Are The Champions' and all that, you know? How perfect could it get?'[1]

'We didn't know Bob Geldof at all,' remarked John Deacon in a rare interview.[2]

When 'Do They Know It's Christmas?' was out, that was a lot of the newer acts. For the gig, he wanted to get a lot of the established acts. Our first reaction was, we didn't know – 20 minutes, no sound check!

When it became apparent that it was going to happen, we'd just finished touring Japan and ended up having a meal in the hotel discussing whether we should do it . . . and we said yes.

It was the one day that I was proud to be involved in the music business. A lot of days you certainly don't feel that! But the day was fabulous, people forgot that element of competitiveness . . . it was a good morale-booster for us too, because it showed us the strength of support we had in England, and it showed us what we had to offer as a band.

As Freddie told his old friend David Wigg on the *Daily Express*, on July 12, 1985:

Sometimes I do feel helpless, and this is one of those times I can do my bit. Bob Geldof has done a wonderful thing, because he actually sparked it off. I'm sure we all had it in us to do that, but it took someone like him to become the driving force, and actually get us all to come together. You have got to have a certain status for this kind of show. That's what Geldof realized, and he has succeeded in persuading the world's biggest-established rock-stars to appear for nothing. He is trying to raise as much money as possible, and to achieve that, he needed the cream of the music business.

Freddie had released the third single from his solo album in the UK, 'Made In Heaven', a couple of weeks before 'Live Aid', at about the same time as the single 'Living On My Own' was launched in the States to a lukewarm reception.

Later in the year, for its UK release in September, Freddie combined his 39th birthday party, an excessive £50,000 black and white ball, with a video shoot to film a promo for the single, at one of his favourite Munich clubs, Henderson's. Some 300 close friends were invited, many of them flown in from London, and everyone dressed in drag – except Freddie, who was in Harlequin tights and military jacket, and Mary Austin, who came as a St Trinian's naughty schoolgirl. Brian May dressed as a witch, Phoebe as a gypsy. Barbara Valentin remembers organizing the black and white food for the party – 'black caviare and white mashed potato, with magnums of Cristal champagne, which people carried away from the party under their arms: everybody stole from Freddie. Even two containers of his birthday presents went missing.' Peter Freestone also remembers the theft. There was a massive birthday cake for Freddie in the shape of a grand piano. Barbara also starred in the video, alongside Ingrid Mack, the wife of producer Reinholdt Mack. When we watched the video together in Munich, she pointed out many friends who had not survived.

'He's dead. He's dead. That one's dead. Dead – dead – dead. Really, most of those guys are dead.' In the end, the promo was deemed too risqué to release.

'"Living On My Own" is very me,' Freddie said at the time.[3]

> I have to go round the world living in hotels. You can have a whole shoal of people you know looking after you. But in the end, they all go away . . . When you're a celebrity, it's hard to approach somebody and say, 'Look, I'm normal underneath.' Then what happens is that they tread all over me because by trying to be normal to somebody, suddenly I've come out of my shell and become far more vulnerable than most people. Because I'm successful and have a lot of money, greedy people prey on me. But that's something I've learned to

deal with. I'm riddled with scars, and I just don't want any more.

I was caught up in being a star, and I thought, 'This is the way a star behaves.' Now I don't give a damn. I want to do things my way and have fun. If all my money ended tomorrow, I'd still go about like I had lots of money because that's what I used to do before. I'll always walk round like a Persian Poppinjay – and no one's going to stop me.

It was the day that every rock-star who was anybody danced and sang to feed the world. It has been said many times that Queen's performance at Live Aid was the most thrilling, the most memorable, the most moving – surpassing as it did the efforts of their greatest rivals, from McCartney, U2, Jagger and Bowie, Elton, Madonna, The Who and Phil Collins, who actually played in both venues courtesy of Concorde. Of all Queen's 704 live performances, it remains perhaps their most brilliant moment, their finest hour. Live Aid provided Queen with the perfect opportunity to demonstrate that, stripped of all props and trappings, their own lighting, sound equipment, fog, smoke and special effects, without even the magic of dusk and with only an 18-minute slot in which to prove themselves, they alone, more than any other band or solo artist, had what it took to conquer the world.

'They had rehearsed really hard at the Shaw Theatre on Euston Road for a whole week, while others had just gone on and busked it,' remembers Peter.

'That's why they were the best. And I remember Freddie being stunned when he went out on stage in broad daylight, launching into "Radio Ga-Ga" and seeing all these thousands of hands start going. He was dazzled by that, having never seen anything quite like it before. They had only ever done it in darkness.'

'There was actually nothing very magical about the way we put the set together,' reveals Spike Edney. 'I remember we all sat around discussing what songs to play, and the idea was eventually hit upon that we'd play a medley of Queen hits. No great mystery to it – if you've got a bunch of songs and you can't choose, it's the obvious thing to do. It was all very matter of fact, but on the day it turned out to be amazing.'

The other members of Queen were the first to concede that Freddie had stolen the show: 'The rest of us played okay, but Freddie was out there and took it to another level,' said Brian with enormous pride.

'It wasn't just Queen fans – he connected with everyone.'[4]

As Brian told me in an interview at Queen's Pembridge Road offices after the event, 'Live Aid *was* Freddie He was unique. You could almost see our music flowing through him. You just couldn't ignore him: he was original, special. It wasn't just our fans we were playing to, it was everyone's fans. Freddie really gave his all.'

Former 'Old Grey Whistle Test' producer Mike Appleton, who later collected the BAFTA award for the Live Aid team as producer of the Best Outside Broadcast, remembers Freddie's performance in particular that day as 'fascinating':

For a start, he was not even supposed to go on. Doctors had already said that he was too ill to perform, his throat was terrible, from a cold or something. He wasn't well enough at all, but he absolutely insisted. And it happened that he and Bono of U2 wound up as the most successful performers of the day.

It was so interesting to see Freddie through the monitors – I was shut away in a sweltering Outside Broadcast truck all day long. We were literally building a programme live on air as we went. Come five o'clock and we were flipping live to JFK – alternating 20 minutes here, 20 minutes there, let's put an interview here, a live bit from earlier there, some highlights of the first hour in this bit . . . it's actually very exciting television, and the only way I like to work. Freddie simply came on, took immediate possession of the stage, coolly and calmly, and then proceeded to take possession of the audience.

Queen had at that point been off the boil for a while, having made no significant impact with any album for some time. The Live Aid experience wound up putting them back on the map, and also had the same effect on the music business as a whole. Overall sales went up, and Live Aid proved to be a tonic for the entire industry. As Freddie was the out-and-out star of the day, he was undoubtedly the main ingredient of that tonic. He was more dominant that day than I had ever seen him be before. The day may have belonged to Bob emotionally, but it definitely belonged to Freddie musically.

From that day on, remembers Appleton, people could not stop talking about Freddie's 'genius': 'Personally, I think it's a word that's bandied about too casually. Michelangelo painted the Sistine Chapel, sculpted David – that's genius. Stephen Hawking is probably a genius. But I don't believe that Freddie Mercury was a genius. He was just an extremely professional rock musician. Then again, he did have a quality above and beyond what you usually find in a rock musician.'

In the opinion of Peter Hillmore, Freddie was, that day,

The consummate showman. He really elevated the audience. He and Jagger, I think, had that ability to hold an audience in the palm of their hand. I remember standing there thinking, there was a time when politicians made great orators, but the art has dwindled somewhat this century. When you think about it, rock 'n' roll is one of the few professions left in which one man or a group of people can control an audience of thousands, or hundreds of thousands, with their voice. Film actors don't do it. TV stars don't have to have it. Which makes rock-stars the last great orators of our times. If you stand there performing for billions, live, as Freddie did, and they can't actually hear a word you're saying, it has to be your raw power that holds them.

As Mike Appleton said, 'Although perhaps not a genius, I would say that Freddie Mercury was certainly unique. No one else has been able to do what he did. The only other person who had that same legendary quality was Jimi Hendrix.'

Enthused by the Live Aid experience, Queen could not wait to plan another tour. 1986, Europe: their most ambitious tour yet.

Faced, yet again, with the monumental task of fulfilling Queen's wildest dreams, Uncle Grumpy, aka tour manager Gerry Stickells, rolled into action. Meanwhile, Queen teamed up with acclaimed video director Russell Mulcahy, to produce music for his forthcoming movie *Highlander* starring Christopher Lambert. But again they managed to incur the wrath of the press, for their recording and release, in November, of a one-off single, 'One Vision'. Denounced for 'cashing in on their Live Aid success' with this Top Ten hit, Queen were incensed: they just couldn't win. Would there ever come a day when their every move was not misconstrued? The song, in fact, had occurred to Roger one day out of the blue. It was, he said, inspired by the legendary black American civil rights leader Martin Luther King's speech, not by Live Aid. In defiance, Queen ignored the press, and hit upon the idea of making a mini-documentary of themselves in the studio to use as a promo video for the single. It was the first time they had worked with the Torpedo Twins, Rudi Dolezal and Hannes Rossacher, but it was not to be the last. Collaboration between the band and the Twins from that day forward was both fruitful and profitable. In 1987 the Twins completed their most monumental task for Queen to date: a comprehensive visual anthology of the band's career entitled 'Magic Years'.

Freddie, meanwhile, was keeping out of mischief by involving himself in a variety of projects, including the Fashion Aid fundraising extravaganza for the starving of Ethiopia, in which he caused a stir by appearing on the Royal Albert Hall catwalk as the 'husband' to actress Jane Seymour's 'bride', both in outfits designed by Elizabeth and David Emmanuel who had made the Princess Of Wales' wedding dress. He also made time to lend a hand to a friend. Dave Clark was the eccentric former drummer and singer with sixties pop group the Dave Clark Five, who had often found themselves disregarded as a pale imitation of The Beatles. In fact, the group had its own distinctive 'Tottenham Sound', with hits like 'Glad All Over', 'Bits And Pieces' and 'Catch Us If You Can', and enjoyed several big hit singles in the States. When the group finally folded in 1973, Clark developed a successful career in the business of music, acquiring the rights to the popular TV pop series 'Ready Steady Go'. Clark's latest project was writing, producing and staging an inventive musical at London's Dominion Theatre. Called *Time*, it would star Cliff Richard, and Sir Laurence Olivier in hologram mode. Dave invited Freddie to collaborate on a couple of tracks for an album (also featuring Dionne Warwick, Julian Lennon and Stevie Wonder), including the track 'Time', to which Freddie readily agreed, and for which he would later appear in a one-off stage performance. Meanwhile, as EMI reaped Queen rewards by releasing a luxurious boxed set of Queen albums with a few glaring omissions. Freddie was not enjoying the solo success he had so longed for; the fifth single from 'Mr Bad Guy', 'Love Me Like There's No Tomorrow', didn't even enter the chart.

Queen now had to complete the music for *Highlander*, which would be combined to form their new album, and prepare for the Montreux rock festival before they could even think about making plans for their forthcoming European tour. They finally managed to start tour rehearsals in May, as tickets went on sale. As predicted, demand surpassed all expectation. During this, their farewell tour – although nobody actually knew this at the time – which was to kick off in Stockholm, and would include performances at Wembley Stadium and Knebworth Park and earn more than £11 million gross over 26 shows, Queen would break the UK all-time attendance record by performing to more than 400,000 people. It was as if the fans had an inkling that this would be their last-ever opportunity to experience the Queen magic live.

'A Kind Of Magic', Queen's 14th album and the *Highlander* soundtrack, was launched at the end of May in time for the beginning of their European tour. It went straight to number one. On 4 June at the crack of dawn, 13 huge, heavily-laden trucks of equipment rumbled out of London to begin an incredible odyssey across 11 European countries, where Queen would perform for a million fans 26 concerts in 20 cities: Stockholm, Leiden, Paris, Brussels, Mannheim, Berlin, Munich, Zurich, Dublin, Newcastle, London, Manchester, Cologne, Vienna, Budapest, Frejus, Barcelona, Madrid, Marbella, Knebworth. Special, symbolic, significant for reasons, in the main, known only to Queen themselves. There would never be another rock tour quite like it.

Photographer Denis O'Regan was by now in great demand as one of the best rock photographers in the business. Through Phil Symes PR, he found himself hired by Jim Beach to act as Queen's official photographer on the 1986 European tour, covering Scandinavia, Holland, and Germany as well as the UK shows.

'I didn't really know what to expect from Queen on the road, or how easy or difficult they would be to work with,' confesses Denis:

I'd heard all sorts of things about what they got up to. PR Tony Brainsby had told me that he'd once found Freddie in a dustbin behind the Embassy Club. But they were great towards me, and really I had nothing at all to worry about.

Roger, John and Brian were the lads, and pretty easy-going. Freddie was definitely the most enigmatic of the bunch. There were often times, I'd notice, when he couldn't even keep up with what he was thinking. His brain would be doing 19 to the dozen, and his mind just raced ahead of his mouth. He'd say things like, 'What I want to get is the flow of the, um . . . oh, fuck it!' 'Oh, whatsisname . . . oh, fuck it!' He'd have whole conversations in which it was all just 'Fuck it, fuck it, fuck it!' because he couldn't get his lips round what he wanted to say.

I remember watching television with him once – it was the 1986 World Cup. Germany thrashed Mexico, I think, at which point Freddie leapt up in disgust. 'That's *it*!' he cried. 'I'm going to go out and fuck me a German! Come on, we're *all* going out – the cars are downstairs!' I went back to my room to get my jacket, and when I got back to Freddie's room, someone said, 'All the cars have gone.' Some negotiations went on, Freddie returned, and said to me, 'Don't worry dear, we've sorted it out. We're going to go out in something called "a cab".' That was pure Freddie.

Denis, although not exactly a stranger to the lewd preoccupations of boisterous rock 'n' rollers out on the road, had never come across anything quite like Queen.

I can recall parties in brothels, Roman baths, Turkish baths. There were more lesbian strippers backstage at Wembley, and all those naked women painted to look like they were wearing bell-hop and waitress uniforms at the Roof Gardens party after the Wembley show . . . not to mention what was going on in the toilets. I think Roger was largely Mr Motivator in that respect.

The guy appeared to be really interested in sex. Sex was a big thing with that band. They always had monumental blitzes on tour. And the thing about Queen is that so much of it is unprintable!

Denis was well aware, from what was said and from what he personally observed, that Freddie absolutely loathed touring.

You could just tell, from his demeanour. He was not the happiest person on the road. Not that he had much freedom, and he couldn't ever really do exactly as he pleased. The others didn't have it quite so bad, although each band member had his own security guys, and they were very protected in every way. He told me once that he enjoyed performing, but that he absolutely hated touring. *Hated* it. He didn't want the tour to be extended, to go on as long as it did, he didn't want to go to America . . . that was why Queen faded away over there as a live act, because he didn't want to go there and work it. He started to be pretty much a stay-at-home guy towards the end.

Freddie just seemed so vulnerable most of the time. He was not at all what I had expected. He could be dainty, almost. He was like a little child sometimes, which could be very sweet. I'd see him sit at the end of tables clapping his hands and getting all excited about some forthcoming dinner or other, and everything had to be just so. It was very cute. He was quiet, reserved – quite introverted, a lot of the time. But then he'd go from one extreme to the other, and be completely the opposite. Considering what a big strong guy he looked on stage, he seemed really petite and effeminate offstage at times.

For such a big star, he was very low key. He never really ate out that much. And I think most of his entertainment was 'in-house', so to speak. He kept a fairly low profile. I wouldn't say that he was a difficult subject to photograph, exactly, but he was a surprisingly shy guy. He would never really pose, as such. He would clown around sometimes, or ignore the fact that you were there taking pictures at all, and just 'be himself'. Now and again he would do something like appear at the door wearing a crown, and throw a few shapes, knowing that I was there – but not specifically inviting me to take photographs. He always knew what he was doing, of course, just like he did on stage.

He would frequently get angry, but I never saw him explode. He could be very dismissive. He was always saying things like, 'Tell them all to fuck off!' But he was pretty apologetic a lot of the time. Freddie's magic was all to do with the live performance. And that kind of star quality I think you have to be born with. Not being 'straight', if you like, he almost didn't have as much to prove up there as the rest of them. He didn't have that same sort of macho hang-up, he never worried about compromising his masculinity. He'd just go out on stage and take the piss out of the audience, where the others perhaps might not have risked it. He had obviously been a really wild party animal in his day, but most of that was well out of his system by 1986.

Spike Edney played keyboards again for Queen on the 1986 'Magic' tour, and noticed a number of significant changes:

For a start, I think the separate hotel thing was pretty much a preoccupation of 'The Works' tour. By the time we got round to the 'Magic' tour, that whole mad partying scene had quietened down tremendously. Making a point of two camps staying in separate places wasn't relevant anymore, and we did actually all stay in the same hotel. That was when we turned into the Scrabble Kings.

I had come to the Queen scene quite late, on the 1984 tour, remember. At that time, the guys were still big-time party animals and would go out, *all* the time. But by the 1986 'Magic' tour, they'd been there and done that, and were fed up with most of it. Previously, after every single gig, there would have to be *something* organized, followed by partying on through till dawn in somebody's suite, because that was all part of the fun of going on the road. I must say, an awful lot of dawn stuff went on.

But by the time we got to the 'Magic' tour it had calmed down considerably. Fred, for one, was much more settled, I think. He just didn't have the taste for going out and staying up all night the way he used to. Plus, he was really looking after his voice. He was very conscious about not blowing that. So we'd often end up back in his suite, which had a nickname which is probably unprintable, where we would drink champagne and play Scrabble. Or Trivial Pursuit. Freddie was mad on competitive games, and both Roger and Brian are very competitive as well. We're talking serious shit. I can remember on several occasions being still up at nine o'clock in the morning, just me and Fred finishing off some dodgy Scrabble game, or playing Reverse Scrabble where you have to take the letters off, but still leave a complete word. That one can really fuck you up.

On the final night of the European tour, Fred decided that he wanted everyone up to his suite, all the crew and everybody. There we all were, drinking champagne, shouting and jumping about, when he announced a game of Trivial Pursuit, four teams: between the band; all the musos; the crew; and management and security.

The best one *ever* – and to this day I relish the moment – was a particular game of Trivial Pursuit before the 'Magic' tour. I was never that great at Scrabble, but

I excelled at Trivial Pursuit, mainly because I have an ability to remember crap. Flying out to New Zealand in '85, John Reid (Elton's manager, Queen's former manager) was with the party. I was introduced to him that night, and on the flight out I was summoned up to First Class from Business: 'We need another player for Trivial Pursuit, and you're good at it, so come and join in.' I got teamed up with, of all people, John Reid. The questions were coming round, and every time it was our turn, Reid would just blurt out the first answer that came into his head. And it was always wrong. After a while, having been fairly respectful towards the great man until then, when I realized he knew shit – about Trivial Pursuit, at any rate – it came round to the next question, he started to blurt, and I said, 'Shut up! We're a team. Why don't you talk to *me* first, and let's find out what we know.' Amazingly, he complied. After that, we started to do very well, and Fred and Rog were mightily impressed by all this. Not least, I think, because I had told John Reid to shut up.

After that, in Australia, there were a couple of serious all-night Scrabble parties, and that became The Thing for the Queen tour.

Being the new boy on the tour, I had suffered an awful lot of 'New Boy' gags, but I managed to get my own back. The games got deadly serious – there was honour at stake – and they were played everywhere. On the bullet train out of Tokyo, for example, it was going so fast that the pieces kept rolling off the table, and Fred was there on his hands and knees looking for the pieces between the seats. What amused me was that previous Queen tours had been all about sex, drugs, rock 'n' roll. But by the time they got into the mid-80s, it went into far more intellectual mode. Well – yes and no.

The *Observer*'s Peter Hillmore and I were among the 500-odd guests invited to the Roof Gardens after-show party in July, where, among other things, we were treated to the sight of former Page Three girl Samantha Fox and Freddie singing 'All Right Now'.

'There was a very smart VIP area into which I stepped and got myself a drink,' says Hillmore. 'And Jim Beach – known to his friends as 'Miami', of course – came up to me and said, "What are *you* doing here? Get Out!" and I made him apologize. It was yet another night of Bacchanalian delights – dwarfs, drag queens, topless, bottomless – which Queen were world-famous for by this time. I am certain that I was not the only one to stagger home at dawn, very much the worse for wear.'

'There will never be another band quite like Queen,' commented the band's old faithful American sound engineer, James 'Trip' Khalaf, who was first assigned to work with the band by Clair Brothers Audio US and UK back in 1976, and who at first had laughed at the very notion of a rock band called Queen: 'Queen was the last great rock 'n' roll tour. Queen was the last fun I've had in this business, I think! They were always ready for wretched excess. The parties were always bigger, the women always had larger breasts, the entire thing was on such a stupendous level that I could hardly keep up with it most of the time. We'd wind up being dragged around by huge minders just to get us to the next show a lot of times.'[5]

Khalaf, who perhaps saw more Queen shows than anyone else, was especially fascinated by Freddie:

What a strange person Fred was. I mean, he was a lovely, lovely person. But he wasn't one of us. He was something ... I think it's been said a million times before, but Fred was just a *star*. If he hadn't have been a star, he wouldn't have *been*. He was just a *fascinating* creature. He was funny. On the one hand, he was completely ridiculous. But he *knew* he was completely ridiculous, and he enjoyed being ridiculous.

I think the question of what drives and motivates a pop star is a subject on its own. I've seen a million of them, and they all have their own reasons for doing what they do. Fred's reason for doing what he did was that he couldn't have done anything else! I mean, he had no marketable skills. What else could he have been but this huge bombastic rock-star? But the sonofabitch did a great job.

On 9 August, Queen performed an open-air gig to more than 120,000 at Knebworth Park, Stevenage, in the grounds of a stately home which had often played host to rock performers, including Led Zeppelin and the Rolling Stones. It was their biggest audience ever in the UK, and the celebrations went on well into the night. The only thing missing from the festivities was Freddie. Disappearing discreetly after the gig with his boyfriend Jim Hutton and Peter Freestone – he didn't even hang around to show his face at the band's backstage celebration – Freddie beat a hasty retreat.

'Freddie never liked parties like that, especially record company dos,' explained Peter. 'He didn't want to hang out with all the employees making small-talk. He wasn't to know that Knebworth was to be his last gig.'

It was only in the helicopter flying back to Battersea heliport that Freddie was informed of the fatal stabbing of a fan during the Knebworth show.

'Because of the sheer numbers of fans, it was not possible to get an ambulance to the guy fast enough to save his life,' explained Jim Hutton.

'Freddie was very upset, and the next morning was still subdued as friends were arriving for Sunday lunch. There was great coverage about the concert in the Sunday papers, which seemed to cheer him up a bit, but that fan's death seemed to prey on his mind. He only ever wanted his music to bring happiness.'

Adds Spike Edney, 'The sad thing is that the good times had to stop rolling, of course. But all good things come to an end.'

Reflecting in the months to come on what the 'Magic' tour had meant to him, one gig would spring to Freddie's mind over and over again. If that word, 'magic' had applied to any individual concert on the tour, it had to be Budapest.

Chapter Twenty

BUDAPEST

Queen's live show at the Nepstadion (People's Stadium) in Budapest on Sunday 27 July 1986 was not just another rock gig. It was in fact a minor historic occasion, being the first significant rock show to be staged behind the Iron Curtain, at that time still steadfastly in place. Queen appeared before a sell-out crowd of some 80,000 fans who flooded in from neighbouring states now known by alternative names: from Czechoslovakia to the north, East Germany to the north-west, parts of the former Soviet Union to the east, which was said to be allowing citizens a début bussing over the border into Hungary, although it was later revealed that Eastern Bloc borders had in fact been open for some time – as well as Rumania and Bulgaria to the south-east. Each had paid the apparently bargain equivalent of about £2.00 for the privilege, which nevertheless to some at that time was the equivalent of a whole month's wages. In spite of this, the promoters had been faced with a staggering oversubscription situation of more than a quarter of a million. They could have arranged to stage a second Queen concert, but the authorities refused permission on the grounds that it would have clashed with an exhibition of old motorcycles being held in town at the same time. To hold two such events simultaneously was deemed to be asking for trouble, since it might have over-inflamed the country's youth. This was not Hungary's first-ever rock concert by an international artist. But it was the first stadium gig: the first, anywhere behind the Iron Curtain for that matter, to be held in the open air. Jethro Tull and Elton John had performed there already, as well as Dire Straits, who held the previous record for an audience in the Eastern Bloc at some 50,000. The Hungarian press had become almost hysterical in their coverage as the day approached. The papers even hinted at 'lenient restrictions on audience behaviour' at the Queen gig, which we took to mean that they were going to be allowed to clap. They would certainly not be drunk, drugged, disorderly or potentially violent in the Western sense, the venue being dry except for fruit juice. Even smoking was banned completely on the field. It promised to be a sedate and well-regulated occasion; perhaps the sub-machine guns wedged into the armpits of the police who would work the stadium shift had something to do with that.

Even before the journalists invited to accompany Queen on the epic visit had left London, we were being fed abundant facts, figures and information both relevant and inconsequential by Queen Productions and no fewer than two PR consultancies: Carol Hayes and Associates, and Phil Symes. The PRs' job was to whet the journalists' appetites and 'get press'. Among other things, we learned that 17 cameras would film at the Nepstadion concert, which some reckoned to be Hungary's entire cinematic allocation; that the cameramen would include Gyorgy Illes, aged 71, a revered tutor at the Film Academy – one of his best pupils, the acclaimed Vilmos Zsigmond, had earned an Oscar for his work on *Close Encounters of the Third Kind*; that Queen and crew would enter Iron Curtain territory by water, cruising from Vienna to Budapest down the majestic blue Danube on the Gorbachevs' hydrofoil. One small five-hour float for rock 'n' roll, you might say. But Queen's pending appearance was already being hailed as a giant step for East-West relations. So much so that the eminently gracious Chargé d'Affaires David Colvin, at that time the Acting British Ambassador to Hungary, decided to host a reception at the Embassy for the group and a cautiously selected côterie of guests.

'On the occasion of Queen's visit, her Britannic Majesty's Chargé d'Affaires and Mrs David Colvin request the pleasure of the company of —— at a reception on Thursday 24th July 1986 at seven p.m.', read the hand-delivered invitation, in elegant black thermographic script. One mischievous wag – a member of the band, in fact – inserted an additional preposition before the name of the band, a stunt which caused convulsions of mirth among the troops out of all proportion to its alleged comic worth.

We were also provided with a mind-boggling list of facts pertaining to the Magic tour as a whole, which still makes fascinating reading. This included, for example, the following:

- The stage measures up to 6,000 square feet (dependent on whether venue was indoor or outdoor). The performance area of the stage was carpeted in grey Axminster.
- 8.6 miles of cable was used on each date to connect all instrumental, sound, light and stage equipment to the 5 full power generators, providing 5,000 amps.
- The sound system was powered by over half a million watts, with 'revolutionary delay towers'.

You didn't get that kind of press release from Michael Jackson or Elton John.

Budapest was one of those special assignments which remain in the heart and memory. Then a rock and pop reporter in Fleet Street, I was there in order to convey the buzz, the history, the histrionics, the fun of the fair, to the upright showbiz columns of the *Daily Mail*. Also present, among others, were Peter Hillmore of the *Observer*, a Polish Jew by birth who therefore especially liked the idea of a Queen gig in Eastern Europe; the *Daily Mirror*'s Gill Pringle; paparazzo photographer Richard Young, and Robin Denselow of BBC Television and the *Guardian*.

One or two proffered the theory that this trip was all an attempt by Queen to prove their ability to deal with the media. If so, there were definite arguments for and against.

Our evening at the British Embassy, a beautiful private house in the leafy, elevated Buda district, did not disappoint. Brightly-lit inside, the house boasted antique furniture, tiled hallways, ancient gilt mirrors and crystal chandeliers. The champagne flowed, and there were glamorous women galore.

Says Hillmore, 'It wasn't just young Hungarian rock fans who were excited by the arrival of all this Western decadence. The Embassy hadn't exactly planned a reception for the European Youth Orchestra, arriving the following week. It was Queen themselves who made the impact.

'I rather liked the surrealism of going to the Embassy for a rock 'n' roll party, knowing that they were more accustomed to welcoming a completely different kind of Queen.'

The occasion brought together a seemingly incongruous mix of English expatriates, Embassy officials, Eastern underground musicians, Western rock 'n' rollers, and the usual gang-and-hang set. Freddie appeared bemused by it all, as if he had walked on to the set of a farcical send-up movie scene. One diplomatic wife had clearly been practising rock-speak from a phrase book without having a clue what it all meant:

'Are you a roadie?' she enquired of Roger Taylor, batting lashes so heavily-laden with mascara that she could barely hold her eyes open. Somewhat taken aback by her unwitting effrontery, he informed her that he was, in fact, the drummer. The revelation didn't appear to mean much to her: without further comment, she held out a piece of paper for him to sign. Around the room, diplomats were practically falling over themselves and each other to get Freddie to do the same.

Freddie himself did not appear overly concerned with nor interested in details of Eastern Europe's recent history. He would rather go shopping. The only building in Budapest which appeared to grab his imagination was the Orszaghaz, or Houses of Parliament. Built around the turn of the century to symbolize the grandeur of the Austro-Hungarian Empire, it is one of the most impressive sights on the Budapest skyline, and said to be the most beautiful government building in Europe. Freddie first noticed it one afternoon when the band went cruising along the Danube:

'What's that?' he enquired, pointing animatedly at the Neo-Gothic arches and turrets not dissimilar to the style of our own Palace of Westminster except for a magnificent but incongruous dome which, at 315 feet, is the same height as Budapest's Basilica, thus placing church and state on an equal plane.

'The House of Parliament? Is this for sale? Do they have enough servants' quarters? Oops!' he exclaimed with a cheeky, self-conscious grin as his hand flew to cover his mouth, a familiar gesture.

'Not a good thing to say in this country!'

However much he might feign lack of interest in 'boring' subjects such as geography, history, politics and current affairs, Freddie had always given the impression of being naturally well-informed.

'Look at his education,' reasons Peter Freestone. 'He may not have seemed as brainy as the others, but if he learned in his boarding-school what I learned in mine, he would naturally know more than most people before he even started.'

Nor was he given to superiority or condescension. As Toby Rose recalls,

He was pretty low-key on the whole, wasn't he? When he wasn't 'on', Freddie had this delightful manner, a remarkable humility. He obviously didn't feel the need to prove himself. You were always uncomfortably aware that he knew far more about whatever it was than he was letting on. And whatever it was, he knew far more about it than you did. He wasn't condescending, though. It was enough for him to know things for himself – he didn't need to spout them to other people, or try to impress. He did that just by being his onstage version of Freddie Mercury. You could take any three words he uttered and turn them into a fascinating thirty. Freddie's attitude was, why waste the thirty words when the three will do?[1]

It was almost as if Freddie absorbed knowledge by osmosis without having to make the effort. He had such a finely-tuned intellect that it is said he could assess mood, overtone and atmosphere in a matter of seconds. That same intellect could also cause him to lose patience with things he couldn't be bothered with. He was for the most part apolitical, however. His private views might at times be regarded as somewhat imperialist. Off-duty he was now and then heard to pontificate, and one could not help but conjure the vision, in the mind's eye, of some grand English expatriate gentleman dressed in immaculate white flannels, crooking his little finger as he took afternoon tea on the verandah of his plantation home. Certainly his clipped and precise public school accent fitted the image perfectly. But Freddie, in his wisdom, had learned a big lesson early on. As an international celebrity and globally-adored entertainer, he knew better than to be drawn into sociological or political discussion in public. If ever he was invited to extend an opinion, he would politely refrain from joining in. Leave politics to the chaps who are paid to do the job, he reckoned:

'We're all born the same, and we'll all die the same, dear.'

'That is Freddie to a "T",' agrees Peter. 'If he learned what was going on today with bands like East 17 and Oasis, for example, he'd have no patience with it at all. He even considered U2 too political. He knew that he was in the position he was in because he was an entertainer. He wasn't there to lead people in their political beliefs.'

Elsewhere across the buzzing room that evening, David Quantick from the *NME* was heard to bemoan the fact that Freddie Mercury had refused to grant him an interview.

I was talking to some teenaged Queen fans at the party, who were asking me if I was there to do an interview with Freddie.

'No,' I said. 'I'm from the *NME*, and Freddie doesn't do interviews with the *NME*.' Freddie was at this point across the room, at the centre of a huddle of people, seemingly oblivious to the conversation I was having. But he later sidled up to me and said: 'Apparently you've been telling everyone that I won't do an interview with you.' I didn't know what to say. I just stood there, coughing and spluttering.

'Nonsense, dear boy!,' Freddie retorted. I immediately started fumbling for my tape-recorder.

'No! No! Not with one of those!,' he hissed. 'We're all going off to dinner in a minute . . . Would you like to come?'

I then had the pleasure of being able to stroll up to the PRs to tell them that I was off to dine with Fred. Roxy Meade, the senior PR, came along with the Queen people, as was her wont. And I remember ending up in the back of a limo, Freddie in the middle, me on one side, Mary Austin, his so-called girlfriend, on the other, heading for the hills of Eastern Europe. I'm chatting away like old pals with Freddie Mercury and he's *really* nice. He seemed so concerned about everyone. He was saying, 'I *must* have a dinner. I want to have a party for all the journalists.' Perhaps he had already thought of it, but wanted it to come across to me as if it were spontaneous. It worked on me, I was completely charmed.

Dinner that night was held at a rustic old hunting lodge beyond the city, at which Quantick had the opportunity of identifying at close range two distinctly contradictory aspects of Freddie's extreme personality. 'It was all very pleasant. But I did notice that, every time I tried to steer the conversation into interview mode, such as when I brought up Sun City, Freddie would simply flap his hands, grimace a bit and shrug, "*Oh*! *So* boring, dear."'

The trio were seated at dinner exactly as they had been arranged in the back of the limo. The rest of the band were sitting opposite.

'John Deacon just sat there and said nothing at all, all evening. Brian I don't remember much about. But Roger Taylor was a livewire, very jovial. He was accompanied by an extremely beautiful, young, blonde, Hungarian woman, who looked exactly his type. She was seated directly opposite Freddie, who had obviously taken an irritable dislike to her. Nevertheless he persisted in addressing her directly. It soon became obvious that he was trying to wind her up.'

David reports a terrible vibe between the two, which culminated in Freddie losing his patience and insulting the woman quite nastily. When he could no longer restrain himself he leant across the table, stuck his face almost up the young woman's elegant nose and enquired spitefully, in best pukka English,

'And how big is your c--t, dear?'

Freddie couldn't leave it there, either: 'Can you get it over your head, dear?' he snarled, as if inviting her to attempt the manoeuvre in front of them all there and then.

There was a sort of terrible pause at the dinner

table . . . but the situation was soon defused, as the woman had the good grace not to over-react. She sort of flicked her thumbnail against her teeth – some old, mildly offensive Eastern European gesture – and the unpleasant atmosphere was dispelled.

Peter Freestone laughs at the recollection, while admitting that perhaps illness was beginning to affect Freddie's usual good humour.

'If Freddie knew there was no way of winning out, he would stoop to the most obscene vulgarity at times,' he chuckles. 'Freddie is partly to blame for all that has been written about him in the press, this "rude recluse" that they used to describe, because he did such things. But he was happy to live by it. He didn't care.'

Having witnessed the ease with which Mercury could deliver a cruel blow, David admits that he began to fret for his own emotional and physical well-being. It suddenly occurred to him that he might not be there in a professional capacity at all.

'Out of the blue, Freddie turned towards me and invited me back to the hotel. I must have looked completely dumbfounded because Mary laughed, leaned over and said to me: "It's all right!" She did her best to reassure, and was terribly sweet. It was as if she was saying: "Relax! You're not the shag for the night or anything." I'd heard all the stories, of course, but you never really know what to expect.'

Quantick admits that he had expected their lead singer to be pompous, distant and chilled. 'In fact,' he says, 'I have never met such a nice man, before or since.'

True to his word, Freddie did indeed give the journalists a very elegant party a couple of days later, in his own hotel suite. It was the Presidential Suite at the Duna Intercontinental, no less, despite his earlier dismissive pronouncement that 'all suites are equal'. 'Well, this one's a fucking sight more equal than mine,' retorted Roger Taylor when he came round to compare accommodation.

Arriving at the appointed time that evening from our own hotel, the Budapest Forum a short walk along the river on the Pest side of the Danube, we were nervous as we knocked on Freddie's door. While the rest of the band had behaved throughout like 'Regular Joes', as Toby Rose put it, and had hung out with the gang, there was now the anticipation of being about to be presented to Royalty.

Freddie was the perfect, gracious host, shaking hands with everyone as he welcomed us into his suite. Smaller than he seemed on stage, muscular and fit-looking, he was scrubbed and fragrant and dressed in a brightly coloured floral shirt and tight, pale denim jeans. His hair was impeccably groomed, but one could not help noticing a threadbare patch just starting to appear on the back of his head – not unreasonably, perhaps, for a man less than two months away from his 40th birthday.

'Good evening. Thank you for coming. Have you people been having a good time?' he enquired in a quiet voice and with a polite smile. We stood in the doorway like gauche 12-year-olds, silently urging one another to speak first as we were handed crystal goblets of champagne. He nodded his head and chuckled quietly to himself as we related the experiences of days off around Budapest. He seemed fascinated by the idea of the Gellert baths where we had taken the waters and submitted to excruciating massage, though we later decided that he had to be an old hand at such adventures. There could be little left in life that Freddie had not tried. He wanted to know if we had bought anything, and we filled him in on our various purchases. We gushed, and tried too hard. Freddie was indulging us. It probably amused him to have us around for a while.

'Very good, very good,' Freddie said, waving us into the room towards a sumptuous buffet heaving with everything from lobsters, prawns and caviare to sugared fruits and exotic ice-creams. Our glasses were never empty. At a highly polished black grand piano in one corner, a dark-suited musician fingered twee, un-Freddie-like hotel-lobby tunes. Leaning against the instrument was big Jim Callaghan, a faithful, amiable minder of the band, who had, over the years, ejected the likes of us from a string of backstage parties and private events into which we had blagged our way but at which we had no right to be. 'Can't throw us out tonight, Jim,' we joked.

The sliding glass windows of the Presidential Suite were drawn back, giving open access to a balcony almost as big as the room itself. To one side of it stood Mary Austin, chatting quietly with the group's manager Jim Beach. Jim Hutton was also present, and keeping an extremely low profile, as were the rest of the group and a few of the crew. Night was drawing in, and the petrol blue sky glistened with stars. The view across the river was achingly beautiful, straight out of some romantic feature film: Fishermen's Bastion, the Citadel on Gellert Hill, the soaring, floodlit spire of Matthias Church.

'The whole thing was surreal, wasn't it?' agrees Peter Hillmore:

And what sticks in my mind is how Freddie conducted himself. I had spent time with him previously, in South America and so on, but I think Budapest was the first time I felt I was with the normal person. But then, perhaps, he could say the same thing about me: when you sit and have a drink with them, you're a person. When you write about them, you're a journalist. Freddie knew the difference. Most other rock-stars don't. Their stardom consumes them, goes to their heads. I once got quite pally with Sting, but only at arm's length. He was completely different from Freddie. In a similar party situation he'd be milking the room with arrogance and charisma and machismo, swanning around knowing that everyone thought he was fabulous. Freddie just wasn't like that. He wasn't even pretending to be not like that. It was a hugely endearing quality.

And finally, the event we had all been waiting for and the real reason we were there: showtime. Sunday afternoon saw us all aboard a coach in our best outfits and making for the Nepstadion, uncharitably remembered by Toby Rose as 'that Godawful monstrosity in the suburbs'.[2]

With Access All Areas passes plastered to our chests, we applauded politely as Hungarian folk dancers in red, white and black costumes twirling handkerchiefs strutted their stuff, and waited patiently for the main event. When it came, it was everything we expected. Indeed, we had already seen the show back in London at Wembley Stadium earlier that month. Pomp and circumstance, a kaleidoscope of lights, billowing smoke, the massive, unique Queen sound. Freddie Mercury singing with his whole body, the sound erupting from his mouth like molten lava from a volcano. He was, as always, a sight for sore eyes, and not afraid to flaunt his manly physique: taut buttocks straining the fabric of his white pants, hirsute of armpit and chest, wide muscular back, the merest hint of middle-age belly. Several changes of sweat-soaked top. The jugular veins in his neck standing out as he pounded the piano like lightning for 'Seven Seas of Rhye'. We winced, as usual, at the sight of John Deacon playing the bouncy little boy on his bass, scudding along the stage like someone not quite confident enough to dance. He wore his 'I Dunno' face and an inane grin, and displayed all the gaucheness of Damon Hill; unlike Roger Taylor, the pretty boy of the band, who, someone quipped, was 'sex on sticks'. The fifth member of the line-up, keyboard player Spike Edney, never stopped smiling all evening, and appeared to be enjoying himself more than anyone. Brian, as usual, was all lanky legs and frantic fingers, ripping his silver sixpence plectrum up and down the strings of his old fireplace guitar. He and Freddie had personalized the performance by learning, at the last minute, a popular romantic folk ballad called 'Tavaszi Szel Vizet Araszt'. 'Now comes the difficult bit,' Freddie told the audience as he stepped forward to perform it. The crowd roared in appreciation, and probably didn't even notice Freddie checking the lyrics every few seconds which he had scrawled, phonetically, in pen on the palm of his left hand. The audience had done their share of memorizing, too. Their reaction to 'Radio Ga-Ga' was the obligatory synchronized hand-clapping as they sang, word-perfect, at the top of their voices. In fact, they appeared to know the words to all the Queen songs. The encore was more of a grand finale: Freddie, stripped to the waist and dripping in sweat, reappeared on stage draped in a vast Union Jack. Moments later his about-turn revealed the Hungarian national flag. The crowd roared. Freddie left the stage and the Hungarians thought they'd had their lot. They were not prepared for his dramatic final appearance, in which he sailed regally on to the stage draped in his Diana Moseley-designed ermine-trimmed velvet cape complete with train, and sporting a magnificent jewelled coronation-style crown. A heavy metal version of 'God Save The Queen' to the accompaniment of Brian's inimitable guitar sound was designed to amaze – and it did. As Brian remarked backstage after the show, 'That was our most challenging and exhilarating gig ever.'

'What a phenomenally professional operation it was – as of course we knew it would be,' says Peter Hillmore.

No expense spared. That night, Freddie Mercury ruled the world, even to the long-toothed likes of me. I remember going up on to the empty stage and waiting for it all to happen, and feeling almost sick with anticipation, God knows why. And I remember walking out there to the sound-deck in the middle of the pitch, which was practically collapsing under the weight of freeloaders.

On the lighting podium, I lifted up a couple of tiny Hungarian girls so that they could see better, and their little faces said the lot. Freddie was out of this world – literally. He was, to them, from another planet.

To us, at the end of the day, this was just another gig. Granted, it was Queen being their most professional, a damned good stage act. We had heard all the songs from the 'Magic' album and so forth before, and enjoyed them. But the bulk of the audience had not. And to them it was the most phenomenal spectacle of their lives. They got unforgettable experience as well as famous rock group. There was a great wave of appreciation, none of the cynicism of a Western audience. We hadn't even paid for our tickets. Some of those people had handed over a month's wages.

After the show there was the obligatory party, at which some absurd game with glasses and tequila was played. All too soon it was Monday morning. We wandered back to our hotels in the cold light of dawn. And it was as if the previous night had never really happened. As if it had all been a dream. Once the adrenalin had drained and the sense of occasion had begun to fade, what we had seen, we knew, was just another Queen concert. The wonderment, the incredible ambience, had emanated from the Hungarian audience. The rest was business as usual. On stage, everyone had loved Freddie. But he already knew that his touring days were numbered. The irony of its being called the 'Magic Tour' was just beginning to dawn. It had been a magical occasion for everyone, perhaps, but him.

Chapter Twenty-One

THE COURT OF KING FREDDIE

Meanwhile in Munich, Barbara Valentin had come to terms with her loss and was getting on with her life. So totally resigned to the situation and so completely unprepared for Freddie's reappearance was she that at first she refused to believe it was really he standing on her doorstep.

Quite a long time after he left here – I don't remember when exactly, the months and years just slip away – I was at home putting myself together, getting ready to go out one night when something extraordinary happened. I was going to a launch: a friend of mine was opening a boutique and he'd begged me, please come and do me a favour, for the press coverage. I had agreed, as it wasn't too far from my place. It was about four o'clock in the afternoon, and I was just about to leave when there was a ring at the door bell. I was cursing, who the hell is that now? I thought it was the taxi, and I was there yelling, 'I'm coming, I'm coming.' There was no answer, and I thought, shit, the street door was open, I didn't press a button, I'll have to go down . . .

So I ran down and opened the door. And there's a man standing in front of me, and I'm going, Oh my God, it's a dummy of Freddie Mercury. I was moaning to myself oh no, no . . . yes, yes, yes . . . I thought I was having a hallucination, an apparition or something The man had some little white flowers—

Barbara breaks down in floods of tears as she does her best to conclude the story.

And he says, 'No, it's *me*,' and I said, 'I know! I know! No! I have to go, got to get to my friend's opening of his boutique.' And I shoved him away, because I thought maybe my mind was playing tricks on me. And then I touched him. And I started to go out, left the door open, turned around and said, I can't think why, 'I'll be back in an hour.' When I went outside there was no taxi, and I felt strange. I thought, No, my God, it can't be . . . I didn't drink so much last night, but did I ? These nightmares, I can't stand this . . . I walked off to the boutique, made pictures with the owner and a few actors for the press, and then said, 'I can't stay for champagne, I have to go home, because Freddie is there, or somebody like that.' I actually said that: 'somebody like that'.

I walked back home, and Freddie was still there, sitting on the couch, and playing with the TV remote control. It was then that it hit me. I cried and cried, and he cried, we both cried.

It was not until about a month later that he explained to me why. He had wanted to cut off completely when he left here. The word 'Munich' wasn't allowed to be mentioned, *my* name wasn't allowed to be mentioned; about one hundred of our friends had died of Aids by this time – and *that* wasn't allowed to be mentioned. He said it was like trying to break a drug habit, getting rid of dope. If you are addicted to something and one day enough is enough, you just have to say no and break the habit completely.

'Barbara, I almost died,' he told me.

'How many times I had the phone in my hand and I was dialling your number and then hanging up . . .'

And it was true. Phoebe told me later, everything about me had disappeared. My photographs had gone from the house, my name was never spoken, everything that would have reminded Freddie of me and Munich was gone. Freddie had just wanted to break from those crazy times, start living a calmer, different life, and, eventually, die in beauty. But he just couldn't stay away for ever.

He said that one of the things which frightened him most was that he couldn't be alone. He'd want to be, and he'd *try* to be, but when it happened he just couldn't bear it.

The two began to spend time together in earnest again. Barbara was a frequent and welcome visitor to Garden Lodge, and also made a few brief trips with Freddie. Life was sweet; perhaps all the more so because both knew that those exquisite days of their lives were numbered.

Awards, chart positions, re-releases, video releases. The Queen machine was in perpetual motion, and ever would remain so. Vast income was guaranteed. Freddie, meanwhile, turned his back on touring with Queen, locked the front door of Garden Lodge and resorted to the relatively humble comforts of home with his handful of trusted friends around him.

'I can't carry on rocking the way I have done in the past,' he said. 'It is all too much. It's no way for a grown man to behave. I have stopped my nights of wild partying. That's not because I'm ill, but down to age. I'm no spring chicken. Now I prefer to spend my time at home. It is part of growing up.'[1]

Freddie would continue to party and to entertain, but most of his socializing was now done under his own roof. His 40th birthday party on Sunday 7 September was a modest affair by his standards: a 'Mad Hat' garden party for 200. Designer Diana Moseley had prepared a range of outrageous pieces of headwear for Freddie from which he could choose, and he appeared in a fetching white fur construction with dangly bits hanging from it like a Martian's antennae. Spandau ballet frontman Tony Hadley was present at the 'Mad Hat' party. It was his first visit to Garden Lodge:

'It was a sedate party for him, but lovely all the same. People like the rest of the band, Tim Rice and Elaine Paige, Dave Clark and Mel Smith were there. Beautiful house, Freddie had. He showed me his beloved carpet in his bedroom that didn't have a join in it – he was so proud of that carpet, which he'd had specially made. It had a big star on it – looked like a Star of David.'

'Not quite a Star of David,' laughs Peter Freestone, 'but yes, there was a star, in the middle of Freddie's dressing-room.'

Tony Hadley remarks that it was obvious to him that day that Freddie was now 'living in the bubble': 'I've lived in a smaller bubble in my time, and I know what that feels like. Everything is done for you, and you very quickly grow dependent on others. He had his own cook, maids, a valet, a chauffeur . . . Freddie gave the impression that he had to be surrounded by people, his own instant audience, all the time. It is all to do with vulnerability. You get to that stage and you never want to let your guard down completely.'

'That's perfectly true,' agrees Peter Freestone. 'But I think Freddie felt able to let his guard down with us.'

Jim Hutton, who was contentedly sharing Freddie's life at Garden Lodge, was meanwhile wrestling a little with his odd relationship with Freddie's former lover Mary Austin. Living in her own home a short distance from Garden Lodge, Mary was responsible for Freddie's household and accounts, including the wages and housekeeping cash. She therefore appeared at their house every day. It has often been said that she never came to terms with losing Freddie. How painful it

must have been for her to see the love of her life with the
male lover who clearly worshipped him as much as she did.
Many questioned the sense in her gluttony for punishment.
Life would surely have been better spent attempting to build
true happiness elsewhere – not clinging to something that was
never to be. Some allowed for the possibility that in Mary's
heart, she really believed that Freddie still belonged to her.
It was as if she was certain that he would return to her one
day – though not in life.

'A curious woman indeed,' muses Jim:

Mary had this thing about people in general: she didn't
trust anyone. She hardly ever spoke about her parents
or her childhood. But I got the impression that she
also had a sister. She was very secretive about her own
background, even though we were part of Freddie's
personal household and all saw each other every day.
I never felt that I really got to know Mary, and maybe
that was her intention.

I don't feel sorry for her – even though so many
people seem to. My thing about her is that she'll have
to one day wake up. The life she has lived so far has
not been what you could call real. I've seen her a few
times when she has happened to let her guard drop,
and she's a totally different person. She's not always
such the sweet, nice Mary Magdalene, the one we've
all read about all these years. There's another side to
her. Oh gosh, yes. On a few rare occasions I'd see her
laugh. And I'd think to myself, now that is a *real* laugh,
Mary – the laughter you should always have. But the
rest of the time the smile that didn't reach the eyes was
painted on to her face, especially when a camera pointed.
There were a few times when she saw me copping this,
and she'd change – Snap!—just like that. I could never
hold out against her, and I wasn't actually interested
in trying.

The loyalty of his dearest friends was, says Jim, the thing that Freddie most relied on during the final six years of his life. Although there were many acquaintances, and Garden Lodge parties were invariably packed with glamorous types such as former EastEnders actress Anita Dobson, and Elaine Paige, the circle of those on whom he could truly depend was small: 'Dave Clark. Elton. Barbara Valentin was a very good friend to him. Freddie loved lively people around him; funny people; people who made him laugh. Or, if he was in a mood about something, someone to pull him out of it . . . Barbara could do that, no problem at all. Or Straker, until that all ended.'

However efficient his household staff, however perfect their accomplishments, Freddie never conquered his need to fuss and fiddle and have the final say:

'We had this cleaner who was quite heavy-handed, shall we say, about the house,' recalls Peter. 'She was always bashing things with the Hoover. Freddie used to say that, had they had cleaners like her in the eighteenth century, we wouldn't have any antiques today.'

'Freddie was just like that,' remembers Jim:

And very, very proper and 'British' about most things. He used to go into panics sometimes. It could be hilarious. I remember his parents were coming over once – he was giving a lunch or something – and he was practically having a nervous breakdown. Oh, God! Talk about a mother hen. The food – he'd be in and out the kitchen all morning, and into everything. Then there was the dining-room table. He had to lay that himself; he always, always made a point of doing that. I hadn't realized how important it was to him. One Christmas – now, what was I doing?—I was making up a centrepiece for the table. And the night before, Christmas Eve, there were a few friends around, and Freddie suddenly said, 'We must lay up the table.' For Christmas or for birthdays, the two of us would usually do it together. Anyway, it got left, as Freddie was into having a good time that night. On Christmas morning I was out in the garage when Freddie came down and started throwing a wobbly. 'Where's Jim? What about the dining-room table?' Moan, moan, moan. Peter came out to the garage and said, 'Freddie wants you. He needs you to give him a hand with the dining-table.' Now, neither Peter, Freddie nor Joe had even been *into* the dining-room. So I came on in and Freddie said, very gruffly, '*What* are you doing?' I said, 'I'm making this floral centrepiece for the table. I'll bring it in now, in a second. Finish your cup of tea.' 'But we have to set the dining-room table!' he flapped, very crossly. This was at 11 o'clock in the morning. Lunch wasn't even until two. Say nothing Jim. I came in with this centrepiece, which he admired, and I said, 'Now let's just see if it'll fit the table, make sure that it won't be too big.' I already had the table laid up, of course, and I was teasing him just the little bit. The floral arrangement was nice and Christmassy, red, white and green, and I had also done the table up in red and white. He came into the dining-room, saw everything, but didn't say a word to me. He just went 'Oh'. Then he went fussing around the table, taking ages making sure that the knives and forks were perfectly pointing towards the ones opposite, and that the place mats were all lined up just so. He couldn't just stand back and admire what I'd done without his help. He could be so infuriating in that way. It wasn't until much later on, that evening, that he said to me, 'Where did you get the idea to put the serviettes [not napkins] like that?' Because we normally had them in silver rings. But this time I had put them into quite an elaborate fan shape in the wine glasses. I just looked at him and I said, 'I did once work in a hotel, you know.' And that was it. For all my efforts, that was the extent of his praise. Anything like that – if he had friends coming round for a meal, whatever – oh, he was the absolute perfectionist. And Joe always made beautiful meals, nothing you could criticize. Freddie *knew* he could always rely on Joe to rise to the occasion, but still he flapped and fussed.

Freddie was never at ease when his parents were coming to the house, a situation which was not to change until his dying day:

Freddie's parents came to Garden Lodge now and again. I remember the very first time I met them at the house, and Freddie was so worried about me meeting them – Oh gosh, yes. He didn't exactly send me off for the day, but I was kept out of the way. I was the gardener. We'd had a little discussion about it beforehand. He said, 'Well, my parents are going to wonder who you are, and where you live . . . so if I tell them you live here, you stay in the guest-room, okay?' I didn't mind that at all. Things like that never worried me. He did introduce me to them at some point during the day, but quite casually. There was no formal introduction, I wasn't actually wheeled on as Freddie's partner.

In fact, Jim is certain that Freddie went to his grave without ever having personally revealed his homosexuality to his parents:

He never told me that he *had* informed them. I don't think he felt it necessary to. I wouldn't dream of speaking for Freddie or his parents, but I imagine Freddie's parents probably knew. Jer was like all good mothers; and mothers have an instinct, a second sight, an insight. She had such a lively little face, and a beautiful smile. I suppose what's still unsaid is best left unsaid, if you know what I mean. Coming clean about everything to your parents is not always the best idea. Sometimes it can work for you, and sometimes it can backfire.

Adds Peter Freestone, 'Freddie's parents knew he was gay, but they didn't want to be told. They actually came to the house very rarely. More often than not, Freddie went over to see them.'

Does Jim himself believe that Freddie was by nature homosexual?

Yes. Without a doubt. I suppose Freddie's lifestyle was totally at odds with what his parents might have expected, or were used to, but I never discussed that with them. I'd driven Freddie over to their house a few times. I had afternoon tea with them often enough. I don't know what I expected, but their house was conventionally Western, and so were their clothes. They had pretty much taken to life here.

I did have a couple of run-ins with Roger, the husband of Freddie's sister Cash. Silly things: in the garden, I knew all the common names of plants, and that was about it. But he would turn up knowing the botanical ones. Freddie said, 'I'm sure he reads up on all these plants before he comes here.' I had to agree with him. Cash, I always got on with. I rather liked her. She played things straight down the line.

Although the so-called 'Court of King Freddie' has often been portrayed as being a cross between the household of Henry VIII and some Middle-Eastern Sultan, Jim insists that everyday life, though grand by the standards of most ordinary folk, was most days not at all exotic, and much more relaxed than has been implied. Granted, Freddie was the boss, the one around whom daily life revolved. The reason they were all there was to see to his needs and keep him secure and happy. But both Jim and Peter report that there were no politics as such, nor any kind of hierarchy or pecking order. Everybody who lived under Freddie's roof was treated with the same respect, and there were no specific 'rules': 'The only unspoken rule was that you didn't bring anyone else back,' said Jim.

No pals, no overnight partners. It was very much Freddie's domain. For security reasons of course, but also because people can be light-fingered and you can't be too careful.

We were more a family bunch than Freddie's staff, if you like. But it all ran along pretty much on an even keel. Joe the chef got away with blue murder. He could be a sweetie, but he had his tantrums. One thing I always think back on which I think is rather funny, we were out doing a video shoot, can't remember what track. I'd asked Mary that morning if Joe could clean the filter of the pond out. I'd said, it's very simple, it's mechanical, you don't have to worry about anything. Later that morning Joe phoned me up to say, 'Jim, the pond has half-emptied.' I said, 'Did you switch the filter off?' and he went, 'Oh – shit.' Then he said, 'I've noticed there's an awful little white, like frogspawn, in the pond,' and I told him that was from the fish that had been spawning. 'Would you get a load of the eggs out for me and put them in the tank?' 'Certainly not!' he snapped. 'I'm a chef, not the gardener!' Maybe Joe thought he was a cut above the rest. But we all had our specific role. And I wanted mine – I didn't want to just live out of Freddie's pocket. There were times, in the early days, when Joe and I might clash a little bit. For example, when I first moved into Garden Lodge, I might feel peckish and fancy a sandwich, and I'd think, I'll just go down to the kitchen and make my own. And I'd get daggers thrown at me from Joe. Just The Look: it was *his* kitchen. We often ate all together, *en famille*, but mostly it was just Freddie and myself. Joe was a bit of a health freak, so he and Peter might prepare something for us and then eat something else themselves. And if Freddie wasn't there, they certainly didn't have a problem preparing meals for me. It wasn't that kind of set-up. And I don't think I gave them any reason to feel resentful towards me.

Everyone had their own room, the same kind of room. Barbara also had her own room there for some time. Her room had been my bedroom, in fact. And then in the later years, when Freddie and I no longer slept together, I moved back into that same room. There was no favouritism. Whenever Freddie's friends came back for a few drinks, everyone who was in the house was included in the party. People were not expected to withdraw discreetly from the proceedings – none of that. Garden Lodge was very much everybody's home, to all of us equally who lived there.

We had some quite beautiful dinner-parties there. Joe and Peter would always sit at the table on Christmas Day. The rest of the time they were generally in the kitchen, and so that was where they ate. Freddie might say to Joe, we're having so many round for dinner tonight, and Joe would go, 'Okay, what would you like?' But Freddie would never come in saying, 'Do this, cook that.' He didn't fling his weight around and give orders, it was all much more relaxed than that.

Throughout all the fun, the frolics and the wild times Freddie and Jim enjoyed together – a one million pound holiday in Japan, the madness of Live Aid, the tranquillity of Switzerland – and the tender love they shared until the end, Jim says he derived the most satisfaction from Freddie's creativity.

Freddie was more or less permanently creative. He was always into something. Not so much playing the piano and singing in the house all the time, but he could be sitting there, you might think in cloud cuckoo land, dreaming, but he'd be planning, planning. I'd look at him and I always knew his brain was doing overtime. I'd think, what's he cooking up now? There was always something going on. First, it was Garden Lodge to finish. He then bought the mews house. When that was completed, he was off to buy a place in Switzerland. He could never rest. Nothing was ever finished. He had to be doing, doing, all the time.

He didn't talk to me much about his music. But when it came to lyrics, he'd talk to anyone who was there who would listen. He'd come along and say 'I've got this idea,' or 'I've got these words,' or 'Now dear, help me out with this line here.' He was always scribbling things down – on anything at all. The back of a used postage stamp if nothing else was to hand. He never sang around the house – only occasionally in the bath. But not Queen songs. I've got a video of him actually in the jacuzzi, and he's just warbling away at the top of his voice.

Professionally, he was as meticulous in the studio as he would be in the house if he was preparing for a party. But he wasn't serious all the time. There was a fun side to him which he couldn't keep down. He'd like to make up different, cheeky words to a song, for example. He would occasionally lose his rag in the studio, but only because he got frustrated, if something wasn't going right as far as he was concerned. He would explode, and then he would seethe. He was like that in his personal life too. And it could go on for days, a week, two weeks. And you'd think, what the hell is this all about? Most of our disagreements were over absolutely nothing. Fun making up? Hmm . . . sometimes. That's what married life, or partnerships, is all about. It's one way of getting to know your partner – through a series of clashes.

Freddie had promised his lover the legendary 'holiday of a lifetime' in Japan at the end of September 1986. And Freddie always kept his promises. A breathtaking time was had, with Freddie particularly relishing the fact that for once he could enjoy Japan as a tourist, and they shopped until they dropped – after which the pair returned to London and settled down to an orderly domestic life at Garden Lodge. His cats, koi carp and closest friends soon became Freddie's primary preoccupations, not necessarily in that order. He had his lover and small côterie of staff for permanent company. What else did he need? Little was he prepared for the shock the *News Of The World* had in store for him.

The newspaper's revelations on Sunday 13 October 1986 were short and to the point: Freddie had allegedly taken a secret Aids test towards the end of 1985. Although he denied it emphatically, those closest to him noticed a distinct change in mood. There was a hint of panic to Freddie's voice whenever the subject was raised, which was rarely – not least, perhaps, because he had recently been informed of the deaths of two previous sexual partners: an airline steward named John Murphy, and young Tony Bastin, the courier he had picked up all those years ago in Brighton.

In America, the falsification of death certificates had by now become prevalent, so many prominent people having perished from Aids who had persuaded their doctors to preserve honour, dignity, and posthumous public image. Even as the pianist Liberace lay on his deathbed, his spokesman continued to insist that the star was suffering the ill-effects of a 'watermelon diet'. Archetypal macho heart-throb Rock Hudson, 'last of the traditional, square-jawed, romantic leading men', and former romantic screen sidekick of movie queen Doris Day, had become the first major Hollywood star to openly die of Aids, in October 1985. In Britain, 264 cases of Aids had been reported by 1985. Aids was declared the most serious health threat to the nation since the Second World War, and Minister for Health Kenneth Clark announced new laws empowering magistrates to order hospital isolation of Aids victims who persisted in careless sexual activity that rendered them a danger to society. It was a ball with which the sensationalist press intended to run and run. Attacks on homosexuals were frequently reported, and misinformation spread like forest fire. When one London gay switchboard failed to cope with the influx of 'Aids Scare' calls and its lines went down, BT engineers refused to mend them in case they picked up the disease from the wiring. And *Burke's Peerage*, the revered published guide to the British aristocracy, made the sinister announcement that in order to preserve the 'purity of the human race', it would not list families in which any member was known to be infected with Aids. There were plenty of reasons for Aids sufferers to keep a low profile. There was also, for Freddie, Queen and Jim Beach, the not inconsiderable question of their recording contract with EMI. With albums still outstanding, the last thing they needed was the suggestion that Freddie might not live long enough to fulfil the obligations of the band to their record company. Freddie, for his part, ignored the stories and the gossip and got on with his life as he saw fit. That Christmas, 1986, Queen's 'Live Magic' album was released, featuring live recordings of many favourite hits, after which the band planned to take a year off to rest and concentrate on solo ventures. Domestically he became a confirmed 'stop-at-home': 'We began to lead a very quiet life together at Garden Lodge,' reports Jim Hutton.

'Most Saturday evenings Phoebe and Joe went out, and left the two of us cuddled up on the sofa watching television. Some nights we'd even be in bed by 10 o'clock, though that never meant Freddie got up any earlier the following morning. Freddie liked to have a cup of tea in bed about eight in the morning, then doze for an hour or two before getting up.'

Jim maintained a good relationship with most of those close to Freddie. Remarked Spike Edney, 'I haven't a single bad thing to say about Jim Hutton. He was always a very charming man. He was a genial, affable guy who, as a non-musician hanging out in a musician's world, seemed to cut quite the right balance of being involved but not overbearing.'

Christmases were romantic affairs surrounded by close friends. Adds Peter Freestone,

Depending on how many you call 'close friends'! We did Christmas dinner for 30 once, and only Joe and I cooking. We were never off duty in those days, 24 hours a day, seven days a week. But we never minded. It was enormous fun. Once, there were 15 people for Christmas Day, and Freddie insisted that everyone brought a present for everyone else. It didn't have to be much – a pair of socks, whatever – but there had to be a present for every single person from everyone there. They were all put under the tree, and what a fantastic pile they made. Jim was always responsible for the Christmas tree. He went out, picked the tree – it was always 14 or 15 feet – then dressed it and looked after it for the whole of Christmas. Freddie loved his Christmases. He loved the ritual and the ambience, and it was a joy to watch him.

Anniversaries of any kind were important to Freddie. On St Valentine's Days, he and Jim exchanged romantic bouquets. And much was always made of birthdays in the household. It was a happy existence. Freddie appeared, by now, to have struck the perfect balance between socializing and work. He'd get up late, perhaps have a few people over for brunch, or go out somewhere local for lunch, chat at the table for hours, and then perhaps spend the evening having a dinner-party at home or at some smart restaurant with the same people or a few new additions. He was happy to work in the studio into the early hours. Some days he might make the short journey to the Queen productions office in Pembridge Road, off Notting Hill, make time for a couple of business meetings, maybe pop in to Christie's or Sotheby's to assess whatever was coming up for sale in the way of antiques or oriental art. He was, remarked one friend, 'always busy but seldom rushed. It was a pleasant convivial life.'

Leee Johns, the vivacious former lead singer with eighties funk-soul trio Imagination, had got to know Freddie in the mid-eighties and was also a guest at his home.

'I have a very special story, I call it my Magic Moment,' says Leee.[2]

I'd often bump into the guys from Queen during the eighties, and they were always complimentary about Imagination and how well we were doing. I'd also long been a great pal of Peter Straker, who was very close to Freddie. Their friendship seemed to me very respectful. They looked after each other, did things for each other. I met up with Peter on one occasion, and he told me they were all going off to Heaven to pick up Freddie. Oh! I hated Heaven! I'd been there years earlier when it was Global Village, but I'm not really into that steamy gay club scene, drug-taking and so on. I never understood why Freddie liked it so much – but even he got bored with it in the end. Anyway, Peter insisted that I tag along, because they were all going back to Freddie's house to drink champagne. I remember Marc Almond being there that night. The music wasn't at all my scene – I much preferred melody and soul.

Then I saw Freddie. I had long been a fan. Queen wasn't the music I was into, but I really adored Freddie's voice and theatrics. Freddie ran up to me, saying, 'Oh, darling, I know you, I know you!' I'm going, 'Who, me?'

'Yes, you!' he said. 'We've got to talk about your voice, darling – your voice, your *tone*!' I remember thinking that he reminded me in a funny way of Ken Dodd – his teeth, the way he spoke.

One thing led to another and we all got in a cab. I was singing in the cab as we went along – Leee is always singing, baby. When we got back to his house, Freddie said to me, 'Now come on, dear, with me, come upstairs.' I said, 'Look, I'm not into all that, I don't do drugs.' But he wanted me to go up to his music room to hear something.

According to Peter Freestone, 'The music room was actually the balcony, a minstrels' gallery on top of the sitting-room, which itself had originally been built as an artists' studio.'

'I remember these two gigantic speakers,' continues Leee.

We sat there and talked about music – soul, jazz, funk, everything, it seemed like for hours. He played me some tracks he was going to do with Michael Jackson – 'State of Shock' – and 'Victory', and 'There Must Be More To Life Than This'. Really funky soul tracks. Brilliant. I think Jagger did that one with Jackson in the end. I sat there in amazement, and we just talked, exchanged stuff, sang along, did some riffs together. Then, before we went back downstairs, he asked me what my influences were. 'Motown,' I told him mine. 'Classical,' he told me his. He said that the secret to the complexity and delivery of music was to be found in the classics: 'The opera,' he said, 'is all.' At that time I didn't understand what on earth he meant. But now, I do. It was as if he saw something in me, and he was trying to give me something more. He said, 'A word of advice: as a performer, you needn't do half as much as you are doing. You don't have to dance so wildly or sing so crazily. Less is more.' And he kept on saying to me, 'Great voice, great voice!' That was amazing, coming from him, and I told him so. But he shrugged, and said, 'Darling, what you must understand is that my voice comes from the energy of the audience. The better they are, the better I get.' I thought that was priceless.

Yet still Leee could tell that Freddie was not pleased when they rejoined the others downstairs. Something was up:

He still couldn't work out where my vocal sound came from. It was as if he'd become obsessed with finding out. He started putting on all these music videos – Supremes, Four Tops, Temptations, Martha Reeves and the Vandellas – he was convinced that I had got my sound from Diana Ross. But Eddie Kendricks of the Temptations had been my main influence. That was where the inspiration for my falsetto came from: sing high and make it speak to you, not shriek to you. Ah! Freddie was now content. He had worked out where I'd got it from.

Freddie then went to his 'wine cellar'.

'We always had a good stock of wines and champagne in the utility room, plus a bin shed outside the house which we had locks put on so that we could keep more wine in it,' explains Peter.

Freddie returned with a fine bottle of vintage champagne. Everybody in the room stopped talking and looked. Those accustomed to his ways knew they were about to witness a special moment:

'He made me open it and drink it,' says Leee.

'It was exquisite. A little later, he had his chauffeur drive me home. And for the first time in my life, I felt like a star.'

Chapter Twenty-Two

BARCELONA: WHO WANTS TO LIVE FOREVER?

Undeterred by the less than ecstatic reaction to his first solo album, Freddie remained keen to record more work of his own. Up at London's Townhouse Studios, he experimented with a version of Buck Ram's classic song 'The Great Pretender', a huge hit for The Platters way back in 1956. It was his first-ever cover of a hit by another artist, and Freddie was so delighted with his efforts that he decided to film a lavish £100,000 video to promote it. For the three-day shoot he even shaved off his moustache for the sake of the slick image he decided to portray in the promo film, which mirrored a series of classic scenes from earlier Queen videos. A number of sequences featured Freddie in the same costumes he had worn for those original shoots. He amazed himself and everybody by demonstrating that he could easily get into them. In one scene Freddie dragged up, along with Roger Taylor and his friend Peter Straker. Model Debbie Ash also appeared, in an armchair, and enjoyed the questionable pleasure of having Freddie jump on top of her. The video did the trick: the single was released in late February and rose quickly to number four. An even more outrageous video was released a month later, depicting the making of 'The Great Pretender' in all its garish glory.

During the 'Magic' tour in August 1986, when Queen were performing in Spain, Freddie is said in previous biographies to have given an interview to a Spanish television channel in which he mischievously 'revealed' that the primary purpose of his visit to Spain was that he was angling to meet his all-time favourite opera star, Montserrat Caballé. In fact, confirms Peter Freestone, who had himself been responsible for converting Freddie to opera and who had spent many hours explaining characters, plots and sub-plots to Freddie as they worked their way through his record collection:

'Freddie had done a *radio* interview, on which they asked him, "Who has the best voice in the world?" Freddie replied, "I'm not saying this just because I'm in Spain – but as far as I'm concerned, Montserrat Caballé has the best voice of anybody in existence."

'Montserrat heard about what Freddie had said,' remembers Peter.

At that point, she had already been approached regarding the 1992 Barcelona Olympics, Barcelona being Montserrat's home town. The idea was created that perhaps the combination of Freddie Mercury and Montserrat Caballé would work rather well for an Olympic anthem. Jim Beach had also had discussions with Carlos, Montserrat's brother and business manager. It was then put to Freddie, who readily agreed, as it would give him a longed-for opportunity to work with her. He was also completely seduced by the idea of another worldwide television audience – he had got the taste for that doing Live Aid. So a meeting was duly arranged in Barcelona, for March 1987. In the meantime, Montserrat sent Freddie some videos of her performing, and in turn had asked for the complete works of Queen.

Freddie was unusually nervous as he flew to Spain with

Peter, Jim Beach and producer Mike Moran, whom Freddie had originally met on Dave Clark's musical *Time*. They waited around in the Ritz Hotel that Tuesday for what seemed like hours. Montsy, as Freddie would eventually feel comfortable enough to call her, was late – as was her well-known habit.

'Lunch took place in a private garden dining-room with a piano in one corner. The hotel had also set up a little stereo system in the other corner,' recalls Peter.

'Freddie had a rough tape with a song and a few little ideas on it, which I had to guard with my life. There was "Exercises In Free Love", plus what would become "Ensueño", and some ideas for other tracks. I noticed that Freddie and Montserrat were both very much in awe of each other, but excited at the prospect of working together. They hit it off, and lunch was a success.'

A few days later, Montserrat had an engagement at the Royal Opera House in London, after which she visited Freddie at Garden Lodge.

'Mike Moran was there, and it didn't take long for them all to hit the piano,' remembers Peter.

'It was an unforgettable night. Freddie and Montserrat were completely natural with each other. They drank champagne and fooled around, just jamming – if that term can be applied to an opera singer. Their formal studio work together was never as relaxed as that night at Garden Lodge.'

The following month, Queen were awarded another Ivor Novello for their 'Outstanding Contribution to British Music'. Soon afterwards, Freddie settled down to concentrate on his album with Montserrat. The process would not be that simple: Montserrat was in great demand at opera houses and concert halls all over the world, and could not take time out to experiment and dabble and work with Freddie in the studio the way he liked to do. Much of the production was done long-distance over about nine months, with Freddie despatching tapes of near-completed tracks for her to add her vocals. As far as Freddie was concerned, this was not the easiest way to work. But the end result was, in his opinion, one of the greatest achievements of his career.

May brought devastation in the shape of sordid kiss-and-tell revelations in the *Sun*. These had been sold to the newspaper for an alleged £32,000 by the trusted personal assistant who had held Freddie's hand on the road for years: Paul Prenter. The story included details about two former lovers who had died of Aids, and also named Jim Hutton as the current paramour.

'Freddie couldn't bear the betrayal,' confirmed Jim. 'He couldn't believe anyone who had been so close to him could behave in so mean-spirited a way. The story continued for a few more days, stories about Freddie and drugs, Freddie and men, it got worse and worse. Freddie got angrier with each new revelation, and never spoke to Prenter again.'

Although the former assistant made a point of calling his ex-employer at Garden Lodge to try and explain why he had done such a dreadful thing, Freddie would not take his calls.

'It crushed Freddie's ability to trust others, except for a select few,' said Jim. 'He certainly made no new friends after that.'

Said Peter Freestone, 'Freddie had taken Paul on when the band got rid of him because he was no longer needed – even though he knew that Paul was taking advantage of him, financially and so on. That made it all the harder to bear.'

Added Spike Edney, 'Oh God, some terrible things went on there. Prenter was the one who had always taken advantage of Fred's forgiving nature, to the point that people used to stand around going, "how does he get away with this shit?" And yet Fred still maintained their friendship.

'Fred got shafted by more people over the years than anyone I've ever known.'

'Not as many, perhaps,' says Peter, 'as other people might have thought.'

But Spike was disgusted by what he witnessed.

You can actually think that somebody is on your side, and you trust them for years, only to find out they've just stabbed you in the back. Considering that Fred was a pretty shrewd judge of character, it's amazing how many untrustworthy leeches actually got through the net. I think in some ways he was a little naïve and gullible, and people who perceived that were able to get close to him who perhaps shouldn't have been able to. Each time he was stitched up, that made him twice as suspicious about anyone new coming in. I used to stand on the edge and watch them all vying for status and favour, and I'd think to myself, 'His is a position you would not want to be in.' He never actually had any true privacy – ever. People like Prenter saw to that.

Later that month, Freddie departed with Jim, Peter, Joe and Terry Giddings, his chauffeur, for a much-needed break in Ibiza. As he was by now aware that he did indeed have Aids, having recently tested positive and having confessed as much to Jim, they took with them, on the advice of Freddie's trusted GP, Dr Gordon Atkinson, a small medical trunk which would henceforth form a vital part of their luggage on all foreign trips. As well as basic First Aid requirements, it also contained Freddie's preparations for Aids.

Freddie's holiday party stayed at the exquisite Pike's Hotel, a converted 500-year-old farmhouse. There, they played a little tennis, lounged by the pool, and ventured out to a few gay clubs and bars at night. According to Jim, 'Freddie developed a bad wound on the bottom of his right foot. It would dog him for the rest of his life, and eventually made it increasingly difficult for him to walk.'

Towards the end of their holiday, Freddie was due at the famous Ku Club outside San Antonio where he had an engagement with his new bosom pal. The 'Ibiza 92' festival, staged to celebrate Spain's hosting of the forthcoming Olympic Games in 1992, was to be closed by Freddie and Montserrat Caballé with a rendition of 'Barcelona', their special duet. Also on the bill were Marillion, Duran Duran, Chris Rea and Spandau Ballet, whose lead singer Tony Hadley was well pleased to see his old pal, if shocked by his obvious ill-health.

'There had been all these rumours flying round, and when I saw Freddie there, I realized that he was probably not very well. We gave each other a hug and stuff, and he seemed on great form. But he had become noticeably more withdrawn.'

The champagne later flowed at the Ku Club, and into the night at Pike's. Freddie partied into the early hours just as he had done in the good old days.

Freddie spent the summer working frantically on his house and acquiring two adjoining cottages in Logan Mews, which were then gutted and renovated. He also planned a conservatory next to The Mews. Jim remarked that it was as if Freddie wanted to leave his own little bit of paradise on earth. September saw them back at Pike's Hotel on Ibiza, accompanied by Phoebe, Joe, Terry Giddings, Peter Straker and reporter David Wigg from the *Daily Express*. The other members of Queen were already ensconced on the island with their families – Roger owned a glorious, secluded holiday home there – and Freddie was planning to celebrate his 41st birthday away from London's prying eyes. The party, to be held at Pike's, was to be a joint affair with Queen's ex-manager John Reid. But Reid inexplicably pulled out at the last minute, leaving a miffed Freddie to cope with all the joint arrangements: dual-name firework displays, shared, Gaudi-inspired chocolate birthday cake, the lot. 'Fuck Reid,' was his only comment. A chartered plane carrying dozens of his friends was due to arrive at any moment, and Freddie was not about to let it spoil his fun.

After the outrageous party, Roger, who was by this time

working on a solo album with his own band The Cross, invited Freddie to contribute to a track to be recorded at Maison Rouge studios. Freddie would be delighted. The Cross diverted from Ibiza to Montreux, and shortly afterwards met up with Freddie in London. Spike Edney was also there:

> The track was called 'Heaven For Everyone'. We were at Maison Rouge studios, messing around with it, and Fred was going to come down and then we were all going to go off for dinner. Whenever you recorded with Queen it was great: you'd go into the studio at about two o'clock in the afternoon, you'd have some lunch, sit around and talk about doing something, generally tinkle about. At seven o'clock you'd open a bottle of wine, then you'd go out for dinner . . . and then, if you felt like it afterwards, you'd go back to the studio all vibed up and do some work. And then go out somewhere. You'd actually do about an hour's work. Anyway, Fred was due down that particular day, to tinker around with this song, and do some backing vocals on the chorus. Suddenly he said, 'Oh, bollocks to this, let me sing the song – I know it now!' So he sang it – and that is the version that you hear, the very first single released from the 'Made In Heaven' album. And of course, Freddie's version is fantastic. But he wasn't actually allowed to be singing on a Roger Taylor solo album, because of his own solo recording contract, which all gets very complicated. So Fred couldn't be credited. Consequently, on that first Cross album, called 'Shove It', you hear this track called 'Heaven for Everyone', and it's in fact Freddie's vocal . . . but when they released it as a single, they had to release the *Roger* version.
>
> Virgin Records owned that track. And what amazed me was, when Freddie died, they didn't even know they owned a track with Freddie Mercury singing on it!

Freddie's and Montsy's acclaimed duet, 'Barcelona' was released in Spain on 21 September. In under three hours, 10,000 copies of the single had walked out of the shops and there was talk of the song being chosen as the official Olympic anthem. The record was released in the UK the following month, stunning Freddie's most vociferous critics into silence. Possible the first collaboration by a rock 'n' roll star and an internationally-acclaimed opera diva, you either loved it or hated it.

Christmas 1987 saw the arrival of two new inmates to Garden Lodge – another pair of kittens. The tortoiseshell, whom Freddie immediately named Delilah and for whom he later wrote the song of that name, would become Freddie's favourite cat. And she knew it: she soon took to sleeping at the foot of his bed. The other, a little dark brown ball, was named Goliath. As Freddie's illness took its toll and life had to be lived at a more sedate pace, it was in his cats that he found solace.

Working whenever he felt strong enough, Freddie was collaborating during that period with Mike Moran and Tim Rice for the 'Barcelona' album. Rice's girlfriend Elaine Paige had expressed an interest in recording an entire album of Queen covers, imaginatively called 'The Queen Album', about which Freddie was very enthusiastic and on which he promised to assist. In January 1988, Freddie, Brian, Roger and John reunited at the Townhouse studios to commence work on their next album, 'The Miracle'.

Brian, Roger and John were by this time only too aware of the fact that Freddie was gravely ill. The horrifying signs were there for all to see. At first, they said, the subject was discreetly ignored. But eventually, finding the embarrassing silences unbearable, it was Freddie himself who sat them all down and made his tragic admission.

'We talked about it, and first of all he said, "You probably realise what my problem is – my illness," said Brian.

'And by that time, we kind of did. It was unspoken. And

then he said, "Well, that's it. I don't want it to make any difference. I don't want anything to be different whatsoever. I don't want it to be known, I don't want to talk about it, I just want to get on and work until I can't work anymore." I don't think any of us will ever forget that day. We all just went off and got quietly sick somewhere.'[1]

As Roger added, 'Freddie knew his time was limited, and he really wanted to work, and keep going. He felt that was the best way for him to keep his spirits up, and he wanted to leave as much behind as possible. We certainly agreed, and backed him up right to the hilt. For "The Miracle", he wasn't that well but he wasn't that ill. But it was an effort – a long album to make.'[2]

Losing himself in his work was precisely Freddie's style. As Mary Austin was to explain it after his death, 'I think it was the one thing that gave him much happiness. It made him feel alive inside, through the pain that he was experiencing. That fed the light inside. Instead of things becoming dull, and life becoming painful, looking at each morning, there was something else that he was working for. Life wasn't just taking him to the grave. There was something else he could make happen, and he did.'[3]

There was also another obvious consideration:

'I think Freddie did feel safe in the environment of the group,' was Brian's assessment of the situation. 'Things were just as they always had been. Probably we all tried too hard. But we tried to make things just very normal. It seemed to work.'[4]

Freddie arrived in Barcelona on 8 October for the huge open-air festival La Nit in the presence of Spain's King Juan Carlos, Queen Sofia and Princess Cristina, during which the city would ceremoniously receive the Olympic torch from Seoul. Freddie and Montsy were due to sing with the Barcelona Opera House Orchestra and Choir, but 'singing' was not what you could call it. The fact that the duo were miming – probably due to the return of Freddie's painful throat nodules, although this was never publicly admitted – brought to a resounding, anticlimactic close a strange evening which had already featured a most unlikely combination of talents: Spandau Ballet, José Carreras, Eddy Grant, Jerry Lee Lewis and Rudolf Nureyev.

Going through the motions in front of backing tapes left Freddie's and La Superba's audience somewhat high and dry. Tony Hadley, who perhaps had not realized that they were miming, comments, 'Freddie was performing with Montserrat Caballé and there was some technical cock-up. Freddie was not very pleased. I saw him in his dressing-room afterwards, and he was really annoyed and upset, throwing a complete wobbly. I said, "Look, Fred, you were great. You're always great. And by the way, mate, it's a fantastic song." There was I, Mr Old Hat, giving Fred the pep talk this time. It was usually the other way round.'

Two days later, when the pair faced the press at the Royal Opera House Covent Garden for the launch of their 'Barcelona' album, Freddie was defensive when asked why they had not sung live in Spain. 'This is a very difficult thing for me. They're complex songs, and we just didn't have enough rehearsal time. If my voice was to go, or not come up to scratch, I'd be letting Montserrat down. I didn't want to take any chances.'

The rest of 1988 passed quietly, with the band all involved in individual pursuits. By January 1989 'The Miracle' album was almost finished, the band working more closely and compassionately together than ever before. Bitter altercation and tantrums had famously been the hallmarks of their style. Their 32nd UK single, 'I Want It All', was released in May, followed by 'The Miracle', Queen's 16th album, which went platinum within one week. The next two singles would be 'Breakthru' and 'Invisible Man'. Following the excitement generated by the success of 'The Miracle', Freddie took off with Jim Hutton for Montreux, where, before he purchased his own apartment in 1991, a little late in the day, Freddie always rented the same beautiful lakeside house. It was called The Cygnets for its view of the little swans, 'Freddie's swans' as they were known, on Lac Leman. Freddie would always rush down to see them as soon as he arrived. He had renamed the place The Duck House, but Roger's nickname went one better: Duckingham Palace. Freddie loved to spend hours walking along the water's edge; the mountain air refreshed him, and he felt at peace. Out of sight did not equal out of mind in the view of the British press, however, who concluded that it was unnatural for Freddie Mercury to keep such a low profile for so long, and that something very serious must be wrong with him. Speculation was rife, and splashed all over the newspapers. Freddie simply stopped buying them. In October, the band took a return swing by releasing the fourth single from 'The Miracle', called 'Scandal'.

At the end of 1989, Queen were voted 'Band Of the Eighties' by the readership of *TV Times*, and were presented with their award on a television show with former Merseyside pop singer turned TV personality Cilla Black.

Freddie, still relentlessly creative, turned his thoughts to the promotion of Queen's next single from the album, also called 'The Miracle'. It was agreed that they should use child lookalikes of the band, with the four actual members of Queen putting in their own appearance at the end. Auditioning took weeks, but the result was exactly what Freddie had in mind. The kids Queen chose to play themselves were astonishing.

In the New Year, 1990, as Jim Beach entered into painfully extended negotiations for Queen's passage out of their US recording deal with Capitol and into a new one with Disney's Hollywood Records, the band gathered at Mountain Studios to begin yet another album, 'Innuendo'. That same year, they finally achieved the covetable BPI award for Oustanding Contribution to British Music. Bending time a little to make 1990 their 20th anniversary, Queen threw a huge party for

400 at the Groucho Club in Soho, to which people who had worked with Queen throughout their career in whatever capacity were invited, as well as a host of stars: Liza Minnelli, George Michael, Patsy Kensit, Michael Winner, Rod Stewart. The celebration cake was in the shape of a Monopoly board, with Queen hits pasted in to all the squares.

Freddie's appearance at the celebration was sadly ill-advised: the press had a field day with those gaunt, giveaway photographs. But still Freddie continued to deny the rumours, and flounced off back to work at Mountain Studios.

'"Innuendo" was very much made on borrowed time, as he really wasn't very well,' Roger would reveal after Freddie's death just one year later. 'I still believe it to be a tremendously underrated album. It's much better than a lot of the others we made. There are some extraordinary performances on that one. I find it very strong all the way through. It's quite emotional.'[5]

Some 17 years down the line, quite by chance, animator and Freddie's former college classmate Jerry Hibbert found himself commissioned by Queen's manager Jim Beach to create video promotional material for the 'Innuendo' album on a budget of £120,000. He recalls:

We certainly spent all of that and more, probably. We made no profit from it, as it was a show-reel job, good cachet. We had done a little bit of graphic work for Live Aid; perhaps that's how we got the job. I had heard all the rumours that Freddie was ill, and of course I was very concerned, so I said to Jim Beach at the meeting, 'Are we animating these because Freddie's ill and can't appear in them?' Jim just said, 'Freddie's *not* ill. Where on earth have you heard that?'[6]

It was merely coincidence that I'd been at college with him. None of them had realised that when they were considering us for the job. Why should they? I think they did know afterwards, but the attitude was a little bit 'Oh, really, so what?' I was really hoping that I might get to meet up with Freddie again. But it never happened. I had actually become something of a low-key Queen fan by then. I'd bought the records, but never actually saw Freddie perform live. What was really gratifying was that the video we did for 'Innuendo' won several awards, and I went to New York to receive one of them.

When he died, I felt so sad that I hadn't been able to meet up with him while I was doing the video, because I really wanted to do a nice job for him. It would have been great to get together. Surely he wouldn't have avoided me deliberately . . . I put it down to the fact that he was ill. I wonder if he ever thought, 'It would be nice to see Jerry again, because he's working on this thing, but I feel that I'm too ill, and he may not want to see *me* . . .' I'll never know. When he passed away, it was a great shock. I remember thinking my chance has gone. I felt very sad. Not for me, for him.

As for the phenomenon of Queen, Hibbert says that he was not at all surprised by the band's extraordinary success: 'He, and the others, especially Brian May whom I had also met, simply had what it took. Great musicianship, of course. But it does require an element of intelligence, and a sense of knowing exactly what you are trying to do. You've got to be focused. Freddie was an extremely intelligent man. They all were. That intelligence reflects itself in the quality of their music. That's what makes it last.'

Freddie's 44th birthday party was celebrated somewhat sedately at Garden Lodge with a special dinner-party attended by about 20 of his favourite people; Mary came with her boyfriend Piers Cameron, Jim and Claudia Beach, Mike Moran and his wife, Dave Clark, Barbara Valentin, Peter Straker, Dr Gordon Atkinson, as well as the usual members of Freddie's loyal household. It would be Freddie's last proper birthday party, and he knew it: he commemorated the occasion in style by presenting each guest with a special gift from Tiffany's.

'The dress Barbara had on was something,' laughs Peter Freestone. 'It was a frock she had worn in one of her early films. Freddie had insisted that we all dress up. And usually, when Barbara dresses up, she wears leggings that glitter as opposed to leggings that don't. This time had to be a bit more special.'

Barbara herself tells how living with Freddie through his illness, watching this man she loved so dearly wasting away before her eyes, was almost impossible to bear:

> There were times when he hated me, you know, at the end. His mind wasn't right. He was very crazy – nothing was clear, nothing was straight, everything was around corners. It was so hard to understand. He was weak, he couldn't function. He wanted to come to Munich again so badly. I said, 'We'll get a private plane, and I'll have a limousine with black-out windows to meet you on the runway, and bring you straight to our apartment, where you can stay in private. We need never go outside the door, and nobody need ever know that you're here. He agreed. He wanted to come. But in the end, it was too late.

Montreux, during that last year leading up to Freddie's death, proved a haven and a godsend. Jim Beach, a permanent Montreux resident, was to comment after Freddie had passed away: 'Certainly in his latter years he came here partly as a refuge, there's no question, because the paparazzi were camping around his house, and he couldn't really go out to a restaurant in London or anything without somebody trying to take a photograph of him. His private life had completely disappeared. This gave him a haven.'[7]

The single 'Innuendo' was released in January 1991 and went straight in at number one – Queen's first for 10 years, their last having been 'Under Pressure' with David Bowie. The album, released early in February, had the same effect on the charts. Both single and album scored similar success in countless countries, including a number one in South Africa. Also in February, Queen regrouped with the Torpedo Twins in London to film the promo video for their next single, 'I'm Going Slightly Mad', in which an extremely gaunt, over-made-up Freddie aped a crazed Lord Byron. 'Headlong', their 39th single, came out in May, after which Queen again made straight for Montreux to begin work, yet again, on yet another album – 'Made In Heaven', which would eventually be released some four years after Freddie's death. They had barely paused for breath. Freddie was unstoppable. He wanted to leave as much behind as possible, and the band had pledged to do everything in their power to help him. Despite his rapidly dwindling strength and energy, Freddie was driving himself as hard as ever. It was business as usual. Brian later discussed aspects of working in the studio on that final album with Freddie in Montreux, particularly 'Mother Love', quite literally his 'swan-song' – the last song that Freddie ever recorded:

A lot of it was strangely enough quite joyous. It sounds odd to say that, and people will probably hate me for saying it, but I know Freddie had some very good times in those last periods. He was able to put it to one side and just get on. And I think maybe there was a part of him that thought the miracle would come. I think we all did. I suppose you do, don't you – you never give up hope. And Freddie was certainly like that. I never saw him lay down, put his head in his hands and let it all get on top of him. We had some very funny times. We were very focused, very together as a group. I think we all realized how precious those moments were going to be.[8]

Fred, as normal, got to some point and said, 'No no no no no, this isn't good enough, I'll have to go higher here, I'll have to put more into this, I'll have to get more *power*.' So he downs a couple of vodkas, stands up, and just goes for it. And you can hear the middle-eight of the track 'Mother Love' just *soars* to incredible heights. This is a man who can't really stand any more without incredible pain and is very weak, has no flesh on his bones at all . . . and you can hear the power, the will that he's still got.

Adds Peter Freestone:

Those were very sad days, really, but Freddie didn't get depressed. He was resigned to the fact that he was going to die. He accepted it: we were all going to die someday. And anyway, could you imagine an old Freddie Mercury? He had always laughed his head off at the way The Who and The Stones kept getting together and going out on tour. He'd say, 'I'm not going to dance on stage when I'm 50. I'd look ridiculous.' Anyway, he knew Queen's time was up when they started getting what he called 'dino-saur awards' – the Lifetime Achievement-type things. Once that starts, he always felt, you really should think about giving it all up.

At home in London, dogged by illness, knowing, in his heart, that it couldn't be long now, Freddie suddenly redis-covered an urge to paint and draw. It was something he had not really attempted since his Ealing Art College days.

'Freddie certainly had the urge to paint,' confirms Peter Freestone:

And Jim went out and bought a watercolour set and brushes and so on for him. It's true that he would sit for hours with his little supply of artist's materials, trying to do a portrait of Delilah [his cat]. It proved too much for him. But he did manage a couple of abstracts. That was

Matisse. We were looking through a catalogue one day, and there was a Matisse going for £10,000. 'Ten grand?' Freddie cried. '*I* could do that!' And he went swish, swish with the brush, and said 'There you go, one each,' to me and Joe. 'See how much that's worth,' Freddie chuckled. I suppose they could be worth all of that now.

At about that time, I started to suffer the most amazing guilt. Freddie was sick, Joe was sick, and Jim had come back and said he was HIV positive. I just didn't know what to do. I'd been around during the same years as them, doing the same things as everybody else. And it was great fun – that's *all* it was. But I'm okay. It took me two or three months at least to come to terms with it. No, I never had a relationship with Freddie. But nobody can say for certain who gave who what. Back in the early eighties anything went in America, while in England you couldn't even look at anybody. Now, it's the total opposite.

But whose place is it to judge? I learned that from Freddie. Because of his own lifestyle, Freddie never judged anybody.

In August 1991, news reached Garden Lodge that Freddie's former aide Paul Prenter had died of Aids. And In September, Jim gave Freddie his last-ever birthday present: a set of Irish crystal champagne glasses which Freddie had wanted for their flat in Montreux.

'Sadly,' remarked Jim later, 'those glasses never did make it to Switzerland.'

It was the quietest birthday of Freddie's life. The only present he really wanted was privacy, but it proved too tall an order for the press. There would be one more dinner-party at Garden Lodge. One more trip to Switzerland, by private jet.

Says Jim, 'Until he died, we continued to live our life as normally as we could. We were in Switzerland just three weeks before he died, and while he wasn't in full health, he was well enough to be there. He was in a recording studio, for

God's sake. We never talked about how long he had left. But I think, if you have a terminal illness such as Aids or cancer, there comes a point when you have a pretty good idea.'

How Freddie had longed to spend Christmas at his swish new apartment. But everyone around him now knew for sure that it was never to be.

'Perhaps it does seem a little pointless now that he got his own flat in Montreux so near the end,' admits Peter. 'But Freddie loved doing up houses. The place in Montreux was just something else to keep him going. It was in the process of being bought, but when he died before completion it simply reverted back to the bank. Freddie had all these wonderful plans about what he'd do to each room, and he bought a lot of furniture from Sotheby's for it. But he never got to live there.'

It was then that Freddie informed his friends that he wanted to stop taking his medication. 'He had to tell us – we were the ones giving them to him,' says Peter.

He stopped everything except painkillers. He never really talked about being afraid of dying. There was no point in being frightened. There was nothing he could do to put it off. He never let the disease take control of his life. As soon as it looked as though that might happen, he took control again. *He* was going to decide when he was going to die.

There were also outside factors. The press all knew that something was going on. For weeks, 24 hours a day, they had camped on his doorstep. Several cars remained out there the whole time. He was basically a prisoner in his own home. But he did not get angry about it – anger was a waste of emotion. Nothing could be done about it, except, perhaps, what he did do – which was let go.

I know what stopped him going outside Garden Lodge at all about a month before he died. It was partly that there were people camped there all the time like vultures, and partly that his sight was going. We had been to Phillips the auction room one day. As you come out, there are these white marble steps, and Freddie found that he could no longer judge where the steps were. After that incident, he stayed at home.

Peter describes how painful it was to see his friend suffering such agony: 'It's painful to talk about it now. Just watching someone die, and knowing that you can do nothing in the world to prevent it.

'I think Freddie's only regret at the end was that there was so much more music inside him. That was the reason why he kept going right up until the end. But that was about it.'

Queen's 40th single, 'The Show Must Go On' backed by 'Keep Yourself Alive', was released in October just weeks before Freddie's death, and was almost an admission that it was all but over. Still the band, management, PRs and Freddie's entourage denied the rumours and insisted that nothing was remotely wrong. Still EMI continued to pump out the product. Queen had never appeared more prolific in their entire lives. A Greatest Hits Two album, Greatest Flix Two video – it never stopped. Just the way Freddie would have wanted.

Back at Garden Lodge, Peter Freestone found himself following in his late mother's footsteps as he set about nursing Freddie during his final weeks:

I learned to do it. I had to. There was nobody else who could have done it. Freddie had now begun to cut people off. He just didn't want to see certain people. His parents, for example; they had been to the house in those last two or three weeks, and they wanted to come again on the Saturday before he died. But he said, 'No. I've seen them.' Part of it was, he didn't want them seeing him as he now was. He'd prefer to be remembered as he had been. That was the reason he turned his back on so many people during the last year. Sometimes it would be a silly argument or something; but he knew the real reason, and so did I.

There were a few really close friends around at that time, who were all wonderful to him: Dave Clark, Elton, Tony King. And Joe and I, who were nursing, had help from the Westminster Hospital where Freddie had been treated: an oncologist who tried to relieve his Kaposi's sarcoma, and a skin specialist.

I've said it before, but it's amazing how quickly you learn things you had never expected to have to do. Freddie had a Hickman line inserted into his chest, for example, through which we were able to give him his drugs. That way, they go directly into an artery.

One comfort is that one of us was with him all the time – Jim, Joe, myself – even through the night. During those last weeks, Freddie was never left alone.

On 23 November a statement approved by Freddie was issued from Garden Lodge, finally admitting that the star had Aids.

Explained Peter, 'Freddie didn't make that statement because he knew that he was going to die the next day. He knew that he was dying, but he thought that maybe he had another week or so left. He'd stopped eating, he was barely drinking. There was no way that it could be long.'

Said Roger Taylor, 'I think the last thing that he wanted was to draw attention to any kind of weakness or frailty, which was all too obvious anyway. He didn't want pity, and he was incredibly brave. Having said that, he didn't want to be usurped . . . He used to say, "Look, I might pop off at any moment" – having not announced it. So it was absolutely right to do it at the time that it was done.'[9]

Twenty-four hours later, Freddie Mercury was dead.

Chapter Twenty-Three

TO ETERNITY

'We'd spent so many years making sure that Freddie was presentable before he left the house. The last thing I could do for him, in preparation for his final departure, was to make everything as perfect as I possibly could.'

In charge of all the funeral arrangements, as Jim Beach was actually out of the country when Freddie died, Peter Freestone recalls that he was amazed by his own calm collectedness.

'Strangely, I wasn't sad. Freddie died on the Sunday, and I think it was the next day that it hit me: his death was a relief. Freddie wouldn't have to go through it anymore.'

Knowing that his days were numbered, Freddie had seemed unconcerned with the specifics of funeral arrangements. He had never actually sat the members of his household down to discuss the details or particular wishes pertaining to his burial.

'Peter had a pretty good idea of what Freddie was like and what his preferences would be,' explains Jim:

The only thing Freddie ever said to me was that, when he died, he wanted to be taken straight out. He wanted everything to be over as quickly as possible, with as little fuss as possible. Had we been able to arrange it, he would even have liked to be cremated the same day. Get it all over and done with, so that everyone could get back to normal. Once you're gone, that's the end of it. If there *were* specific wishes, it was Peter who carried them out.

Freddie had this belief that, when your loved ones pass away, you have to get back into the land of the living as fast as you can. You mustn't go with them – it's not your turn. Freddie never wanted people to go around tearing their hair out or gnashing their teeth. Get on with life – that's what it's for.

As he had been attended by doctors throughout, a post-mortem to determine cause of death was not required. Peter went ahead and made all the arrangements: 'I had consulted with his parents, who had to be considered. We were burying a rock superstar, but they were burying their son. Naturally they wanted things done according to their Parsee tradition, and their requests were all taken into account.'

Holding fire, earth and water sacred, Parsees are not supposed to cremate or bury their dead. Bodies are placed within Towers of Silence for a celestial or 'sky' burial, and picked clean by vultures. If a Zoroastrian priest does not attend to say prayers at the time of death, it is believed that the soul will not leave the body after two days, and everlasting peace will elude the deceased. There was much speculation and discussion in Bombay during our visit as to how and where Freddie was buried, or his body otherwise disposed of. A celestial burial would obviously not be possible in England. Therefore his soul could not have left the body, and consequently he cannot, in Parsee eyes, be at rest. Such a consideration may explain his family's sustained unhappiness.

'They had to make do with cremation, this being England,' says Peter. 'It had to take place as soon after death as possible. And because of cremation, two doctors had to sign the death certificate. First thing Monday morning I went to Chelsea Register Office to register the death.'

The cause of death was given as 'a. Bronchopneumonia. b. Aids', as certified by Dr Atkinson. Peter's own signature appears on the death certificate.

'Then I went on to the funeral directors.' Freddie's funeral was actually quite difficult to arrange, not knowing how many people to expect, how many cars. I had to book two sessions at the crematorium, knowing full well that we wouldn't get done in half an hour with all the people that were bound to turn up.

The flowers just kept on arriving and arriving at the house. In the end there were five floral Daimler hearses purely for the flowers. Freddie would be in a Rolls-Royce hearse, and there were three or four cars after that.

He was cremated on the Wednesday morning at West London crematorium. And considering how distressing it was for all concerned, everything went very smoothly. Freddie's family went to the funeral directors' at 8.30 a.m. to start their Parsee proceedings. And the floral hearses and friends left Garden Lodge at 9.40 a.m. for the 10 o'clock service. We didn't need mobile phones and stuff to organize things, it was all very dignified and worked perfectly, almost like a military operation. It was perfect – just the way Freddie would have wanted it.

The coffin went in, and we all followed. There were some 14 on the 'friends' side, and about 30 relatives on the 'family' side.

Elton John had arrived in his green Bentley. The remaining members of Queen were all present. Brian came with Anita Dobson. Mary Austin, pregnant with her second son, came with Dave Clark.

'The music was "You've Got A Friend", sung by Aretha Franklin, which played as he went in, said Peter.

Then there was more of the Parsee service, and then his

oak coffin, with just a single red rose on top, disappeared. When it did so, we played a recording of Verdi's 'D'Amor sull'ali rosee', an aria from *Il Trovatore*, sung, of course, by Montserrat Caballé. That had been Freddie's favourite of all musical pieces ever. He'd often go into the studio, put it on and turn it up to such a volume that you could hear the musicians turning the pages of their music and moving their chairs.

It was incredibly moving, and I was rather upset. It's a time when you need to be on your own. My mother is buried at that crematorium, and I remember I ran down to where her ashes are buried and just asked her to look after him.

Floral tributes covered more than a quarter of an acre outside the crematorium. Freddie's parents had sent white dahlias and lilies with the message: 'To our very beloved son Freddie. We love you always, Mum and Dad.' There was a star in white carnations from Gary Glitter, yellow roses from David Bowie. Elton John had sent a heart of salmon pink roses bearing the message 'Thank you for being my friend. I will love you always.' Boy George's flowers came with the words 'Dear Freddie, I love you.' Mary Austin's wreath was a yellow and white pillow of roses. Her card read 'For my dearest with my deepest love, from your old faithful.' Another wreath from her little son bore the message 'To Uncle Freddie with love from your Ricky.' Roger Taylor's carried the moving words: 'Goodbye, old friend. Peace at last!' All the flowers were later distributed to Aids hospitals throughout London.

Jim Hutton has sketchy memories of the day of Freddie's funeral: 'I still to this day can't remember certain things. I can remember after the cremation, there was a crowd in the house, friends and what have you, drinking champagne and carrying on and I couldn't be doing with that.'

'There *were* a group of people back there, but only doing what Freddie wouldn't have minded – basically wishing him well,' adds Peter. 'Roger, Brian, Jim Beach, Terry Giddings, Dave Clark . . . I'm not 100 per cent sure if Mary was there, or if she just went home.'

Jim found that he could not handle the crowd, and wandered out to the garden by himself.

For me – and I suppose this stems back to my childhood – a bereavement day is rather a solemn day, where people meet, offer each other condolences and chat about the person who has died. Although I had previously lost my father years earlier, I wasn't here in Ireland when it happened. So I suppose you could say that Freddie was the closest person to me who actually died – and it hit me *very* hard.

I remember going into the garden and sitting in one of the little summer houses with the cats, and what I thought about I don't know. It is a total, absolute blank.

Jim does remember being particularly incensed by the deeds of significant others in the weeks following Freddie's death. Not least Dave Clark, who apparently recalled to the press that he was the only person in the bedroom with Freddie when he actually passed away.

'No – Dave was *not* the only person in the room,' Jim states firmly. 'He initially said that to reporters after Freddie died, and Dave Clark will never backtrack. It was quoted and quoted all over the place to the point that he could not take it back.'

Yet the error must have perturbed Clark. 'Some time later,' recalls Jim, 'I received a beautiful card on my birthday from David, which I still have.'

The inscription he has written inside is 'You *were* there'. I don't know why he said otherwise. I'm not saying that Dave wasn't brilliant when Freddie was very ill. He would come round to the house all the time and muck in.

I myself wasn't nursing Freddie, it was Joe and Peter who did that. I cannot stress enough how much they did for Freddie. And Dave would come around, and he wouldn't actually say, 'Come on, lads, I'll sit here, you go off and have a break,' but that was what he was doing there. And yes, he did sit by Freddie's bed for hours on end. So he *was* involved. And the actual night that Freddie died, Dave *was* in the house. But he had left the room; and myself and Peter were left *in* the room. Freddie's favourite cat was Delilah – there wasn't anything he wouldn't do for that cat. And I noticed that she hadn't been on his bed all day, which was strange: that was where she slept, that was where she lived, practically. But that evening she was at the foot of his bed, on the floor, and I picked her up. Dave, at the time, was holding one of Freddie's hands. So he took Freddie's hand and stroked Delilah with it. And there was a glimmer of recognition from Freddie as he did so. And then Freddie expressed a wish to go to the toilet. I flew downstairs to get Peter to come up and give me a hand, and I'm afraid Freddie wet the bed. I said to Peter, 'We'd better change his sheets and clothes before he wakes up.' And at that stage, for the sake of dignity, Dave went to leave the room. And Freddie passed away.

Dave was always an oddball. I met him a couple of times after Freddie died. He said he'd come to my barbecue, and didn't. I ran into him once or twice in garden centres.

Dave also apparently made comments which appeared in the newspapers, along the lines of 'Freddie never wants his music to die'. But, I can assure you, Freddie never said to *anyone* that he never wanted his music to die. It just wasn't the type of comment Freddie would make. Queen music will never die anyway, and I'm sure Freddie knew that in his heart. He would never sit at home listening to Queen music, either.

Even now, Jim finds it distressing to talk about his lost lover.

There are still times when I can be pottering around in the garden and Freddie's facial expression when he died will come into my mind. It can pop up anywhere. I can consciously blank out what happened, but not subconsciously. It is impossible to forget. Meeting Freddie changed my life. I learned such an awful lot from him. He goaded me into doing things – like my little bit of woodwork. Freddie's attitude was always, 'But you can, don't you see? You *can* do it. Put your mind to it and you'll see what you can do.' That was one of the loveliest things about him – that he was so *positive*.

Had Jim never met Freddie Mercury, where does he think he might be now? 'I really don't know where. Possibly I'd be still a barber at the Savoy Hotel.

'I'm hugely grateful, and still amazed, at some of the things I experienced through being with Freddie. I was taken to places I could only dream of . . . not *even* dream of.'

In Munich, Barbara Valentin was forced to deal with her grief alone. She had bought 'the black outfit' and her plane ticket, and was preparing to set off for London when the phone call came telling her that it was better if she stayed away: Mary Austin was to be 'the widow'.

I couldn't even be there to bury him, you know? After all we had been through. The pain was terrible, and I have never got over it. The love I had with Freddie I had never had before, and I've never had since – not that I've ever gone looking for it again. Once was enough. He was the greatest love of my life. For my heart, he was. And he still is. I never had such warm, close feelings for anybody –

certainly not any of my husbands. And since my sexual relationship with Freddie ended, I have never touched a man ever again. I can't do it, and I can't help it. Anyway, I had enough in my life, I can't complain. Twenty women would have to live a hundred years to have what I had. It's better to stop at the right time. I guess that's what he did too.

Things at Garden Lodge never did 'get back to normal'. As Mary prepared to move in, as was her right according to the will, it was plain that she wanted the others out – immediately.

'I would have loved to know why, after Freddie died, Mary totally blanked me out,' says Jim. 'And that was long before I had the idea to write the book. She made a promise to Freddie concerning me which was never carried out: that I could stay at Garden Lodge just as long as I wanted.'

Adds Peter:

And me. And Joe. We really didn't have somewhere else to go, and needed a while to sort things out. Freddie knew that we wouldn't take years to leave, we would have left soon enough of our own accord. Mary actually asked me if I would stay on and look after the house, and I agreed. And I'd booked a holiday for the third week of February. But just before I was due to leave, I was told that I was expected to leave the house at the end of February. I had just one week to find somewhere to live when I returned from my holiday. Mary's behaviour was certainly baffling.

Freddie had also told Jim that when he did decide to leave, he could have whatever he wanted:

They were the words that Freddie told me when he called

me into the garden one day, to tell me that he had given me a wage increase. He also informed me that he had told Mary. None of it was ever in writing, although I had suggested to Freddie that he might take that precaution. He obviously trusted Mary sufficiently that he felt he didn't need to.

Mary didn't stick to verbal promises. Had she done so, she would soon have seen that we would all have left in our own time anyway, and all this bad feeling could have been avoided. How on earth could the three of us be treated the way we were, after all we had been through with Freddie? It didn't make sense.

I left that house with nothing, but knowing that at least I had good friends outside Garden Lodge and nothing to do with the Freddie court whatsoever. That's what kept me going.

Why did Jim think that Mary had wanted to cut off so drastically and finally from the past they had all shared?

Lots of reasons, I think. There was some suggestion that she was worried about her two children not having friends at school because of people in the house being HIV positive. Things like that. But she had not shied away from such things in the past. When her first boy was to be born, Mary went and had an Aids test and made a big thing about announcing that it was 100 per cent clear. If you think about the relationship between Freddie and Mary, Aids can take 10 to 15 years to take effect. And Freddie wasn't faithful to her, either. That also begs the question, how long ago did their relationship really break up?

Jim, of course, could have made trouble in the years following Freddie's death had he so wished. To do so was never a real consideration. But many aspects of Freddie's will continue to puzzle him.

The world still thinks he left everything to Mary. *Why* did he leave everything to Mary? Well, because he had promised her. A promise was something he never went back on. Pity she didn't feel the same. I believe Freddie actually rewrote his will in the September or the October before he died. There seem to have been a few versions of the will, though. At that stage, Freddie already knew that I was HIV positive. He knew that Joe Fanelli had Aids and would die soon. He had to be realistic. Had he left the bulk of his estate to me, where would it have ended up if I passed away?

I often think, if I'd had enough money myself, would I have contested the will? Had I been a woman, I would have been regarded as the common-law wife – I was Freddie's live-in partner, after all – and I could have contested it by rights. My solicitor even suggested it, as a trial, a test case. We could have made legal history. But he also warned me that if I were to do it, it could possibly take up to 10 years to come to court, all assets in the meantime would be frozen, and none of the others would have received a penny of what was due to them until the whole thing was resolved. You might win these things, or you might lose horribly. I couldn't risk making things terrible for the others, particularly Joe, who didn't have long to live, and deserved to live out his last years in a bit of comfort without having to worry about money.

On close inspection of the will [of which the author has a copy] there do appear to be a number of clauses which raise eyebrows. Jim remarks:

I never saw the complete will. But from what I have

learned from solicitors, the way it is worded is open to question. Money seemed to become such an issue after Freddie's death, which was so sad, because it had never been so in his lifetime. There was always enough to go round. Joe's medical bills, like my medical bills, had always been taken care of. Freddie had arranged for them to be paid automatically, and all bills were sent directly to John Libson the accountant. After Freddie died, my bills started coming directly to me.

Peter Freestone ruefully tells a similar story.

Then there were the lengthy wrangles over Barbara's apartment in Munich:

'Freddie and Barbara came to an arrangement when they bought that flat in Munich, and it was a 50:50 deal,' agrees Jim.

Now I don't know the whole ins and outs of it, but I believe the agreement was whoever should die first, the other one got to own the entire flat. There was a document to prove this, which Freddie had to sign. And which he *did* sign – but unfortunately he didn't date the damned thing. The paperwork was put in Freddie's bedside drawer. After Freddie's death, Peter had a call from Barbara saying that Jim Beach, the accountants and the legal people were questioning her rights to the flat. Peter phoned me in a panic to tell me all this, and said, 'Did Freddie actually sign those documents?' And I said, 'Yes he did. And as far as I'm aware, they are still in his bedside drawer. So you should phone up John Libson and tell him where they are and that they *are* signed by Freddie.' Which I presume he did. Poor Barbara had been having a really bad time through all this. When they got the documents, they discovered that he hadn't put the date. But if one had examined the signature on the document, compared it with a later signature of

Freddie's, they would have deduced that Freddie had signed this when he had his full faculties and was fully aware of what he was doing.

Thanks to the kindness and honesty of her friends in Garden Lodge, Barbara did eventually receive a letter from Libson and Beach, which she showed me in Munich along with two fat files of correspondence. In words to this effect, it said the following: 'Dear Barbara, you will be pleased to know that the documents pertaining to the arrangements you made with Freddie over the Munich flat have come to light . . .'

Barbara maintains to this day that it is thanks to her friends at Garden Lodge that she kept her home. Both Jim and Peter agree that she would have done exactly the same for them.

As 'The Myth Of Freddie Mercury' mounted with each passing day, those who had been closest to him during the last years of his life were totally ignored. Neither Peter, Jim nor Joe was acknowledged publicly for the way they had devotedly cared for Freddie until the end. The Court Of King Freddie was systematically dismantled. Soon, it was as if it had never existed. Jim says that it was his anger that the truth was not being told, not money, which originally motivated him to write his book.

'I think Jim Beach, especially, was angry that my book ruined "The Myth of Freddie". It returned Freddie to his original status of Human Being. It told the truth. I think Jim Beach much preferred for fans to believe that Sweet Mary Austin was the love of Freddie's life, and what a great, tragic, romantic tale it all was. But I believe the fans don't give a monkey's whether Freddie was gay or not. And I also believe that fans prefer to know the truth, good and bad.'

Peter Freestone agrees.

Freddie would be horrified to have seen all that has gone

on since his death. Maybe he does know, but he can't exactly do anything about it. Still, those concerned have to live with themselves. Mary once said of Jim Hutton that he 'had a very vivid imagination'. I would suggest that maybe she should look at herself. I have known Jim a very long time, and have never known him to be anything other than totally honest. Jim's conscience, like mine, is clear.

There has been much speculation since Freddie died as to what eventually happened to his ashes. 'He did remain at the funeral director's for a long time afterwards,' remembers Peter.

'After that, I know for a fact that he was back at Garden Lodge. But what has happened to him since, I could not say for sure. There are so many theories, and I would not put money on any of them. I know where Freddie *wanted* to be: under his cherry tree in Garden Lodge. But as we have seen, what Freddie wanted and what he got after death didn't always tally.'

What is certain is that Freddie's family went to great lengths to conceal from the public the whereabouts of their son's final resting place. But did not Freddie's millions of fans have a right to know where they could go to pay their last respects? For years so many of them have wandered in the wilderness, making their sad pilgrimage to his London home because there is nowhere else for them to go. They do not even know if he is there. Most of them know for sure in their hearts that he is not. According to rumours, Freddie's ashes were variously in Montreux, Switzerland, buried beside his beloved Lac Leman, Lake Geneva; in a small, insignificant urn on his parents' mantelpiece; scattered over the ocean off Zanzibar. According to Freddie's lover Jim Hutton, they *are* buried beneath the cherry tree in the grounds of Garden Lodge, in keeping with Freddie's wishes. Although this has never been officially denied, Jim Beach politely refused a request to reveal the actual place of burial, explaining that he had to respect the family's wishes that it should remain a well-kept secret. Mary Austin has maintained her usual silence. But Gita Choksi, Freddie's old friend from St Peter's School in Panchgani, was able to throw some light on the mystery when she visited me in London: 'I had the most incredible experience about one year after Freddie died,' she said.

I was over in London to visit Dad's grave for the first time, at Brookwood Civil and Military Cemetery in Surrey. My father unfortunately died in England in the late 1940s. A lot of American soldiers were buried there too. I had never before been to Dad's last resting place. I went on the train from Waterloo to the Parsee plot of this huge cemetery about half an hour by train from London, and found Dad's grave, which was terribly overgrown and unkempt. It was an emotional time for me, and I was very upset. As I was walking away from the grave, the graveyard caretaker happened to point out an unmarked plot nearby with no headstone or anything to identify it, and said, 'Do you know who this is? It's that rock-singer Freddie Mercury.' I was completely shocked and overcome. The caretaker obviously had no way of knowing anything about my connection with Freddie, and no apparent reason to lie. I had not seen my old school friend all those years, and here he was, his ashes buried just a few feet away from my own father's. I am absolutely sure that it is the truth. I really don't think the caretaker would tell me, another Parsee like Freddie, such a thing if it were not true. It was the most extraordinary thing to happen to me in my life. But I was very grateful for it.

My first visit to Brookwood turned up little in the way of clues. My second, made on a brighter day in the company of a Parsee friend, allowed me to locate the grave of Gita's father: Homi Dhunjishaw Bharucha, born 12 March 1908, died 22 August 1948. The plot number was 212583. Close by we examined a few unmarked plots, but found nothing to suggest that any of them might be Freddie's grave. Spotting a caretaker, who gave his name as John, we told him that we were looking for an unmarked grave of a Parsee by the name of Freddie Bulsara.

'I know who you mean.' He smiled at us. 'It's that rock-singer Freddie Mercury, isn't it? Come with me.'

Walking with us back to the spot, he pointed at a patch of ground and said:

He used to be there. For ages he was there, and it was just marked out with a stick with a number on it and a little vase of flowers. This small blonde woman [presumably Mary Austin] used to come up here all the time and put fresh flowers, and she came to me and asked me to keep an eye on the grave.

Quite a long time after that, a new grave arrived. [He shows us the grave in question.]

We presumed it was one of their family. They all come down here late one evening, not many of 'em. All stood round, Tony [another caretaker] come to me and says lend us a spade, I've got to go in under one of them graves. And he went in under, and they put Freddie's ashes in there. They obviously didn't want anybody to know where he was.

Examining the headstone in question, it made perfect sense. To anyone who knows anything about Freddie's roots, there are obvious clues. Not wishing to invite desecration or damage, I choose not to identify the grave here. Indeed, there is nothing to confirm the presence of Freddie's ashes. There is not even an entry in his name in the cemetery office records. But as the secretary explained to us, 'That plot belongs freehold to the Zoroastrian Society, and they can do what they want up there. Bodies which are buried have to be recorded, but you can do what you like with ashes.'

She was right. If you can scatter them over the sea or off a bridge up the M1, you could certainly slip them unnoticed into somebody else's grave.

Peter Freestone was not at all surprised to hear this story, although he was unable to confirm it.

'I simply don't know,' he said. 'I suspect that his ashes were divided, and that perhaps the parents got some, and Mary got some . . . but who's to say? Only they know for sure.'

On 20 April 1992, the rest of Queen gave a huge Freddie Mercury tribute concert at Wembley stadium in loving memory of their friend. Although all the stars involved would perform Queen songs, Brian, who described Freddie's death as 'like losing a brother', was the first to stress that this was not Queen. The show kicked off with live footage of Freddie doing his vocal scales. Annie Lennox and David Bowie performed 'Under Pressure', Roger Daltrey 'I Want It All', Extreme 'Hammer To Fall', George Michael and Lisa Stansfield 'These Are The Days of Our Lives'. Elton John and Axl Rose tackled 'Bohemian Rhapsody', and Elton said that Queen were 'the most important figures in rock 'n' roll'. Seal chose 'Who Wants To Live Forever' and Liza Minnelli sang 'We Are The Champions' – brilliantly.

'A lot of people are changing the keys to these songs because they find that they can't do a Freddie,' remarked Robert Plant.

Mike Appleton agreed: 'I think to say that these people were not a patch on Freddie would be unfair,' he says. 'These were not their usual songs, and nobody could sing them as well as Freddie. Except perhaps George Michael, who demonstrated that day that he really does have the makings of a superstar in the Freddie vein.'

George Michael, who also performed 'Somebody To Love' with the rest of Queen and stole the show just as

Queen themselves had done at Live Aid all those years earlier, remarked at the time: 'When I think of Freddie, I think of everything he gave me in terms of craft. Just to sing those songs, especially "Somebody To Love", was really an outrageous feeling. It was probably the proudest moment of my career. Living out a childhood fantasy, I suppose.'

Mick Ronson and Ian Hunter, formerly of Mott the Hoople, performed a moving tribute in the form of 'All the Young Dudes'. But why was the 'heavy metal' element, which Freddie had never fully embraced, emphasized? There were also a few notable absentees: where was Dave Clark? Tony Hadley? Leee Johns? Where was the 'Out Gay' element representing that side of Freddie's lifestyle: Boy George? Erasure? Or even Lily Savage, as camp compère? Where were the operatic arias, and the classical singers he so adored: Pavarotti? Domingo? And above all Montserrat Caballé? The day overflowed with emotion nonetheless, not least when Aids campaigner and Hollywood legend Liz Taylor came on to address the crowd:

'Don't worry, I'm not gonna sing,' she quipped.

'We are here to celebrate the life of Freddie Mercury. We are here also to tell the whole world that he, like others we have lost to Aids, died before his time.'

Liza Minnelli was more succinct:

'Thanks, Freddie,' she cried. 'We just wanted to let you know that we were thinking about you. Stay safe.'

Added Brian, 'I know for a fact that Freddie would have been excited to be working with these other people. If he's up there looking on, I know he's into it.'

As Spike Edney remembers,

The concert was bloody hard work, but a wonderful thing. It was truly a labour of love. If anything, the rehearsals, in Bray, were more magical than the actual day. The very first time Annie Lennox and David Bowie got up to sing 'Under Pressure', it was absolutely spine-tingling. It didn't come anywhere near it on the day, even though it was still great to watch. George Michael too. Singing at the rehearsal with no audience, he had far more intensity and magic than his actual performance, if you can believe that, because he was mind-blowing at Wembley. Lisa Stansfield shone through – that was a great moment for her. It was an amazing concert, and I still like to watch stuff from it, but for me the greatest moments happened in that hangar in Bray.

It may not be fair to say that none of those great artists could sing any of the songs as well as Freddie. But I know a lot of them felt as if they were there in his shadow. Of course, he would have loved that! He would have loved to see them all suffer. As well as appreciating it for what it was – a great tribute – he would have really relished the agonies they all had to go through, not managing to match his keys.

The whole thing was summed up when we went to the after-show party at Browns. And I was absolutely shagged by the time I got there, after all the weeks of work and the gig itself – which was pretty slick, all things considered. I remember being upstairs at Browns, and I saw Rog propped up against the wall, just staring into space, and then I spotted Brian a couple of feet away doing the same thing. I went up and said 'How d'you feel?' and they said 'Can't feel anything.' Nobody could remember anything about it. You just couldn't take it all in. And once it was over, it was, 'God – what have we actually *done* for the past month? And what do we do *now*?'

The Mercury Phoenix Trust, established in 1992 to deal with revenue from the Tribute concert and other sources, continues to raise cash for Aids causes throughout the world. 'Bohemian Rhapsody' had been re-released as a single for

Christmas 1991, soared to number one, and more than a million pounds was handed to the Terrence Higgins Trust Aids charity as a result. Also re-released in America, profits from the single were distributed among Aids foundations across the States (through the Magic Johnson Foundation). George Michael, Lisa Stansfield and Queen later donated royalties from the 'Five Live' mini album to the Phoenix Trust. Additional money flows in constantly (as when the Royal Mail bought Freddie's stamp collection – for £3220 – in 1993). Spike Edney, for one, is responsible for regular donations from collections at his 'Spike's All Stars' gigs, and hundreds of Queen fans hold their own fundraising events around the country throughout the year. The money is used to help aid-projects and fund research worldwide.

Since Freddie's death there has been another Queen album – 'Made in Heaven', a massive-selling number one hit and an all-time Queen great, which features in particular, his haunting vocal on the track 'Mother Love'; his statue has gone up in Montreux; his photograph exhibition has gone on the road; and a specially-choreographed ballet, incongruously entitled 'Le Presbytère N'a Rien Perdu De Son Charme Ni le Jardin De Son Eclat' ('The presbytery has lost none of its charm, nor the garden its sparkle') by French choreographer Maurice Béjart, has been performed in Freddie's honour in Paris. It featured 16 original Queen songs and four Mozart compositions, and costumes were designed by Gianni Versace. All royalties were donated by Béjart in perpetuity to the Phoenix Trust.

The remaining members of Queen have done their best to keep going, but know better than anyone that things can never be the same. The Queen Productions offices in Pembridge Road, Notting Hill Gate, are now closed. Mountain Studios have been sold, and Queen, to all intents and purposes, are no longer a working group. It is possible that EMI will see fit to release a further Greatest Hits album in time – there remains a wealth of tracks which have never made it on to a compilation. If it happens, Queen will be the first band in history to have released three Greatest Hits albums. At the end of 1996, the Queen Fan Club magazine reported that not only have the band sold over six million albums in the 1990s, but they remain the only group to have had two separate Greatest Hits albums sell in excess of two million copies each. Commercial chances are that there will also, before long, be another 'Boxed Set'. Meanwhile, Montserrat Caballé has recorded a new album with Mike Moran and friends, which includes her version of 'Bohemian Rhapsody'. And a Broadway play about Freddie's life and work is currently in pre-production. In his music, and in the hearts of his millions of ever-faithful fans, Freddie lives on.

'Freddie was my best friend,' Roger Taylor said to me recently. 'I have never got over his death. None of us have. I think we all thought that we would come to terms with it quite quickly, but we underestimated the impact his death had on our lives. I still find it painful to talk about. For those of us left, it is as though Queen was another lifetime entirely. Our present and our future without Freddie are still impossible to contemplate. I deal with it day by day.'

Concluded Peter Freestone,

When I think of him now, I think what a charmed life he had. Freddie was one of those very rare, very fortunate people who could actually afford to do *whatever* he wanted. Who wouldn't envy him for that? He could afford to indulge his exquisite taste, and bring pleasure to so many others at the same time. How often do you get people with boundless wealth but no taste, or incredibly good taste but no money to indulge it?

I personally have learned so much through Freddie. Looking back on our life together now, I can see that Freddie was the teacher and we were all the school kids. Now that school's finished, we have to go out into the world with what we've learned.

Barbara Valentin, who understood the real man behind the superstar perhaps better than most, says that at least Freddie did what he always said a star should do:

> He quit while he was ahead. Freddie always used to say to me that you can never afford to fall from the top, be not as great as you once were. This is what he did. Fame had made him the loneliest person in the world. To compensate for this, the life he lived became wilder and wilder, until it controlled him. He was only over-compensating for his loneliness – Freddie did everything to extremes. The price he paid in the end was the most terrible, and I know for sure he wouldn't have planned it quite like that. But you'd have to say, he had his way. Immortality was what he wanted, and immortality was what he got.

SELECTED SOURCE NOTES

Full details including dates have been listed where poss-
ible/applicable.

Please note the following abbreviations:

EXCL/LAJ   exclusive interview with the author
Anon   Anonymous, 'Rescue from Bondage: Freedom for the
            Fettered', *The British Empire*, BBC TV Publications
            partwork/Time Life, 1973.
Gunn/Jenkins Gunn, Jacky, and Jenkins, Jim, *Queen: As It Began*,
            Sidgwick and Jackson, London, 1992.
Hodkinson   Hodkinson, Mark, *Queen: the Early Years*, Omnibus
            Press, 1995.
Palmer   Palmer, Robert, *Dancing In The Street – A Rock and
            Roll History*, BBC Books, London, 1996.
Rider   Rider, Stephen, *These Are the Days of Our Lives*,
            Castle Communications, 1991.
St Michael St Michael, Mick, *Queen: In Their Own Words*,
            Omnibus Press, 1992.
Watson   Watson, Peter, *Nureyev – A Biography*, Hodder &
            Stoughton, London, 1994.

Chapter 1 *Introduction*

1 EXCL/LAJ

Chapter 2 *Spice of Life*

1 Anon.
2 EXCL/LAJ

Chapter 3 *From Zanzibar to Panchgani, from Panchgani to London*

1 EXCL/LAJ
2 Rider.
3 St Michael.

Chapter 4 *Ealing*

1 Gunn/Jenkins.
2 EXCL/LAJ
3 St Michael.
4 Palmer.
5 EXCL/LAJ

Chapter 5 *Queen – the Beginning*

1 *Today*, 15 January 1991.
2 St. Michael.
3 Hodkinson.
4 St Michael.
5 Hodkinson.
6 *Today*, 15 January 1991.
7 EXCL/LAJ
8 Hodkinson.

Chapter 6 *Freddie Comes On Board*

1 St Michael.
2 Hodkinson.
3 Ibid.

Chapter 7 *And It Was Mary . . .*

1 *Daily Express*, 20 April 1992.
2 St. Michael.
3 *Daily Express*, 20 April 1992.
4 St Michael.
5 *Daily Express*, 20 April 1992.
6 St. Michael.

Chapter 8 *Early Days, and the Trident Years*

1 St Michael.
2 Ibid.
3 Ibid.
4 As told to Tony Brainsby.
5 St. Michael.
6 Ibid.
7 Ibid.

Chapter 9 *All the Young Dudes*

1 Gunn/Jenkins.
2 EXCL/LAJ
3 EXCL/LAJ
4 St Michael.
5 Ibid.
6 EXCL/LAJ
7 Hodkinson.
8 St. Michael.

Chapter 11 *Mona Lisa and Mad Hatters*

1 'Tantrums and Tiaras', broadcast ITV 7 July 1996 (producer David Furnish, Rocket Productions)
2 Ibid.
3 EXCL/LAJ
4 As told to Mick Rock.

5 EXCL/LAJ
6 EXCL/LAJ

Chapter 12   *Fame*

1 EXCL/LAJ
2 John Blake, *Evening News.*
3 EXCL/LAJ
4 EXCL/LAJ
5 St Michael.
6 EXCL/LAJ
7 Watson.
8 EXCL/LAJ

Chapter 13   *Queen Limited*

1 EXCL/LAJ
2 As told to Rick Sky.
3 St Michael.
4 *Evening News*, 27 February 1980.

Chapter 14   *Queen of the South*

1 EXCL/LAJ
2 EXCL/LAJ

Chapter 15   *Bavarian Rhapsody: My Funny Valentin*

1 *Daily Mirror*, 23 October 1981.
2 St Michael.

Chapter 17   *Under Pressure: Sun City Rollers*

1 St Michael.

2 EXCL/LAJ
3 EXCL/LAJ

Chapter 19   *We Are the Champions*

1 Interview for BBC Radio One documentary about Queen (producer Stuart Grundy for Unique), broadcast 10 December 1995.
2 St Michael.
3 *Daily Express*, 12 July 1985.
4 St Michael.
5 Interview for BBC Radio One documentary, op. cit.

Chapter 20   *Budapest*

1 EXCL/LAJ
2 EXCL/LAJ

Chapter 21   *The Court of King Freddie*

1 EXCL/LAJ
2 EXCL/LAJ

Chapter 22   *Barcelona: Who Wants To Live Forever?*

1 Interview for BBC Radio One documentary, op. cit.
2 Ibid.
3 Ibid.
4 Ibid.
5 Ibid.
6 EXCL/LAJ
7 Interview for BBC Radio One documentary, op. cit.
8 Ibid.
9 Ibid.

Appendix I

<u>CHRONOLOGY</u>

5 September 1946	Farrokh Bulsara born on Zanzibar.
1951	Farrokh attends Zanzibar Missionary School.
1955–1963	Farrokh boards at St Peter's School, Panchgani, India. Changes name to Freddie.
1963	Freddie returns to Zanzibar to complete his schooling at St Joseph's Convent School.
January 1964	Revolution on Zanzibar. Freddie's parents flee to England with their two children.
September 1964–Easter 1966	Freddie enrols at Isleworth Polytechnic School to study for art A Level.
September 1966	Freddie joins Ealing College of Art to begin course in Graphic Design and Illustration. Leaves home. Meets Tim Staffell, who plays in a band with Brian May.
July 1969 onwards	Freddie leaves Ealing College with Diploma; runs a stall in Kensington Market with Roger Taylor; hangs out with the bands Smile and Ibex. Freddie launches his first band, Wreckage. Freddie meets Mary Austin.
April 1970	Queen launched, comprising Brian May, Roger

445

	Taylor and Freddie, who soon changes his surname to Mercury. (John Deacon joins in February 1971).
18 September 1970	Freddie's rock idol Jimi Hendrix found dead.
1972	Queen sign deal with Trident Studios.
Spring 1973	Queen sign recording contract with EMI Records.
July 1973	Queen's début single 'Keep Yourself Alive' and début album 'Queen' released.
November 1973	Queen tour UK supporting Mott the Hoople.
End 1973	First official Queen fan club launched.
March 1974	'Seven Seas of Rhye' single and 'Queen II' album released. Queen's first headlining UK tour.
April 1974	Queen suport Mott the Hoople on US tour.
October/ November 1974	'Killer Queen' single and 'Sheer Heart Attack' album released. Before the end of the year, both break the US Top Ten.
1975	Queen's first headlining US tour. First tour of Japan. Freddie wins Ivor Novello Award for 'Killer Queen'. Queen pull out of deal with Trident. Elton John's manager John Reid takes over.
31 October 1975	'Bohemian Rhapsody' single released.
21 November 1975	'A Night At The Opera' album released.
25 November 1975	'Bohemian Rhapsody' makes Queen's first number 1 in UK, and wins Freddie another Ivor Novello Award.
1976	Queen's second US tour.
February 1976	All four Queen albums in the UK Top 20. Tours of Japan and Australia.
18 September 1976	Queen's massive free concert in Hyde Park.

December 1976	'A Day At The Races' album released.
1977	Queen tour the world.
October 1977	'We Are The Champions' single released. 'Bohemian Rhapsody' wins Britannia Award. 'News Of The World' album released. Lawyer Jim Beach negotiates Queen's exit from contract with John Reid. Beach takes over management of Queen's legal affairs. Queen put together their own personal management.
1978	European tour.
October 1978	Queen's outrageous Hallowe'en Party in New Orleans to celebrate launch of album 'Jazz' in November.
1979	Queen start recording at Musicland, Munich. 'Live Killers' album released in June.
October 1979	Freddie performs in charity dance gala at London Coliseum with Royal Ballet. Meets his future personal assistant, Peter Freestone.
1980	'Crazy Little Thing Called Love' single hits number 1 in countless countries, gives Queen their first US number 1. Freddie acquires Garden Lodge in London. Epic US tour. 'The Game' album released in June – becomes Queen's first US number 1 album. 'Another One Bites The Dust' single number 1 in US and numerous countries. Two Grammy nominations. Queen enter *Guinness Book Of Records*. 'Flash Gordon' album released.
1981	Queen tour South America. Freddie's five-day birthday party in New York City. 'Greatest Hits' album released in November.
1982	Queen sign new contract with EMI for further six albums. 'Hot Space' album released May. 'Under Pressure' single with David Bowie makes number 1. American tour. Queen receive Keys of the City of Boston 23 July.

1983	Freddie meets Winnie Kirchberger in Munich. Meets Jim Hutton in London. Begins first solo album in Munich.
1984	Freddie meets Barbara Valentin in Munich. 'The Works' album released UK and US in February. Queen win 'Outstanding Contribution to British Music' Award in June. Spike Edney joins Queen as touring keyboard player. Queen's controversial dates at Sun City, South Africa, October, cause them to be blacklisted by Musicians' Union.
1985	Queen headline at Brazil's 'Rock In Rio' festival, January. Queen tour New Zealand, Australia and Japan from April. Live Aid, Wembley Stadium, July. Freddie quits Munich to live in London.
1986	Queen's farewell 'Magic' tour of Europe. 'A Kind of Magic' album, the Highlander soundtrack, released, June. Freddie retires from live circuit to set up home at Garden Lodge with Jim Hutton, Peter Freestone and Joe Fanelli.
1987	Freddie releases cover version of 'The Great Pretender', February. Freddie meets with Montserrat Caballé in Barcelona to discuss musical collaboration, March. Former Queen aide Paul Prenter sells kiss 'n' tell revelations about Freddie's lifestyle to the *Sun*. Freddie performs at La Nit Festival, Barcelona, before King and Queen of Spain, October. Mercury/Caballé collaboration 'Barcelona' released, October.
1989	'The Miracle' album released, May. Queen voted 'Band of The Eighties'.
1990	Queen awarded BPI's 'Outstanding Contribution to British Music' award.
1991	'Innuendo' gives Queen first number 1 single for 10 years. 'Innuendo' album released,

February. Work commences in Montreux on Queen's final album, 'Made In Heaven', eventually released in 1995.

24 November 1991   Freddie Mercury dies.

Appendix II

QUEEN DISCOGRAPHY

Compiled in association with Queen expert Jim Jenkins, this list is the first complete discography to feature in any Queen/Mercury biography.

ALBUMS (dates given in brackets = U.S. releases)

Queen	13 July 1973 (4 September 1973)
Queen II	8 March 1974 (9 April 1974)
Sheer Heart Attack	8 November 1974 (12 November 1974)
A Night At The Opera	21 November 1975 (2 December 1975)
A Day At The Races	10 December 1976 (18 December 1976)
News Of The World	28 October 1977 (1 November 1977)
Jazz	10 November 1978 (14 November 1978)
Live Killers	22 June 1979 (26 June 1979)
The Game	30 June 1980 (30 June 1980)
Flash Gordon original soundtrack	8 December 1980 (27 January 1981)
Greatest Hits	2 November 1981 (3 November 1981)
Hot Space	21 May 1982 (25 May 1982)
The Works	27 February 1984 (28 February 1984)
The Complete Works	2 December 1985 Limited edition boxed set containing all Queen's albums to date except *Greatest Hits*, and includes a special album, *Complete Vision*, featuring tracks unavailable at that time. (not released in US at that time)

451

A Kind Of Magic	2 June 1986 (3 June 1986)
Live Magic	1 December 1986 (not released in US)
The Miracle	22 May 1989 (6 June 1989)
Queen At The Beeb	4 December 1989
	Re-released May 1997, as a double album, remastered, including every song Queen ever recorded for the BBC. (Not released in US) originally, but released 7 March 1995)
Innuendo	4 February 1991 (5 February 1991)
Greatest Hits II	28 October 1991 (not released in US)
Classic Queen	(3 March 1992 US only)
Live At Wembley '86	26 May 1992 (2 June 1992)
	The 12″ Collection was included with *Box Of Tricks* 26 May 1992 (not released in US at that time)
	Greatest Hits (different track listing) (15 Sept 1992 US only)
Made In Heaven	6 Nov 1995 (7 Nov 1995)

FREDDIE MERCURY SOLO RELEASES
ALBUMS

Mr Bad Guy	29 April 1985 (7 May 1985)
Barcelona (with Montserrat Caballé)	10 October 1988 (released in US after Freddie's death 14 July 1992), and re-released in UK 10 August 1992
The Freddie Mercury Album	16 November 1992 (in the US released as *The Great Pretender*, 24 November 1992)

SINGLES

As Larry Lurex:

I Can Hear Music	29 June 1973

Freddie Mercury:

Love Kills	10 September 1984 (11 September 1984)
I Was Born to Love You	9 April 1985 (23 April 1985)
Made In Heaven	1 July 1985 (not released in US)
Living On My Own	2 September 1985 (2 July 1985)

QUEEN DISCOGRAPHY

Love Me Like There's No Tomorrow	18 November 1985 (not released in US)
Time (title theme of Dave Clark's musical)	6 May 1986 (not released in US)
The Great Pretender	23 February 1987 (3 March 1987)

FROM 'BARCELONA' (with Montserrat Caballé)

Barcelona	26 October 1987
The Golden Boy	24 October 1988
How Can I Go On?	23 January 1989

POSTHUMOUS RELEASES

Barcelona	re-released 27 July 1992
How Can I Go On?	re-released 12 October 1992
In My Defence	30 November 1992
The Great Pretender	re-released 25 January 1993 (12 November 1992)
Living On My Own	re-released 19 July 1993

This re-release of *Living On My Own* was Freddie's biggest-selling hit single ever. It topped the chart on 8 August 1993 – the first time any solo single released by a member of Queen had reached number 1.

INDEX

455

INDEX

461

INDEX

gay scene, 10, 197–201
New York Native, 267
New York Times, 267
New Zealand, 341–5, 347, 361
Nicks, Stevie, 3, 120
A Night At The Opera, 187, 192, 193, 218
19, 152
1984 (amateur band), 97–8
Norman, Philip, 176
Novello, Ivor, 171
'Now I'm Here', 216
Nureyev, Rudolf, 203, 206–12, 406
Nutter, David, 177
Nutter, Tommy, 177

Oasis, 371
Observer, the, 22, 335, 362, 367
'The Old Grey Whistle Test' (television
    programme), 145, 146, 184, 193, 219
Olivier, Sir Laurence, 355
Omar, Hamari, 28
Onassis, Jackie Kennedy, 211
'One Vision', 1, 354
O'Regan, Denis, 77, 159, 193, 216–18,
    356–9
Osbourne, Ozzie, 333
O'Shea, Miss, 54

Paige, Elaine, 382, 384, 404
Palkhivala, Nani, 41
Palmer, Robert, 87–8
Park, Merle, 233, 234
Pavarotti, Luciano, 316, 317, 433
Pearson, Rosemary, 111
Peel, John, 144, 147, 159
Peter, Paul and Mary, 83
Phil Symes PR, 356, 366
Picture Power, 212
Pink Floyd, 100, 188
Plant, Robert, 433
Platters, 397
'Play the Game', 243–4
Prenter, Paul, 216, 221, 235, 254
    dies of Aids, 413
    as F's personal manager, 177
    in Munich, 269, 271–2, 274, 276
    in Rio, 333, 337–8, 340, 341
    sells revelations about F's lifestyle,
        400–401
'Le Presbytère N'a Rien Perdu De Son
    Charme No le Jardin De Son Eclat', 435–6
Presley, Elvis, 2, 35, 62, 83, 108, 173
Pringle, Gill, 368

Quale, Johnny, 98
Quant, Mary, 83
Quantick, David, 371–3
Queen
    arrogance, 331
    and *As It Began*, 63
    'Band Of the Eighties', 407
    Beach takes over management of legal
        affairs, 221

blacklisted by the Musicians' Union, 327
and charities, 6
confidence, 130, 138–9, 150, 222
controversial dates in Sun City, 251,
    320–21
Edney joins, 321
enter the *Guinness Book of Records*, 4
European tours, 223, 226, 315
fan clubs, 161, 318, 340
fans, 154–5, 157, 160, 161, 164, 168–9,
    170, 220, 248–50, 263, 318–19, 333,
    363, 365, 435
first album *see Queen*
first appearance on television, 162
first ever stadium concert in the Eastern
    Bloc (Nepstadion concert, Budapest), 5,
    18, 364, 365–9, 371–8
first gig (1971), 117
first headlining UK tour (1974), 162–3,
    164
first international performance, 157
first manager, 78
first number one single, 4, 192–3
first number one single for ten years, 410
first (official) single, 145, 147, 148,
    149, 415
first promo video, 147–50
first single, 94
first US number one album, 244
first US number one single, 241
Hallowe'en Party in New Orleans
    (1978), 225–6
headline in 'Rock in Rio' festival, 5, 333–6
Hyde Park free concert (1976), 4,
    215, 216
and Japan *see* Japan
last performance (Knebworth Park, 9
    August 1986), 2, 5, 13, 18, 356, 363
launch of, 117
at Live Aid, Wembley Stadium (1985), 5,
    17, 347–9, 351–4, 433
logo, 116, 153
'Magic' tour of Europe (1986), 5, 17, 354,
    355–60, 363–4, 365–78, 398
and Maradona, 258
and the Marx Brothers, 218
and the media, 18, 151–4, 158, 161–3,
    166, 225–6, 248, 257, 313, 366, 367–8
Mountain Studios bought, 6
named, 114–15
new approach, 231–2
office in Notting Hill, 16
'Outstanding Contribution to British
    Music' award (1990), 399, 407
party for twentieth anniversary, 407–8
receive Keys of The City of Boston, 315
records at Musicland, Munich, 227, 241
Reid manages, 177, 186
royalties, 6
sign new contract with EMI for further six
    albums, 314
sign recording contract with EMI (Spring
    1973), 145

INDEX